COLD GLITTER

THE UNTOLD STORY OF CANADIAN GLAM

ROBERT DAYTON

Cold Glitter: The Untold Story of Canadian Glam © 2025 Robert Dayton

9781627311540

All rights reserved

Feral House
1240 W. Sims Way
Suite 124
Port Townsend, WA 98368
www.feralhouse.com info@feralhouse.com

Design by designSimple

THE UNTOLD STORY OF CANADIAN GLAM

HEAVY INTRO *10*

CHAPTER 1: BRITISH COLUMBIA • *20*
SWEENEY TODD • *22*
NO FUN • *32*
TOYS & POLLY • *40*
TIM RAY & A/V, PHIL SMITH & CORSAGE • *48*
THOR (AND FRANK SODA) • *50*
TWITCH • *61*
RIFF RAFF • *71*
BABY STRANGE (AND A TOUCH OF SLAN) • *75*
SLAM • *80*
TROOPER AND PRISM: AN APPRECIATION • *83*
SINGLES! • *86*
FACES: THE PLACE IN VANCOUVER • *86*

CHAPTER 2: ALBERTA • *92*
STAMPEDERS: AN APPRECIATION • *95*
BUICK MCKANE • *99*
SPUNK • *107*

CHAPTER 3: SASKATCHEWAN • *110*
THE NERVE • *112*

CHAPTER 4: MANITOBA • *122*
THE DAVE WEBER BAND • *124*
GUESS WHO'S "GLAMOUR BOY" EXAMINED • *126*
K-TEL • *127*

CHAPTER 5: ONTARIO • *134*
TORONTO ROCK N ROLL REVIVAL '69 • *136*
JOHNNIE LOVESIN • *139*
THUNDERMUG • *148*
FLUDD • *156*
ROUGH TRADE • *164*
STREET LIFE AND TOBY SWANN • *178*
DISHES AND DRASTIC MEASURES • *184*
FLIVVA • *199*
THE CLICHETTES • *209*
CHIKKIN • *220*
LYNX • *225*
JUSTIN PAIGE • *234*

CONT'D

ZWOL & BRUTUS • *240*
ROBBIE ROX • *251*
CRACKERS • *263*
TRIBE • *272*
TRIBUTE TO MAX WEBSTER'S HIGH CLASS IN BORROWED SHOES ALBUM COVER • *276*
LAURICE • *279*
NEIL MERRYWEATHER • *287*
BONUS TRACKS! ODDS, SODS, AND ONE OFFS • *297*
HOLLYWOOD BRATS • *298*
ERSATZ '50S • *302*

CHAPTER 6: QUEBEC • *306*
MACK • *308*
DANGER • *313*
ANGELO FINALDI • *320*
AUT'CHOSE • *338*
LEWIS FUREY • *350*
THE WACKERS AND ALL THE YOUNG DUDES • *360*

STANLEY FRANK • *370*

BONUS TRACKS! ODDS, SODS, AND ONE OFFS • *377*

NEW YORK DOLLS IN CANADA
OR JOHNNY THUNDERS APPLESEEDS • *378*

CHAPTER 7: MARITIMES • *382*

**CHAPTER 8: NEWFOUNDLAND
AND LABRADOR** • *386*

MUMMERS AND PETER FRANCIS QUINLAN • *388*

**CHAPTER 9: NUNAVUT
AND THE REST OF CANADA** • *396*

JIMMY EKHO • *398*

OUTRO: GLAM NOW AND FOREVER • *400*

CREDITS AND THANK YOUS • *406*

HEAVY INTRO

"WHAT IS CANADIAN GLAM?" they ask, hungry faces all aglow. "Is there such a thing?" I am so glad that questions such as these are raised. It means that I can answer affirmatively.

Nothing entices me more than the nebulous—and what could be more nebulous than the words "Canadian" and "Glam"? Seemingly contradictory, they rub against each other, causing friction to keep us warm these long winter months (is it summer right now? I don't know). Perhaps the chill comes from

being under the shadow of Canada's powerful neighbor, the USA, plus from being rendered further ineffectual by still having a British monarch on all that Canadian money. For such a vast land mass (second largest!), Canada tries so hard to be unassuming. If we think nobody's watching, why be uptight and repressed? Maybe it's the spread; this isolation can sure make you feel lonely.

A little glitter on our faces could surely help our problems.

Canadian Glam provides relevance in my own here-and-now frustration with Canada's perpetually unchanging, culturally conservative climes. Step foot into Canada. Look down. Sun on snow making sparkling glitter. What's that crackling stomp? Look up, it's the Northern Lights. Broad swaths of smeared makeup shimmering across the after-hours sky. Canada, how Glam you are! Canada, you sure are Glam.

Canada is a construct formed out of some very nasty business. Using the word "Canadian" feels odd in general. So, even though this is a history book, it is also an urge to encourage others to create something new, and perhaps a guidebook on how to be more fabulous.

Glam was an allergic reaction—bursting out in glitter instead of hives—to shaggy, drippy 1960s rock machismo. It was time to play with identity. Granted, much of this onstage play was done by white guys; however, the importance and influence of Suzi Quatro in her black leather cat-suit creating heavy stomping belt-alongs should not be underestimated. Still, norms were thwarted and boundaries were stretched. *It's okay to be different!* Gender play was creaking the door open, working against gender norms and towards turning fantasy into reality.

Much of this gender play was initiated by women. The Glam Rock movement was born in England with either Marc Bolan's wife June or his publicist Chelita Secunda (sources vary as to exactly who it was) applying glitter to his cheeks before he performed "Hot Love" (part of his new sound furthered the shortened bursts of rock 'n' roll energy with the addition of strings and Flo and Eddie helium backup vocals with ambiguous, cosmic lyrics) on the popular television program *Top of the Pops,* inspiring his adoring fans to follow suit: glitter on everything! Angela Bowie used femme fashion dictates for hubby David and his band. In the United States, the GTOs, a.k.a. Girls Together Outrageously,[1] taught the Alice Cooper Band how to dress in boas and gave them a heads-up on unusual finds such as old sequined Ice Capades outfits for sale at a quarter a pound in a thrift store, as well as lending their innovative, spidery eye makeup stylings to the lead singer, Vince Furnier.[2] The Alice Cooper Band member Dennis Dunaway's wife Cindy did much of the costuming as well.[3]

The American gay underground scene also influenced Glam, with such foreshadowings as Jack Smith's 1963 experimental film *Flaming Creatures,* which was so beautiful that it was deemed obscene by Canada Customs[4] at the time and was so shimmery that one doesn't know where the delicate, adorned naked bodies end or begin, all their bejeweled genitals and makeup—so much glitter and glamor created on no budget, influencing Andy

---

1 This Los Angeles girl group recorded a brilliant album, *Permanent Damage*, with Frank Zappa in 1969 for the Bizarre label.

2 Better known today as Alice Cooper himself.

3 Thanks to Reg Harkema and Cindy Wolfe from the 2014 documentary *Super Duper Alice Cooper* for this info.

4 In the United States, screenings in the 1960s resulted in raids and arrests. In Canada, *Flaming Creatures* was seized at the border (Customs being a strong arm of Canadian censorship), leaving the film unseen in Canada for years. The Toronto programmer and curator Jim Shedden notes, "The Film-Makers Co-Op responded by refusing to ship any films to Canada, hence a major ripple act of self-censorship. This went on until the late 1980s when the Innis Film Society was able to get them to reverse their policy."

Marc Bolan of T. Rex. Image courtesy of the *Hamilton Spectator*, September 23, 1972.

Front cover of *The Rise and Fall of Ziggy Stardust and the Spiders from Mars*, David Bowie (RCA, 1972) autographed by Ziggy Stardust's partial name-sake, the Legendary Stardust Cowboy himself ("the Ledge"). Author's collection.

Warhol and on and on and on. John Vaccaro used bagfuls of glitter in the unbridled and subversively comic productions of the Playhouse of the Ridiculous, stating that he had been using it since the 1950s.[5] In the very late 1960s over in San Francisco, up sprang the Cockettes, the unhindered, gender-fluid, glitter-packed, camping and vamping stage musical force. In 1971 the transgressive Warhol play *Pork* used the antics of the eccentric members of Warhol's Factory in New York as its basis, then further exaggerated their character traits. The cast of *Pork* were often naked and entwined with each other on stage. Angela and David Bowie were sitting in rapt attention in the front row at the debut for the

---

5 As described in Barney Hoskyns's book *Glam!* (Faber and Faber, 1998), one of the very first books to even regard the Glam genre.

Front cover of *Transformer*, Lou Reed (RCA, 1972). Author's collection.

London production and were so inspired by the brazenly flaunted fabulousness that they subsequently hired those New Yorkers involved with the show—including Jayne County and Cherry Vanilla—to work at MainMan, the new company that managed Bowie.

Unlike the earnest posturing hippie musicians who wanted to dress like their audience to show they too were part of the movement, Glam rock performers dressed as outrageously as possible. The predominantly female audience followed in kind, making shows a participatory spectacle. The sound itself was visual, designed to emanate larger than life from the speakers—PLAY LOUD!—creating total sparkling energy. This wasn't hippie head music; this was the sound of the body: lucid and lithe and ever shifting.

Gender play and a honed sense of camp were not going to fly in mainstream America and certainly not in Canada, where touring regional Glam acts were often chased out

Cover of 1978 edition of *Against Nature (À rebours)* by Joris-Karl Huysmans.

of town by plaid-clad and workboot-wearing burly boys who were not into having aesthetics and heavy mincing infiltrate their townships, even for just one night. Glam gender play and visuality in Canada were more subdued, with nary a dress to be seen. Some acts didn't even own a razor. Canada, in general, often didn't *get* camp. However, in his 1994 essay "Not Just Some Sexless Queen: A Note on 'Kids in the Hall' and the Queerness of Canada" for Semiotext(e)'s *Canadas* book, Thomas Haig writes particularly of the actor Scott Thompson's Buddy Cole character, and then more generally of Canada, that it is a somewhat queer country existing under the shadow of the larger American culture, stating, "camp culture and Canadian traditions of satire and irony can be understood as remarkably similar responses to the experiences of marginalization and lack of voice."

All too often Canada imitates the American status quo. Plus, I have heard established Canadian artists bemoan that their careers suffered because they were "too camp."

In the early 1970s an article in the Canadian gay magazine *The Body Politic* about the lack of gay music in Canada reports that RCA Records initially were not going to release what is regarded as a key Glam album, Lou Reed's *Transformer,* in Canada because they didn't see a market for it. That 1973 album, produced by David Bowie and Mick Ronson, is seminal because of the songs' subject matter, the camp humor sung in Reed's deadpan style, and the musical arrangements. Even the title, *Transformer,* is significant, as the lyrics address themes of transformation, including makeup application, gender play, total body changes, and geographical moves to the cosmopolitan big city.

Because it documents the '70s Glam era and its mainly Eurocentric influences, this book contains a lot of white men in makeup. Though freaky, Glam is, admittedly, pretty white. The impact of '50s Black American music on Glam is key to understanding a genre that includes Little Richard and Chuck Berry riffs galore and the synchronized outfits, dance steps, and harmonies of Motown girl groups.

And when it comes to cosmic themes, wild costumes and makeup, personas, stage shows, and humor, American funk acts such as Funkadelic come to mind. Alas, I have found very little Black Glam in Canada and I *have* dug for it—but that doesn't mean it isn't out there.

Glam was also influenced by the decadent 1884 French novel *Against Nature* (*À rebours*) by Joris-Karl Huysmans. *Against Nature* was probably the "poisonous French novel" mentioned in Oscar Wilde's *Picture of Dorian Gray* and, while its amoral protagonist's self-created world comes crashing down in the end, the denouement feels like a tacked-on moral spanking that is at odds with all the multitudinous examples of splendidly detailed nature-improving artifice in the preceding pages. Glam is all about artifice. Canada positions its identity in relation to its perceived landscape, pure and unsullied natural beauty, even as it extracts and destroys that environment, which can be perceived as a false authenticity. As a monolithic construct like a nation-state, this stance of *natural* is not to be positioned with nature itself, but within the so-called normative status quo, against what *they* deem "unnatural" or "different," that which shifts or changes depending upon the mood, the light, and other factors. I would be remiss if I did not admit that Canada's sweeping natural expanse is indeed lovely. Glam itself was full of confusion and contradiction, and what better contradiction of both "Nature" and "Against Nature" than Canadian Glam? Glam Rock was a pastiche of past and future, 1950s rock 'n' roll and space age synth swooshes. Canadian Glam even shaded into seemingly disparate genres, especially the bearded head music of prog rock, occasionally going full-on Dr. Frankenstein and merging that bearded head of prog to the full body of Glam Rock. Canadian Glam was even more confusing and contradictory than American and English Glam Rock.[6]

European Glam Rock in general—especially of the Junkshop variety of Glam Stompers—loved mimicry, and an influx of one-off acts imitated the form in countless pop singles. Rooted in colonialism, the constant looking to England and the U.S. for cultural cues is very much a Canadian trait, but nothing in this book is as derivative as European Junkshop Glam. The Canadian mutt of Glam is more ineffable.

Where does one draw the implied line? Some Canadian Glam acts saw themselves as Glam, some didn't, but they were all wild and even fun, misfits with an abundance of offerings checking whatever boxes they felt like. It is with plum glee that so much great Canadian Glam has been uncovered for inclusion in this book! Some of these artists didn't even play music, making innovation across the spectrum of multi-disciplinary art and into magic, comedy, and more. Glam is the most slippery of genres; knowing that catch-alls are often a quick fix, I hope that we can be flip about it.

Like many of the best Glam acts (Bowie, Roxy Music, etc.), some of these artists transcend the loose margins of Glam. Some may not fit anywhere else and may be best defined as Freak Rock. I am not a fan of terms, genres, subcultures, and countercultures as they can be elitist and confining. Glam is the loosest of genres and I use the term loosely. Honestly, it's nice for those who get called different or who feel different to feel okay for a while. And Glam often feels good. You can look like a million bucks and don't need much to

---

6   Though Bowie had also dabbled with prog rockers, using musicians such as Yes's Rick Wakeman on his albums.

achieve a Glam look. Waitasec, allow me to coin a new term for that: PIZZAZZAMATAZZ! You're welcome.

Canada is known for reacting rather than acting; this is a Commonwealth country getting smacked against the U.S. of A. Canadian culture can also often be a delayed reaction to American and English influences. EXCEPT! when its cultural innovations are ignored by Canada itself; see, for example: the 1980s Vancouver musical act Slow paving the way for grunge, Vancouver's still-going-strong Mecca Normal and their influence on the riot grrrl movement, the invention of noise rock over fifty years ago by the Nihilist Spasm Band of London, Ontario, the coining of "cosmic consciousness" a hundred years before that by Richard Bucke, and the coining of the word "psychedelic" in the flat farmland of Saskatchewan[7], and on and on and on.

Pinpointing exactly when Canadian Glam begins and ends isn't easy either. For the purposes of this book, I've set an endpoint of 1980, yet a few notable artists ripple past that date. Who said history had to be tidy? Glam wasn't included in the punk rock history books as a legitimate influence until Todd Haynes's 1998 film *Velvet Goldmine* showed the fictionalized relationship of characters inspired by Iggy Pop and David Bowie. Until then, Glam's influence on punk wasn't seen as valid as it didn't fit the tired argument that punk was a reaction against prog. Canadian Glam is not only disreputable, it is full of dispute! If you're seeking genre purity, look elsewhere. This mutt licks!

---

[7] Where, as a nursing student, my own mother was asked to take part in early LSD experiments (she claims that they had already found enough volunteers but I do wonder . . .).

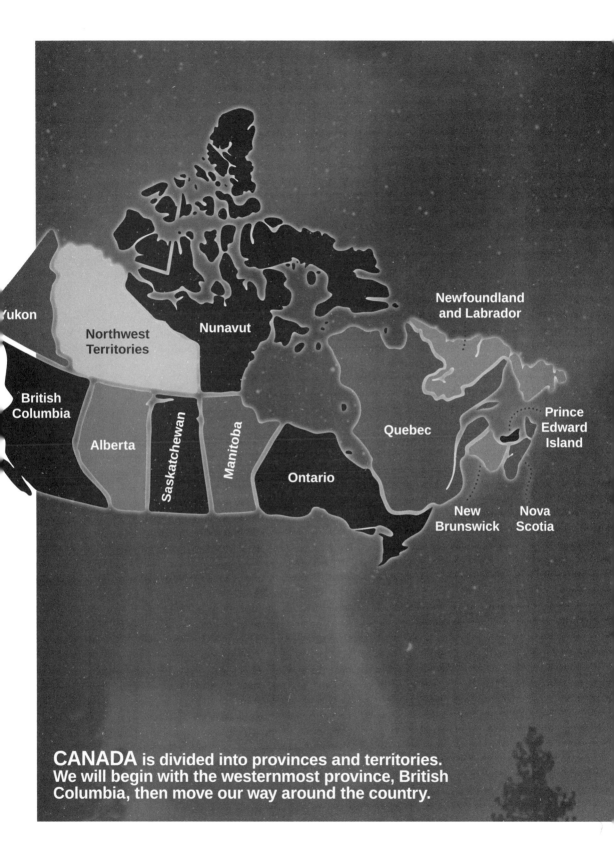

CANADA is divided into provinces and territories. We will begin with the westernmost province, British Columbia, then move our way around the country.

CHAPTER 1
BRITISH COLUMBIA

Sweeney Todd concert poster (1974) featuring early promo photo of them in makeup. Courtesy of Rob Frith.

SWEENEY TODD

WHEN MUSIC FANS, EVEN DIE-HARD fans of Glam, are asked to name a "Canadian Glam act" they often can think of only one: Sweeney Todd from Vancouver, British Columbia. Sweeney Todd was as glittery as it got, in or outside of Canada. They were chock full of swaggering Glam with undisputed classics of the form performed by white-satin-clad lads in soft focus with the founding singer Nick Gilder's *Tiger Beat*–ready good looks and incredible upper range front and center on stage.

Sweeney Todd's roots were dank and proggy, forming out of a band called Rasputin. Lucky for us, they soon discovered—as growing boys do—gobs of makeup that they wore expressively very early on, so heavily that one could hardly tell there were lineup changes. Opening for Chuck Berry, one of the early bassists dressed like a pleated angel, wings and all (ever wonder what an angel wears under the robe? hint, as he lifts his robe on stage: not a thing).

Though the bar scene was sewn up by the rosters of the noted music business management heavies Bruce Allen and Sam Feldman, Sweeney Todd did get early plum gigs opening for major acts such as Flo and Eddie and New York Dolls at the Commodore Ballroom.

Whilst shifting from their grotesque makeup to a more nuanced shimmer in the late summer of '74, they also found a much more permanent bassist in Budd Marr, a teenager doing the thing that musicians in need of a band do: putting up a sign at the local Long & McQuade[1] music shop, thus landing him in Sweeney Todd, where he stayed for a very long time, along with a new drummer, John Booth, joining from Holy Smoke, a band from the nearby island city of Victoria. Holy Smoke had Glammy overtones in its own right, star-eyed makeup, mustache-dabblers who did a heavy guitar version of the Canadian National anthem "O Canada." Furthering their cred, Holy Smoke had previously opened for T. Rex in Vancouver.

Sweeney Todd's first album was underway when Marr joined. Two tracks, "Short Distance Long Journey" and "Daydream," had already been recorded with the previous bassist, Drummond Eveleigh-Smith, who remained uncredited, which is a shame as his name looks scrumptious in print and sounds as angelic as his attire.

This album was very much a group effort, with Gilder and the guitarist James McCulloch contributing, according to Marr, "like ninety percent. Dan [Gaudin, the keyboardist] would put in little bits and he got credit on one song, 'The Kilt': he pretty much wrote it all, but it is derived from a classical composition. . . . They went down and registered the songs under their two names and didn't give us any writing credit. At the time we didn't really care, we just wanted to get the record out, get some money for beer and get some chicks. . . . We never got any royalties for any of this stuff."

The first Sweeney Todd album, released in 1975, has a faux art deco sleeve all sheen and preening. The total platform strut of the smash hit opener "Roxy Roller" is filled to

---

1 Long & McQuade is a music store with multiple locations across Canada.

the brim with innuendo ("she gets bubble gum on her knees, down between the seats sometimes she'll pass you the keys"), tasty guitar fills, the moist squelches of synths (none moister than on the cut "Juicy Loose"), and evocations of Glam signaling—even using the word "Roxy" is a heavy nod to Roxy Music, who themselves acknowledged classic cinema as Sweeney Todd does on the song "Broadway Boogie."[2] ("Broadway's calling me back, star of the screeeeeen . . . .") "Sweeney Todd Folder," with its shimmery beauty, is an example of self-referentiality, a quintessential Glam touchstone. Gilder's voice is quite possibly the coyest and most sensual voice in all of Glam. No one else preens and pouts quite like Gilder. Those little oohs and operatic trills in "Short Distance, Long Journey" slip up and down the spine. The rushed sounding production cannot detract from the well-rehearsed rock energy and dreamy melodrama. This self-titled album has no duds—okay, the instrumental "The Kilt," with its fake bagpipe synths, might be, but it certainly is audacious. The album closer "Let's All Do It Again" makes us eager for more. Will everyone all do it again?

Apart from the odd platformed heel and brightly colored hair-dye job, Sweeney Todd's fans were mostly normal teenaged kids. Marr points out that this was because of where their manager Barry Samuels booked them: "Every time someone meets me for the first time, [they say,] 'You played at my high school!' I know! I played at everybody's freaking high school in the whole Lower Mainland. I'm sure we didn't miss a one."

In 1976, Gilder, along with his songwriting partner, the guitarist James McCulloch, both left the band for a solo career in L.A. on a U.S. and worldwide deal, just as "Roxy Roller" was about to hit number one in Canada, a pivotal time for the band. Sweeney Todd swiftly got themselves a top-notch new guitarist by the name of Skip Prest. Auditions were held for the coveted singer position. One future member of the Glam band Toys was so nervous at the prospect of filling Gilder's shoes that he left a trail of Hall's lozenges scattered behind him. The producer moved fast, forcing an unknown guy on the band to be the front-man. The band, in turn, teased the new singer mercilessly. This guy, a bit of a burly boy named Clark Perry, got to tour as far as the oil town of Fort St. John, British Columbia, and even got a chance to record "Roxy Roller" for the U.S. market. It was quite a couple of months for Clark. "Really nice guy and a good singer," says Marr. "The voice wasn't quite right for us. The look was definitely not right. He wasn't a thin white duke by any means. And that's when Bryan Adams went to our manager and said, 'I can do a better job than that guy.' One day we did sound check two hours early at the Port Coquitlam Arena Hockey Rink. Adams came out on the stage and sang a bunch of the songs, and we went, 'Yup, you are better than the other guy.' I don't remember who told Clark. He was feeling it from day one. People were making fun of the way he looks. We went and played Calgary with Bryan the first time and someone yells out from the audience, 'Hey, they got rid of Baretta!' because he looked like Robert Blake a little bit."

---

2   Numerous classic cinemas have been named the Roxy and Broadway.

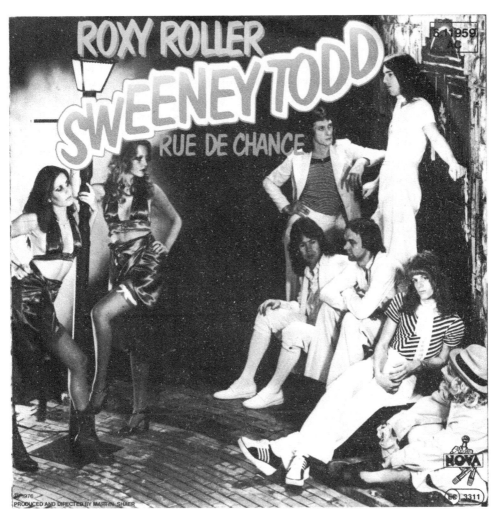

Roxy Roller, Sweeney Todd (Bryan Adams era) German single sleeve (Nova, 1976). Author's collection.

This teen dream—going by his full name of Bryan Guy Adams—had been washing dishes at the Tomahawk Restaurant, but his sights were focused up to the stars. Not yet clad as the famed everyman in jeans, with his strawberry blond locks cascading out from his top hat and tails, Adams also got his chance to record "Roxy Roller" for a single release.

A few months after Sweeney Todd's single "Roxy Roller" hit number one for three weeks running on the Canadian charts, their label presented them with a gold record and little else at Nathan Phillips Square in Toronto. Says Marr, "It was the biggest selling record in Canada that year *period*; over Paul McCartney and Queen, it sold more records than anybody. There's 20,000 kids in Nathan Phillips Square, it was frightening. We made 200 bucks for the week. That was the most we had ever made. It's usually like 75 or 100 bucks a week. The Nathan Phillips Square one was the biggest crowd I'd ever played. We had a limo driver who did funerals. He had to drive us in. There was no place, no security, just a sea of fifteen-year-old kids. By this time, they've already had five bands. A frenzy develops. We finish our set, and we have to get out of there. There's no path, no fences, just people. He's got his car and it's surrounded by teenagers, and we have to get into his car. The only way is to pass through the crowd. I'm in the back seat of this limo and I've got my feet in, and a road manager has got my legs. Some little girls have my hair. They're trying to pull me out of the car and he's trying to pull me in. And I'm thinking, 'I don't think I want to do this for a living, it's terrifying.'"

Let's take a time out to talk about "Roxy Roller." All the versions of "Roxy Roller" can make your head spin and I can't guarantee you'll walk away any less dizzy after this explanation. I created an FBI wallchart with rubber bands and bits of string to figure out all the perpetrations and I still get baffled. Although the song kicks off their debut album, this future classic wasn't Sweeney Todd's first single. Nor their second. "When you're in the middle of something you really can't tell," says Marr. "Sometimes you think something's great and then it just flops and then other times it's a surprise. It was popular: we'd been playing it for almost a year in the bars and people liked it. I guess we thought it was too simple. We wanted something more proggish like 'Sweeney Todd Folder' [the second single] which is much more leaning towards Yes or something—as opposed to T. Rex—which it's nowhere near of course," adds Marr in full self-deprecating fashion.

For the Canadian hit single version, they took the album track, shaved off a minute, then re-mixed it for your sashaying pleasure—with a completely new guitar solo, one with a more modern polish and a Cruella de Vil theme-song influence, no longer sounding like the raunchy boogie of before. Not long after Gilder and McCulloch moved to Los Angeles, Sweeney Todd re-recorded and re-released the single with Perry singing and Prest's energized guitar playing for the U.S. market, since Gilder owned the master tapes from the first recording. Then, a month or so later, Sweeney Todd swiftly erased Perry's vocals, replacing them with Adams', and released "Roxy Roller" again, both versions reaching the Billboard Top 100 in 1976. The European-released sleeve shows the lads hanging out on a simulacrum "Rue de Chance" (the B side song) having a satin-clad face-off with a pair of women draped around a ye olde style streetlamp showing leg and dressed like streetwalkers, betraying the fact that the photo was not taken anywhere near Europe, but in a studio in North Vancouver.

But what of Gilder? About the same time as the Perry version was released, he released "Roxy Roller" under his own name with the words "ORIGINAL VERSION" plastered up top. This is definitely not the original version, but yes, it uses the original tracks, heavily remixed. There are new overdubs (crazy backups and whispered "Roxy"s on the solo). Gilder sings the second verse the same as the first but skipping the lyric about her "Daddy, the Commissioner"—and whooshing and pulsating those synths way up in a whoahhh wow kinda way. And yet the version that he put on his solo album (which does not appear on the Canadian pressing in any form at all) appears to be the original Sweeney Todd single from 1975. At least five different versions of "Roxy Roller" by Gilder and Sweeney Todd were put out into the world. Not only am I confused by it all, but the public was too. States Marr, "The radio program directors got the two versions and dropped it saying, 'You guys figure this out. We're not going to play two records that are the same by two different people on two different labels.' They could have arbitrarily picked one, but they were so identical they couldn't."

"Roxy Roller" also crossed oceans. In 1977 the innovator and inspiration Suzi Quatro recorded her own version of "Roxy Roller," released in the U.K. and beyond as a single showcasing Quatro belting it out with the bass up high giving it an entirely different groove. Though Quatro was in the Glam HQ of England, she was originally from Detroit, just a ride across the Ambassador Bridge from Windsor, Ontario, where she received rock 'n' roll, soul, R&B, and Motown transmissions from the important and influential CKLW Radio, also known as 'the Big 8' in its heyday. In an email interview in Quatro's all-caps style: "I am Detroit through and through . . . weaned on Motown and CKLW." In terms of Canada in the Glam era, "I played there all the time, one of my most successful areas." As for her version of "Roxy Roller?" "It was my record company boss and mentor, Mickie Most . . . he liked the song and played it for us . . . I was in between not working with Mike Chapman and working with him again, Mickie took over the reins for a year."Mike Chapman—who had been half of the legendary Glam production team Chinnichap—would later produce Gilder's hit "Hot Child in the City." Quatro inspired innumerable musicians, including the Runaways, whose own Cheri Currie would also cover "Roxy Roller" in her solo shows. Over in France in 1978, Linda Keel did it in French and did it very well, titled simply as "Roxy," along with Gilder's "Rated X" translated into a song called "La Fille des Magazines." In 2000, Gilder, with his backing band Time Machine, updated the song with more of an electro sound and brand-new futuristic lyrics. When the Covid pandemic hit in 2020, Currie, Quatro, and Gilder released a brand-new Zoom video conference version of "Roxy Roller" for Currie's solo album *Blvds of Splendor*.

There was even an answer song to "Roxy Roller." Released during the second half of the '70s in Vancouver, the single "Baby Roller" by the one-off group Free Wheels has "be prepared" lyrics about "bubblegum kneepads" as a reply to the original's "bubblegum on her knees." This child of Roxy has a faster T. Rex groove coming in with a staggered

Sweeney Todd (Nick Gilder era) promo photo. Image courtesy of *Alberni Valley Times*, December 19, 1975.

Suzi Quatro, *Roxy Roller*, Japanese single sleeve (RAK, 1977). Author's collection.

beat then takes off soaring. The chorus is similar to "Helen Wheels," Wings' Glammiest number. The Free Wheels writer and singer J. C. Stone was doing soft folk-pop songs around this time and had a couple of singles out on London, Sweeney Todd's label, and later released a solo album, *Stealin' the Night,* on the Leo label with an album cover of a woman reclining on top of a hot-wheeling fancy car, but it has no horsepower; the album is pedestrian power-pop. As well, the Canadian AOR rock band Streetheart's standout 1982 song "Snow White" could be "*Roxy Roller*"'s kid sister with its rousing sha la la las.

Flipping Gilder's "Roxy Roller" single over, we get the song "Prophet's Tale," which only ever appeared as a B side. Gilder intones, "In case of confusion, let's set the record straight"—but it still doesn't sound straight, not with this, the closest he came to art rock with loads of distorted bass. "Running around with your lies and deceit . . . a prophet's tale so close to complete . . . a sense of allegiance if you have the time." Is this a Glam Rock diss track? What most likely was a diss was the cover of Gilder's first solo album, *You Know Who You Are,* with Nick pointing directly at the camera, a red-haired clown puppet beside him. That puppet was said to be a mocking representation of Adams.

On *If Wishes Were Horses*—the second Sweeney Todd album—Adams is resplendent in shiny white satin tux and tails; he doesn't just return Gilder's insult by looking so good. In a song written by Adams, he addresses Gilder, whom he had never met, with the lines, "This is a song for a star . . . if you really are a star. Here is a song for you all, take a lesson before you fall . . . Could have been the start of it but this is just the start of it, now." This beef was made all the more peculiar due to Adams' gilded Gilder-style vocals. Thanks to the passage of time, according to Marr, "It all smoothed over."

I once saw Adams pricing Basquiats at a gallery opening in the late '90s and called out to him, "I really love the second Sweeney Todd album!" (This is the ivory-colored album with the female red-nippled albino centaur on the cover, by the way.) Adams turned around, walked up to me, and said, "You and one other guy. He kills bugs for a living." I pressed Adams for album details, factoids, and sordid tidbits but he responded, "I was sixteen years old." I kept pressing and he repeated emphatically, "I was sixteen years old."

This version of Sweeney Todd sounds epic, the recording budget sounds bigger. Martin Shaer produced both albums and wrote the grandiose stage-setting opener "If Wishes Were Horses." Adams captures and replicates the soft-focus high pitch of Gilder in his butterfly net. Unreliable sources claim that there was studio manipulation of Adams' voice, which is totally untrue. It sounds natural (as natural as Glam can be)—balls not yet fully dropped for the signature "authentic sounding" vocal style that Adams became known for. My oldest brother saw this lineup and said that Adams held his own vocally. Although Gilder and McCulloch had vacated Canada, they did leave behind a number or two to alleviate any potential second-album curse, including the single "Tantalize," which also appears in an entirely different version on Gilder's fabulous first solo album. Who played it better? I can't decide. Gilder hits those high notes in tandem with strings soaring to the stars. But the doo doo doos and phasing and rock energy of the Adams–Sweeney version are fabulous, Prest's guitar playing is so great . . . . ahhh shucks, I don't know. They're both awesome. Describing how the album fared, Marr asks, "This went Paper, I think. It sold like 38 copies. Remember A&B Sound on Seymour Street? Under the racks of the record store there were boxes and boxes and boxes of this album with holes punched in them, 99 cents. And these were two hundred bucks at the end of the '80s when Bryan Adams was at his peak. I should have bought a box of those!"

On the back of his first solo album, Gilder wrote us all a touching note in gold ink thanking us for showing our encouragement as he rewards us with songs about porn stars and dancers and rock fans all aglow with handclaps and cheers. His love-lost ballad "Genevieve" showed up earlier in a radically different form on a 1976 single with electric guitar atmospheres and ambient swooshes instead of the power chords. Flip the 45 over for "She's a Star (in Her Own Right)," written by the Canadian ex-pat Philip Rambow of the pub-rock-sounding Winkies, Brian Eno's live backing band during his Glammier early solo era. With consecutive albums, Gilder smoothly shifted into a solid, straight-shooting power pop direction. Gilder became a songwriter for other acts until his eventual return to Vancouver in the '90s where he made a rootsier, reflective solo album.

Adams did not intend to stay with Sweeney Todd forever. Marr notes, "The first time we went out to Toronto he was already making the rounds. 'This is who I am, this is who I play for, I'm looking to get a deal of my own.' He was so driven and so convinced that he was going to be the next big thing. We were like, 'Yeah right. Whatever. You're just the sub.' He is one of those people, super hyperactive to the point of driving you fucking nuts, that's why Skip [Prest] left the band. He was annoying. He and I hung out because I was

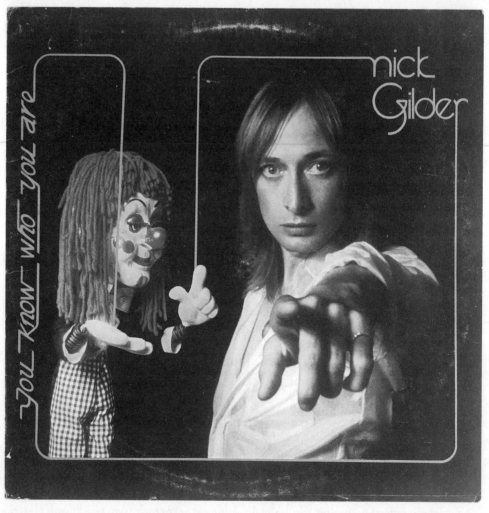

Front cover of *You Know Who You Are*, Nick Gilder (Chrysalis, 1977). Author's collection.

Front and back cover of *If Wishes Were Horses*, Sweeney Todd (London, 1977). Author's collection.

the young guy in the band before him. I was nineteen when I joined the band and by the time he came along I was twenty-one and he was seventeen. We spent a lot of time playing backgammon and Risk. Smoking cigarettes at his mom's dining room table at the house of people who don't smoke."

Prest left the band in late 1977 and was replaced by Grant Gislason, who had previously played with John Booth in Holy Smoke. Sweeney Todd continued touring hockey rinks around western Canada, opening for Trooper, as well as a stint where they headquartered in Ontario. Then, in 1978, Adams left. Booth, the drummer, was blessed with a set of twin brothers, and both boys joined their brother's band, with one of them, Chris, replacing Adams as singer for a few months, and the other, Phil, as guitarist replacing the short-lived tenure of Gislason, along with a new keyboardist, Robbie Gray. Still with me? Then, with the departure of Chris Booth, the band became a four-piece. Marr moved center stage into front-man position with his bass, writing and recording a suite of songs based on the band's namesake, the infamous nineteenth-century penny dreadful *The Demon Barber of Fleet Street*. This was the year before the famed composer Stephen Sondheim premiered his musical version, titled *Sweeney Todd,* in 1979. Says Marr, "We didn't want to do a whole concept album, it was lame by then. Then myself and our keyboard player and the guitar player at the time wrote a bunch of rock songs and they're okay, they're mostly filler." These album demos shift more towards a light prog sound; however, a total knock-out version of "Goldfinger" lays on the bombast, liberating it from its original context as a James Bond movie theme. Here, Sweeney Todd pays proper rock tribute to the musical greats John Barry, Leslie Bricusse, and Anthony Newley, who wrote the song, and to Shirley Bassey, who famously belted it out. These ten demos remained unreleased as the age of interested record companies faded into the band's past.

Ultimately, Sweeney Todd fizzled out playing their last show in what was advertised as "a teen event" on April 27, 1979, at Kerrisdale Arena.[3] Notes Marr, "In the early '80s I would never want to tell anyone that I was involved with that band, I wouldn't wear the t-shirt. It was frowned upon. Punk was the thing. I tried to join Pointed Sticks and I did that for a couple weeks but they didn't have any gigs. I need to make a living, I can't just be a punk on the street, I was twenty-five years old!"

In the '90s, Marr was playing in a country band. One night he asked Gilder to come up and sing "Roxy Roller." And, oh, that bug! It was back!

On August 26, 1998, I went to the Pacific National Exhibition. After eating some whale's tails,[4] I saw the reunion of Sweeney Todd featuring two original members: Nick Gilder and Budd Marr, along with a very un-Glam-looking band, performing just downwind from the petting zoo. Gilder was wearing a velvet purple dream coat, and "Roxy Roller" turned into an ill-advised medley with "Roadhouse Blues" by the Doors. In an impromptu phone interview a week before the show, Gilder promised me a cover of Jesus Jones's "Right Here Right Now," as it seemed prescient to him (the song was about seven or eight years old at the time). It didn't happen. A planned special appearance by Bryan Adams was leaked to the media. That didn't happen either (was it going to?). Gilder also told me that we should do lunch and that also didn't happen. It was still cool to see them perform. I sure wanted more.

A year or two later, Prest approached Marr to join this new incarnation of Sweeney Todd, having never actually played with Gilder. Marr states of this hybrid of two Sweeney Todd eras, "He was in there for a couple years. That was probably the best band I was ever in with Nick Gilder; Skip Prest, Rick Fedyk on drums, and Lee Worden played guitar and keyboards." Marr left the band in the early 2000s, other members came and went and came again. As of this writing, Sweeney Todd featuring Gilder still tours today.

NO FUN

LAUGHTER WAS THE SPARK. You can hear it on No Fun's very first recording, "Planned Disaster," a song that is fast and distorted and screamed and, yes, a lot of fun and even sounds rather punk, except some may say it's too early for punk—it's 1974—and sets the precedent for doing whatever the hell you want to. David Matychuk, known to No Fun fans simply as David M., elaborates, "We'd been trying to finish Jimmy Hamelin's new song, and he was frustrated by trying to sing and play his ten dollar electric guitar at the

---

3 Chris and Phil Booth moved to Washington State to form the band AlleyBrat, which bridged over into Glam Metal with a *Clockwork Orange*–inspired version of "Singin' in the Rain." AlleyBrat relocated to L.A. in 1980, where Chris and Phil did soundtrack work.

4 Whale's tails are a brand of locally made Vancouver fried dough covered in powdered sugar found mostly at carnivals and fairs. In Ontario, the brand is known as BeaverTails. In parts of the United States this confection is known as elephant ears.

same time. Without knowing what he was trying to do, I suggested letting me try it. The next two minutes ended with Jimmy laughing hysterically, and No Fun officially began." Before this, David and Jimmy had been playing together in a band called the Pandas, but naming themselves after the Stooges song—an energetic "dance around in your underwear" song about not having fun—was most fitting beyond form. David M. and Jimmy Hamelin kept recording. A lot. All new, all different kinds of songs, the kind that people who don't want to be bored would like. They started bouncing tracks on to Jimmy's Uher tape recorder, but only once or twice—any more bounces and there'd be too much noisy build-up. They recorded seven albums that way, along with two "greatest hits" and an EP with Ned, the ten-year-old kid brother of David M.'s oldest friend (Ned still goes to their shows) (he isn't ten anymore), before they got a four-track and then recorded four more albums, including *Hi, We're from the Gay Club* and the ninety-minute *No Fun to Spare*. These albums were all done before 1978, yet No Fun were just getting started.

David M. explains, "No one we knew was doing this. Boredom is crucial. That's why kids do it [rock 'n' roll] so much, because they're so bored and not having sex and they're losing their minds and they're frustrated. And what can we do? Rock and roll is like that, most creative fields are full of stuff where somebody is young and they're just losing their minds because nothing is happening and let's do anything other than be bored and then they're doing it the rest of their lives. Anything to alleviate the boredom."

No Fun had a most unique method of distribution for these early albums: they'd play them for basically whoever wanted to listen to them, very personalized, person to person, practically monogamous. Okay, okay, they'd dub and pass a few copies out to musician friends, but this was at a time when barely anyone had cassette players. David and Jim, who were close friends, were the two other full-time members, with other folks passing in and out to perform and record. The guitarist Dan Vere officially joined No Fun in 1977 after playing on early album sessions. David M. explains, "We're all friends as well. There was a certain Surrey [B.C.] music scene that kind of coalesced around us that was separate from trying to get in club bands. People knew right away that we were doing something that was different."

In November of 1977, No Fun ambitiously sent tapes out to record companies—not just any record companies, but the kinds of record companies that they liked. They received a rejection letter from the Canadian cueball Glam rocker Walter Zwol, then an A&R man for Attic Records. Zwol writes, "If you ever feel you would like to make your music more contemporary, please keep me posted." No Fun were so unimpressed by this letter that they later quoted it verbatim in their fast-paced song *No Fun Bio*. The following month they received a response from Virgin Records in England stating, "No Fun, we like your stuff, contact Jumbo for an appointment." Due to mail rerouting shenanigans, Jumbo van Rennen thought that No Fun were living in Surrey, England, and not Surrey, B.C.! Oh no, what a mix up! Jumbo basically told David, "Well, okay, if you're not coming to England, let me suggest this. What people are doing here is they're pressing up their own records and they put them out, and they put them in a little sleeve." David M. already owned a fair number of such singles, having bought a bunch from the import section at Quintessence Records in Vancouver. But Jumbo put the idea in his brain: do it yourself.

David M. took his four-track down to a garage studio run by Stan Cayer, whose career goes back to before 1963 when he recorded a record in Nashville with Elvis Presley's band. Cayer got the No Fun recording mastered and even arranged the pressing. And thus the first No Fun single was born in 1978. One thousand copies. Orders started trickling in immediately from the U.S. and Germany, all due to a review in *Trouser Press* ("Puts a grin on your fizz while you engage in some lively head banging"), a magazine that would also write up R. Stevie Moore, Shoes, and others on similar home-recording journeys across the continent. Thanks to their boredom, No Fun crammed in wallops of diversity with hard rockers (the title track "Fall for a Cliché" and "China Shop Raid"), a fake lute instrumental ("Interlute"), heavy psych with backwards and forwards guitar ("Paisley Brain Bolts of the Mind"), a screamer ("Now I Ain't Got No Face"), and the cosmos ("Planet," the actual name of the synthesizer patch they used).

The Ontario-based producer and manager Gary "Pig" Gold[5] sent David M. a copy of the first Simply Saucer single on Pig Records from all the way across Canada and suggested, "Hey, let me know if you want to swap records. You can distribute our record there and we'll distribute yours." Doing it grassroots style, they sent each other two boxes' worth, with David M. sticking the Simply Saucer single in record stores throughout Vancouver.

No Fun released their second single, "No Fun at the Disco," in 1979, equally jam-packed and diverse, with accordion, a little girl named Suzy singing about "Suzyside," a gentle country jingle with mooing ("Cowtown"), synth promptings ("Don't Get Uptight"), more hard rockers ("Snog"), folk ("The Man Who Collected Diseases"), and no actual disco music (the run-out grooves literally state "THIS IS NOT A DISCO RECORD" and "WE HATE DISCO")—though they did include a business card stating "No Fun, Disco Dance Music for All Occasions." Those jokers! They certainly were creative enough to create special occasions of their own.

All the No Fun material was released on their label Werewolf T-Shirts Records. After that *Trouser Press* review, Greg Shaw of *Bomp* magazine in L.A. ordered half the run of both singles for his record distribution company. When David M. visited L.A. with his friend Lester Interest in June 1979, they stopped into Tower Records, a place that Lester called "the best record store in the world." After David M. got a nice little thrill finding the No Fun EP in the No Fun section (a whole section!), he said to Lester, "I believe you about this being the best record store in the world."

Like their fellow trailblazers Simply Saucer, Rough Trade, and the Dishes in Ontario, a punk scene started springing up around them. The rock critic Tom Harrison asked David M. to bring his four-track to record the three-day long *Georgia Straight* Battle of the

---

5   Gold is also a musician and a writer, publishing the early music fanzine *The Pig Paper,* which began in 1973.

Business card insert from "No Fun at the Disco" single (Werewolf T-Shirts Records, 1979). Author's collection.

Bands in June 1978. DOA, Tim Ray and A.V., Doug and the Slugs, and No Fun all lost but continued on to much greater heights. No one remembers the band who won with their selection of Lynyrd Skynyrd covers, which was perhaps the least noteworthy thing that a band could do at the time, whatever their prize was—let's hope they savored it. Alas, only half of No Fun's energetic rock set was recorded because they were still figuring out how to make the four-track work (hey, *you* try it), but DOA released the recording of their set as *Triumph of the Ignoroids*.

In 1979 the *Vancouver Complication* album, featuring a who's who of the Vancouver punk scene, was released, and it keeps getting reissued. With a dramatic, suspenseful guitar intro moving into a strut followed by a low-lit pub sing-along chorus, No Fun's "Mindless Aggression" is definitely not *just* the Glammiest track on there, it is also the greatest by far! Their other contribution, "Old," is thirty-seven unsettlingly effective seconds of creepy voices and whistling.

No Fun often get written out of this punk history because, as David M. says, "It doesn't fit the narrative." He continues, "We're kind of like Zelig, right? We're there. You look at the pictures, we're right there." They came along before the mold was even set, doing their own thing, and, though such freedom has its price, it sure is much more of a pleasure to listen to.

One day Hamelin decided that he didn't want to do it anymore, simple as that. Then Vere was gone too. Would this stop No Fun? David M. continued on undaunted. He was casually playing with a group of guys who said, "Let's put together another band," and then immediately this new No Fun incarnation went and played three nights at the Smilin' Buddha in November 1979, quickly followed by six nights at the Cave, where a camera from the local station CKVU was there to film the lads, with club management staunchly opposed to David M.'s red nylon autumn jacket. ("My Dad got me this jacket.") The jacket stayed on.

Around this time, the band Toys were on a one-year sabbatical. The Toys guitarist Paul Leahy was delivering pizzas for Venus Pizza around the corner from David M.'s place, "so it was perfect for me. I would just walk down there about eight o'clock when it's starting to get

No Fun live at the Cave, Vancouver, c. 1979, featuring David M. in his red jacket.
Photo courtesy of David M. of No Fun.

dark in the summertime, and ride around all night with Paul delivering pizzas. We got to be really good friends. I was kind of in a similar boat." Though Leahy had already done some recording with No Fun over the previous few years and was playing live with them—even doing a six-night run of four different sets a night—Leahy was determined to see how Toys would play out. A year went by, Toys did get back together, and it went miserably. After a disastrous Toys band meeting, David M. went to see Leahy while he was delivering pizzas.

"How'd it go?"

"Well, I quit."

"So, okay, you want to join No Fun?"

"Okay."

The '70s were over. Leahy's first recording as an official No Fun band member is on the *Ghost Paper Boy in Robin's Gay Trailer Park* cassette album, released in 1981. David M. notes, "The first song I got him to play was 'It Came from Heaven' because the song is like an exact cross between T. Rex and Creedence Clearwater. Paul's a huge Marc Bolan fan." This song was subsequently re-recorded for their 1981 single, which was just commercially palatable enough to get plenty of local radio airplay.

David M. had the utmost respect for Leahy and his years and years of guitar devotion and training, which he described as a mastery that became second nature. "He could play exactly like Mick Ronson and that's not easy, bending notes. I've got a great photo of Paul sitting in my basement; he is sitting really close to a TV intently watching Mick Ronson."

The ambitious double cassette album *Snivel* contained much more than a few Glam gems, like "Direction" and "Tyger," that Leahy wrote for Toys but were never used: their loss was No Fun's gain, fitting in rather well alongside the songs "Say It with Mink," "Oh, to Be on Heroin," and "Ream Me Like You Mean It." These songs more than live up to their titles, and many have a lighter feel. No Fun's output was consistently great, of a much higher water mark than their more heralded home-recording peers. They may have done whatever they wanted, but their songcraft only makes them all the more listenable—the only drawback being that the amount of music they produced can be daunting for listeners. This isn't a case of a lost legendary act that recorded one song and vanished. Prolific and persistent, the music continuously flowed out of them.

No Fun's *1894* cassette album moved away from a full band sound and became their most popular release, selling over four hundred copies. David M. speculates, "I think, because the whole concept behind it was 'Let's do something that's really basic that sounds like us in the basement. But let's make sure "Be Like Us" is on it because we were already doing it.' People liked the song." "Be Like Us" was No Fun's anthem, a catchy song that tells you to "kill your parents . . . eat human flesh . . . burn churches . . . dance to rock music" and so much more!

No Fun live was now just David M. on acoustic guitar and Leahy on electric guitar playing melodic, deceptively simple leads bursting into solos like a full-blown band. This approach seemed more direct and less confusing for the audience, who were often invited

Paul Leahy watching Mick Ronson on television. Photo courtesy of David M.

No Fun with Gorgo.
Photo courtesy of David M. of No Fun.

to sing along on the lifestyle mantra "Work Drink Fuck Die." People described them as "Glam Folk," a wide-ranging catch-all. David M. comments, "We were friends, that was the main thing. That's all it is, the No Fun that you know, when you would see us play, didn't you think we were friends?"

At the tenderized age of sixteen, my then friend Ken took me to see No Fun perform. I nervously sneaked in, but no one batted an eye, and I was soon put at ease once No Fun hit the stage: maybe we were meant to see this—a positive influence on the youth—get some proper subversive culture. They were my first club show ever and I thought that's what all club shows were like and that all bands were friends. I was so fucking naïve.

Some of the more aesthetically presbyterian types could dismiss No Fun as musical comedy, and certainly they have songs that would be in the best of that genre—more sardonic than milk-spraying-out-your-nose funny—but they were also much more than that, no pin downs. Nevertheless, live No Fun got goofier as the '80s progressed: there were the theme shows "*No Fun on Drugs*," "*No Fun in Love*," and "*No Fun at Christmas*." In the mid '80s, David M.'s girlfriend Penny Borg joined No Fun as a regular performer, becoming the "chanteuse" Pico, with parts being written just for her, a refreshing addition to the group. Also, Leahy met his wife Kimiko Karpoff through Borg, who was a mutual friend. Pico appears on a few of their albums, most notably on *The Night Smells Like a Dog*, but she left in 1996 when she and David M. broke up.

One day in 1985, David M. found a new obsession. It was at his local 7-Eleven that he came across Gorgo, a "Cosmic Green Chew Bar with Fizzy Fruit Flavour." On the package was a green alien overlord, one dripping sticky hand coming out of a large bubbling cauldron, the other hand throwing in the black fizzy lime bursts. There was nothing quite like it. Honestly, it was the kind of thing that you'd dream of seeing on the candy shelf. I can still taste it all these years later. Gorgo was intensely good and inspired No Fun to come up with their very own Gorgo parody jingles, some of which are sprinkled throughout the *No Fun on Stage* cassette, such as "Gorgo Days," sung to the tune of Bruce Springsteen's "Glory Days." On *Nightlines*, the eclectic, adventurous, late, lamented all-night CBC radio show that aired direct from Vancouver all across Canada, the host David Wisdom often brought No Fun in to perform, always including their tributes to Gorgo.[6]

The noted Vancouver writer and historian John Mackie dubbed No Fun "the Beatles of Surrey." Surrey—a part of Metro Vancouver, the poorer next-door neighbor city that is still the unfortunate butt of many jokes—was No Fun's hometown. Walking around Surrey lately, I have made numerous attempts to take "the scenic route," only to find that there is none.

By the mid '80s, No Fun was garnering a fair bit of press, and much of it mentioned Gorgo. David M. gathered up these clippings and sent photocopies to Gorgo's Scottish candy manufacturer. Lo and behold, he soon received a package full of Gorgo t-shirts and posters, along with a phone call from nearby Langley, British Columbia. "Hi, I distribute candy. And I am wondering why this candy supplier I deal with is telling me to give you whatever you want." David M. explained the situation and got the invitation, "Come out here and get some Gorgo." Loaded up with boxes of Gorgo, No Fun now had Gorgo to throw out to the delighted crowd when they did their Gorgo jingles.

At Expo 86, a World's Fair held in Vancouver, No Fun performed shows and gave out Gorgo for the whole world, as David M. describes: "little kids are running down to get it and I'm faking them out and throwing it. And actually, that guy [the candy distributor], he later became mayor of Langley, and he was kind of a right-wing, hardline Christian guy. He said, 'You're playing at Expo? I'm coming to see you.' So, he came to the first show. He phoned the next day and said, 'I gotta tell you, it was just terrific. I really enjoyed it. I would just ask that you watch the obscenities and the blasphemies,' and I said, 'Hey, we always do.'" As a candy, Gorgo was just too good to last, its green light shining all too brightly, called back to its home far away from earth. However, David M. has a secret stash in his fridge.

Though their last album, *The Night Smells Like a Dog* (which closes with the poignant seven-minute opus "Entering Bikini Area," its ribald double meaning sung ever so plaintively), was released in 1990, No Fun did record a CBC Radio session in 2000 of mostly new material, featuring many of the songs that were to be on their proposed album *Great Name*. However, their live audiences were beginning to dissipate.

After decades of service, Leahy's last No Fun show was on the ominous date of June 6, 2006 (made more ominous written as 06/06/06.) Still paying tribute to Gorgo—long gone but not forgotten, well, not by No Fun at least—with the Queen parody "Gorhemian Rhapsody." David M. states, "Paul never quit No Fun. If we got offered a show, I would call him. In 2015, we were offered a thing at Khatsahlano Festival and so I called Paul, and the thing is, he was sick for a long time. I said, 'Yeah, they're asking for No Fun, do you want to do it?' And he said, 'Well, let me think about it.' He knew he never had to explain anything to me about anything. 'Just tell me, tell me what you want.' And he said, 'No,

---

6 This was just one aspect of a show that I would try my best to stay awake listening to as a teen in an isolated northern B.C. town, affecting me heavily. One never knew what Wisdom was going to play from his own record collection. The ultimate free-form deejay, he wisely avoided the CBC record library like the plague, as his taste was wide ranging. There were things played in the middle of the night that scared me, but I kept coming back every weekend.

no, I always want to know when we're offered something, just case by case. But just give me a few days.' So, he thought about it for a few days. And then he said, 'I don't think I'll be able to do it. But I want you to do it.' And I said, 'Well, I don't want to do it. Other than as No Fun.' And he said, 'Well, no, no, I want you to do this. I want you to do the show.' So that is the one and only No Fun show where he insisted that it still be called No Fun."

On January 27, 2017, the day after Leahy's death, David M. showed up at "The Super Duper Show: A Tribute To Paul Leahy" and played a few songs alone on acoustic guitar specifically related to his departed friend.

In recent years, David M. has started using the No Fun name again as the No Fun Gang, comprising people who have been involved with No Fun for decades, including Lester Interest. Lester was there through everything, being close to both David M. and Leahy. Lester was billed to play the No Fun Gang's "Paul Leahy Jam Session" on May 6, 2019, but died suddenly of cancer that very day. "Him and Paul, I have no way to recover from those personal losses in my life. When I'm playing and I'm doing a show it's very similar to what we were doing all along, Paul and I—and I do feel their presence literally. I don't know those people without No Fun. Everything in my life comes directly from No Fun, my work situations, where I'm living, everything."

In 2022, the American label Fractional Farthing started the Atomic Werewolf sublabel, which has been releasing a flurry of No Fun reissues on CD, cassette, and vinyl.

TOYS AND POLLY

IS NOW A GOOD TIME? Is there ever a bad time to throw on a few songs by Toys? It feels good! Take the infectious Glammy power pop of their song "Hello!" So inviting! Hello! Isn't there a Glam Rock band called Hello? Why yes, there is.

Toys' ballad "It's Gotta Be Love" is by turns swoony and squelchy while maintaining a pleading come-on, wanting to get tender and even classy by setting the scene with candlelight and a French red wine. What vintage? '70s. 1970s. At least one button became undone, guaranteed. You can catch the influences on "Sweet Theme" when the singer goes, "as Roxy turns another trick," with a little razzle-dazzle piano. Is this a "Roxy Roller" answer song? Isn't there a Glam Rock band called Sweet? Yes, there is. Clutching their pearly headphones tight, the listener implores, "Why haven't I ever heard these gems before???" I'll tell you why: because they weren't released.[7]

One must not underestimate the cultural impact of the shocking, subversive, and wildly funny films of John Waters, particularly the widely distributed comedy *Pink Flamingos* from 1972. Its break-out star was Divine, who did a new, creative kind of drag utterly un-

---

[7] Only one song, "Hello," has seen release as of this writing, available as a bonus track on the Polly *Make It a Smash* EP.

shackled from celebrity impersonation, societal standards of body norms, and "lady-like" behavior. *Pink Flamingos* came right out of Baltimore and became a hit on the Midnight Movies circuit. After reading about the dogshit-eating scene, David M. figured that the only way he would get a chance to see the film was to drive across the U.S. border. Luckily, he didn't have to go too far, just another short journey from Surrey to Vancouver.

The young owners of the Rembrandt, an independent Vancouver repertory cinema, took a chance—one that very few other theaters in Canada took—and started playing *Pink Flamingos* on April 24, 1975, more than three years after its release in the U.S. The censorship boards of several Canadian provinces had edited the movie down, with the more offensive bits removed,[8] as was the case when it had earlier screened at the Original 99 Cent Roxy Theatre in Toronto.[9] *Pink Flamingos* was banned outright in the province of Nova Scotia until 1997.[10] In Vancouver, *Pink Flamingos* played the Rembrandt for months.

David M. and Hamelin went multiple times, dragging everyone they could to these midnight screenings at the Rembrandt. David M. still thinks that *Pink Flamingos* is the finest movie ever made, stating, "I mean, you can live your life based on what is suggested in that movie. If you are what you are, then you're going to be okay, it will even save you if you're in trouble. But if you're trying to be something you're not then it will destroy you and I still think that's true." Hamelin and the future No Fun guitarist Dan Vere made the journey to the Rembrandt without David M. one night, bringing along their friends Leahy and Bruce MacKenzie.

Pink Flamingos so inspired Leahy and MacKenzie that they named their band Babs Jonson, a misspelling of Babs Johnson, after the alias that Divine's character uses to hide from scrutiny. A few lineup shifts later and Babs Jonson became Toys. This was a name more befitting their youthful charms, denoting a ring of young playthings, as well as being a nod to New York Dolls, whom both Leahy and the new singer Rex-Jackson Coombs loved. Coombs had previously been in a band with Tim Ray[11] and once auditioned for the vacant lead-singer slot in Sweeney Todd. Coombs was even offered the job but "I ran it past my dad who rather emphatically said, 'NO WAY ... are you quitting school?' So, I had to decline the offer." This Sweeney Todd audition was how Leahy caught wind of Coombs, who passed the audition in MacKenzie's parents' home to join Toys.

---

8   In an interview with the *Toronto Star*, Waters stated that he received a note from the Ontario Censor Board about his 1970 movie *Multiple Maniacs* that said, "Destroyed."

9   Though they had the tux-clad musician Nash the Slash as the valet for the premiere and the promoter Gary Topp played many John Waters movies straight from the source, Topp even called Waters up to say, "You got to get into punk rock and you got to see this guy Stiv Bators," Soon after, Bators was cast in Waters' *Polyester*. The Original 99 Cent Roxy screened lots of wild stuff, and Topp would often play Roxy Music albums before the movies.

10   In the '90s, the pop culture aficionado Ian Marshall brought his friends to a screening at the University Art Gallery in Guelph, Ontario. All of the tickets were bought up by a bunch of nuns—and maybe a priest or two—who sat in folding chairs with their backs to their screen. Thankfully, another informal screening was added, no nuns.

11   Tim Ray was later known for releasing what is deemed the first Vancouver punk single in 1977—"Space Race" b/w "Time Waves."

Toys promo photo, c. 1977. Image courtesy of Kimiko Karpoff.

Toys' main songwriters were Coombs and Leahy. Like Leahy, Coombs's tastes ran towards Glam, as well as power pop and avant-garde rock. The rest of the band members leaned more towards prog. David M. notes that Leahy's favorite Glam Rock album of all time was *Queen 2,* saying, "It is a singular achievement in the Glam Rock field." *Queen 2* was the common ground among Toys members, providing inspiration for their unifying black-and-white visual aesthetic. Paired with scarves and tight white jeans, their matching white and navy-blue striped shirts came from Samson's, a men's clothing shop owned by the father of Coombs's friend Steve Samson.

David M. says about Glam at the time, "I would go see bands and mostly they weren't doing it. Toys were thin and could be dolled up and made up to look like Glam Rock, so they could do it. But thin was crucial. And you know, good looking. And you needed a lot of hair. It's a young man's game. It's a thin man's game." Coombs notes, "Initially we wore make up for only the larger or weekend shows. We had a girl named Gay do our 'slap.' She was a friend of Bruce's, and she would come out and tart us up for the shows. The idea was to look like oversized Toy Dolls." It was 1976 and the Bay City Rollers were teen idols that the girls all screamed for. With Toys being no slouches in the cute department themselves, the Bay City Rollers certainly influenced their image.

After learning a lot of covers—Bowie, Mott the Hoople, Queen, Sweeney Todd, even Styx—Toys hit the road with a massive PA and lighting system, their management booking them into countless clubs and a few showcases, with just a bit of time to record a demo of original material. One original, "Rich and Famous," may just be the most ridiculously camp thing ever, with tinkling ivories and Coombs coyly singing, "Boop boop ba doop." Performed live and on CKVU, it was never recorded, which is a damned shame. Being underage at the time, Toys weren't legally allowed in the establishments except to perform on stage. The rest of the time was spent in the dressing room or—in the case of the small pulp-mill city nine hours north of Vancouver, Prince George—in the dressing room of the strip club downstairs. The strippers adopted them like children. As Coombs put it, "Our relationship with the stripping fraternity continued until I left the band. They were great fun and always had our back."

Their recorded originals were very much in the same bag as Sweeney Todd. As for their covers, Coombs said, "We soon got the reputation for doing Todd better than Todd. A lot of people got not only the bands confused, but Bryan and I confused. We swapped girlfriends, dated the same girls at one point or another. After Bryan left Todd . . . they offered me the job for a second time. I again respectfully declined."

Toys made a few regional TV appearances, including a telethon, during which, Coombs recounts, he and Leahy got separated from the others: "Panicked, we went through a door that said 'Auditorium' thinking we could get to the stage that way … We came up in the middle of the audience. It was as close to experiencing Beatlemania as I will ever come. The girls were on us before we knew what was happening. They were ripping our shirts off, hair out . . . clawing us to pieces ... We dove for the stage and clambered to safety just in time for the cameras to spin around to catch us climbing out of the mosh pit having been ravaged by 'ankle biters.'"

Toys got their picture in the "More New Bands" section of *Rock Scene Magazine*, the Glammiest mag of all. Unfortunately, *Rock Scene* mixed up the caption with that of another band. Fortunately, that band happened to be the now very legendary art rockers Simply Saucer, the same band whose Pig Records single David M. would soon be distributing across Vancouver, as related earlier. The caption read, "The Toys may hail from Canada, but their recent Japanese tour showed they might well be contenders for the Rollers' crown. Or so Lisa Broughton and Valerie Spanier of the Toy fan club tells us . . . "

You read it right. Toys flew to Japan for what was to be a six-month tour. Sounds too good to be true? Coombs states that the first show was in a supper club, opening with the white noise of "Hello" accompanied by flashpots going off, causing cutlery to rattle. Diners were in shock. The plug was pulled after just three songs. Goodbye! Coombs elaborates, "What did happen in Japan should stay there. I can tell you this, we were not ready for it. The promoter had been running ads about the band and, as we stuck out like a sore thumb, we began to garner a great deal of unwanted fan attention. We did several big shows and another quick stint in a club until the authorities told the promoter to either lay on more security or send us home, which he did. We were obviously more trouble than we were worth. We came back in serious debt and with our tail between our legs. We thought it was going to be the first step to a big recording deal." For these Japan shows, as Leahy later told his son Finn, Toys alternated with a flamboyant boy band from the Philippines. David M. says, "Leahy described it to me as like some kind of Japanese mobbed up prostitution, drugs for rich guys or something." The six-month tour wound up lasting less than two weeks.

After Japan, their management sent the lads on the road for more grueling touring, performing their big Glam Rock show in small bars across the land. Leahy's wife Kimiko Karpoff remembers the stories that both Leahy and Randy, the lighting guy, told her. "They drove cars that sounded like they barely drove. They're driving from Regina in a car that has no heat in the wintertime. When they stopped, he couldn't open his hands because they were frozen to the steering wheel. He talked about staying in hotel rooms or band rooms and those were the days where bands got money, but they weren't making any money—they had to pay their promoter." As Toys relentlessly toured, all the money went towards expenses—even getting charged for the weekend self-help seminar scam that their manager forced them to take! I am trying to imagine these young rock musicians locked in a hotel conference room alongside various middle management business types, all forced to endure intensive personal growth sessions led by the EST-like cult Lifespring, who made no new converts out of Toys.

Toys believed that if they wanted to make it they needed to stop touring and shift their focus to writing and recording more original material. Coombs sums it up: "As the new songs were shaping up it became clear that we were headed in different directions. It was at this

Toys and Simply Saucer switcheroo in *Rock Scene Magazine*, February 1978. Photo courtesy of David M.

point that the band decided that I was not going to cut it as a vocalist, did not like my material, and sacked me." David M. elaborates, "The manager could see that mutiny was going to happen. So, it was better to stop and wait." It was decided that Toys would take a one-year break.

When the group came back in 1979, instead of finding another singer, Toys decided to become a prog band, alienating any fans that they may have had even further by having the drummer do most of the singing. Though he no longer fit in, Leahy stayed with them, wisely leaving the stage for their one cover, a version of Emerson, Lake, and Palmer's "Hoedown."

David M. loved the exuberant showmanship of the first incarnation of Toys but now started going to see them for different reasons. "It was kind of interesting to see how they're playing somewhere, and people are just hating them, booing. They were doing originals and most of the originals were terrible. But Paul would get his one song per set to sing, and people would snap to attention because he knows what he's doing, he's putting on a show. They had this one song called 'Music of Men.' I think it was their attempt to do something like 'We Will Rock You' because it was so repetitive, but what they did with it was make it this ten-minute thing, [strums] 'Play the music of men, play the music, play the music, play the music of men . . . ' and there was nothing else to it, there'd be long solos and that was it. They had this one ballad called 'It Doesn't Take Much.' And again, on and on, like ten minutes, and it would stop in the middle and the singer would be singing very gently. 'It doesn't take much. It doesn't take much.' You could hear hate just in the air and the song has been going for a couple of minutes already, and they're stopping and they're

The students at Queen Elizabeth Senior Secondary School had an early start celebrating Valentine's Day, with a dance last Friday. The Bobs Johson group made its debut as a band. Three of the musicians are students at the school.
At the front are Peter Trutzak, bass, at left; vocalist Brent Belair.
Back row — Paul Leahy, lead guitar and Ron Nociar, percussion

Debut photo of Babs Jonson featuring future members of Toys. Misspelled as "Bobs Johson group." Image courtesy of *Surrey Leader*, February 12, 1976.

dragging it out with this quiet part. And it was kind of awesome. It was immediately after that they were getting fired from gigs. This is the second reason I was going to see Toys, not just because it was a train wreck, but because I wanted to support Paul. I wanted to see him happy. I didn't want to see him miserable because this thing is a big disaster. So, after a couple of months of pretty abject failure that they were not used to, their manager called a meeting. They're like, 'We want to take some time off, hire a singer and work up some Top 40 stuff and get back into that and then go from there.' And Paul said, 'That wasn't the deal.' And he quit. That was it." After all his devoted hard work in the band for barely any pay, Leahy had to give them back his black Les Paul guitar and stack of Hiwatt amps. This treatment by the music business changed Leahy's attitude. He joined No Fun. As David M. says, "Let's just do something worth doing." Leahy continued with No Fun for well over two decades. What happened to Toys after Paul Leahy left? Who fucking cares.

It was while Leahy was working part-time at a candy shop in the late '90s that the owner, Valeria Fellini (a former member of the '90s cuddle-core band Cub), formed the Transvestimentals in 1998 as a showcase for the songwriting talents of Leahy and the candy shop's co-manager Nicole Steen of the noir rock band Coal, along with the bassist Adrian Bolden. Fluid and raw and high energy with wig swapping and drawn-on facial hair, the Transvestimentals released a cassette in 1998, which included the Leahy-scribed song "Cosmic Planet Rock." For this project Paul had been using the stage name Polly.

Leahy's next project, Pleasure Suit, a tight power trio with Eric Napier and Marc L'Esperance, recorded tracks in 2002 for an album that was never completed as the band had already moved on. Pleasure Suit foreshadowed the more overt Glam of his next project, Polly. Polly began after Leahy had surgery for throat cancer. Karpoff explains, "He had a really hard time because he couldn't sing very well, and he couldn't really talk. He was kind of depressed thinking maybe he'd never be able to make any music again." Leahy found a small studio right down the street from his home. Karpoff continues, "He just went in there and he said, 'I want to try a thing. I want to record a song. I just want to do it on my own. So, we'll do it in in layers, record tracks track by track. I have a little song I thought

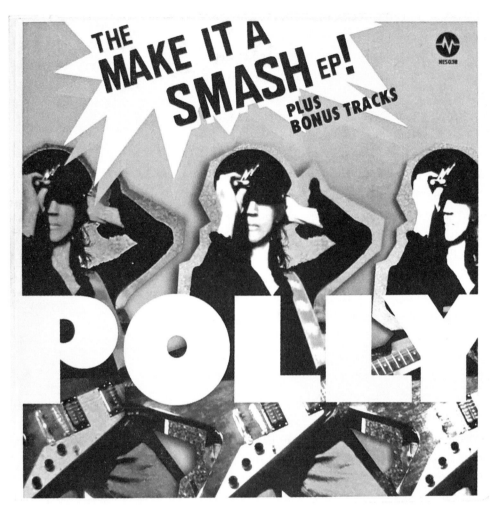

The *Make It a Smash* EP, Polly (Northern Electric, 2016). Author's collection.

I would just come and try it. Are you game to help me try this experiment?' They did 'Roll 'Way the Stone.' And then they thought, 'Okay, well, so that worked. Let's try another.'"

Polly was the purest expression of Paul Leahy. The album took him two years to make. Paul plays everything on it. Released in 2012 on Northern Electric, *All Messed Up* is not just the greatest Glam Rock album of that decade, but it would fit in very nicely with the original Glam era, an era that Leahy himself was there for. With all that Leahy had to overcome, one would never know it from listening to Polly. He is in perfect form, a pure, joyful form. Everything on the album is Paul. The coyest vocals, harmonies, multiple tracks of his incredible guitar playing—so rich and so lustrous, plus bass and drums and keyboards, letting you know exactly the intent with the opener "It's a Glam Glitter World." It's hard to believe that this was all done by one man. Leaving us exuberantly drained and wanting more, Polly closes the album with "Roll 'Way the Stone." The apostrophe in the title winks saying, "No, this isn't the Mott the Hoople single, but why don't you throw this one next to it on your mix tape?"

The Northern Electric label put a live band together for Leahy consisting of members of the pivotal Vancouver punk band Pointed Sticks. This lineup fell apart after a rocky tour to Vancouver Island because those Pointed Sticks still liked to party a little too hard. But the feelings weren't so hard. Agreeably, Leahy let them go and got a new lineup. Of Leahy's live presence Karpoff states, "There were people who didn't recognize him. They would see him after the show and not actually know that that was him. He was super shy, painfully shy. When you saw him on stage, he was bigger than life, jumping around singing, big voice."

On December 1, 2015, Leahy's birthday, he noticed that something wasn't right. He had it checked out and it was oral cancer. The cancer had returned. He had so much energy that cancer seemed like a thing of the past. Leahy had just performed a big show at the Rickshaw three days before. Karpoff notes, "I missed it because I was working the next day. Of course, I didn't know at the time it was going to be his last." In early 2016, Leahy started recording again, knowing that he was sick. He recorded until he could no longer sing, releasing the five songs as *The Make It a Smash EP!* Short but oh so sweet, *Make It a Smash!* is one helluva last hurrah. Opening with Glam stomper drumbeats, romping through five songs, two of which have "Super" in the title, including the very appropriate "Super Duper Star" and closing triumphantly with "Theme from Elvira Madigan," a variation on Mozart's Piano Concerto No. 21, showcasing his outstanding harmonic guitar tones. A CD bonus track, "Pomp & Circumstance," is absolutely everything you would hope it to be, like a candelabra outstretched into far-reaching lighters in the sky, little vocal squeals and ohs singing, "We really made a mess this time."

Karpoff explains, "He had surgery in April 2016. And the surgeon said, 'It went as good as it can go,'

TIM RAY & A/V, PHIL SMITH & CORSAGE

There are a couple of Vancouver bands centered on distinctive personalities that some people tell me fit more into Glam than the punk just warming up, with their sound veering closer to post-punk or oddball power-pop but also so uniquely their own thing they were in danger of getting written out of history, or not getting written in at all in the first place, snubbed from the gala again. So here I am placing my write-in ballots: one for Tim Ray and one for Phil Smith.

Phil Smith's band name Corsage was a play on the New Romantic band Visage and, though the New Romantics had a powdery Bowie fixation, Corsage is really a much Glammier name. Zulu Records' very first release, *The Phil Smith Album,* from 1983, collects earlier material including "The Shame I Feel," with its saxophone and a million psychoanalytical things going on lyrically. There's an incredible music video for it made from commercial film ends and someone's meager inheritance, with members of the first Vancouver all-woman punk band, the Dishrags, singing and appearing in it, as well as street dancers, the artist and one-time Corsage member Rodney Graham, and a little person named Angel blowing sax in a clown costume. Angel was a Bulgarian circus performer who claimed to have escaped to the West from the Moscow Circus by hiding in the bottom of a lion cage. Prior to filming, Smith and the production searched high and low for a little person until at the very last minute they found Angel, who was imploring, "I need work, any kind of work." Angel provided his own costumes and would join them dancing on stage for live shows, taunting the audiences on the mic. Some of Corsage's live shows featured a ten-piece band, including dancers and projections, with Smith all over the stage, not holding back. Of this he says, "Things happen." On a family trip to England during the height of T.-Rex-mania—"Oh my God, the general hysteria around Marc Bolan"—a teenaged Smith saw Alice Cooper at Wembley Stadium. He describes, "It was just off-the-charts amazing! I think I was thirteen or fourteen. Opening for them was this new band called Roxy Music and at that stage it was with Eno—and with their leopard-print suits. I knew 'Virginia Plain' a bit because it was on the radio. I knew nothing else. But they ended with this song that was just mind-blowing, just a kind of drone riff that built and built and then later I found out it was 'Remake/Remodel.' That was pretty revelatory, I have to say, and seeing the visual so fused with the conceptual—even though at thirteen I didn't know those terms—but you felt it." Alice Cooper's stage persona also appealed to him: "That you could fuse drama,

but he probably wouldn't have been able to sing again because he lost a lot of his tongue and a piece of his jaw. Then he healed really well." In late summer, Leahy knew something was wrong. After Thanksgiving they finally got in to see the oncologist, who said, "No, it's cancer and we have no treatment for it." Leahy entered palliative care for pain relief on Remembrance Day and never went home.

While Leahy was in palliative care, a fundraising tribute show was organized for January 27, 2017. In the months leading up to the concert, Leahy's son Finn came up with the idea of making an elaborate box set for it containing CDs of Paul's various groups, including never before released tracks by Toys and Pleasure Suit (mixed by Marc L'Esperance working from Leahy's notes specifically for the box set[12]). Karpoff and a friend put it all together including postcards, buttons, and fridge magnets. It was called *The Polly Package*. Finn Leahy comments, "Mom didn't get the dick joke, but dad and I were like, 'heh heh.'"

With the tumor growing, Leahy entered hospice on December 2, 2016. "Then he died on the day before the tribute show," shares Karpoff. "There were people at the tribute show who didn't know he died. They were like, 'Oh, when's Paul coming?' But it was a great night of music. Finn performed. He was fantastic." Says Finn, "I sang 'Kooks' by David Bowie, as well as 'Jet Jet & the Golden Feather' with the hodgepodge of people who played with dad in the band." Pointed Sticks performed the Polly song "Put a Little English on It," then recorded it two days later. They still perform it at every show. Karpoff says, "Paul had a Glamminess, and he loved that genre, but I think he transcended it."

---

12 These songs are on Bandcamp as the *Put It On* EP.

THOR
(AND FRANK SODA)

THERE ARE NUMEROUS THORS covering the globe, chafing deep within the hard-to-reach areas. Some Thors are many centuries old, carried forward by word of mythy mouth, some are in faded four-color newsprint, but here now in this very book that you are holding, dear reader, we are focused on one Thor and one Thor alone: Thor, the Rock Warrior. His combined love of bodybuilding and rock music came to him early on. One need not get all Nordic when trafficking in the entwinements of Adonis and Dionysus, those noble twin pursuits. You may be asking, "What is bodybuilding?" According to Wikipedia, "Bodybuilding is the use of progressive resistance exercise to control and develop one's musculature for aesthetic purposes." What does that mean? Go ask your mother. Hope you like muscles!

Jon-Mikl Thor started entering physique contests at the age of thirteen. Says Thor, "I was influenced a lot by Elvis Presley, and I was also a bodybuilder. If you remember, in 1970, '71, he wore very glittery, glam type of jackets and garb and I started wearing that stuff on stage because I had a band called the Ticks and then it evolved into Centaur and then I got more heavy with a band called Man. And Man was sort of Glam up before Glam was really that popular." Promoting concerts at Lasseter's Den, a live music venue with a large devil painted on the door, Thor says, "I would put on concerts there and bodybuilding shows, and I would combine them with Mr. Western Canada and other bands. Then I would come out in these gold capes and strange headdresses and masks, and it was pretty wild."

Vancouver's big supper-club scene was at its zenith. Glowing warmly at night, Vancouver was a city lit by multi-colored neon, calling one in to get dinner and a full-blown show. Some of these shows were elaborate burlesque stage shows enhanced by a cornucopia of showmanship from burlesque dancers using magic,

theatre, music, art into some kind of performance piece." Smith later did two years as a theater student in university and returned to academia in 1999 as an art-school lecturer in humanities, media history, and Interdisciplinary forums.

Corsage came about after the dissolution of Smith's seminal

Phil Smith, 1983. Image courtesy of *The Vancouver Sun*, June 24, 1983.

punk band Wasted Lives. The band members of Corsage were Smith, Bill Napier-Hemy, and the Dishrags—of whom he says, "They were so influenced by Bowie and Lou Reed—even to the look." In fact, the Dishrags recorded a cover of "Vicious" by Reed. Corsage first appeared on a compilation of "fuck bands," a humorous Vancouver punk tradition—though Corsage transcended with legs!

At the Pacific National Exhibition in the Summer of 1981, Ron Obvious set up a temporary recording studio called the Fishbowl. Some of the material from *The Phil Smith Album* was recorded there. Smith describes, "Literally it was open glass to the concourse, and there'd be kids eating cotton candy, farmers with their animals, just watching us record. I kind of loved it because you know what recording studios are like—we're talking about with performance, it's hard particularly for vocalists to really get the same energy level—but this was great, there was tons of people watching—some were thumbs up, some were giving us the finger, whatever. The warmth of that studio, it was amazing. That studio, I swear it had some of the best, warmest sound." One can only imagine the crowds' response watching Smith roar upon roar on the audaciously slinky "I'm a Lion," aided and abetted by a hallucinogenic red wine. Corsage has continued to make music with a healthy Bandcamp page and a rare show in 2023.

Tim Ray released what is often noted as the first Vancouver punk single in 1977, but, like most people on the ground floor, including No Fun, it didn't fit punk. The music is smart and poppy. Future members of Pointed Sticks, including Bill Napier-Smith, were in the first lineup of his band A/V. Alexander Varty was in a later lineup. Varty recalls seeing the former Sweeney Todd singer Bryan Adams pull up to drop off his friend Ray at band practice in a

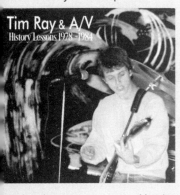

bright white sportscar—just like the Glammy Trooper song of the same name. A CD collection of Ray and A/V's music was put together and released by Ron Obvious titled *History Lessons, 1978-1984*. It is twenty-five solid, punchy songs long, including the unreleased EP that fell through due to lack of money, leading Ray to move to New York. Ray is a painter, so his music could be filed under art rock. Varty's liner notes describe Ray as a "former glam fancier."

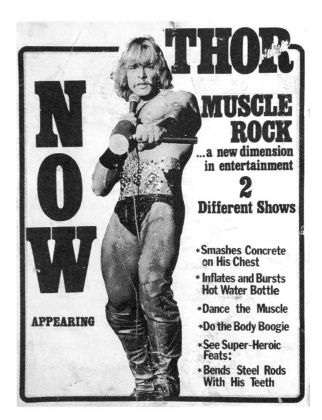

Thor Muscle Rock poster, c. 1976. Courtesy of Rob Frith.

live animals, bubbles, and more.[13] Isy's Supper Club advertised one particular musical revue as "Boys will be girls/It's unisex all the way!" It may seem kooky, but there was once a time when sleeping did not rank high among the city of Vancouver's interests, and yet it all looked like such a dream.

On the movie set of *The Groundstar Conspiracy*, a plastic-surgery amnesia thriller starring George Peppard, Thor met the costumer Clyde Dubois. Designing costumes for the burlesque dancers, Dubois was the go-to guy, reputed for his impeccably flashy, glittery outfits. The man really knew his way around a sequin. Says Thor, "I would don these glam outfits that he made for me. And that's when I started getting out of the suits and ties of the Ticks, the British Invasion look, and getting

---

13 Becki Ross, *Burlesque West: Showgirls, Sex, and Sin in Postwar Vancouver* (University of Toronto Press, 2009), p. 104.

more flamboyant. I got in with Isy Walters, the owner of Isy's Supper Club, and a lot of the strippers at that time. Jayne Mansfield would come in and perform there. Vancouver was trying to sort of have their own Las Vegas in Vancouver. I took all these concepts and then incorporated them into my show, and I wanted to become more flamboyant than just the four guys standing there playing music." As Glam moved in, Thor became influenced by that too: *Ziggy Stardust and the Spiders from Mars,* Alice Cooper, KISS, and so on, so forth.

Comic book bodybuilding ads promoting desire and, if not physical alteration, then at least voyeurism are a running theme in Glam. And then there's the homoeroticism. The hit Glam Rock stage musical *The Rocky Horror Show* outright quotes these ads with the lyrics " . . . in just seven days I can make you a man . . . "[14]

"We are Body Rock, we will sonic shock!" goes the theme to Thor's bodybuilder band Mikl Body Rock. In the Summer of 1974, they performed at the Commodore Ballroom for *the* Canadian Glam event! The Vancouver weekly the *Georgia Straight* ran a review of the show by Rob Geldof who later became Bob Geldof then later still Sir Bob Geldof after being knighted by a Queen. He was unimpressed by the openers, Twitch and Seattle's Ze Whiz Kidz, but when he saw Mikl Body Rock he was practically salivating. In his concert review "Sand Gets in Your Eyes" in the *Georgia Straight* he wrote,

"Basically, Mikl Body Rock consists of John Mikl [*sic*] otherwise known as Mr. Canada and Mr. U.S.A., Jim Essex aka Lord Jim aka Mr. B.C., Mr. Pro N.W., and Renaldo Rainier alias Mr. North America. Then of course there is Wonder Woman or Patty as she's known to those 'in the biz.'"

(She was also billed on one show poster as 'Runner up in the MISS NUDE WORLD CONTEST.') Geldof continues,

" . . . these four refugees from a Fellini movie began what can only be described as a hilarious extravaganza of fathomless decadence. First, Mr. N.A. and Mr. Pro N.W. appeared romping from the edge of the stage in silver sequined shorts, leather thonged sandals into a mad parody of a Socratic Olympian Grecian evening. The boys proceeded to launch into a calisthenic dance routine while the tapes play behind them and Mr. U.S.A. comes rushing on stage dressed in black caballero style and sings through his acceptable vocal cords some aging rock tune totally incongruous to the whole, yet it seems to fit somewhere into this crazed act. Mid-way through the opener Wonder Woman rushes on stage and rips Mikl's clothes from his vast body. The lads dance on, body oil glistening, muscles flexing, and Mr. U.S.A. stands glorious in black sparkling sequined JOCK-STRAP: Mr. U.S.A. and JOCK STRAPS? Well, yes. Apparently, the circus was in town at the Commodore. Mikl flashed his muscle-bound bum at the crowd and had his arse go through the most incredible paces I have ever witnessed. They flexed and flicked, postured, and posed, and no-one there would have kicked sand in their faces . . . "

---

14 In fact, before casting Tim Curry, *Rocky Horror*'s creator, Richard O'Brien, was looking for a muscleman who could sing.

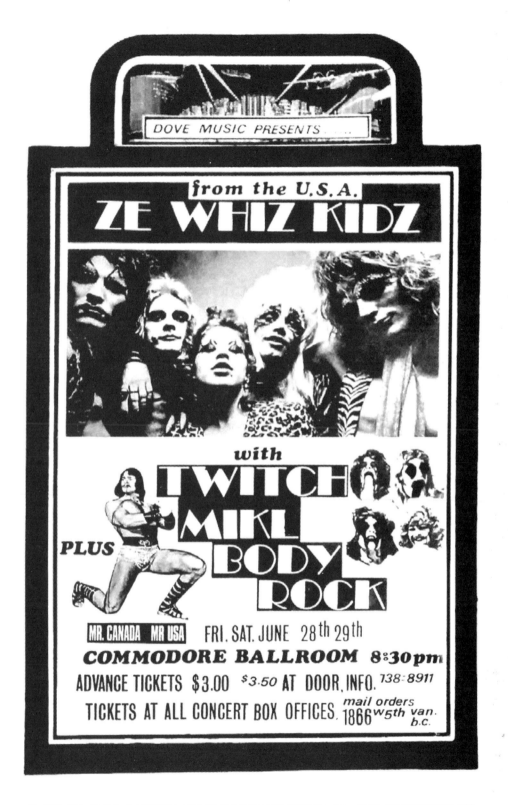

Ze Whiz Kidz, Twitch, Jon Mikl "Body Rock" at Commodore Ballroom, June, 1974. Courtesy of Rob Frith.

In a post-show mini-interview with Thor, Geldof asks,

"But why did you want to be a Mister Something or Other? 'Well, I always wanted to be a superman when I was a kid and now I am one.' So saith John Mikl [sic] who continually flexed and brushed himself in the mirror while I talked to him. Isn't it a very narcissistic thing? 'No, not really.' And Wonder Woman says, 'He's nicer to hold in bed.' Nicer than what? 'Nicer than ordinary men.' Do you get off on muscles? 'Well, it looks healthy.' What about other women? 'Oh, they all rush the stage, especially in places like New York, but we do a lot of other things as well, like simulated sex and gladiator things, y'know.'"

Further elaborating on the Mikl Body Rock show, Thor tells me, "And then there was also a band wearing Glitter Rock outfits to play the music. Maybe a couple of times we would incorporate some recording, backing tracks, but for the most part when we did our shows, it was a live band."

As Thor's manager, Isy Walters sent him to do a tastefully tawdry show in Hawaii, then on to a tour of British Columbia where he met Frank Soda and the rest of Soda's long-hair cover band. Soda elaborates, "We were going to be his backup band. And he had just come from Hawaii, and it was just snowing like crazy. And they were all totally dark and tanned. He would do some Elvis and some whatever stuff but he was always saying, 'I want to get into the original stuff.'"

Apart from Thor, the Frank Soda band were little guys and thus christened Thor and the Imps as they toured their way east with new songs like "Do the Muscle." To coordinate with Thor, the Imps donned white makeup and lightning eyes rocking out in the luxurious glitter jacket finery of Dubois. With lines out the door at all the clubs, word of Thor had spread!

Thor explains, "It was just really freaky for some people and the whole muscle thing. Me bending steel bars and getting guys worked up, they would challenge me all the time. There was one guy who grabbed the steel bar out of my hand, a big guy at one of the shows in a small town and he put it in his teeth, and he tried to bend it with his teeth like I did, but I wrap a towel around it, so I don't break my teeth. He broke his teeth. All his front teeth snapped, he started screaming, going crazy.

"I think a lot of it at that time was, the girls were really getting into the show and screaming and going crazy and then it was this whole thing with the boyfriends, the jealous boyfriends, who eventually really got into the show as we got more and more popular. Because the girls would come to the show, the guys would follow. Once I tried to lift up a 400-pound person with my neck and the platform broke and just rolled into the crowd. Mayhem broke loose. You have to be really careful with the pyro-techs as they were in their infancy at that time, we sometimes used hockey pucks and soup cans for the flashpots. Many times, Ontario venues would be downstairs in the bar and the rest of the place is a hotel. We did too many flashpots and the whole place was full of smoke up into the hotel

Thor and the Imps, c. 1976. Courtesy Rob Frith.

rooms and the owner just went berserk. He had the police escort us out; said we were trying to burn the hotel down. We did use a bit too much flashpot that time. And, you know, dancing with Frank Soda in the audience was pretty wild."

Dancing? "Yeah. So, that was one of the things I did, I would balance him in the air with two hands and then eventually hold him while he played guitar. I held him up with one arm. I couldn't do that with him now, but back then he was really light. Then I would dance right into the crowd holding him up with one arm while he played guitar. I don't think too many guitar–singer teams, whether it's Mick Ronson and David Bowie or Robert Plant and Jimmy Page, would do that kind of stuff. We were wild and we had good songs."

In 1976, Thor and the Imps auditioned for KISS's management company, who invited them to open for KISS at Maple Leaf Gardens, leading a raucous procession of fans known as the KISS Army—these fans were so devoted, they weren't even drafted, they freely enlisted—out onto the stage. That same year Thor and the Imps headed into the studio with the guitarist Stacy Heydon, who had just gotten off a world tour as Bowie's lead guitarist, and recorded four songs, including the grooving thud of "I Gotta Eat," with plans for a full album. A very limited-edition cassette and vinyl EP on God of Thunder Records was sold at shows. Canada proved difficult, as Thor states: "I knew we had to go to the USA to try to make it. I was too wild. I wasn't that many people's cup of tea being so flamboyant and crazy and being a guy to boot. I'd have reviews like 'He sings like a muffler.' And I listened to my tracks back then, I didn't sing like a muffler, I had a pretty good voice you know, but then the image, right?"

Thor was sent to Las Vegas to be part of a comedy-variety revue called *Red, Hot and Blue,* leading to his appearance on the popular American polyester-blended TV talk show *Merv* (hosted by Merv Griffin, always good for a chuckle or two), singing a big band version of "Action" by the Sweet, pausing midway to blow up a hot water bottle using only pure lung power. Thor explains, "Frank Soda and the Imps stayed in Ontario and toured. I tried to get them on the Merv Griffin show, but Merv thought they were too hip. And so I ended up using the Mort Lindsey Orchestra. All the while I kept trying to bring the Imps out to Las Vegas. But you know, it was a different kind of place and more family oriented, they didn't want the heavy rock that we were doing."

Now without Thor, Frank Soda and the Imps took to creating their own brand of showmanship with Canadian cueball Glam as an accidental result of those pesky flashpots. Soda explains: "We shaved our heads when we didn't have to—now I have to, but then we didn't. I'll tell you what ended up happening. We were playing the Gasworks in Toronto—if you don't know that place, the ceiling is kind of low and I was doing the pyro stuff on my head. My hair was regular at the time and what happened was, that I had a big round thing on my head like a big Moon Man. It was a round head, it had the eyeballs and all that and I was playing and playing—"

Wait, it had eyeballs? "Flashing eyeballs. What happened was the black powder had spilled down, the bomb was right about up here [gestures to an invisible place about two feet above his head], and it was supposed to shoot upwards, but some of the—"

It's supposed to spray like flames? "Yeah, huge twenty-foot flames. And normally from here down [motions to indicate top of head to bottom of feet] nothing would happen. I had protection and everything, but because he overloaded it, some of the powder was spilling as I was moving and as it went off, I could see it, just a big white thing in front of me and I saw it going and I lifted and I threw the thing [giant headpiece with eyeballs] right off. You know that hair-burning smell? The eyebrows never grew back. It could have done way more damage because I felt it coming. I did burn my hair. And after that, I had a big spot here [points to top of head]. So, I just shaved it right off and then the other guys in the band did the same thing."

Besides the Moon Man, Soda would wear an exploding (more flashpots!) television set on his head inspired by his song "TV People" and shown on the cover of the Imps' 1979 live album *In the Tube,* on Tube Records. Frank Soda and the Imps signed to the Quality Records label with *Soda Pop,* the album cover featuring a cocktail waitress and Frank's arm offering the record buying public a large and fizzy can of pop. Frank then went solo for his 1981 album *Saturday Night Getaway* before the label imploded.

Frank Soda has always been Frank Soda: it's his name from birth, so when he donned a red and white Coca-Cola jumpsuit it just made perfect sense. He changed out of the

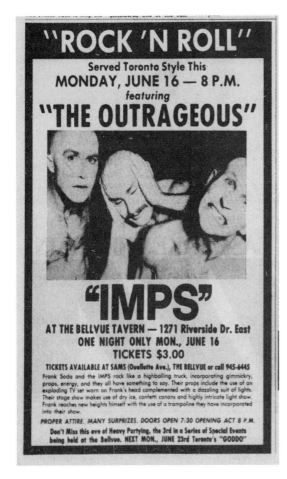
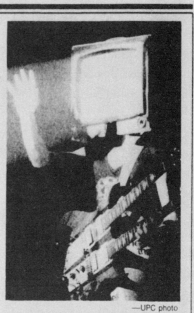

Left to right: Frank Soda and the Imps show ad. Image courtesy of the *Windsor Star Ottawa Citizen*, June 14, 1980. Frank Soda wearing his TV head. Image courtesy of the *Ottawa Citizen*, September 8, 1983.

jumpsuit and into a superhero costume for the picture disc *The Adventures of Sodaman* in 1983. The second side of the picture disc shows him back in the TV head as a topless woman faces him looking into her reflection to apply her lipstick. Ever ambitious, there was an accompanying long-form twenty-minute video. Some scenes were filmed on an impressively accurate replica of the *Star Trek Enterprise* bridge set, originally built for Toronto Star Trek '76, Canada's first *Star Trek* convention. The *Sodaman* video had some semblance of a plot. Frank describes, "This guy comes in from another planet and goes, 'I gotta go check out what's happening on Earth.' There's been no sex for so many thousands of years up on the other planet, so he wants to go check out what's going on and that type of thing."

Video became a much more interactive part of Soda's show in the '80s, touring with two large video screens and a video crew. "I'd be running in the audience, and I'd do a guitar battle with myself on the screen and have this wild guy on the screen, like, a demonic type of guy. And I'd be out in the audience, and I'd be doing a battle, like way ahead of its time."

At one point, Terry Watkinson, the pivotal former keyboardist of the popular Canadian rock group Max Webster, was part of the band. Soda and Watkinson took to performing as a duo called Diet Soda, with Watkinson dressed as a wild professor behind the keyboard, pre-programming the bass and drums.

In the late '80s, Soda moved to Vancouver to take care of his dad. Soda then formed an all-woman band (well, except for him) called Frank Soda and the Pop Tarts.

* * *

After his Vegas stint, Thor returned to Canada in 1977 to make *Keep the Dogs Away* with RCA. This album came with a poster of bare-chested Thor holding on to a pack of dogs. What kind of dogs? They look like guard dogs, but I am sure that Thor would do just as well without them. The visual effect, though. Whether canine or human, this album makes its own gravy, its own work-out mix with a couple preening cooldowns thrown in. It sounds like KISS but without the pouting-lipped front-man Paul Stanley, like eggs stored in the armpits, marching, never strutting, careful not to drop a single egg, yet roaring like the wind. A song called "Thunder" crackles! Years before the "Superman Song," Thor details what becomes of them all on "Superhero," then asking, "What becomes of me?"

Moving into other media, including getting photographed in his animal-print skivvies by the legendary Robert Mapplethorpe (gelatin silver print no less), along with other, more provocative (ooh!) photos by the mysterious Vancouver commercial photographer Dick Oulten, the eye of the camera was infatuated with Thor's physique. He had the body of a superhero, so it seemed only natural that he would have his own comic books. In 1979 Ken Landgraf released the newspaper format *Rock Comics* #1, with one story by the influential comic artist Neal Adams (having done pivotal runs on *Batman, Green Lantern/Green Arrow*, the list goes on) depicting Thor's not-so-secret origin (he loved comic books, he lifted weights, he loved rock). Landgraf himself is a gifted artist with an appealing style who has worked on a wide range of comics, from Marvel's Wolverine to the decidedly more independent Doctor Peculiar, from fetish comics for Eric Stanton to educational Christian comics. In 1982, Landgraf drew a comic book for Thor's short-lived band Vikon. With the release of the black-and-white *Rock Warrior* #1 comic book in 1983, Thor and his bandmates are given superpowers in a full-blown adventure—again, drawn magnificently by Ken Landgraf. In it, Thor uses his sonic sword to fight evil demons from another dimension. The comic book ends on a cliff-hanger telling us to watch for Jon-Mikl Thor in an upcoming feature motion picture. *Rock Warrior* #1 came with a free ticket for two to see Thor perform songs from his new 1983 album live on stage at midnight in New York City! Four years later, the promise of Thor's movie came true. *Rock 'n' Roll Nightmare* is an inexplicable, low-budget horror film about a rock band recording in a weird

Front cover of *Keep the Dogs Away*, Thor (RCA, 1977). Author's collection.

old Mississauga, Ontario, farmhouse full of monsters. In the movie someone asks, "But why Canada?" Thor replies, "Because Toronto's where it's happening, man . . . the music, the film industry, the arts."

Time marched on, and Thor made a smooth move into hard rock and metal, a harder sound, but with the stage show intact. A hiatus. A sustained hiccup. In 2000, Thor made a triumphant comeback. At one of these Vancouver shows, I saw a surprise guest hit the stage: Frank Soda, in his Coca-Cola jumpsuit, exploding TV head and all! And Thor was still as much a showman as ever. A 2015 documentary, *I Am Thor,* is a rock redemption tale that highlights Thor's lows. European audiences began to embrace Thor in the 2000s. New albums were released and old ones re-released. Thor continues to ceaselessly tour. And on many of those dates his old friend Frank Soda joins him.

Rock Warrior #1, page four, art by Ken Landgraf (Thunder Productions, 1983). Author's collection.

TWITCH

DO YOU ENJOY HORROR INTENSITY? British Columbia's own Twitch were very early adopters of corpse paint and took it further into proto-black metal before it was even a thing to do. They would also coat themselves in gold and silver paint and donned a great many wigs. In 1974, Twitch took a page from the Grand Guignol playbook and used crosses, fog, fake blood-drenched sacrifices of their drummer, and screaming witches being burned and resurrected as part of an elaborate occult rock opera. It was a reaction against "head music" isolated from the body, an antidote to the old "nothing to see here, folks" mentality, a jump kick away from the cool toward the hot, often bringing in actual flames and plenty of smoke. Wow, what a show. How do I know all this? Research. Let's give a bit of credit here. I heard about, and heard, Twitch via the Canadian label Supreme Echo, which did all the heavy lifting to put out previously unreleased recordings from this era of Twitch as the LP *Dark Years*, with an informative booklet documenting their story and lots of wild photos.

Twitch's performance and costume elements evolved naturally. Before Twitch, Ian Steeksma, one of its founding members, had a band called the Invaders in 1964. The Invaders were rock—garage rock—covering Them's "Gloria" and the Sonics' "The Witch." The other Invaders were reluctant when Steeksma suggested they cover "The Witch," wondering who in the band could scream like that. Steeksma replied, "I can do that." Playing a high school sock hop, Steeksma avoided opening with lighthearted introductions and instead screamed, "Testing!" into the mic, then right on into "The Witch." It immediately got everyone's attention, and, as Steeksma noted later, "And that's what took our little band off." The Invaders also loved Paul Revere and the Raiders and the matching outfits that set them apart. Steeksma knew that they had to dress up too, and then they added the choreographed moves typical of many Motown acts. He had seen too many bands standing like statues on stage, which immediately made him think, "No, no, you've got to do something to keep people's attention. And to give them something to look at while you're on stage." The Invaders disbanded in 1965 when Ian formed a new band called Cry for Justice in Nanaimo, B.C. They dissolved in late 1967, then Ian formed a whole new Cry for Justice in Vancouver, but they didn't last long.

Forming in 1971, Twitch covered the fuzzed out, frenetic "The Witch" for a spell as well. Twitch's song "Things" was the natural next step, with its slowed-way-down thud and dank bass metronoming through. "Things" is a classic in its own rite—I mean, right. It was released as a single, and its flip side, "Pick-Up Is Illegal on 401," refers to the highway through Vancouver where the song's protagonist watches "all my brothers leave town." The song takes its name from signs posted all along Highway 401 warning drivers not to pick up hitchhikers. Steeksma explains, "It was more or less sort of a protest song, but not really. It was to give people a commonality with us that we would write something like that. And back in those days, it wasn't long after the hippie era and people used to hitchhike all over

Twitch "Wiggin Out" promo pic. Courtesy of Jason Flower/Supreme Echo.

the place." Though pressed in a small quantity, this single soon thumbed its way onto jukeboxes across the Lower Mainland. A second single followed, with the post-jangle of "Sweet Thursday" on side A. The flip, "Country Tune," starts out as just that, then switches with a yowl into fuzzed-out rock! If you look at the cover photos to the more recent, less limited but still limited, Supreme Echo 7" reissue you will see the original incarnation of Twitch going all in on the makeup, with the drummer split right down the middle into white and black all the way to his gut but no further—don't want to mess up his nice, satin trousers. The other two have their droopy mustaches mixed with thickly made-up brows and eyes dripping down and curling around, a variation on the spider eye styles of the GTOs and Alice Cooper.

Steeksma says, "The original Twitch was Bernie Mulatz, who was on the drums, myself, and a great guy named Rick Laing who played bass and sang as well. Rick was a really good guy but incredibly quiet, really quiet guy, funny, but very quiet. He and Bernie came from a Mennonite or something background in Saskatchewan, I think. I suggested to them, 'Let's wear a bit of makeup and make ourselves more attractive on stage,' because I didn't feel that we were that great of musicians. Everybody went along with it for a while until I started wanting to get it to be more and more of an experience for people to watch us as well." Theatrical alienation caused lineup shifts with Bernie and Rick leaving the band. As well, Twitch added a second guitarist to better fill out the sound. They now needed a new rhythm section.

Ian's brother Colin was at first reluctant to join the band, being more of a guitarist than a bassist, but, Ian Steeksma says, "He was an incredible bass player and he took that spot with relish and went along with absolutely everything his crazy brother wanted to do." Many of their costumes were made by their wives and girlfriends. It usually took over an hour for them to apply their makeup. A makeup artist named Emma who had worked for the CBC suggested the full silver body paint for the new guitarist, Steve Perry, though he was worried that his circulation would be cut off à la *Goldfinger,* but he was just fine. Their booking agent/manager in this era was Barry Samuels of Axis Entertainment, who also handled Sweeney Todd. In fact, Ian Steeksma recalls that Samuels told them about Twitch, which influenced Sweeney Todd's early heavy makeup applications.

Twitch sang in four-part harmony. The 1974 recordings that comprise *Dark Years* gets into the heavy rock, a foreshadow to stoner metal. The album itself, with songs like "Litany to Raise the Dead" and "Satan's Blood," is pure rec-room shock rock veering into the chugging dunder boogie woogie boogie boogie woogie woogie boogie (hey, it's proto black metal—no rules yet) of "Roaring Drunk." Then there is "Jessica," a ballad about a woman from Salem, Massachusetts, who was accused of witchcraft and burned at the stake in 1705. Ian Steeksma was the Wizard ("Still am ha ha," says Steeksma) and in "The Wizard" he proclaimed, "I am the Wizard!" The song "Sex with Mother" was left un-released. When I asked Ian Steeksma about that one, he replied, "It was pretty . . . pretty vile. People were aghast."

The Canadian Glam Rock event to be at was held in 1974 at the legendary Commodore, the infamous big-band club with the bouncy castle floor! Curiosity seekers came out, along with a couple of fans in Twitch makeup. Whoever put this bill together was divinely inspired. Not only did Twitch open, but Thor's early bodybuilding band Mikl Body Rock was also on the bill. The headliners Ze Whiz Kidz came all the way from Seattle—a three-hour drive away if the border guards aren't being pricks.

Ze Whiz Kidz are the connecting thread between the proto-Glam pioneers the Cockettes and punk, thanks to Tomata Du Plenty. Tomata took the legendary, glittery gender-blending, wild stage shows of San Francisco's Cockettes—of which he was an early member—and put them to good use with Ze Whiz Kidz, which he formed soon after moving to Seattle. I could get deep into Tomata's Brechtian performance qualities as a member of the synth punk pioneers the Screamers—I mean, oh my God—he is missed. It'd have been wild to see what his dragged-out earlier theatrical performances were like. Mixed-gender members of Ze Whiz Kidz, with such names as Stormy Weather, Cha Cha Samoa, Rialto Bijou, and Chicken Delight, made the trek to Canada—without Tomata, who moved to New York City for a stint in 1973, though he and Twitch would later cross paths.

Describing the heavily theatrical shock-value antics of both Twitch and Ze Whiz Kidz, Bob Geldof—who, we will recall was during this period a music journalist for the *Georgia Straight* newspaper—dismissively described their sets as full of illicit sex, blasphemy, necrophilia, and homosexuality. He also skipped half of Twitch's show, claiming boredom. He wrote, "Although Twitch and Ze Whiz Kidz tried hard, it was fairly obvious that all that glittered was definitely not gold. However, if one were to examine the differentials between the decibel level and the glitter/decadence ratio, one would be forced to the conclusion that they were both equally loud and raucous, which, depending on your taste, can be a recommendation or a turn-off."

Reviewing the show for the *Vancouver Sun,* Don Stanley noted that Twitch's leader "growled in a voice calculated to frighten stormtroopers. The bassist's face suggested an open wound, the guitarist was covered head and torso with Goldfinger paint, and the lead singer was merely animalistic. . . . Scattered among Deep Purple and Slade imitations were original songs centering on a girl named Jessica, who entered into illicit relationships with beasts!" [*sic*].

People loved Twitch because they were so different, yet some bad eggs in the crowd felt otherwise. On one western Canadian tour, they performed in a small hall in rural Saskatchewan, where, as Ian Steeksma described it, "Tons of people showed up. I'm standing there [on stage] and at that point in time I had my big high boots on. I'm singing and I'm trying to look as tough as I could—even though I'm a wimp. And this one guy comes up to us and stands in front of me. He just takes this switchblade out of his pocket then proceeds to bury it in the stage floor between my feet. Like throw it. And, of course, because of the image that we projected, I couldn't go, 'Oh, my God, what's happening? I'm running away from this. I'm not dealing with this.' I had to stand there as he kept doing it. He'd get closer and

Twitch, *Dark Years* era with crosses, c. 1974. Courtesy of Jason Flower/Supreme Echo.

closer to the toe of my boot. Then he backed away when he saw I wasn't going to react." Dressed and in his scary Wizard persona, Ian Steeksma had the power and it couldn't be easily taken. Twitch never broke character on stage.

Twitch attracted both women and men. Ian Steeksma explains, "I think the reason is because the guys liked the spectacle and the shock and the girls liked the look of the band, but there wasn't anybody you'd love because we did not look lovable. I think the girls were kind of shocked as well. But to some degree, you know, some of them were slightly, I wouldn't say frightened, but they wouldn't want to get too close to us because—just because. However, that changed in the *Dark Years* era, when we played at Oil Can Harry's in Vancouver on Grey Cup weekend.[15] By this time, people had heard of Twitch and they showed up in droves, lined up around the block. It was standing room only. Because we drove people into a frenzy, especially towards the end of the set, with the cauldrons and the drums and the burning crosses and all that stuff, they picked up on that as violent. There were a couple of times where I

---

15 A popular Canadian football event.

Twitch Live *The Wizard: Dark Years* era featuring Ian, Steve, and Mike, c. 1974. Courtesy of Jason Flower/Supreme Echo.

had a girl who's sitting on the shoulders of her boyfriend come up right up to the stage and wasn't wearing anything on top at all. In my persona, I stuck my head out fairly close to her, and she drilled me in the face with her fist. It was not too long after that that we said, 'Hey, you know what, this part of Twitch needs to change because we're inviting something that we don't like here.' We were on the verge of, I think, inviting, for lack of a better word, some kind of evil spirit type aura. We had a couple of incidents that happened on stage that wouldn't normally happen where we finally said, 'Oh, you know what, we got to stop this.'"

But making changes didn't mean a move away from showmanship itself, just a shift away from all that occult imagery stuff. They weren't going to stop putting on a show.

With the drummer Mike Selby-Brown and the guitarist Steve Perry gone, Ian and Colin continued on and enlisted new members. For what Supreme Echo has deemed their "Good Time Punker" era, Twitch softened their look and made their pancake makeup more smiley, almost like literal smiley faces. No, they weren't clowns—just smiley. Their new logo was a smiley face with a black eye, emblazoned on bright yellow t-shirts for the fans to buy to wear to the shows or wherever they pleased—hey, it's their shirt.

This new lineup of Twitch put on a rock opera described as "*West Side Story* meets *Clockwork Orange*." The stage show changed as well, and the new version took over two hours to set up. The backdrop was a dead-end alley brick-wall motif. The drum riser was set on garbage cans, and underneath it was built a jail which doubled as a costume-change area. Set against this backdrop, the band were framed as punks hanging out in the alley who just happened to play music. The villains were the cops because, well, ACAB. The cops were represented only by sirens and flashing lights accented with smoke and fog; they were not human but an abstract authoritarian force. The show incorporated covers of the Sensational Alex Harvey Band's version of "Framed" and, for the finale, "Midnight Moses." Steeksma elaborates: "When it [the song] talks about the cops beating him, our lead guitarist Gary would make like he was hitting me with the head of his guitar. That was usually the end song for the set. I had a blood bag in my mouth, and I'd squeeze that, and it would come out all over the place and people would crap. They'd end up helping me off the stage and I'd be staggering all over the place and people thought I was really damaged."

Twitch did record a fair number of their original "Good Time Punker" era songs in the studio. I have heard the songs "County Jail" and "Chevy Dream" and they are cartoony Canadian Glam stompers! As of this writing these songs are unreleased. The upcoming Supreme Echo release of these sessions will be most momentous.

Twitch now had an infamous "manager"[16] and booking agent named Harvey Borley, of Accident Productions. Borley dazzled Twitch as he was known for bringing in a lot of big bands to play large venues. One of these bands was Nazareth, from Scotland, who were on

---

16 Putting quotation marks around manager is how Ian Steeksma would describe Harvey Borley's role. Colin Steeksma describes him as the "Donald Trump of '70s promoters," citing Borley's "narcissistic hyperbole" on Borley's own blog.

The Return of Twitch concert, January 1976, the Mabbett Room, Port Coquitlam Recreation Centre. Courtesy of Jason Flower/Supreme Echo.

a world tour, with their Canadian leg ending in Victoria after a massive Vancouver show. But Nazareth missed the ferry to Victoria and were no-shows, disappointing thousands of waiting fans. Nazareth claimed that they cancelled the show because of ferry delays from fog. Borley claimed that it was because the band stayed in Vancouver to party at the Deep Purple concert that Borley himself put on. Borley penalized Nazareth by temporarily confiscating their gear—gear that they needed for the Australian leg of their tour. Feeling ripped off, Nazareth was inspired to release the song "Vancouver Shakedown" in 1976. Not to be outdone, Borley quickly wrote lyrics, booked studio time for Twitch to record the song, and then released it as a single on his own Astro Records, the label's only release (Supreme Echo reissued this single in 2016). Colin Steeksma notes that this retaliatory song was Borley's main reason for picking Twitch up. Nazareth's "Vancouver Shakedown" ain't no great shakes. Answer songs are usually weaker than the songs that inspire them, but look what Twitch had to work with: they came out on top with "Mess'n with the Bull (Gets the Horn)," making good use of Borley's lyrics, "We'll always be there to please our fans." And then there's the B side, "Spunk." Oh my gosh, it makes me blush. Moving on . . .

Borley sent Twitch out to high schools throughout the province. These school shows allowed them to use all their stage props, which didn't always fit into the smaller rock clubs. In April of 1977, Twitch went on a four-day Vancouver Island tour opening for Wenzday, who were then riding on their minor hit cover of the British Glam boy band Kenny's "Fancy Pants." They shared trade secrets: Wenzday wanted to know how Twitch made their explosions (gunpowder in flashpots in garbage cans) and Twitch wanted to know how Wenzday made their fog effect (pesticide fogger from Sears loaded with mineral oil).

Borley booked Twitch on a grueling itinerary that the band nicknamed the Borley Torture Tour. In June and July 1977, Twitch traveled long distances up through the Interior[17] of British Columbia with a week of shows in Prince George suddenly cancelled, then a few dates opening for Long John Baldry, then an intense car accident outside of Hope on a substandard road with a steep shoulder causing minor injuries and over two thousand dollars in damages (though Colin's bass actually sounded better after it had floated down the river). The band successfully made it to their destination of Humboldt, Saskatchewan, two provinces over, and the gigs went well. They then went back a province and played the Executive Inn in a rough part of Edmonton, Alberta, but were fired halfway through their two-week stint (Colin Steeksma notes that one of their roadies had had too much to drink and threatened the club booker with a rolled-up newspaper). At the end of July, Twitch played the rec center of Ma-Me-O Beach, a summer village in Alberta.

In September 1977, Twitch sent Borley a letter cancelling their contract due to three thousand dollars in unpaid debts. Borley retaliated by stealing their band equipment. As evidenced by the Nazareth incident, Borley had a history of this. Colin Steeksma notes, "I had to go to court to try and get it back."

Twitch returned to having Barry Samuels as their booking agent. In 1978, Samuels booked Twitch for a series of dates down the West Coast on their way to record in Los Angeles. Opening for the Screamers in July 1978 at San Francisco's historic Mabuhay Gardens, Twitch were billed as "Canadian punks." Says Ian Steeksma, "At that particular point in time we were doing face makeup. But basically, all we were doing was just for the 'Good Time Punker' look, we had our studded jeans and our low-cut tops, they were black and that kind of thing. So, nothing really overboard. We went out and played our set. People started throwing things at us. They were throwing popcorn. They were spitting. They were throwing the odd beer bottle, but not really hard, at us. Afterwards, I said to the manager, 'I'm really sorry. They really didn't like us.' 'Oh shit, no. They loved you.' That's what they were used to doing. When we were down in Los Angeles,[18] we played the Starwood in Hollywood; the Starwood was totally different. The first time we played there, word got around and people came out to see us, even celebrities like Steve Tyler and Linda Ronstadt. The reception was so much different. It was standing room only, they were jumping and yelling and clapping and, you know, taking us backstage and saying how great we were, and they'd never seen a band like us before, etc."

Samuels got Twitch a plum gig opening for Blondie in January 1979 at the Commodore

---

17 The Interior refers to the non-coastal parts of British Columbia.
18 Another Canadian Glam connection: while in L.A., Twitch stayed at Nick Gilder's place.

Ballroom in Vancouver, but they had to tone it wayyyyyy down. Ian Steeksma says that this was done at Samuels' request: "He didn't want us to upstage her act." Besides limiting their theatrics, they reluctantly went clothes shopping for a brand new 1930s look just short of spats. They did get new shoes, peaked hats, and suspenders too. During the show, one band member was subjected to a guy in front yelling, "Nice shoes, you ——!" Well, you can guess the succinctly homophobic rest of what he said.

I asked Ian Steeksma when Twitch dissolved. "Oh, gosh," he replied, "in my opinion, we kind of never did." They did more recording, some with Randy Bachman, transitioning into a studio project called Blind Date. In 2004, they played a reunion in Mission, B.C. Although they didn't dress up, they did mostly play their "Good Time Punkers" era material. More recently, Colin moved to a place closer to his brother Ian, affording them the opportunity to resume playing together, doing "maximum classic rock" under the name Dutch Courage.

RIFF RAFF

NOTHING QUITE SAYS GLAM like having a hair stylist in your band. Such was the case with Riff Raff. They formed in August 1973, a week or two after a customer named Jim Dyck sat down in the stylist's chair at the Vikings, one of the first men's hair sa-

Riff Raff live with Paul Wickett holding penis balloons, includes Jeff Taylor (drums), Jim Dyck (guitar), c. 1975. Photographer unknown.

The Vikings Men's Hair Designs ad. Image courtesy of the *Vancouver Province*, Aug. 11, 1971.

lons in Vancouver. This was the spot if you were a man desiring something other than the rigid barber shop haircut. Dyck bonded with the hairdresser, Paul Wickett, over their love of Glam Rock—David Bowie, Lou Reed, and Mott the Hoople. Wickett didn't just cut hair; he also sang and had ambition. The guitarist Jim Dyck affirms, "The next week he found local Kitsilano lads Jeff Taylor to play drums and Jim Bescott to play bass, and we had a first get-together. Our bass player Jim Bescott, probably the most creative one in the band, came up with the name Riff Raff. He suffered from bipolar disorder and when manic came up with all kinds of ideas. One such idea was to put on a 'History of Rock' show."

This show was the height of ambition, comprising four sets of music devoted to the history of rock, beginning with '50s rock 'n' roll covers, followed by the British Invasion, then a set of West Coast hippie stuff. Riff Raff would do costume changes for each set—removing white tees and jeans to don collarless suits, then switching to paisley. Jim Dyck describes the culmination: "The final set was the Glam set. We'd all come out in colorful silk and gold lamé, as well as SOME, not a *LOT,* of make-up. Then we would do the David Bowie, Lou Reed, Mott the Hoople stuff, as well as our originals which Paul and I wrote." These four sets were chosen to keep the crowd, with its diverse tastes, interested, as well as charting rock's movement in time, positioning Glam as *the* current event, as the living end. Dyck continues, "For performance antics, we generally used the 'moves' of the day during our four sets. Trying to do a few Elvis moves in set one, Beatles moves in set two, and just stand there like stoned hippies for the third. For the Glam set, Paul would come out wearing a trenchcoat with his pants rolled up so all you could see were bare legs under the trenchcoat. The rest of the band would be on stage, and he'd peek out from behind the curtain and then tiptoe out with his back to the audience. Then he would 'flash' the band by whipping open the trenchcoat, kind of like a conductor. When the coat was open the band would play a crash-and-burn style chord with a bunch of drum rolls. When he closed the coat, we'd stop. Then he'd look over his shoulder at the audience

Riff Raff later era band photo featuring Jim Dyck (guitar), Kevin Redden (bass), Paul Wickett (vocals), Dave Senior (keyboards), and Jeff Taylor (drums), c. 1976. Photo by and courtesy of Hans Sipma.

and raise his eyebrows a few times, turn back to the band, and flash again. To the audience, it was supposed to look like he was a pervert flasher. But as soon as the first tune started he'd throw off the coat and jump into the tune. It was our signature antic."

Due to the realities of existence (day jobs), Riff Raff mostly kept close to Vancouver, venturing as far as Boundary Bay and Richmond, just a stone's throw away, for weekend concerts. Plus, lots of high school dances, including York House, a girls' school. As Dyck recalls, "There were a lot of 'unwed mothers' who went to York House at the time. For guys our age, that was intriguing." The Pender Ballroom, a venue infamous for having hosted a legendary Iggy and the Stooges concert in August 1973, was a regular spot for them, bringing the sax player Ken Lerner along for a show. Riff Raff seemed like trouble right down to their name—yet performed for well-heeled attendees on New Year's Eve at the Bayshore Inn. Riff Raff often had penis clown balloons as stage decorations. A high school vice-principal sent them a letter thanking them for their "professional manner" (despite the presence of the penis balloon loosely tied and dangling down from the microphone stand). On Canada Day 1974, they played shirtless (it was hot) on a flatbed truck driving onto the track between drag races at Ladner's Boundary Bay Raceway. The audience dressed in swimsuits for a high school pool party show at the North Vancouver Rec Centre while swimming to the sounds of Riff Raff (no electrocutions reported). Between all these gigs, Riff Raff even found time to make a silent 8mm movie on the railway tracks filmed in fake "old timey" sepia tone.

A couple of years in, Bescott left the band, going on to form the iconic Vancouver punk band the K-Tels with Art Bergmann in 1978. It was with the K-Tels that he made punk history by convincing the Smilin' Buddha Cabaret to book punk bands, with the K-Tels being the first, cementing the club's reputation as a legendary punk venue. Soon, the K-Tel Corporation applied legal pressure (maybe even waving one of their "As Seen on TV" all-purpose slicer-and-dicers around for incentive) and the K-Tels changed their name to Young Canadians.

Moving forward with a new bassist, Kevin Redden, and the addition of Dave Senior on keyboard, Riff Raff went into a home studio to record four original numbers. These off—in the least off-putting way—songs had wonky energy, sounding like Riff Raff really were riff raff, loose and upbeat, foreshadowing the punk to come. Flanged the fuck out songs featuring sexual subject matter with names like "Magazine Lover," "Angel in Heat," and "An Inch Is a Mile"—a dreamy little ditty about an encounter with a hitchhiker culminating in a warbly synth solo; a Riff Raff guitar pulling strong rock riffs, then switching into dreamscape setting. Acidic vocals. On everything, including the mid-tempo rockers, frenetic hot-air-popper-styled drums ricochet so fast they turn into lasers. These songs were never formally released, merely used to score gigs; it is a shame, as the songs are quite a treat.[19]

When Dyck and his wife decided to trek across Europe, Riff Raff opted not to continue. While Riff Raff only lasted for three years, ending in August 1976, Dyck and his wife are together to this day. A few years after Riff Raff dissolved, Senior died way too young in a car crash. Many of Riff Raff's original songs were not recorded, and what live recordings there were burned in a massive fire at Bescott's mother's home in 2005. Mere weeks after that terrible news, there was greater tragedy: Jim Bescott died falling beneath the wheels of a grocery truck at a supermarket. Fortunately, Jim Dyck and Paul Wickett still keep in touch every week and, as of this writing, they both recently visited Jeff Taylor.

---

19 In recent years the songs have been uploaded to https://www.soundclick.com/riffraffcanada.

Baby Strange promo photo, c. 1974. Photo by Chandler Keeler.

BABY STRANGE (AND A TOUCH OF SLAN)

A CANADIAN GLAM BAND NAMED AFTER A T. REX SONG? Yes, please! Oh, we mean, to quote Bolan, "a one and a two and a bubbly bubbly boo boo yeah!" Baby Strange went through a near-death experience and lived to tell about it! In the accident (we'll get to that later), did their short lives flash before their eyes back to the beginning of the band? Baby Strange formed in October 1973 after Steven Weakes, Dave Rodger, Chris Ainscough, and Jed Harrison had been playing in various prog-oriented projects in high school. Prog didn't exactly thrill and excite audiences, as Weakes, the keyboardist, says: "It's way too much work for the average listener. We enjoyed doing it, but it kind of fell flat with the crowd." For this project, they needed a singer and Helen Frost fit the bill. Frost, then in her first year at the University of British Columbia, was encouraged to audition by a friend. Frost had a strong background in music, having written and performed both solo and in a duo since she was sixteen years old.

Ainscough, the bassist, explains, "And so we just kind of convinced her. I mean, she's absolutely stunningly gorgeous. And one of the nicest people you'd ever meet in the world. And I think in hindsight, maybe we felt a bit a bit bad about leading her down this rock 'n' roll path. But she enjoyed it."

Baby Strange was Glam right out of the gate. They were all in, dressing for the stage, putting creativity over expense, doing it themselves. As Ainscough says, "We were all about the show, and because we didn't have much money all we could do really was to make outfits. I think for us it was just a natural part of performing. We're going to make the show the best we can possibly make it and so that included costumes, that included getting dressed up, make sure your hair was great. And if you need a little eyeliner or something or a little rouge, then that's what you did because that was the standard of the industry as far as we're concerned—certainly our heroes, that's what they did. And it just looks good on stage. And certainly for Steve, you know, his tradition of his parents in the theater, there's nothing unusual at all about going on stage and pumping up your face for the lights—it looks better."

Frost describes their outfits: "They were Glam, especially the guys, they out-glammed me every night. Our lead guitarist [Jed Harrison] was also very Glam looking. I think a lot of his performing clothes were made by his girlfriend. He was kind of the boa king of the band. He always had a feather boa around his neck."

Ainscough took a pair of cobalt-blue corduroy pants and cut them all the way up to the knee, inserting black cloth to turn them into huge flares. He paired this with a woman's halter top that he bedazzled in fake gems. The band members' parents were helpful and supportive; Ainscough's mother would even run costumes through the sewing machine.

Frost performed in striking costumes, many of which were made by her and her mother, including a white halter dress ensemble and a Halloween witch costume that she "absconded" from her younger sister, then modified. Says Frost, "And a lot of the accessories came from shops like Beau Brummell in Gastown and a lot of boutiquey shops. It was kind of fun to search for old vintage jewelry."

Weakes often wore a navy-blue jumpsuit. Completing the look was an old tutu worn around his neck, fastened with a brooch. Cheap jewelry was borrowed from his girlfriend at the time. "I mean, that was the other part of it, too, is in those early days that the girlfriends often had ideas or things for clothes because that was their thing, right? And they would say, 'Try this, try that.' And we wore boots—a lot of us did, high boots, knee-high boots. I had a pair that were platform runners that were quite high. It helped me because I'm only five eight. We just sort of pieced it together from a thrift store."

They even made their own silver glitter speaker cabinets, thinking, "Hey, this will look good in the lights." Weakes says, "Everyone was eager, but we're all quite new and testing our ability and so on as a performer, as a player, as a singer." They soon developed a repertoire covering current Glam hits, including a lot of Bowie and Slade, as well as old rock 'n' roll standards like "Roll Over Beethoven" and "Blue Suede Shoes." Frost adds, "And then we would close every gig with [Elton John's] 'Saturday Night's Alright for Fighting' and, for whatever reason, it always brought the house down."

Barry Samuels of Axis Entertainment took notice. He was the booking agent for a roster of acts, including Sweeney Todd and Heart, acts that inspired members of Baby Strange

(Samuels also managed Twitch). Says Frost, "I do know when Barry said he would manage us it was like winning a lottery. We were so excited. Because he was the cream of the cream in Vancouver."

Ainscough explains, "Heart would go and do a gig in a high school and if they couldn't afford Heart, they would get us." At the time, Heart was primarily doing covers. "The best cover band in the world. No question. And the nicest people in the world. We would go to Oil Can Harry's and see them if we could and, in the break, they would come and sit with us and chat, both Ann and Nancy [Wilson] and Roger [Fisher] and all the other guys." Frost relates, "Nancy was an absolute doll and couldn't have been more generous. I can remember on one occasion she joined us during a break at a club they were performing at to share some guitar riffs. I know I was star struck. They were all such gifted musicians." Just a few years on, the title track of Heart's 1980 album was called "Bébé le Strange."[20]

Samuels' promotional hype sheet for Baby Strange describes them: "They dress in customized outfits and, all in all, loads of appeal . . . Very attractive and subtly seductive lead singer named Helen Frost . . . Her voice is rather unusual with a certain tremolo." Frost's vocal style was more operatic, as she explains: "I had a lot of classical training. I think in the end it kind of served us well, because it was a little bit more of a signature of the band. It lent itself to a lot of what was happening in the Glam music scene at that time, too. I think while we tried to really find our own style and voice, we still emulated a lot of our idols. Freddie Mercury was certainly one of them."

Pointing to himself in the band photo, Ainscough laughs and says, "We were huge fans of Queen at the time. I went into Crimpers hair salon downtown, and I took the Queen album with me, and I said, 'I want my hair cut like this.' He says, 'I can cut your hair like Freddie Mercury. No problem.' . . . And it wasn't." As close as Crimpers was to a Glam hair salon with British accents and everything, they just couldn't quite get Ainscough's hair to the Olympian heights of Queen.

In 1975, members of Baby Strange narrowly escaped death in a car crash en route to a show in Chilliwack, B.C. When I spoke to Frost, Ainscough, and Weakes separately, the incident was brought up by each of them, without prompting. Jammed into the car were Frost, Harrison, and Weakes, along with Weakes's friend Fred who would be running lights and sound and was doing the driving, while Ainscough and David Rodger, the drummer, traveled separately with the gear in a rented truck. Frost explains, "We were in a little Morris Minor, very old, and it didn't have any seat belts. We were just headed onto the 1, the Highway 1, north up toward Chilliwack. We were travelling about seventy miles an hour, the wheel literally came off the car, the car flipped over, and we landed upside down. None of us were wearing seatbelts. But we all survived."

---

20 In a 2016 interview with *Rolling Stone,* Ann and Nancy Wilson claimed that the inspiration was a San Francisco dive bar they'd drive past called Jacques Le Strange, but it seems more likely that Baby Strange the band had seeped into their psyches.

Weakes takes up the story: "When it rolled over, my eyes closed for a couple seconds. I guess I was in panic mode probably and this vision said to me, 'Everyone's going to get hurt but you. The rest of them will all be hurt somehow but you won't.' Boom, the car stops. Nobody was getting out right away and I was able to finally kick the door open because it was kind of wedged. The other three were all injured in one way or another. I was not—not a scratch on me."

Ainscough says, "Me and the drummer ended up at the gig with the truck and we had to load all the gear in and get set up and then they took a cab in from the hospital to the gig. And Helen didn't know that she actually had a broken collarbone." Frost explains: "We literally made it to the gig on time. We performed. Our lead guitarist had a huge gash in his leg. And I knew that I had injured something because I couldn't move my right arm at all. So I just shifted my tambourine to my left hand."

Weakes continues: "We had a move planned where Jed would come running up behind Helen and pass his white Stratocaster through her legs as she would pull the guitar up in front of her. And then he comes from behind and takes it back from her, all in one sort of grand move—a big showbizzy kind of thing. And we'd rehearsed it a little bit, but I didn't think we'd actually go through with it. But we thought, 'Let's try it tonight.' So he goes running through, he passes the guitar through her legs like he's supposed to do, but he doesn't let go of it. She's pulling it all she can, finally he lets go, and the thing flies up and the tuning pegs slit her eyelid open. She's bleeding in the middle of the tune now with a big dress on and makeup and the whole bit, right? So we finish the song." Frost elaborates: "I ended up with a gash on my head from the botched guitar stunt but somehow we made it through the song and the entire evening. Amazing what you can do when you're nineteen or twenty."

The show must go on! As a result of her broken collarbone, Frost performed with her arm in a sling for the next six weeks.

Baby Strange had a chance to open for Iggy and the Stooges at the Pender Ballroom. Ainscough says, "And that was gonna be awesome! What we'd heard was that he would order a private ambulance to take him to the gig so that he could breathe the oxygen on the way in. And that all the gear on the stage were 'all bets are off,' because he would just smash whatever he wanted." Not wanting their equipment ruined, Baby Strange declined.

After Weakes left to join another band, they moved into a band house in North Vancouver and decided to go for a two-guitar approach à la Queen and began auditioning dozens of guitarists, including fourteen-year-old Bryan Adams. However, his rhythm guitar playing wasn't quite up to snuff, so Ainscough asked him, "Well, can you sing? Do an Elton John song or something." As Ainscough related later, "Holy crap, he can sing! We already got two or three people that can sing well in the band. We didn't need another singer, but we got along great."

They did find a young guitarist who played quite well and was handsome to boot! Says Ainscough, "But again, nobody had any money at the time. He was working in a steel factory, and he called one day, he had done the all-night shift, and he'd run his hand through one of the things and he said, 'My hand's broken, man. I won't be able to play for at least six months.' Oh, no. So then we had to go back to the drawing board and find another guitar player. And at this point, I'm just going, 'Oh boy, this is not very good.'"

Alas, there is no recorded legacy. Baby Strange just fizzled out in the spring of 1975. They were oh so close to doing original material, says Frost: "I feel like we were on the cusp of that happening and then the band broke up. Chris included all of us in a group email a couple of years ago and attached a treasure trove of Baby Strange memorabilia (pictures, our Axis promo material, my handwritten set list, and gig lists, to name a few). We all responded with the same sentiment: 'Those were some of the best times of my life.' I think it was a great time to be a part of the music scene

SLAN were formed after Drew Arnott put an ad in the paper in 1973: "Wanted—An uninhibited rock vocalist interested in joining the glitter brigade." Darryl Kromm answered. Arnott and Kromm later formed Strange Advance, who still perform today. Darryl Kromm (vocals/guitar) in white, Craig Soon (bass) to his left, Edwin Dolinski (keyboards, synths) up top, then Drew Arnott (drums) on the right. Photo courtesy Drew Arnott.

in Vancouver, watching bands like Heart with the mega-talented Ann and Nancy Wilson emerge as rock royalty and I'm forever grateful to the guys in the band for offering me a chance to be a part of the rock 'n' roll world."

Today the members have continued to be creative in their respective fields. Helen Frost is now based in California, writing films, Chris Ainscough is writing soundtrack music for film, and Steven Weakes is also in film, recording and mixing sound. David Rodger is high up in the airline business. Jed Harrison is a scientist at the University of Alberta; when he arrived there, he was the youngest professor at the university and subsequently developed a microchip.

The band Weakes left Baby Strange to join was called SLAN, who were also managed by Samuels. As the replacement keyboardist, Weakes didn't need to change his attire. They too dressed for the stage—think formal evening wear with a touch of flair: shiny shirts, black opal cufflinks, and big velvet bow ties. SLAN was into the European side of things: when they covered Bowie, they did "Space Oddity" and the deep cuts, along with the Genesis opus "Watcher of the Skies." The slender, curly-maned singer Darryl Kromm moved like Bowie but tried to maintain an aloof, brooding artist mystique. Named after an old science fiction pulp novel by A. E. Van Vogt, the name often confused audiences, especially when in a loud bar. Says Weakes, "People would ask you on the break what you're called, and I'm telling you every single time they would get it wrong. I used to dread that part of the night." He would have to spell out the name, S-L-A-N! With the more sophisticated material, it was difficult for SLAN when they played the out-of-town gigs where the crowds wanted to boogie to "Sweet Home Alabama." Weakes lasted two years in SLAN, long enough for them to go new wave, covering the Cars and Elvis Costello. Members of SLAN moved on to form the heavily synthesized new wave band Strange Advance. After SLAN, Weakes toured with Bryan Adams in 1980.

SLAM

WHEN I BEGAN THIS BOOK many people—some reputable, some not so much—would ask me, "Canadian Glam—is there even such thing?" While keeping to my tailored qualifiers—tight where it counts—this book has become a beast, almost savage and difficult to wrestle, going further than I ever thought. As I dusted off my satin-covered knees, thinking my work to be pretty much done, the owner of Neptoon Records, Rob Frith, dropped me a line from his basement. This record store has existed for decades. Frith has such a vast collection of posters and memorabilia that even he is uncertain of all that he has—including a mystery find, a poster of an incredibly Glammed-to-the-nines band called SLAM. Hazed out electric yellows and sepia brown, a pale crimson logo with a lightning bolt, and the band, oh the band, the lads have their faces on! A mustache and makeup combo pack for practically everyone. A cape gently draped. In the foreground is an elaborate platform boot going all the way up one member's leg. Just below the boot, Frith's poster was neatly autographed by someone named Gary Mons. Mons was the drummer and longest-standing in a long succession of members. And, as I found out, he is still based in Victoria, B.C., and still involved in music as an active member of the Victoria Blues Society.

Mons has been playing since he was six years old. He explains, "I was on the pots and pans and the parents kicked me out into the yard and I had suitcases out there and I was drumming and drumming and drumming until they finally bought me a set of drums. I mean, I started at six years old, and I even had a marching band going up and down the street. I had a drum, and all these baton twirlers were behind me because they were all practicing, and that's kind of the neighborhood I grew up in." It was such a creative neighborhood that the future Sweeney Todd drummer John Booth lived just up the street. Drummers galore!

Mons formed the Jimi Hendrix tribute band Armadilla with the guitarist Mark Stadnyk at Victoria's Esquimalt High School, opting out of Phys Ed to practice in the high school gym locker room. Stadnyk emulated Hendrix in the guitar playing as well as the performativity: smashing the guitar to bits, lighting the guitar on fire, jumping on a stack of

SLAM poster, c. 1974. Courtesy of Rob Frith.

Marshall amps. Playing high schools in the region, they'd rent the biggest PA they could from Booth's band Holy Smoke, who'd subsequently watch their shows, flabbergasted that Stadnyk would smash his white Stratocaster to bits! Mons reveals the switcheroo: "When Mark would switch his white Stratocasters for his white Kent guitar they wouldn't know, they would think he's still got the Strat in his hand. We couldn't afford to smash a good guitar. He had a Kent guitar painted up."

The bassist soon went off to the Juilliard School, later returning to Victoria with his doctorate to take up the bass position in the Victoria Symphony. SLAM sprang out of Armadilla after finding a singer, Jack Day, from their usual source: Esquimalt High. SLAM wasn't always Glam, but they most certainly always rhymed with Glam! Their booker was named B.C. Sound Productions and with a name like that SLAM never went further than B.C. Wait. That's wrong. They did leave the country once. SLAM continued doing the Hendrix numbers that they began with Armadilla and took the act all the way down to Hendrix's home town, Seattle, for a show at the University of Washington. Also in their set were covers of the rather un-Glam Doobie Brothers and Lighthouse, along with Deep Purple, but also Bowie—but just the Bowie you could boogie to. And Slade. Oh, how they loved covering Slade's "Gudbuy T'Jane."

That Slade influence helped take the performance one step further into their stage apparel. Mons explains: "Mark was definitely the one that got the Glam going because his mom was a seamstress. She made a gold lamé suit for me, totally gold. And then he had a silver suit, and he had the high snakeskin boots." The women applying SLAM's stage makeup, including a teardrop drawn on Mons's cheek, were also looking at Alice Cooper. Who were these women? Gary answers, "Girlfriends of the band. I think one of them was a wife—the guys didn't last very long with their marriages." These guys didn't last very long with their marriages? "I remember the one guy, he was locked out of the house at four in the morning and he had the makeup on still and the sister-in-law looks out the window and says, 'Oh my god, what are you doing with this man coming home at four in the morning and he looks like this???' and next thing you know he's divorced." So, she didn't help apply the makeup, I guess? "No."

In April 1974, SLAM backed up Chuck Berry at the Memorial Arena (today it is more commonly known as Save-On Foods where the music is now pre-recorded and piped in; you can also purchase groceries if so inclined; to use the bathroom type in the code 7658). Sweeney Todd opened. Mons describes, "It's a new arena, so it's probably the worst arena just about you could ever want to play in because of the echo in there. It was so bad that Chuck Berry stopped playing after three bars. He walked up to me, said, 'We got to change this.' Turned his amplifier right around to me, not out to the audience anymore. And there's six thousand people there. It was packed, the floor and the stands, it was just jam packed in there. He wanted me to hear him so I can keep the beat properly—not to hear an echo coming back at me." Par for the course with Berry, who never rehearsed with the local band backing him at a show. "He shows up with his guitar, he had been drinking and he was a little—a little on the juice and he was out of tune. But he wasn't going to tune up with us because he was, you know, just kind of rebellious about that. Mark had tuned up all the guitars with his tuners and he was bang on. Chuck was a little off. And that was the way it was gonna be. This is the way that guitar is and that's it." It was the legendary pioneer of rock and roll Chuck Berry, and it was great, and everyone loved it, so much so that he even played for an extra half hour with the promoter telling Mons, "He never does that." Mons explains, "I mean, the crowd went wild, and they had actually shut it down at one point because we had streakers, one guy who just got onto the stage naked [unsure if this was a result of Berry performing his then-current single-entendre hit "My Ding-a-Ling"]. And I still know some of the bouncers from back then and they were kind of shocked at what was going on in that concert because people were just doing wild stuff. And at the end, when people started coming onto the stage, that's when they shut it down. So, Chuck Berry took off, and we were still playing. I thought, well, this is our chance to play now. But then they unplugged the PA."

Mark Stadnyk left SLAM when he moved to Vancouver, where he had a band called Rage. His inventiveness with creating new and wild guitar sounds then led Bryan Adams to hire him as his guitar tech for seventeen years. SLAM got a new guitarist and further lineup changes but kept its Glam style, as evidenced by the poster described earlier. Most people got a chuckle out of their appearance. Some, however, were not amused. Mons says, "It's like you're in redneck country all of a sudden. Just like *The Blues Brothers*, you know, people are throwing beer bottles at you. That's why we needed some pretty hefty bouncers in the bars there. And we had probably the toughest bouncers you'd ever see. I mean, six foot four, could pick a guy up and throw him down the stairs."

SLAM dropped the Glam and, after a few years, disintegrated. Mons drummed for a reasonably recent SLAM reunion—a surprise birthday party at a lodge for ScatCat, a.k.a. Christa Rossner, the drummer in the Victoria band the Curl. It was a good party!

TROOPER AND PRISM
AN APPRECIATION

THE RADIO-FRIENDLY ROCK ACTS Trooper and Prism both have songs that really pump up the synth and sound great whilst rotating around the roller rink.[21] Trooper's and Prism's hits are—like the best of hard Glam—dumb and strangely grandiose. Trooper even toured with Sweeney Todd. Trooper still works very hard touring to this day. Their 1979 greatest-hits album *Hot Shots* sold four million copies. Trooper is a Greatest Hits band. And the hits? Faux-rebel lighter wavers with high pitched fey vocals and a big thump-and-thud backbeat. Trooper's self-titled debut album from 1975 consists of numbingly bland low-impact blues work-out filler, yet it has this one song and ooh, such an upbeat song: "General Hand Grenade" is full of nursery-rhyme schemes and dreams about two faintly sketched-in characters named General Hand Grenade and Isabella Band-Aid. What does it all mean? Ha! Who's asking? Just turn it up.

Trooper's reasonably improved second album, *Two for the Show,* has two key Glam album cover sleeve hallmarks: fake hand colored photo tinting and two women who are definitely not in the band; à la Roxy Music, none of the band is pictured at all. Canadian *Country Life*. With Glam one can create mythical fantasy characters such as the ones who

---

21 Apart from Trooper's rather lead-footed cash-in song "Roller Rink," ironically enough.

Front cover of *Two for the Show* by Trooper (Legend/MCA, 1976). Author's collection.

fill up T. Rex's "Telegram Sam." With their hit song "The Boys in the Bright White Sports Car," Trooper created the hoser archetypes Jerry the Garbage Man and Jack-of-All-Trades Stan as if they had leapt from the pages of *Alligator Pie*, the brightly colored classic Canadian children's book.[22] I have heard more authoritative folks argue that Trooper really were not Glam but let's look at live footage of "Boys in the Bright White Sports Car" from 1975 showing much satin and the guitarist's silver and black pseudo–Ace Frehley space jumpsuit. They got moves; they work the crowd. Another Trooper big-league chewer, "Raise a Little Hell," is pretty much a footie anthem, suitable for all sporting events: it sounds like it coulda woulda been sung by Noddy Holder, in multiple shades of Slade in spades and,

---

22 The original edition of Alligator Pie with the tripped-out Frank Newfeld illustrations only, please. This 1974 children's poetry book should be in every Canadian Glam library.

like Slade's creative spelling-bee shockers, it really should have been called "Rayz a Lil 'Ell." As much as Trooper's hits fulfill Canadian-content requirements for Canadian radio, we can't deny that they are real fist-pumpers.

Prism took the Sweeney Todd vibe and put that heavy rock on a van to the stars—and not just any van but a van with shag-carpet artistry and an airbrushed mural of a deep sunset on the side inviting you in—smooth shine and lube. A band of lads clad in sprinklings of pink satin and even a slightly foreboding pair of black gloves, their name sounds cosmic—as if an alien came down to bum a smoke. Prism's main symbol was a pyramid with colorful lights refracted through it to produce a rainbow that has absolutely nothing at all to do with Pink Floyd, so don't even think of asking.

Prism's 1977 smash hit "Spaceship Superstar" isn't space rock—it's rock in space! Ladies and gentlemen, we are cruising in space! "Got a solar powered laser beam guitar!"

Front cover of *Armageddon* by Prism (Ariola America, 1979). Author's collection.

They had plenty of other solid smooth rockers, like their other space-themed number "Take Me to the Kaptin." The 1979 song "Armageddon" gleefully foretells the end of the world as caused by the death of Elvis Presley, the King of Rock 'n' Roll. Before it gets all kick-ass, ominous aircraft fly above a stately procession building the tension, salivation occurs while we line the streets to greet the '70s future past.

As cosmic as it all seems, Prism is more of a star council really, starting out as an early session project put together by the big-name rock producer Bruce Fairbairn, along with the songwriter Jim Vallance (famed as Bryan Adams's songwriting partner) briefly in the mix. One member came from Trooper, and one member joined Sweeney Todd. This is the kind of band that, at various points in their long career, has had no original members.

FACES: THE PLACE IN VANCOUVER

ANYONE WHO CLAIMS that Vancouver had no Glam scene was obviously not looking in the right places. Faces was gay-owned and -operated and an iconic part of Vancouver's large gay scene. One need only follow the trail of glitter down the block to find it. Faces was on Seymour, located right around the corner from Beau Brummell and just one door over from Ruby's, both places where many of the more Glammed-out clientele would conveniently shop, including a few Bowie wannabes (or Fauxies, as some liked to call them). It was hip.

Faces was begun by the former proprietors of the wig shops Gone with the Wig and the Wig Wam, who realized that wigs weren't going to be big. After being open for just a couple of months, Faces was failing—it needed a lift. After the manager quit, the owners knew that they needed a visionary to get the place happening. In the final week of 1969, they asked a part-time em-

SINGLES!

JAM—"TAKE ME BACK OME" 7"
A Vancouver band doing a reasonable cover of the Slade song, not belting it out like Noddy but more loungey. They add some pretty sweet fuzz guitar, though. The A side is not Glam at all. They sprang out of a band called Spring. But the absolute greatest thing that the band member Bob Buckley did was co-write the tuba—and whistle-driven A&W Root Beer theme, a.k.a. "Ba-Dum Ba-Dum."

THE HOOD—"'CAUSE WE'RE IN LOVE"/"SWING IT" 7" (GOLDFISH RECORDS, 1974)
It's really a Terry Jacks one-off with a '50s good-time rock 'n' roll riff, saxophone, and some deep oh-yeahs, but done with his moody 'shroomy production styling. The B side, "Swing It," is a breezy near-instrumental with vocal manipulations, slowed down and sped up like a Chipmunks B side. Jacks had a reputation for recording some pretty wild B sides, often using vocal manipulations. On "She Even Took the Cat," he intentionally parodies Neil Young, and then there's his infamous B side "Put the Bone In"—the flip to "Seasons

in the Sun"—where you can faintly hear the drummer Kat Hendricks intone, "Oh, no," at the very end (Canadian version only) while the Vancouver Canucks do a group chant in the middle. When I interviewed Jacks, he told me that after his double A side with the Poppy Family, "Where Evil Grows"/"I Was Wondering" split airplay and thus split sales, Frasier Jamieson, who ran London Records Canada with Alice Jamieson, told him, "Look, Jacks, whatever you do for the next record you put out, put something terrible on the flip side." And Terry Jacks really went wild with it! He describes them as strange records, "things that nobody would play." With "Seasons in the Sun"/"Put the Bone In" now in millions of homes, Frasier told Jacks, "Oh, man, you've really done it." As a result, they became cult records. Another peculiar Canadian cult entertainment you may want to track down is the *Seasons in the Sun* movie made years after the song was a hit. Jacks plays Terry Brandon, a pop star who gets a brain tumor right before his Madison Square Garden concert, moves to a houseboat on the island, then gets chased by Russian spies.

Dennis Robbins, manager and DJ at Faces Dec, 1972.
Photo courtesy of Dennis Robbins.

ployee, Dennis Robbins, to step in as manager: "They knew that I knew a lot of people because I was going to the bars. I was pretty young then. I was only twenty-two and I wasn't sure that I could do something like that. But I said, 'You've got to change the music.'" With a budget to work with as Faces' music buyer and DJ, Robbins would make regular trips across the border to Seattle as well as San Francisco, often with his roommate, the popular Faces DJ Jerry Cole, to get the latest R&B records before they hit Canada, throwing in some of the latest British rock. This blend of music naturally anticipated disco. Robbins notes that the cutting-edge late-

Faces Christmas Show with the Facettes, Dec. 1972. Photo courtesy of Dennis Robbins.

night FM radio disc jockey J. B. Shayne would show up "just to hear what we were playing." Faces got busy rather quickly—people were lining up, and the place was packed right until 4 AM on weekends.

Robbins oversaw some cannily extensive renovations, installing a state-of-the-art sound system pumping out a lot of danceable Glam mixed in with early proto-disco R&B such as Donny Hathaway and George McCrae to keep the crowded dancefloor moving. The dancefloor was built up and opened up so that the dancers were the stars. Says Robbins, "It became a stage so that people could go up there and perform and dance. It was fun!" The room was transformed.

Though not a live venue, there were performances. Robbins was inspired by San Francisco's Cockettes, the legendary proto-Glam gender-blending performance troupe who took a page from Jack Smith's underground film *Flaming Creatures* and rode it all the way to the tinfoil-covered cardboard stars. On one trip to San Francisco in 1972, Robbins had dinner with Sylvester and Hibiscus of the Cockettes and subsequently started the Facettes, featuring Faces staff and friends. Robbins notes, "I remember seeing the Cockettes around. They were seen out on Castro Street and going around bars. The Facettes weren't quite like the Cockettes—they were a take-off on the Cockettes. The Facettes just put on a few shows at Faces." Robbins didn't perform in the group, but Cole was a mainstay as the ranks varied from show to show, with magical names like Ruby Tuesday, Cherie Ripple, Peach de Vogue, Mabel, and

Top to bottom: Facettes Valentines Day show at Faces in 1973. Facettes as cheerleaders for Lou Reed, 1973. Photos courtesy of Dennis Robbins.

David Divine joining in, depending—often decked out in dresses and glitter beards, some members having seen the Cockettes themselves on visits to San Francisco. These shows were all themed, with Halloween being the first in 1972, then moving on to a very memorable and glittery Christmas show. The fashion historian and collector Ivan Sayers provided some of the costumes, including the '20s-themed outfits for Valentine's Day, the Facettes singing and dancing along to "I Wanna Be Loved by You." Another Facettes performance featured a '50s theme.

There was one special show that took place outside of the Faces nightclub. Four of the Facettes dressed up as cheerleaders for Lou Reed's concert at the PNE Gardens, touring the landmark Glam Rock *Transformer* album. As people arrived, these four Facettes set up impromptu, right in front of the stage, and went into their special cheerleading routine. On one cheerleader's outfit was an L! and one had an O! and one had a U! and one had BABY! What does that spell? LOU BABY!!! During Lou's set, right as the band went into "Walk on the Wild Side," he looked at them, pointed, and said, "Sick little girls."

Robbins observes, "A new crowd was emerging in 1972 and 1973 that were very much into glitter and very much into David Bowie. I was myself—I wasn't into glitter but I had satin shirts. There was a crowd of people that started to dress very cool—a younger group."

Eventually it was time for Robbins to move on: "I quit in '73 and I moved to London, England, for a year. I was burnt out after three years. I was so naïve when I started. I was not when I left, I tell ya. But it was a great experience. I just needed to get away. London always appealed to me. I worked over there and went to the gay bars over there. I saw the live performance of *Rocky Horror Show* on Kings Road with Tim Curry! It was amazing!"

Thanks to an obviously fake ID, the artist Roy Arden was a regular at Faces early on. Arden states, "Every night they ended with the Lou Reed song 'Goodnight Ladies.' When I went there the crowd was very gay. It was mixed, open. You just had to be cool to get in." Faces' reputation spread not only all the way to the gay scene in California but also to the nearby Vancouver suburbs, where the residents would drive down just to harass the people out in front of Faces, yelling homophobic epithets and throwing things at them. Some of the wilder Faces regulars hanging outside, like the handsome character Randy Rhinestone and Oliv, wouldn't take their redneck shit and would yell and throw things back at them. Oliv later became a long-term fixture in the performance-art world and was photographed for *House of O,* a photographic installation by the artist Oraf, noted as "one of the first artworks that took the drag queen as subject."[23]

Arden continues, "The true freaks who wanted to go to a place like that were so few, the dancefloor wasn't very big, so you could get a real party vibe really quickly." With Vancouver's Draconian liquor laws, Faces was a "bottle club," where one would have to bring one's own bottle to check at the bar for the bartender to pour. It wasn't just booze,

---

23 Glen Alteen, "Beyond Haute Camp: The Interplay of Drag and Performance in Vancouver," in *Live at the End of the Century: Aspects of Performance Art In Vancouver*, ed. By Bruce Canyon (Visible Arts, 2000), p. 127.

Arden adds: "Everybody was on drugs. It wasn't like they were all doing the same drug. One person would be on Mandrax, one person would be on pot . . . " But the main thing was dancing. People would make their entrances and go right on to the dancefloor. In 1976, Faces expanded, taking over Beau Brummell's vacated location.

By the early '80s, Faces was fading. When someone from the club came in to L'Espresso, where Arden was working at the time, Arden said, "'Why don't you let us take over and bring a whole new scene in? It might be quite straight but there'll be cool people, they won't be homophobic or anything but we'll play hip-hop and new-wave music.' The guy said, 'Sounds great. Do you have a DJ?' 'Yeah, Stan.' Stan said, 'What?'" The now world-renowned artist Stan Douglas was quickly convinced to DJ and in this new incarnation Faces had a second life, lasting for a couple of years.

CHAPTER 2
ALBERTA

New quadraphonic format to make the Stampeders entertaining

A combination of several changes in format promises for an entertaining evening with the Stampeders when they debut their "Quadraconcert" here in the ADSS auditorium Oct. 9.

The three-man band — Ronnie King, Rich Dodson and Kim Berly — are the first Canadian group to use the sophisticated quadraphonic sound system which actually places the audience right in the centre of the sound.

Another highlight of the evening will be a light show featuring 24,000 watts of color-light energy.

A change in the last half of the show will be a six-man back-up band which includes up to five trumpets at one time, with the use of extra bass, guitar, organ and synthesizer.

"As far as dynamic rock is concerned the addition of the quadraconcert system, new material, and the solid back-up of six extra men will make every concert one of the rock'nest performances anyone will have ever seen," says Mel Shaw, the group's manager.

Appearing with the Stampeders will be a seven-year-old rock and roll band, Thundermug, that plays, according to Rolling Stone, "defiantly unpretty rock and roll. Like the early records of Little Richard, Eddie Cochran, and the Who, the (LP) shudders with a power they seem to emanate out of pure frustration."

Also accompanying the Stampeders will be the Incredible Laughing Band of B.C.

A jam with all the musicians on stage will conclude the concert. The internationally acclaimed Stampeders have had a recent smash single, "Hit the Road Jack" followed immediately by another hit, "New Orleans". These, and the 30-city Western Canada tour of which Port Alberni is a part, signify the successful result of a philosophy held by manager Shaw.

"I believe the band must be seen regularly by the public from coast to coast," he says.

"I also feel that spacing our records correctly is very important. We always wait until a record has gone up the chart and is heading back down again before putting out another one."

Although the group has been together for a dozen years — a phenomenally long time in a business where three-day wonders and overnight success abound — their hit record action did not start until 1971 when "Carry Me" became a hit in Canada.

Their first important album, "Against the Grain", contained a new song, "Sweet City Woman" that blew the lid off the recording scene for the Stampeders. It became a million seller in Canada, spread to the United States and Europe and became a world-wide hit. Over the last six years, they have had 17 singles hit Canada's top 100 charts, including "Carry Me," "Sweet City Woman," "Devil You," "Wild Eyes," "Running Wild," "Hit the Road, Jack," and "New Orleans."

Image courtesy of *Alberni Valley Times*, October 3rd, 1975.

STAMPEDERS: AN APPRECIATION

THE VERY IDEA OF CONJECTURE can be more troubled than the teens in the group home across the street (and those kids are getting the help they need, man) but okay, okay, here we go: what if the hard rocking British Glam acts Slade or the Sweet had come from the big cowboy town of Calgary, Alberta? What would they be like?

I'm talking aboot Stampeders, a power trio named after Canada's most popular rodeo event, the Calgary Stampede. The Stampeders themselves, though burly boys, are not full-on yee-haw. Oh sure, their early albums are truer to their Alberta roots, tinged with K-Tel country, as they cautiously, gradually gravitate towards the rock. You probably know the hit 1971 song "Sweet City Woman" from listening to music. And not sour music either—there are no sour notes in "Sweet City Woman." It's the one with the French lyric, "Bon c'est bon bon c'est bon bon," which my grade-two French teacher translated as "Good it's good it's good good" because it is good! Such a good song! French is one of Canada's two national languages. "Sweet City Woman" is bilingual—just like Canada!

If you listen to the early Stampeders number "Man from P.E.I.," you could even say that it is a Canadian cousin to the Sweet's "Alexander Graham Bell," also from 1971, except the man from the teeny tiny province of P.E.I. (Prince Edward Island) didn't invent the phone, he stood in the pogey[1] line. Plus: Stampeders use "Dudes" in an album title—*Rubes, Dudes & Rowdies*, a total Glam move, dude, a full two years before the Glitter Band came out with their 1975 album *Rock 'n Roll Dudes* across the pond in England.

Stampeders were prolifically pumping out albums and singles with their producer and manager Mel Shaw riding herd to keep the hits coming. He named them and dressed them in cowboy hats and denim dyed in bright colors by his wife Fran.

1973's *From the Fire* opens with the heavy-beaded thud of "Manitou," about the Native North American spiritual force. That thud pulsates and permeates this long player, then subsides as chinooks blow in long gusts, giving us warm dreams. "Chariots of the Gods" takes its name from the popular book about ancient aliens having staked their claims in Earth, influencing human technology so much that this very album was the result. Thanks, aliens.

And then came *New Day*. The skies broke. On this album our boys still keep warm in burly buckskin, but now our holy Northern trinity (Rich Dodson, Ronnie King, Kim Berly) are all pimped and jump-suited out. Stampeders' most Glam moment is the smash 1974 single from that album, "Wild Eyes," an all-out rock attack pulling a T. Rex with the addition of strings to meld with that steel-belted thud made radio-perfect. For a few minutes *A New Day* even gets cosmic. How do we know it is cosmic? Synths! Synths = cosmic. The song is called "Brothers of the Universe." Whoa, deep.

---

1 Canadian slang for the office that distributes unemployment checks.

Front cover of *From the Fire* by Stampeders (Capitol, 1973). Author's collection.

Heavy chugging live, these dudes would play any high school gymnasium—even when they had massive hits on the charts. However, they also played heavy rock to 13,000 fans at the Toronto Forum as documented by their live album *Backstage Pass*. Unfortunately, the album has no actual backstage shenanigans whatsoever. Oh, to know what was happening back there—were there shimmering stubbies[2] of beer on ice and boxes of Old Dutch potato chips?[3]

Next up was the hard Glam stomp of 1975's *Steamin'*, which took the meat and potatoes of the fellow Canadian-content providers Bachman Turner Overdrive and removed

---

2   A short, round bottle of beer popular in Canada in the 1970s.

3   Old Dutch is a popular Canadian potato chip company known for their large boxes containing two bags of chips.

Inner cover of *New Day* by Stampeders (Music World Creations, 1974). Author's collection

all that long-winded soloing, keeping it short and bon. They're not winded, they're working—they're *steamin'*—for us, the fans! Maybe Stampeders were a BTO for the pre-teen set—I dunno. Like any good Glam act, they throw in flashback nods as evidenced by their wacky cover of "Hit the Road, Jack," featuring a guest appearance by the wild rock 'n' roll disc jockey Wolfman Jack, fresh from the retro flick *American Graffiti*. The single was released the same year as the Guess Who's ode "Clap for the Wolfman." Did Wolfman Jack do both songs on the same weekend excursion to Canada? Let's imagine yes, though it's probably no.

Stampeders' next album, *Hit the Road,* is solid, with a wide array of choices for the dancefloor including "*C'est la vie.*" (In case you still don't understand French, they sing "Thaaaaaat's life!") No longer a trio by this point, they had expanded to become a sev-

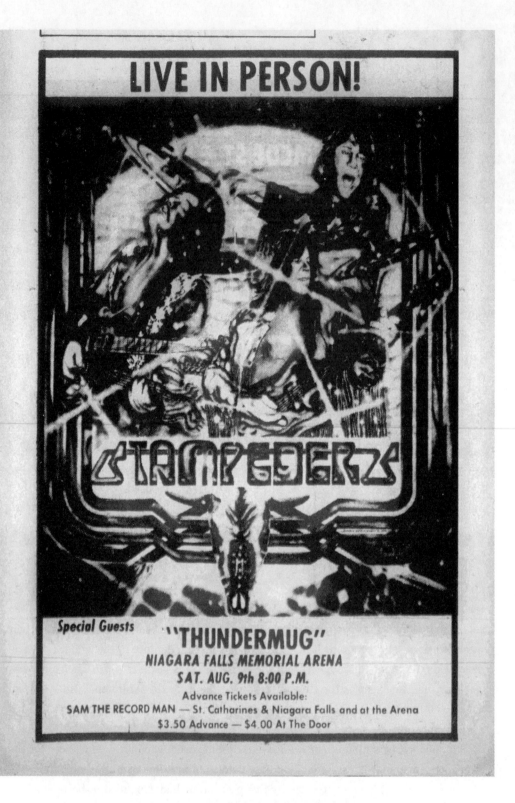

Stampeders with Thundermug concert ad. Image courtesy of *Niagara Falls Review*, August 8, 1975.

en-piece band. And now the bassist, Ronnie King, was stepping up his songwriting, contributing half the songs on the album, including the hit "Playin' in the Band." Guess what that one's about? This album, while still stomping, moves towards a groove with the addition of horns. Soon these Stampeders followed the Glam lead of embracing soul on into disco (see Bowie etc.). They kept the horns but lost a pivotal member (goodbye, Rich Dodson) for the 1977 album *Platinum* (it never went there), and at that point they just stopped doing it for me. Then another pivotal member of the original trio moved on (goodbye, Kim Berly) before the meat-no-potatoes album *Ballsy*. Stampeders clearly stopped doing it for lots of people, because the band just sort of petered out. So what? They left a legacy of damned good dollar-bin finds! Want more good news in these troubled times? The main three boys are back together (breaking news: as of 1992) and may be playing a rodeo fairground near you![4] Ronnie King passed in 2024, but the band continues.

BUICK McKANE

I MAY BE GOING AGAINST GLAM PROTOCOLS with what I am about to pronounce, but why not affront? Here goes. The most quintessentially Canadian piece of music is the theme to the *Kids in the Hall* TV series. Simultaneously maudlin and cheerful, yet goofy, this twangy number nods to Canada's country music roots as well as its punk history. And it's used for one of the funniest Canadian television shows ever made. The song really is something special. Originally released in 1985 by Shadowy Men on a Shadowy Planet, the song, "Having an Average Weekend," is just one of their numerous great instrumentals. But this chapter isn't about them—well, actually, it kind of is. Shadowy Men on a Shadowy Planet's beginnings are as a Glam Rock band in Calgary.

Rob Wynne and Bob Keast were classmates in the Dr. E. P. Scarlett High School pop music class taught by Leo Snye, or—as some students preferred to call him behind his back—Uncle Leo. The brothers Grant and Reid Diamond weren't even in the class but hung out playing piano during their spare block when the four of them met and formed a loosely knit band. This unnamed band had mild competition from another high school band with Brian Connelly and Scott Reed—who *had* joined the pop music class and were the Diamond brothers' neighbors. Out of this mix, in the Summer of 1974, came the short-lived first incarnation of Buick McKane, with Rob Wynne on drums, Bob Keast on guitar, Reid Diamond on bass, Brian Connelly on guitar and vocals, and Grant Diamond as band manager. Soon enough, they went from two guitars to one: Keast was out; he just wasn't excited by covering—let alone discovering—the music of New York Dolls. Grant Diamond describes him: "He was more of the type of guy who

---

4   Shout-out to the artist, writer, and musician Plastic Crimewave for casually coining "Canadian Glam" when he shoved a Stampeders album under my ungainly schnozz and planted the seed for this entire project.

you see probably playing guitar in maybe a Chicago cover band. You know, that's more where you see him and teaching guitar at a strip mall . . . he did end up doing that." Scott Reed subsequently became Buick McKane's lead singer, allowing Connelly to focus purely on his guitar playing.

In Glam Rock tradition, Buick McKane wore their influences on their sleeve with a cheeky twist, brazenly nicking their wrap-around bolt logo from the crunchy Canadian rock band Thundermug, and their slogan "Maximum R & R" was an overt reference to the Who's "Maximum R & B" slogan, and, of course, their very name came from the thunderous and wondrous T. Rex song "Buick Mackane," intentionally misspelled for a bit of flairful differentiation. They used the tools and supplies of the Dr. E. P. Scarlett High School shop department to silkscreen the Buick McKane logo onto bundles of t-shirts, bumper stickers, and business cards, with Grant Diamond freely admitting, "The guys weren't even enrolled in shop class. They were driven to succeed."

Buick McKane band photo, c. 1977. Top: Reid Diamond, Brian Connelly, bottom: Scott Reed, Alex Koch. Photo by and courtesy of Grant Diamond.

Reid Diamond on bass. Photo (probably) by Grant Diamond, courtesy of Don Pyle.

As connoisseurs of rock, Buick McKane had an ear for covers that were swaggering, often Glammy, always gritty, and always rock. Grant Diamond notes, "My brother Reid's big influences were the Who's John Entwistle and Dennis Dunaway, the bass player for Alice Cooper," naturally leading them to cover material by both bands. Scott Reed explains their song selection process: "Reid was famous for going to the used record stores and finding all sorts of bands that nobody had ever heard of before. If the band had some great tunes on the LP, then we would pick one and just never tell the audience who the song was by. A lot of them thought that they were songs that we wrote, but we just never said anything."

Examples of the fast ones that they pulled were "The Cops Are Coming" by the Heavy Metal Kids—complete with flashing cop light, "Hello New York" by Silverhead, "T.N.T." by AC/DC in the days before anyone knew of AC/DC, and "Roxy Roller," which had hit the airwaves just in time for them to quickly learn it for the CKXL Radio "School's Out" Summer Picnic. There were thousands in attendance, eager and excited for summer to begin. Of this "Roxy Roller" rendition Reed notes, "I think a lot of the young girls that were out there watching us thought we were *the* actual band. I mean, I could copy his voice pretty well." They also covered songs by the Sweet and Slade and "Vambo" by the Sensational Alex Harvey Band, which they later went and recorded at a highly amped up pace.

Buick McKane wasn't initially booked to play the CKXL "School's Out" Summer Picnic. Without a proper booking agent like Alberta's largest booking agency, Studio City, Buick McKane was limited to playing high schools but were desperately eager to expand. Grant Diamond called CKXL Radio up and asked, "What time are we on?"

"You're not playing it."

"We were promised by Studio City that we would be on the gig. You know, we're just going to have to go to Studio City and say you guys are welching. And I don't know what they're going to do with the other bands, there's going to be other bands on the bill with Studio City as well."

With this outright lie and implied threat, the radio station put them on first and they blew the audience away, which led to them actually getting signed to Studio City's roster. Knowing the importance of having the right look, Connelly borrowed his dad's camper for the concert to use as a dressing room for them all to get done up in: Reid Diamond in his custom-made white and black satin jacket, Scott Reed with his long satin scarves draped around his neck and mic stand, Connelly with his sailor look. Some of their clothes were purchased from fashion shops in the Penny Lane Mall. If Reid Diamond wasn't getting clothes made, he would purchase them from the boys' department, a blessing of his smaller size. Scott Reed's mom made him black velvet trousers and a black glittery shirt, which he wore with a matching glittery scarf. As Scott Reed recounted later, "A lot of that push to wear that kind of stuff came from Grant Diamond." They also knew the importance of good hair. Rob Wynne was getting his hair cut all the time, while Reid Diamond and Brian Connelly got their hair cut downtown by a stylist that they both had dated. Scott Reed's hair influence was the porcupine chic of Stuart "Woody" Wood from the Bay City Rollers, with bits sticking up on top, cut by the hip stylist sister of the CKXL Radio DJ Dieter Stachow.

Of the live dynamic, Grant Diamond elaborates: "With Scotty up front, he was a great front-man, he really could sing. Robbie Wynne with his great big set-up a little bit off the block, which would have eight tom-toms. And it was just as much part of the show. I mean, you had to have a big Marshall amplifier, Reid had to have Ampeg SVTs. You know, the lights and the smoke and the flashpots. It was all part of it, all part and parcel. Reid drove a lot of the music, to be honest. But it was one of those interesting things that, when I look back at it, we had just a ton of fun. Even playing some little town in some community hall, we'd trip up there, and there'd be like, crickets, there'd hardly be anyone there!"

As manager, Grant Diamond was also responsible for onstage effects, which included the smoke-bombs and homemade flashpots full of gunpowder. Buick McKane usually ended their shows with these smoke-bombs because if they went off any earlier they would choke Scott Reed, and because they tended to set off the fire alarms in high school gyms and auditoriums. "We were pretty saucy in those days, and it was kind of all led by Reid and Brian,

Buick McKane live crowd shot, c. 1976.
Photo (probably) by Grant Diamond, courtesy of Don Pyle.

they had that punk attitude, I was always kind of, 'Maybe we should stop.' No, we didn't stop. They opened the doors and cleared the smoke out and, once the smoke was all cleared out, they turn the lights back out and we started playing again. It was beautiful," says Scott Reed, adding, "I think they were smoke-bombs left over from the war that Grant bought at army surplus."[5] The homemade flashpots were not without incident either. Once a careless helper asked, "What's this switch do?", then pulled it without waiting for an answer, immediately setting off a flashpot aimed right at Connelly's crotch. The epitome of cool, Connelly stepped back and continued playing. Many times, after a show, Connelly's fingers would be bleeding from his constant Pete Townshend–style windmills, even cracking his white Gibson SG guitar after butting it into the side of the PA. This happened more than once.

Beginning in 1976, Buick McKane toured Saskatoon, Saskatchewan, in two-week stints, with one week at Yip's, another at Jack's—both of them Chinese restaurants by day and music clubs by night—complete with the band staying in the grotty bunk beds above Jack's. Across the street was the A-Four, the biggest club in Saskatoon, where the hit-making, plaintive soft-rockers Edward Bear happened to be performing at the time. While in Saskatoon, the two bands spent a bit of time together. The members of Edward Bear were really into Scientology, and one afternoon Scott Reed was told by their singer Larry Evoy

---

5   Yes, World War II, which meant those were, in 1975, thirty-year-old smoke-bombs.

that he used to be someone before this life and to "Close Your Eyes"—which was also the name of one of their hits from the album of the same name and had liner notes promoting Scientology on the back cover. Edward Bear was from London, Ontario, a Scientology hub in the early '70s when people were open to new, spiritual ideas and less alert to their dangers.[6] "I still got that book, man. They gave me the book." Clearly Reed never joined up because he added, "I should see if he ever signed it."

Though still Glammy, it was now 1977 and punk was edging its way in. Buick McKane was adding "Blitzkreig Bop" and a punk version of the *Monkees* theme into the set. Scott Reed and Rob Wynne were close buddies. One day, Wynne told Reed, "Well, I'm out. I'm basically quitting the band, going to get in a band that plays Boston and Kansas and all that sort, Styx . . . " These irreconcilable differences led Reid Diamond to find Alex Koch after a record store proprietor told Diamond that Koch had the first Sex Pistols jacket in Calgary (actually, it was just a jean jacket with an iron-on patch). It wasn't just jibing tastes, states Grant Diamond; "Alex was a really tight little drummer. He was amazing," Not having met them, Koch was scared of Buick McKane, thinking they were big, lunking bullies due to their reputation of going to shows to heckle and throw things at the other bands. Koch says, "So I met Reid and Reid is like four foot nothing. He turned out to be a real nice guy and we learned songs right away. And the first gig I did with them was at the Airliner and we played a set and then their old drummer got pissed off and phoned the people and said that the drummer was underage, so we got shut down. Later, we dumped a whole bunch of stuff on his parents' lawn."

Platform boots were Glam *de rigeur*. Reid's diminutive stature meant the four-inch platform heels gave him a lift and packed a wallop. Grant Diamond says, "I remember one night when they were playing the Airliner Hotel in Calgary and the Airliner, they used to pack the place; I don't know how many it held, it was like 300 or whatever. It was one of those great big old beer halls. I remember this one guy was giving Reid a really rough time. He was saying very uncomplimentary things, calling him a 'f*g' and all this kind of stuff and how he was going to kick the shit out of him in the parking lot. He didn't like the look of the band, I guess, and had too much to drink. And the guy decided that he was going to hoist himself up on the stage and take a run at Reid. I remember the guy putting his hands flat on the stage, and it was about chest height, to hoist himself up to get on the stage. And Reid taking one of his big, beautiful platform shoes and kicking him right in the face and knocking him on his ass then stepping up to his microphone going, 'Security.' The guy was down for the count."

The heels weren't worn just for shows. For Koch's eighteenth birthday (the legal Alberta drinking age), they went out to a big bar called the Highlander. "We had some girls with us. This guy comes up and grabs me around the neck, some mustached old guy. We

---

6   The London, Ontario, born movie director Paul Haggis was on his way to a London (Ontario) record store when a Scientology member stopped him, starting his decades-long membership until he very publicly left the cult. I have been told that members of Edward Bear have also left Scientology.

Ad for Buick McKane at The Airliner Inn, c. 1977. One of Alex Koch's first gigs with the band. Courtesy of Alex Koch.

get into a fight, and he drags me to the ground, and when he gets up, he's all bloody. I'm thinking, 'Geez, I didn't think I got him that good.' Turns out, while I had him down, Reid booted him in the head about two times with his big four-inch heels." Calgary can be rough-and-tumble and hard drinking; being the hub of the Canadian oil industry, people come far and wide to gain employment in Alberta where natural resources are exploited and extracted from the land.

Sometimes the band would have to concede to the starchier tastes of the bars on the circuit that their booking agent sent them to and throw in the radio hits of the day, the worst being "Two Tickets to Paradise" by Eddie Money. Reid Diamond and Connelly giving each other "Oh my God" looks as they worked their way through it. Even with these musical concessions, the band would drive down the dark highway late at night after shows and get chased by cars and trucks trying to run them off the road. The lads had no choice but to hightail it to the nearest police station for safety.

Buick McKane did have fans, more women than men. One, Leeanne Betzler, wore intricate, colorful eye makeup. The future Kid in the Hall Bruce McCulloch was tight with Reid Diamond and often attended their shows. They both would drive around Calgary in thirty-below weather squirting people in the face with squirt guns. Scott Reed elaborates,

Saskatoon ad for Buick McKane at Yips. Image courtesy of the *Star-Phoenix*, August 21, 1978.

"Bruce was a real cheeky little bastard. I would weekly threaten him to kick the shit out of him. He'd always lip me off and Reid would step in because I had him by the throat and up against the wall and Reid would say, 'Leave him alone, leave him alone, he's okay.' So, yeah, that's me and Bruce McCulloch. Real love-hate relationship."

As Buick McKane's ambitions grew, they were outgrowing their city and started writing more original material. This was at a time when most Calgary bands couldn't get away with doing originals in Calgary without actually getting away from Calgary. In 1978, they recorded a five-song basement demo bursting with rock energy, catchy and explosive. Six months later Koch said, "This isn't going to do anything here." After seeing punk bands in Toronto, he knew that was the place to be. So, they packed up and moved to Toronto—that is, everyone in the band but Scott Reed, who said, "I'm out." Reed reflects, "I regret that. I regret it because I know that even if we couldn't have done anything with Buick, it would have led to opening doors to possible other gigs and other bands." Grant Diamond agrees: "If Scott had gone with them, they probably would have gone in a different direction maybe. But I think that they still would have done extremely well and landed a good recording contract. As the years went on in Toronto, they got to be more talented, they honed the writing skills much better, which I think Scott missed out on, in my opinion."

Scott Reed joined a band called City Kids who covered a lot of power pop, evolving into the Kids, with the former Buick McKane drummer Rob Wynne, to become the top Calgary band of 1980. Scott Reed left the Kids, and they then recorded an album of soft, more powerless pop originals with an abundance of synth flourishes; Reed sings back-up vocals on it. Scott Reed eventually did move to Toronto and, after a long hiatus, currently plays in an all-covers band called Tangent.[7] Wynne remained in Calgary and became a recording engineer.

In Toronto post–Buick McKane, Reid Diamond, Connelly, and Koch met up with Don Pyle, a pen pal of Koch's brother Steve. Pyle joined them as lead singer and they

---

7   The drummer's dad is John Gibb of the legendary rock 'n' roll clothing store Long John's.

became Crash Kills Five, a punk band with a Ramones-y sound, throwing in a couple Buick McKane originals such as "Oddy Knocky." Reid Diamond eventually left Crash Kills Five, the band continued for a spell, and then it broke up in 1981. Koch next joined his brother Steve, who had been playing in the Viletones and the Demics, to tour Ontario in a rockabilly band called One-Eyed Jacks. Koch has been living in Vancouver for over twenty years, most recently playing and recording with Tony Balony and the Rubes. Koch concludes, "Then I lost my drums to the pawn shop man about three or four years ago, so I haven't played for a while now. I think I paid for them about three times over. I finally decided, when you're not playing why are you still paying? Just get rid of it."

In 1984, with Reid Diamond on bass, Connelly on guitar, and Pyle on drums, but sans vocals, something new was formed and voilà: Shadowy Men on a Shadowy Planet. After a very successful run, including numerous singles and a couple LPs, they broke up in 1996. In 1993, Reid Diamond and Pyle formed Phono-Comb with Dallas Good from the Sadies, initially to back up Jad Fair. Connelly toured and recorded with Neko Case and Her Boyfriends and formed Atomic 7. In 2001, Reid Diamond died at the age of 42 after a long battle with brain cancer. In 2012, Shadowy Men reunited, with Good on bass, and continued to play sporadically. They recorded music for the new *Kids in the Hall* TV series, a treat for comedy fans, and the band is shown in the opening credits. Months before the show aired in 2022, Good died at the age of 48.

SPUNK

MEMBERS OF BUICK MCKANE REVERED SPUNK like an older Glam brother. Grant Diamond says, "They were a little bit harder edge, but they were a campy band in many ways." How so? "I guess it's kind of camp when you start tossing an inflatable doll around the stage." Spunk played a car show that also had an info booth for the Hell's Angels, it went okay! Diamond continues, "They [Hell's Angels] loved them. Everybody loved Spunk. They had a bit of a harder edge to them, and the Angels were grooving to them, so it was all right. They had a sense of humor and, as they developed, they became better and better and better musicians and had a really tight sound."

Scott Reed says that Spunk played the top gigs in Calgary, noting that the lead singer, Mike Rynoski "was always cheeky with the crowd. I'll never forget he said one time, 'This one's for all the girls with yellow panties in one spot!'" Rynoski and Craig Blair were the two main members of Spunk, with Jake Stolz and Bob Wagers rounding out the lineup. Reed adds, "Rynoski was just flat-out cool, they were just a great band to go watch. They wore the velvet and the satin and the platform shoes and we kind of had that look going on as well." Alex Koch notes, "I loved them. We wanted to be like them with all their big heels."

Spunk "World Of Wheels" ad. Image courtesy of *Calgary Herald*, May 10, 1975.

Spunk did a lot of covers, including "Vambo" and "Midnight Moses" by the Sensational Alex Harvey Band. Towards the end, though, they started writing their own songs. Blair left in 1976 to join a later lineup of the basic hard rock band Hammersmith which Rynoski subsequently sang for briefly when they had two lead singers. With his incredible pipes, Rynoski did a stint in Toronto as the replacement singer for the band Moxy, playing on their fourth album *Under the Lights* from 1978.[8] He went from being in Spunk ("You got spunk, kid!") to Moxy ("You got moxy, kid!")! After this, Mike shortened his last name to Reno, enjoying fame in the band Loverboy.

---

8   Moxy went through a lot of members. Terry Juric, who would go on to play with Thor and Stanley Frank, was a founding member of Moxy. Woody West from Brutus joined Moxy briefly in 1978.

CHAPTER 3
SASKATCHEWAN

THE NERVE

NEAR THE END OF ONE OF OUR PHONE CALLS, right before signing off, P.J. Burton told me, "I am fabulous!" This is not an opinion. This is a fact. Burton was born in Winnipeg, Manitoba, and lived there until the age of twelve when his father got a job transfer to the much smaller community of Dauphin, Manitoba. And there he grew up, stating, "It was an extremely transformative time. Dauphin's a wonderful little town." With an encouraging arts and music community, it was actually quite progressive. Burton says, "I was there throughout grade eight to twelve and still have a lot of friends from that era who either made their living in the arts or still at it, be it visual or theater or music."

Through new neighbors, Burton became fast friends with a Saskatchewan musician named Brian Lowe who was in a band that needed a drummer. Burton had previously been drumming in a high school psychedelic band named Fred. This first-and-only-name-basis band was perhaps too psychedelic for the high school dances they played. Fred didn't have a lot of songs, but the songs Fred did have were very long. Manitoba is right next to Saskatchewan. Dauphin was somewhat en route to Saskatoon, Saskatchewan, from Winnipeg, the capital of Manitoba. Among the marked similarities between Winnipeg and Saskatoon are a quiet weirdness (no one is looking), brick beauty, and nature. It is a five-hour drive to Saskatoon from Dauphin, speed limit depending, smooth sailings across flatlands—these are the prairies. Burton packed up and joined the band Deacon Brodie in Saskatoon.

Deacon Brodie was named after a real man, the inspiration for *Dr. Jekyll and Mr. Hyde*. Although such transformations were to occur later, this particular band played Jethro Tull and Allman Brothers Band covers and other typical hippie rock stuff at high school dances in the region. However, the keyboardist, who played the Hammond B3, had access to vitamin B12. This keyboardist was being treated by Dr. Abram Hoffer, a proponent of megavitamin therapy for schizophrenia. Hoffer had also worked with Humphry Osmond on LSD research in Saskatchewan, where Osmond coined the term *psychedelic*. In order to get away from work early, Burton would dip into his bandmate's supply and pop B12 pills which would transform him into . . . a different color. Burton recalls his work telling him, "P. J., you look terrible. You're all red." Burton remembers saying, "Don't worry about me, I'll just do my shift." And then being told, "No, no, you better go home, you look terrible." And off Burton would go, into the band bus waiting out front, then off and away to play the gig.

A confluence of factors led to Burton's next band, the Nerve. It was previously noted that the town of Dauphin had a strong arts community. To elaborate, Dauphin had a *commedia dell'arte* program for high school students organized by a brilliant shop teacher and theater expert named Gary Nicholson. They met in the harlequin-decorated rumpus room of his and his wife's bungalow every Wednesday night. The productions the troupe put on were many steps above your average high school play. This meant that there were a lot of costumes.

CREDITS

P.J. Burton . . . . Drums, Vocals, Successive Regeneration, Miracles
Gary Law . . . . 2nd Guitar, Vocals, Holy Snappers
John Mair . . . . 1st Guitar, Vocals, Technical Data
Barry Muir . . . . Bass, Vocals, Teen Appeal

Studio B Productions . . . . Lighting
Bodies . . . . Generic Influence, God
Management . . . . H.E.L. Music, Saskatoon—244-6319

Nerve promo pic and hype sheet, c. 1974. Courtesy of Barry Muir.

Burton admits, "So, we absconded with the outfits that included things like capes, colorful this, that, whatever, and then that became part of the repertoire in the bands in Saskatoon." His other favorite outfit was "this black fishnet kind of shirt with a black boa sewn around in it. It was really sparkly, shiny, slinky, sexy stuff, that was what it was all about."

Besides the stage attire, Burton put freaky flair and finesse into his street clothes. This was facilitated by his job in the Midtown Plaza mall at the unisex clothing outlet Big Steel. Not only did the fact that it was a unisex store make it a great place for Burton to meet girls, but staff discounts also made much of the sparkly, shiny stuff affordable for him. His boots came from an outlet that sold Fox & Fluevog. Girlfriends would make clothing for him. Burton favored satin pants and t-shirts with spider webs and sequins—all of it tight—accessorized with chokers and chains and "all kinds of fucking bracelets halfway up your forearm and trinkets," along with black nail polish and eye makeup.

I did have to ask Burton about his mustache. He admits, "Just the mere presence of it was idiotic—you know, shave already, if you're going to be wearing makeup, shave. It just doesn't square. It's sort of like, well, I'm hip. And I'm into the future. But I still have one leg in the '60s. That was dumb, I don't know why I had the stupid mustache—antithetical." I personally feel that the stars on his face offset the facial hair.

Burton says, "And the thing that can never be forgotten is that every boy worth his salt loves to put on eyeliner. To this day in one form or another people love to wear makeup, for obvious reasons, because then you look even sexier than you are, and the hair and all of these other elements." Having hairdresser friends helped. After making a living applying blue rinse to the older population by day, these hairdressers would dye Burton's hair an ever-changing array to black, silver, blonde ... All of this allowed Burton to become B.D.O.C. (Best Dressed on Campus) at the University of Saskatchewan, where he was enrolled as a student majoring in Education. There he met more like-minded people, people who were different.

Burton lived in a few places. In and around 1972, he lived at his theatrical friend Mike's. Mike was going through a marriage break-up. This created the perfect opportunity to throw Glammy parties with elaborate themes like "Santa's Suicide" and "Death and the Future." The Nerve would often perform in the basement. Both Mike and Burton would actively seek out albums by the Stooges, Bowie, Lou Reed, and New York Dolls, making special orders at the local record store, perfect for the house party hi-fi. It was a very hip, well-dressed bunch of party attendees, including a group of young women called the Space Cadets.

When I asked Burton what they all did he replied, "Well, we all just drank around and had sex and did gigs and went to bars and whatnot and wore our outfits." They sought out anything Glam or at least Glam-tangential (Saskatchewan A.O.R. like Cambridge—which became Queen City Kids—and Kenny Shields's bands Witness Inc. and Streetheart) at the local venues Jack's and Yip's. The Red Lion nightclub leaned towards showbands.[1] Burton

---

1   In Canada showbands often wore matching outfits, played covers of popular songs (including medleys), and played lounges.

and friends would see the Glammier ones, such as Free Spirit, a touring L.A. band, who they bonded with over hair and nail polish. They favored anything that was more urban and decadent. A favorite bar to hang out at was the Ritz, officially named the Apollo Room of the Ritz Hotel. This was Saskatoon's unofficial gay bar at the time. The bar itself had crimson décor, and the room featured a giant photo of an astronaut on the moon. The Saskatoon Public Library's Facebook page states, "The management and staff welcomed the new LGBTQ customers and dealt quickly and firmly with anyone harassing patrons." The Ritz lasted until 1985. Burton describes it: "And this bar featured a waiter who was like some kind of time travel, like a guy from a drawing of an art deco era with the hair really shiny, parted on the side. And the waiter uniform."[2]

Although Saskatoon is far more cosmopolitan than people who have never so much as stepped foot there give credit for, the only Glam band that I could find for the entire province of Saskatchewan was the Nerve, who grew Glammier and Glammier over time. Burton often sang and drummed at the same time, but he needed to move out front at times, noting, "It's such a waste to have great boots and the right pants if they're hidden behind drums." There were other drummers on occasion to offset the singing drummer syndrome. One band member, Barry Muir, recalls, "Then what we'd do is for some of the showstopper tunes, he'd come out front, and Dave Cummins would drum." Muir says of Burton, "And a real treat to play with and a great singer, he had a really cool voice. But I have no idea what happened to him. He is the most unique individual in Canada. I swear."

Amidst much onstage prancing there were props and effects cues administered by the deaf roadies. As Burton explains, "You would use sign language to tell them what you want next." The roadies were long-haired, like-minded music fans, close friends who attended the Saskatoon School for the Deaf. Burton says, "And it was great because when we just went to bars you can talk to people with sign language. It didn't matter how loud the band was." Immersed in this community, Burton also went out with a couple of deaf women.

One of the props was a mannequin equipped with blood bags that Burton would stab. I asked if he was doing a deliberately scary stage persona and he replied, "Just sort of indefinable, or like a bit manic maybe. Campy! Campy would be good." The roadies, dressed in black with white made-up faces, would then carry the mannequin away in a stretcher.

As an early member of the Nerve, the keyboardist Craig Jarvis remembers, "People didn't know what was hitting them when we came on with all the makeup and what we did—which was kind of funny—is we would come on with our street clothes in the first set and warm ourselves up, we'd come on and we play and we'd keep saying, 'Hey, there's a

---

2 Although completely unrelated to Burton or the Nerve but deserving mention in this, the only section on Saskatchewan, is the Cave, which opened in 1973 and still exists today, just outside of time. This restaurant's décor seemed Flintstones-inspired, each booth being just like a small cave, but with the civilized trappings of seating! "The Cave" written in a sort of stone cursive font on the front over a window with large circular wooden doors set in cement greets you. Inside there are few ninety-degree angles to regiment you; it's all curves, nooks, and crannies galore. Faux stalactites hanging down, edges softened. Blue and purple lighting curving around the ceiling of the bar, foliage in the center. Peas and spaghetti on the menu.

The Nerve in Edmonton. Image courtesy of *Edmonton Journal*, May 23, 1978.

great band coming on here right after us called the Nerve and they're gonna wow you and everything.' And we just played in our street clothes. So, we went backstage and changed and came back out front and then did the show with the makeup. Then we'd run back stage and we'd take the makeup off and people would come to try and get in the back room. We'd go, 'Oh, they've left already.'" Due to the Nerve not getting a lot of gigs because of club owners being scared of them, Jarvis moved on to the more lucrative, regular gigging, straight-ahead cover bands—including one called Legend.

The Nerve had a few originals and mostly garagey covers of "Search and Destroy" by the Stooges, "Personality Crisis" by New York Dolls, plus lots of the Sensational Alex Harvey Band and Alice Cooper. In May 1974, Burton and other members of the Nerve witnessed the KISS-like spectacle of, well, KISS on their very first tour to Saskatoon. Burton recalls scoring tickets to the show through his job at Big Steel: "I was there for their soundcheck so I actually saw KISS without their makeup on, but of course we didn't realize it." The showmanship of KISS's synchronised moves and fire-breathing deeply affected Burton. The Nerve, in turn, became more KISS-like. The makeup thickened. Burton pranced higher. If their tongues weren't dangling out, they were at least in cheek.

The band briefly adopted noms de guerre. Burton's was Joy Synapse. In their mid-'70s press photo, Burton was credited with "Successive Regeneration and Miracles." He explains, "And so, of course, nerves regenerate at a certain rate, and so that's where you get that regenerative thing with a band called the Nerve. Nerve cells actually regenerate." Muir joined the Nerve as bassist when he was in grade eleven to become the youngest member; he is thus credited in the photo as "Teen Appeal." Muir had a case of nerves about joining the Nerve until Burton gave him a pep talk: "We really like you and I think you're gonna be just great." Muir says, "And I was so pumped up . . . and I'm so glad. That if Rick[3] [P.J.] hadn't talked me into staying in the band, I would probably still be living in Saskatoon." Muir subsequently moved to Vancouver and, after doing some session work for Bob Rock, joined the Payolas in 1982 to go on a massive North American tour of arenas and ballrooms playing shows with Cheap Trick and the Go-Go's. Mick Ronson produced them and even played in the band for a spell. Muir joined the late Billy Cowsill's band The Blue Shadows in 1992, a greatly respected act that played original country music with a moody, romantic tinge.

The Nerve mostly stuck to the more urban city of Saskatoon, but the odd venture to outlying small towns could mean trouble. Notes Burton, "I mean, if you're prancing around with makeup in the early '70s in small towns in Saskatchewan, watch out!" Jarvis remembers getting chased out of towns on more than one occasion, including a police escort out of Rosetown for their safety. Muir mentions that many people in these farm towns were genuinely helpful in setting up gear. He describes the guitarist John Mair as a farmer

---

3   Muir refers to P.J. as Rick, stating that P.J. is more his stage name.

from Rosetown, saying, "He just made like tens of thousands of dollars farming. And so he was always buying stuff and it was great. The band had no shortage of equipment. He'd basically finance the whole band and he'd get paid back by us gigging. But it was nice to have that kind of upfront money."

Both Burton and the bassist Gary Law left Saskatoon for Edmonton, Alberta, where they continued the Nerve, taking it in a punk direction. Edmonton was a boom town. Money was to be made. Burton worked various industrial jobs during his year off from university. A near fatal accident working at a pulp mill prompted him to become a frontman full-time. A giant three-quarter-ton roll of paper fell on him, nearly killing him. Burton was severely injured, with his kick-drum leg broken. Moving out front, he made the cast a part of the show, further bandaging himself and pouring on the ketchup as fake blood. Burton says that this was when he realized he was an egomaniac: a frontman he stayed. Attending the University of Alberta, he was newly flush with cash from worker's compensation and walking with a cane. Burton says, "So very mysterious. Who's this moneybags with the cane?"

The drummer Joe Kelly's best friend was a genius prop whiz. "He made this giant razor blade, like a Gillette safety razor. And so I could straddle it, sort of like you're literally cutting your nuts off." This prop master also made a giant mock detonator that Burton would plunge as smoke-bombs went off on cue. "That, and a huge giant safety pin that he made fully workable. I could actually safety-pin the bass player and the guitar player together—it was that big." The Nerve released a single of the songs "Penchant" and "Preludes" in 1978 that is on many a punk record collector's drool list.

Burton felt it was time to change and move on musically from the Nerve to the Smarties, a more synth-driven new wave band. Smarties are also known as tiny round chocolates in a colorful shell—popular in Canada, virtually unknown in the United States, now unfortunately manufactured by the evil Nestlé Corporation.[4] Burton and the guitarist enlisted the bassist Joy Toyota to leave the band Spunk. Burton says, "She was great. She was about four foot ten. Her bass was practically as tall as she was. That was her real name, Joy Toyota, a gorgeous little Japanese woman with really, really bad PMS who would kill you. I mean, the first time that I met her she made her own skull bleed by smashing the pegs of her Fender into her head—long, black Japanese hair. And then during the break she was drunk and PMS[-ing] and therefore had no choice but to kick her husband in the balls a number of times as she's bleeding and crying and yelling and freaking out. Yeah, so we knew that was the bass player for us."

Burton describes the response to the Smarties: "We were snapping our spandex, much to the chagrin of the punks, who saw us as complete betrayal. And there's nothing quite like walking down an alley in Edmonton and seeing graffiti on the wall that says, 'HATE PJ

---

4 This Smarties confection bears no connection to the chalky pastel-colored discs that Americans call Smarties. In fact, the reason Nestlé can't distribute their own Smarties in the U.S. is because of the name conflict.

P.J. meets Batman, Adam West. Image courtesy of the *Winnipeg Sun*, April 8, 1985.

BURTON? GOOD. THEN MEET US AT THE DOG HOUSE.' The Dog House was a punk club. That's where I ended up starting a riot. Because we were warming up [the band] 999." Coming on stage to face an audience of angry punks, the Smarties sprayed the crowd with air freshener as Burton said, "We just want to clear the air." Psssshhhhhht. Further angered, bottles started flying. And breaking. "One more bottle, we're leaving!" Burton knew full well what the response would be. Smash smash smash smash smash. After egging them on with countless "fuck you!"s, Burton then took a chainsaw to the infamous mannequin that he still had with him from Saskatoon, then threw the head at the crowd. A riot ensued—bathrooms and seats destroyed. Burton advises, "You know, at least once in your life, if you can, have the opportunity to start your own riot. It's a very fulfilling experience."

His 1981 solo album, *P. J. Burton*, written with his keyboardist, Bob Binns, is basically a Smarties album. This album is not fully new wave per se, more mid-tempo than herky-jerky, with synth flourishes, kind of like the Tubes but with a university education.

Songs include "People Change," "Go Subliminal," and "What Does It Mean." The record lists a hair credit: Celebrity Salon, which is still in Edmonton if you ever need a cut.

One night, Burton was bandying about new names for the Smarties. He got a stick and wrote "Chocolate Bunnies from Hell" in freshly poured cement. With the name now enshrined, Burton took the name with him back to Winnipeg—where he was born and still resides—and formed Chocolate Bunnies from Hell.

In August 1989, Johnny Thunders from New York Dolls played a couple of nights in Winnipeg, but he couldn't get his drummer across the border. He couldn't get his methadone across the border either. Thunders was addicted to heroin. Burton called Thunders' hotel room. "Oh, Mr. Thunders, I know that you don't have a drummer, and I'd like to offer my services."

Thunders replied, "You got anything?"

Burton stammered.

Thunders went, "Yeah, well, you got anything?"

Burton replied, "Gee, I don't, maybe I'll try to find—sorry. But anyway, I could drum for you if you like . . . "

"Okay, you got anything?"

Burton arranged to meet him in his dark hotel room that night. Opening the door a crack, he heard Thunders go, "You got anything?"

"Well, no."

Burton explains, "The last thing he cared about was the drummer. He was only interested in getting some smack." At the show and noting that there really was no fill-in drummer—well, no decent one anyways—Burton got behind the drums. As he fondly recalled, "And so I was kind of a little bit in the New York Dolls for, you know, an hour or so in Winnipeg. And that was, I think, one of the highlights of my whole life." Burton never would have expected to go from covering New York Dolls in Saskatoon to now performing with a New York Doll. Burton says, "That was a high-water mark, that was a real landmark." Thunders' bassist, Jill Wisoff, a filmmaker who has worked with the director Todd Solondz—including doing the soundtrack for *Welcome to the Dollhouse*—wrote glowingly of Burton in her blog's tour diary. Wisoff herself later filled in on bass for a Chocolate Bunnies from Hell gig in Toronto in the '90s.

Chocolate Bunnies from Hell still exist today. A seven-inch of their cover of Iggy Pop's "Pumping for Jill" was released in 1986, a CD in 1992, another CD in 2019, with more to come. Putting his university education to use, Burton has been teaching for quite some time. He is currently teaching high school English in Winnipeg, where his stage life is no secret.

CHAPTER 4
MANITOBA

THE DAVE WEBER BAND

FINDING MUCH GLAM ROCK IN MANITOBA has proven difficult even though Winnipeg immediately embraced the 1974 movie *Phantom of the Paradise*, the Glammiest movie ever made, with line-ups down the block during its lengthy run there. I was told of the Winnipeg band Pilot Young, formerly known as Syren, named after the Roxy Music album but with a more creative spelling. They did Glam covers and played a few gigs. To my knowledge they never released anything. But there was one Manitoba act who did and, holy smokes, is it ever something!

Picture if you will a bare-chested elf in a wood-paneled Winnipeg studio using up all manner of spells to conjure up mystical beasts that are hybrids of T. Rex and Led Zeppelin in 40-below weather. Filters and wah-wah on the wicked guitar wailing away through each ear at the speed of light (made scientifically possible through fantasy)! Wah wah wah! Filters and wah-wah! Female Flo and Eddies going off like flares in the background

Left to right: Front cover and back cover of *The Future Is Here* by the Dave Weber Band (Hot Wax, 1980). Author's collection.

(sometimes they sound all too human) (ahhhhhhh ahhhh ahhh) going for sweet tones point-for-point against/with Dave's unearthly *au naturel* vibrato tongue touching the stars. Rec room drum thump, melodic bass haze, sharp synths: all in one studio, but the tracks with producer and exclusive manager John Cartwright adding "Space Effects" are the stand-outs, a whole swath brought through the Lesley organ adjusting the outcome of the voice. When Dave sings, "I really do love you all!" in a high coo you believe him. I love his unique voice. Sometimes he goes "Ah!" like he just drank in something so refreshing, i.e., his own album *The Future Is Here* on Hot Wax Records. So hot the wax, Winnipeg can get hot in the summer, it burns to the touch. It feels hot enough to melt and the vinyl is thinly pressed—when they weighed it a Manitoba butcher put his finger on the scale. What kind of scale? The scales of justice in a cruel world that has not heard this album? Or the scales of a futuristic dragon to take you to space? The vinyl may be flimsy but the album rocks!

On the back cover Dave and the two women in skimpy shiny cosmic clothing literally glow. High cut, low cut crimson and gold lamé, winged elbow-high gloves, boots to go-go. I found Dave and tried to get some answers but the answers were few, the haze was just too strong, multiple conversations, very few answers, too much haze but know this as fact: he is in Winnipeg. What about those outfits? Dave Weber explains, "We were experimenting in the studio and the inspiration came from the album being titled *The Future Is Here*. The costumes fit that idea and, yes, they were worn on stage. We also would have leather costumes, really a lot of changing going on but that was related to what type of music we would be doing. It's really all about the music, and the art as part of the show was added to it to and to the effect." Were the women on the cover the back-up singers? "Yes, they were the back-up singers. I would say the lineup lasted four years or so. We had a variety of people coming out to the shows. Always had, I'm glad to say, a cult following that grew over the years." Dave opens up to me about some of the studio magick: "The pedals used were a flanger and an overdrive effect which added a raunchy effect and to some degree a swirling sound. It was different."

There on the front cover, through a cloud of smoke, Dave's bust in a flying triangle emitting rays that flash on to a bunch of poorly-cut-out but excited junior high school kids (picture Dave hunched over the kitchen table with scissors, collaging and designing the album cover)! Weber says, "We thought it would be interesting to have the younger generation there as they are the future, and we wanted the idea of them seeing the future coming at them. You notice on the album they're pointing to the sky . . . . I always liked space, the Universe." The name of the album is *The Future Is Here* and like all things from the future it came out of Winnipeg (released in 1980). Read the fine print in the top right corner for it actually states: "This album is laser sealed." Time to crack the seal, I say. We are more than ready for the future as relayed by the Dave Weber Band! Flash forward twenty or thirty

THE GUESS WHO'S "GLAMOUR BOY" EXAMINED

Hailing originally from Winnipeg, the Guess Who were an iconic Canadian rock group with a long string of massive hits both in and out of Canada from the late '60s on into the mid-'70s including "American Woman", "No Time", and "Share The Land." The Guess Who were Canada's Beatles! That sounds ridiculous but it also makes some sort of sense. Then there's the Guess Who's 1973 single "Glamour Boy" from their tenth or eleventh album (they lost count) titled *#10* (no, really, they lost count). "Glamour Boy" will tell you how singer Burton Cummings felt about Glam Rock at the time. "Glamour Boy" directs its bitchy ire at Bowie and his ilk. A doughy, soft ditty with troubling lyrics—"For $25,000 you can look like a woman tonight"—then he flaccidly mentions singing an honest song for the people. The audacious "authentic" posturing offends and amuses. The song is redeemed by a great melody with a couple of evocative turns of phrase: "So spin with the archer now and laugh in his face as he cocks his bow . . . " This song, like many in Burton Cummings' repertoire, is simultaneously shitty and great.

7-Up soda Rock Caps contest ad to see the Guess Who live in London. Image courtesy of *Edmonton Journal*, October 6, 1973.

years—depending on how often he updates his website—Dave has become addicted to the substance known as "classic roadhouse blues rock." Come back to the future, Dave—the future is here (1980) and it's wild! His website has a dead link to his art. A mystery. His newer bloooozy solo project Web the Band has some oddly personal comments posted repeatedly and excessively on its YouTube channel by one very angry woman asking such things as, "Where is my money?" Who is she? A mystery. It's all such a mystery. Hopefully everything got sorted out. Weber wraps things up with me: "Thanks for the interest. After all, we have to keep the people Rocking, right?" Ain't that the truth. Keep fantasy alive.

K-TEL

A TWENTIETH-CENTURY capitalist permutation of the essence of Christ died on Wednesday, April 27th, in the Year of Our Lord Two Thousand and Sixteen. His name was Phil Kives. He was eighty-seven years old and handsome, according to the obituary that I am poaching this from. Kives created K-Tel! This bit of Christ consciousness was human. Born in the ever-shrinking hamlet of Oungre, Saskatchewan, he relocated to Winnipeg to perform miracles with such cheaply priced items as hair removers, vegetable slicers, and BeDazzlers—an applicator that Glams up your clothes with studs and rhinestones. K-Tel used the innovation of beaming from the comfort of your TV set (CALL NOW), bye bye door-to-door salesmen.

Winnipeg, the promised land, the home of K-Tel. For music fans, it was the records that they knew K-Tel

Phil Kives, the owner of Winnipeg based K-Tel International Ltd.

Phil Kives. Image courtesy of *Times Colonist*, April 3, 1998.

for. K-Tel gave us the innovation of taking pre-existing songs and repackaging them as compilations, beginning with polka and country, then moving into all sorts (including some Glam—oh, yes), jam-packing the records with so much ear candy that K-Tel would trim the fat à la *Reader's Digest*, editing the songs down to squeeze 'em all in, wrapping them up in the most Glammed-out coming-atcha (sometimes from space) sleeves. WOW! And let us not forget their novelty song compilations *Goofy Greats, Nutty Numbers, Dumb Ditties*, and *Kooky Kountry*—which were all exactly that. Truth in advertising.

K-Tel promoted Canadian talent. The compilation *Canadian Mint* is covered in Canadian coins with a red maple leaf proclaiming "22 ORIGINAL HITS ORIGINAL STARS" and it is an outstanding all Can-Con[1] comp with Fludd, Andy Kim, Stampeders' "Wild Eyes," Chilliwack's "There's Something I Like about That" (the closest they got to Glam, produced by Terry Jacks)... and more!

K-Tel was not exactly known for releasing original albums; why, the very idea practically seems verboten. An original K-Tel album? Absurd. Unbelievable. But I know of at least three. Plus: all of them are concept albums. If you know of more or have any knowledge of these curiosities, please drop me a jot please! Please! Are you ready? No, you aren't. We're going anyways.

ROCK FANTASY LP

Advertised and billed truthfully right on the cover as *Original "Funtastic" Rock Music*—how Glam Rock is that title? Not a dream, not an imaginary tale. It's a *Rock Fantasy*! Those blow-dried pubey-eyed teens holding hands on the sleeve have been pre-Photoshopped into a "land where animals are people" (to quote the guiding mandate tune "The Land Where Animals Are People"). A big part of Glam Rock is the shifting of identities, and this cartoon-bubble Glam concept album takes anthropomorphism to the hilt. The bare-bones credits list such artists as Horace Howell (the Wise Old Owl), Sidney Klunk the Friendly Skunk, Bernie Byrd, and more... and every one of these singers has their

---

1 Short for "Canadian content."

Front cover of *Canadian Mint* by Various Artists (K-Tel, 1973). Author's collection.

own unique personality, with the numbers not only being appropriate to each animal (Sir Dan D. Lyon singing "You Don't Need a Crown") but also laced with the odd aside such as G. Raffe gravelling, "This is me your Long Tall Georgie, your Zip Code Daddy" (huh?) on the heavy Glam topper "Instant Action." That track, along with "Fantastic" by Jack Kass, should be on the essential Canadian Glam comp. This animal album is wild, man.

I was deeply turned on to *Rock Fantasy* by my July Fourth Toilet bandmate, the cartoonist Julian Lawrence. July Fourth Toilet —a musical project that I was deeply involved in for a great many years—performed this entire album in full animal costumes for our tenth anniversary in 2004 and, though we tried to find info from the K-Tel vaults, we came up fairly empty. Maybe this preserved mystery keeps us in the *Rock Fantasy*—maybe these animals were people. We did find that some of this album was made with what sounds to be actual backing tracks of songs by the late, great pop singer Jewel Akens, including

Above: Front cover of *Rock Fantasy* by Various Artists (K-Tel, c. 1975). Author's collection.
Opposite: Front cover of *Funtown, 20 Favorite Selections* by Various Artists (K-Tel, 1978). Author's collection.

"The Birds and the Bees," as Akens's record label Era was eventually sold to K-Tel. Perhaps this was recorded at an elaborate K-Tel staff party? Imagine those parties. We just have to enjoy this album for what it is and oh, what it is!

FUNTOWN: FAVORITE 20 SELECTIONS LP

As a kid, I used to stare and stare at the *Funtown* album while listening to it repeatedly. The circular photos of the puppets would peer out at me—the ventriloquist dummies Archie Wood (wood, get it?), Grandpa Wood, and Tammy True, the cute little dog puppet Petite, and Marvin Mouse. "Who are they?" I'd wonder. "Do they exist beyond this record?" Years later, I found out that *Funtown* was a show that ran for twenty-five years on Winnipeg television. This was a children's institution called *Archie Wood and His Friends* on weekdays and *Funtown* on Saturdays, hosted by "Uncle Bob" Swarts (uncertain just whose uncle; on weekends he was known around *Funtown* as Mayor Bob).

The first time that I heard "Hey Jude" I was seven or so years old and thought that these "Beatles" were ripping off Marvin Mouse and Tuttle Turtle's "Hey Tuttle," and I didn't think that this so-called "Hey Jude" was anywhere near as good! Now, as a nearly fully grown adult, I realize that Mayor Bob was just improvising and character-acting overtop of a track from Marty Gold's *Moog Plays the Beatles* LP.[2] In later years, it was rumored that Mayor Bob was a very heavy drinker and, if true, one can sure hear it on this 1978 album: he stumbles and slurs over stock backing tracks like "Can't Buy Me Love," in which Tammy True—really just Archie Wood in a wig—tries to woo Mayor Bob by giving him

---

2   In tribute, my musical duo Canned Hamm (consisting of Big Hamm and Lil Hamm—I'm the Lil one) took the very same backing track, along with Marvin Mouse and Tuttle Turtle's banter, to make "Hey, Lil' Hamm." Yeah, I'm obsessed.

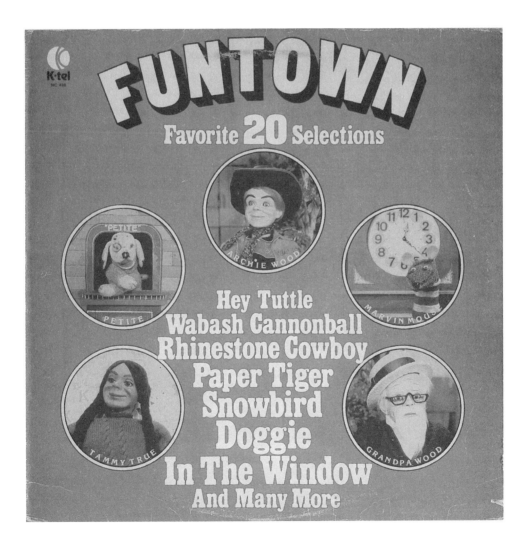

Puppeteer Bob Swarts and Archie Wood. Image courtesy of the *Winnipeg Sun*, February 8, 1982.

ten bucks and singing this song—though Tammy True is really just Mayor Bob warbling in falsetto. Close your eyes and visualize that bit of studio time as this Brylcreemed man in a cardigan nestles the mic. Did he use the puppets to record with, even though only the engineer would have known? There's some deep puppet persona work afoot here. Then there's "Put a Little Love in Your Heart," in which Grandpa Wood literally misses a cue to a verse and has to catch up, leading me to believe that this whole album was done in one take. With Petite, the cute little female dog's vocals aren't just sped up, they speed up the whole stock pop song! "Paper Tiger," "Walkin' My Cat Named Dog," "The Doggie in the Window," and "Mocking Bird Hill"—all of them sped up from a $33\frac{1}{3}$ record to 45 rpm. How brilliantly shoddy. Try to imagine the most way-out album you can think of. What is it? Oooooh wow, okay but THIS EXISTS! Former Winnipeggers tell me that Uncle Bob often used to yell at kids to get off of his lawn. There were actually a few albums made by Uncle Bob, but this is the only one on K-Tel with its far-reaching distribution channels; the others all seem to have been released by smaller labels—not labels per se, probably local Winnipeg furniture stores.

ALEX HARVEY PRESENTS - THE LOCH NESS MONSTER

Alex Harvey of the Sensational Alex Harvey Band was a Glam Rock legend. In 1977, this Great Scot did this spoken word album featuring Harvey's interviews with people who describe their encounters with the Loch Ness Monster for the Canadian K-Tel label. *Rocky Horror*'s Richard O'Brien pops in to introduce the album. There is but one song, a short gentle ditty with whistling and Loch Ness Monster sounds called "I Love Monsters Too." I love Alex Harvey. What's not to love? The man had conviction, humor, and pure rock showmanship.

CHAPTER 5
ONTARIO

Little Richard at Toronto Rock & Roll Revival, 1969.
From *Keep On Rockin'* by D.A. Pennebaker. Courtesy Pennebaker Hegedus Films.

TORONTO ROCK & ROLL REVIVAL '69

ALLOW ME TO PROPOSE A THEORY most preposterous, because the best theories are, aren't they? Yes, they are. Some of those seeds of Glam are in Canada, 1969. 1969 was the year of the hippie rock fest, to which I say fuck Woodstock, fuck Altamont even! The fest to be at was at the Toronto Rock and Roll Revival.

Glam loved to revisit and revive the '50s, and this fest sure did that all up, with Chuck Berry, Bo Diddley, Jerry Lee Lewis, Gene Vincent, and Little Richard made up perfectly in his shiny mirrored top, lights bouncing off it, reverberating around the concert—he was in incredible form, pompadour bigger than ever, energy electrifying. This was not a simulation or a '50s recreation; these acts were the real thing! No, the previous month's Woodstock with the retro act Sha Na Na was not the inspiration; it was actually June's Toronto Pop Festival with Chuck Berry's performance (the Velvet Underground and Tiny Tim also performed) that sparked John Brower, the promoter and impresario of Toronto Pop, to carry the golden oldies further to the Toronto Rock and Roll Revival. The Beatles hadn't even properly broken up yet, the baton had yet to hit the floor, Ringo had yet to boogie around with Bolan, but the Rock and Roll Revival marked the first formal appearance of the Plastic Ono Band, with the soon-to-be-former Beatle John Lennon and the noted Fluxus artist Yoko One doing some of that good ole rock 'n' roll along with their heavy friends. Yes, it looked like hippies playing oldies covers, nothing to write home about, in marked contrast to the actual rock 'n' roll pioneers like Bo Diddley putting on a total show at the same festival, but the second half of the Plastic Ono Band's set where Ono moved into the spotlight was when things got downright next-level avant-garde, alienating some of the more uptight crowd—it turned into a full-on noise show, yeahhh! Deeply emotional screams and feedback and distortion reigned, letting the guitar feedback continue as they exited the stage . . .

Yoko Ono with John Lennon at the Toronto Rock & Roll Revival, 1969.
From *Sweet Toronto* by D.A, Pennebaker. Courtesy Pennebaker Hegedus Films.

Alice Cooper Band with chicken at Toronto Rock & Roll Revival, 1969. From *Keep on Rockin'* by D.A. Pennebaker. Courtesy Pennebaker Hegedus Films.

Wearing makeup and sounding freaky-deeky—this was before the Canadian wunderkind producer Bob Ezrin entered the frame—the Alice Cooper Band made their mark here. Coop is quoted as saying, "We drove a stake through the heart of the Love Generation."[1] During their set a chicken was killed in the process, veering close to carnie geek styles—the story grew distorted (no, Coop did not bite its head off as some urban legends claim; he threw it out into the throng where it was dispatched), making their career. The emcee, the primo glitter-rocker creep and Svengali Kim Fowley announced them as "Alice Cooper, the group of the future!" and ain't that about right. Prior to their own set, the Alice Cooper Band doubled as the back-up band for the '50s rock 'n' roll legend Gene Vincent. Past and future.[2]

Fowley was there in tow with the glitter-rock DJ Rodney Bingenheimer, later of the famed Rodney's English Disco—which wasn't in England, it was in L.A. of course. Both Bingenheimer and Fowley were key glitter rockers who certainly exemplify the creepier and more unsavory elements of Glam culture.

The fest was a confluence of factors and elements that almost didn't happen. And no one knew the Beatles were going to break up a week later.

This event was a way of saying: here's the '50s and here comes the future; we are no longer in the '60s.

1 See the director Reg Harkema's documentary *Super Duper Alice Cooper*.
2 Most of these '50s rock 'n' roll artists were only in their thirties at the time.

Toronto Rock & Roll Revival crowd. Image courtesy of the *Standard*, September 15, 1969.

JOHNNIE LOVESIN

JOHNNIE LOVESIN WAS ALREADY A BIT OF A VET—though not even thirty—by the time "Tonight" was released in 1977, a full-on Glam single on Smile Records with its tagline "Incredibly Canadian!" on the sleeve. More importantly, for his own logo, Johnnie Lovesin's i's are not dotted with smiley faces, nor are they dotted with hearts—no, Lovesin has a flashy logo where the i's are dotted with stars. He's got stars in his i's! And this song sparkles. It's not about tomorrow, it's not even about today, it's about tonight! Always a popular trope and this one has a hint of menace: "Well, I'm ready for a fist fight tonight, I'm looking sharper than a switchblade tonight!" Fierce! He enunciates with his tongue hitting the roof of his mouth and up the nasal passages, relentlessly upbeat-sounding, three minutes soaring by; the B side is the same song in French, appropriately enough, "Ce Soir," identifying him as bilingual. He's from Quebec!

Lovesin hit the Yorkville district of Toronto as a teen singing songs on street corners. Yorkville was full of folkies and hippies. Lovesin aligned with the sharp-dressed Mods: they were very well put together (and, over in England, a major influence on Glam). The head of Yorkville Records, Bill Gilliland, believed in Lovesin and bought him his first guitar. Lovesin's 1971 single "Black Spider" b/w "Letter to the President" on Yorkville Records leans close to Glam but goes deeper as a raw rock 'n' roller to the core, with a major Chuck Berry influence as common touchstone. A full album was recorded, then sadly the tapes got lost.

He was a man of many names. What's in a name? Names are powerful. Lovesin was a subtle yet practical alteration on his then manager's part. He was born Johnnie Lovsin, but the press kept dropping the fact-checking ball, misspelling it "Loosin" ("so long as they spell my name right" goes the old adage). Add the letter e and voilà! No problem. It also added mystique. His later manager Michele Morgan says, "People were always trying to analyze it—'What's it mean? Love and sin?' He really wasn't that deep rooted at the time. And much like a lot of his band names, he had so many band names and he liked to name other people's bands. He came up with cool names, but again, they were kind of based in his reality, he liked anything to do with the cosmos, on the scientific side. And he had so many handles. He was Little Johnnie, he was Johnnie Yorkville . . . " Johnnie Lovesin had a t-shirt listing his numerous band names—all of them playing rock 'n' roll.

Lovesin would joyously almost leap out of his skin on stage, so it was not all that surprising that from a young age he started having terrifying out-of-body experiences. They started as a teen when his mother became quite ill. Possibly relatedly, she too had them in the hospital, floating and hearing the attendants talking about the severity of her situation; thankfully she pulled through. Throughout his life Johnnie kept having these out-of-body experiences, hovering over himself in bed, yet his songs gave audiences comfort with lyrics about romance and camaraderie—again, all rock 'n' roll.

When Bill Delingat first met Lovesin in Yorkville in 1969, he recounts that Johnnie

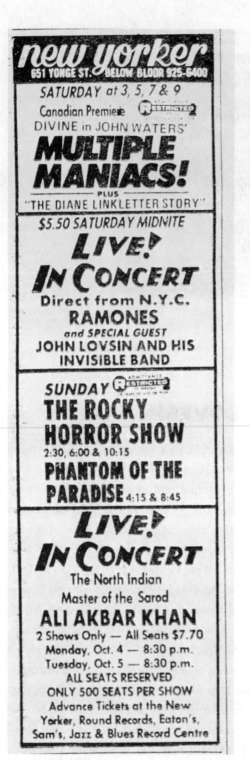

New York newspaper listing ad showing John Lovsin and the Invisible Band opening for the Ramones' first Canadian shows. Image courtesy of the *Toronto Star*, September 25, 1976.

Front cover of *Set the Night on Fire* by Lovesin (Taxi Records, 1980). Author's collection.

said to him, "Okay, you're going to be my drummer. Meet me at the Rock and Roll Revival. We're going to open up for Bo Diddley." Delingat thought little of it, but lo and behold, the very next day he and his friend Michael were at the Rock and Roll Revival hanging out in the grandstands doing the things one does when up in the grandstands when they saw a guy with some security guards pointing up at them! Uh oh. Trouble. Oh wait, no, it was Lovesin in oversized sunglasses with the name of his band, the Kings of Rock and Roll, on a cardboard sign yelling, "There's my drummer! Come on down, come on down!" Soon they were led backstage. Delingat explains, "He really had the gift of gab, charisma. He was really young, a little skinny dude. I'm going: okay, I've never played with this guy." Lovesin reassured him, "Oh, don't worry. We're going to play in between Bo Diddley and we're going to use Bo Diddley's bass player. Just follow the four, I'll count you in." That didn't happen, what with the chaos of famous people like the Doors and John and Yoko flurrying

Back cover and inner sleeve of *Set the Night on Fire* by Lovesin (Taxi Records, 1980). Author's collection.

to and fro—one perk of the fame being a fleet of limos. They jumped in the back of one with the chauffeur asking, "To the airport?" and Lovesin replying, "No, just drive around in circles." Joy-riding and taking some famous rock star's limo. Strong friendships formed. Soon Delingat and Lovesin were playing together in a short-lived band that Lovesin named Black Ballet, for the color itself as well as the art form and the surrounding moods.

Delingat had a band called Draco that went off to try their luck in England. They lasted a year or so. Joe Mavety, their gentleman guitarist, decided to stay there, it worked out, and he later played on Marianne Faithfull's *Broken English* album. The rest of Draco came back and Lovesin filled the guitarist spot, asking, "What kind of name is that? Draco?" And Delingat said, "Well, it's actually a constellation. It's the dragon constellation." He goes, "Yeah, well, I don't know about that name. I'm the Ace from Space." In Draco they wrote a lot of songs together of a hard-rocking nature. Donning a velvet cape in 1974, Johnnie performed solo as the Ace from Space. Other times he was billed as the Electric Kid. Delingat had nothing but glowing things to say about what a creative force his friend was—pausing, then adding, "How can I say it—he was so spontaneous and interesting." Delingat remembers the time there was a band that left Lovesin behind; Lovesin asked them if they had a name for the band yet. "No," they replied. Lovesin said, "I know, why don't you call yourselves the Deserters." And they did! The Deserters went on to record a couple of albums for Capitol Records.

When the Ramones played their very first gig in Canada, it was a pivotal part of Canadian punk history. The Garys (Gary Topp and Gary Cormier) were legendary Toronto show promoters booking three Ramones shows over two nights, including a midnighter. Opening for the Ramones would have been a feather in your cap—it's 1976 and this is one of the first big glimmers of punk—no future, but put it in your scrap book. A lot of people were angling for that choice opening slot. It was thought that Teenage Head would, but Topp knew exactly who to get, someone who had been doing his own rock 'n' roll thing: Johnnie Lovesin. Says Topp, "This kid comes to my theater. He was like a Glam street kid. He said, 'My band is the Invisible Band and it's just me.' I just wanted something different that no one was expecting. He asked Cormier if he could build him a box." Rising from the box was a poster of Jimi Hendrix for Lovesin's Hendrix tribute. Imagine that—a tribute to Hendrix for Ramones fans to enjoy. In the recording of Lovesin's set, some very soon-to-be punk voices could be heard voicing annoyance, but Gary states, "I think he went over pretty well."

The Invisible Band. Get it? The rest of the band was invisible! One sweet piece of swag was oval Invisible Band pins of him in a white jumpsuit, but for this notable concert Lovesin wore all red Adidas from the t-shirt and track pants right on down to his runners. Why this attire? Michele Morgan speculates, "He was really animated on stage. So, maybe that was for practical reasons because he would take these huge jumps off the stage . . . . He would do these moves, all that Joe Tex stuff with his mic stand and the knees. It was pretty crazy and he paid dearly in his older years because his knees were just shot." Besides his stage moves, his banter would rev up the crowds, sometimes with salty language. At the

Mustache in Montreal, the city's premiere rock club, he'd even put his bilingual skills to good use packing the place for his run.

One of the majors took an interest in Lovesin. At the time he was still on the much smaller Smile Records. And there was a guy connected to Smile who wanted to be Lovesin's manager (conflict of interest). Michele recounts that the three men (Lovesin, the wannabe manager, and Smile's co-owner) were flown to L.A. and treated very nicely—wined, dined, put up in a hotel—by this major record label, but in the meeting with them Lovesin's much less experienced label and wannabe manager started getting greedy going, "Well, we want this and we want to keep all the publishing and we want to do that." Morgan remembers, "And Johnnie said that he had it all worked out, it took them so many hours to get from Toronto to LA, from the hotel to this meeting, say, over the course of twenty-eight hours, he said, 'We were in and out of his office in like, six and a half minutes.' You know, 'Okay, gentlemen, thank you very much, I think this meeting's over.' They gave Johnnie the opportunity to stay but showed those guys the door. Sadly, Johnnie chose loyalty over smarts and he followed those guys back home, but oh so close."

Furthermore, it came to pass that it didn't go so well for Lovesin with his label either. Things got messy. Smile Records, which put out "Tonight," was also the Taxi label, which put out the *Set the Night on Fire* album in 1980 without Lovesin's cooperation. Nothing says sketchy like changing the name of your business. Taxi seemed not so much fly-by-night as, more befittingly, a drive-by-night operation, putting out a few things.[3] Though they did have quite a knack for packaging. Lovesin is captured, in the *Set the Night on Fire* cover art, hovering in mid-air over the city, electrified hand-drawn dazzle around him, rocking out on guitar while the city of Toronto—including the newly erected CN Tower—burns behind him, the name "Lovesin" in a gust of smoke. The back cover is a photo album of Lovesin playing Rock Shock, headlining over Teenage Head, opening for the Runaways in 1978, Johnnie Lovesin and the Sidewalk Commandos at the Canadian National Exhibition, and such hype copy as the caption "Johnnie Lovesin and His Invisible Band blow The Ramones off-stage."

While describing Lovesin's great talent, these liner notes bald-facedly mention how he had a falling out with them mid-production, mentioning "contractual terms" and how the label remixed everything and released it without his involvement, patronizingly concluding, "He's still not the rock star he believes he should be. However, he's still playing, still making demos, and still thinking like a rock star."

The album is a hodge-podge, with different lineups (including Greg Godovitz of Goddo) and studios, but the clarity and consistency of the songs (all published by Taxi Driver Music—ahem) transcend it to make for a great rock album—not hard, it's rock, rock 'n' roll, with a romantic quality, sometimes raucous. "Tonight" is included and fits in quite nicely. Along with the street drama of the title track, there's "One of the Boys," "American

---

3   Including a version of "My Guy" by Brandy Stafford, who was known mostly it seems for posing in *Playboy* magazine's "Girls of Canada" pictorial. For this single she was clad in a string bikini.

Miss" (about a "teenage groupie queen"), "Matter of Time" (about checking ID and doing time for not really checking ID), "Teeny Bopper" (it's not what you think; this is a heavy, street-wise ballad about a runaway who fell into a hard lifestyle and was murdered), "Rock All the Way," and more at a steady clip with much Glammy goodness.

Rife with typos and inaccuracies, the liner notes also implore, "We would be pleased if you turn on your friends to Taxi artists but would ask for your co-operation in not lending this album to anyone whose intention is to copy it in whole or in part. Not only is unauthorized duplication an offense but more importantly it deprives both the artist and company of revenue needed to continue bringing their new music to you."

Much before meeting Lovesin, Morgan had seen him perform at the Canadian National Exhibition,[4] and she was in awe of the energy coming from the stage. Later, when she had a boyfriend with a car, they eventually met, giving a hitchhiking Lovesin and his then girlfriend a ride. She recalls, "And I turned around like I was Hayley Mills or something and I'm leaning, I look back at him. 'Oh my god, you're that guy. You're Johnnie!'" She next saw him at a bar and asked, "What's going on? You look so sad." Well, his girlfriend had left him and he was having label problems. Shortly thereafter he was couch-surfing at her place and she naturally became his manager. "It's funny because I was so naive that I would pick up the phone and I would call people as if I'm selling Rod Stewart, so I had so much confidence and then he probably sat in the background and just kind of enjoyed watching me." The two of them eventually started dating.

Lovesin had his guitar in hock and decided that his career was over. That didn't mean he was giving up music—no, he just figured he might as well become a frontman and drop the guitar playing. An opportunity presented itself when he and Morgan were handed the keys to the upstairs section of the Oriental Palace on Bloor Street, a multi-roomed club that would later become Lee's Palace. Morgan describes it: "And the downstairs was a Korean nightclub, with all the clichés: the guy would be sitting there with the cigarette holder really long with a cigarette in it and these young pretty girls would get up and sing very American pop music, but they couldn't speak a word of English—and a cloud of smoke. So, it's just too much. And anyway, we happened to have a friend who was married to one of the daughters of this family." They named the upstairs club the Rock Palace. Morgan did all the booking and event-planning. Looking very much ahead, Lovesin started putting a band together called the Next. Morgan notes, "All these guys who joined the Next were very young, quite a lot younger than Johnny—not the greatest musicians, but really cute. They all had really spiky hair and were wearing eyeliner and Cuban pointy boots. So it was pretty sexy. There were great contrasts between Johnny and his young Next—it drew girls, it always had predominantly girl audiences." And Johnnie could write a ballad to make the girls swoon.

---

4   This is a large fair that has been held every summer in Toronto since 1879. Concerts are one integral part of the CNE, along with deeply troubling deep-fried food concoctions, rides, farm animals, and the popular butter sculpture competition.

Johnnie Lovesin with the Next. Image courtesy of the *Hamilton Spectator*, October 17, 1979.

For their sets the band learned lots of covers—"Tired of Waiting for You," "Sorrow"—that Michele describes as "very sultry, sexy stuff, and he had great stage presence and was still not really big on hair and makeup, but just enough that it was sexy. And so he had this young band and one day they were at rehearsal and he dragged them all to a photo booth down the street. He wanted them all to slick their hair and do rockabilly haircuts and put their collars up. And he wanted a whole new look for the band and these guys were really pissed off because they're all young and current and doing whatever is happening at the time and they don't want to do all this old sort of crap, this old music." Hey, Johnnie loved to rock 'n' roll.

Alternately known as the N.E.X.T. (thought it is uncertain what these letters stood for, if anything), the band themselves wore striped shirts. How did Lovesin dress? Besides finding a frilly tuxedo shirt, unclaimed and set out front of a closing dry cleaners', Morgan says, "He had some guy make him a long purple velvet walking coat," along with tight leather pants for his six-foot-two frame. "Right to the end he always stood out. I mean, even when it was almost impossible for him to walk. He would never go to an event without wanting to be different, putting together his outfit to look extraordinary. He was really getting into a lot of beads and baubles and things. He was always a dresser. He always had a code and it might have been slightly off the mark of what normal everyday people were wearing, but it made him stand out for sure." After the club ended, Morgan was headhunted by a management company where she also managed Lovesin up until their kids were born. She later went into the arts. As she says with a laugh, "So basically my life's always been in the shitter one way or the other."

It wasn't long until Lovesin picked the guitar up again. And then it happened! Headlong into the '80s the producer George Semkiw entered the picture. Semkiw's reputation was first made back when he was cutting lacquers at RCA Canada. He received a Lou Reed track that sounded so shoddy he had to ask RCA in the USA to send it again; they did—still shoddy—so he went to work and cleaned it up and did such an incredible job on it that Reed called him up to personally thank him. Semkiw and Reed started hanging out. Semkiw helped get Lovesin a big record contract with A&M Records. This period is synthabilly, with Semkiw providing modern '80s production, cue sequencers. There was even a twelve-inch dance remix maxi-single of "(I Need a) Working Girl" released in 1983. The sleeve shows Lovesin in a leather jacket with his guitar coming atcha—right onto the dancefloor. Semkiw liked to keep things upbeat. Contemporizing à la ZZ Top or Robert Palmer at the time, the songwriting and vocals retain the rock 'n' roll, but everything else is full-tilt processed, complete with an accompanying neon-lit music video. Album art all done up like Memphis Group BBQ, the songs from Lovesin's 1986 album *Tough Breaks* were performed live at a massive show at the Diamond Club with a horn section and back-up singers—Lovesin stepping out in front of a big band.

Lovesin loved rock 'n' roll—this has been duly noted—not the ersatz-'50s glitz but digging deep into the roots of the music, be it country, blues, or rockabilly, going deeper into blues-rock as time went on. He released his *Ready to Rumble* CD in 1996, with a release party held appropriately at the Rockin' Blues Bar. Lovesin played all kinds of taverns, regularly celebrating his birthday with a show, until his death from hospital complications in 2019. Delingat and Morgan put together a celebration of his life. As Delingat describes it, "everybody who was anybody in the rock scene showed and went on stage and played good old rock and roll in his memory. It was really, really sweet."[5] When I asked about their relationship, Morgan said, "While Johnnie and I were never married, we were a pretty great couple for many years before and after our sons Morgan and Britain were born. Both now are parents themselves ... quite shocking! We continued to be in each other's lives always ... The boys and I really miss him ... all the bumps and grinds ..."

---

5   Delingat died in 2023.

THUNDERMUG

THUNDERMUG HAIL FROM THE MID-SIZED CITY of London . . . Ontario, that is. London is the birthplace of the term "cosmic consciousness," coined when, back in 1872, after a nice visit with the poet Walt Whitman, the psychiatrist Richard Bucke received a blinding flash of light. It lasted only a few seconds but it affected him forever.

What a name: Thundermug. Buzzing energy served here. If you factor everything in without looking at the band, you'd go, "That's Glam!" Remove the velvet blindfold: they're all shaggy, like, like . . . hippies. Then they got some snazzy outfits—well, more on that later . . .

Thundermug sprang out of the lysergically named band Pink Orange, named for the guitarist Bill Durst's two favorite types of acid—though pink was number one. As Durst put it, "It was delightfully euphoric. Yeah. It was very, very nice. It was actually the best LSD I ever had in my life." Though colorless and odorless, the many different permutations of the hallucinogenic drug LSD were often named after different colors and other "trip" descriptors.

Back in 1969, Pink Orange's singer, Mike Curtis, left, so Durst stepped up to fill the void and sing. He didn't really want to. "Our big goal," Durst told me, "became to get a vocalist, and the best vocalist in town by far was Joe de Angelis." LSD is a mind-altering substance; this particular Pink Orange hybrid, though, had after-effects that manifested a larger, longer lingering residue of a more visual nature, bringing on shape-swinging tracers. De Angelis had a name for the band: Thundermug. Durst exclaimed, "God, that's fucking fantastic. That's fucking perfect, it's kind of cuteish but not too much, but it's got a thundering. Come on. It's fucking perfect." Excited, he went home and told his mother —a nice, middle-class woman—the new name. Her response was unexpected.

"Oh, Bill, why would you ever want to name your band after that???"

"What are you talking about?"

"Well, it's the porcelain pot that you put under the bed in the country, you know, when the washroom's outside, and you pee in it in the middle of the night."

Chalking it up to the "confidence of youth," Durst cemented the name by replying, "Mom, if I didn't know that, nobody else does either."

With de Angelis as lead vocalist, Durst was now freed up to focus purely on guitar: "And it was wonderful too, because, you know, for a period of time there was 100% trust between the musicians. So, if the drummer did something, it was cool. You know, it was a really great time period. It was a super ensemble with a total trust in what the other guy was doing. And so then you can just concentrate on the neatest thing that you could possibly do. Which is remarkable."

Glam Rock, in general, represented a shift from the "head music" of the '60s to "body

Front cover of *Thundermug Strikes* (Axe Records, 1972). Author's collection.

music."⁶ Thundermug wanted to be loud. They bought Gbx amps to make it so. "And they were horrible and they broke down all the time. And we were actually at the Gbx factory every single week on O'Connor in Toronto, and the best part was it was right by the Peek Freans cookie factory. So every time you went there it smelled like heaven. And, you know, the amplifier company did not last too long because their amps kind of fell apart and all the rest of it, but we gained a reputation of being really loud and all the rest of that." This reputation landed them a spot in a documentary on noise pollution. "And I'm in the documentary explaining that it's not good enough to just hear the music, you want to feel the music, physically feel it. And we really, really liked that and so it looks a

---

6   See Philip Auslander's book *Performing Glam Rock: Gender and Theatricality in Popular Music* (University of Michigan Press, 2006), which has a chapter on Roy Wood's bands the Move and Wizzard—bands which Thundermug has unintentionally much in common with musically.

bit dumb nowadays, you know, what about your hearing? The documentary turned out to be entitled . . . *Another Man's Noise.* And we were made to look quite stupid, but we were quite famous for it, so all our fans thought it was cool."

Feeling the music, the sense of touch, makes the music seem more visual. If there is thunder, there must be lightning. Can you see the lightning? It's a direct hit!

Thundermug's 1972 single "Africa," which kicks off their first album, *Thundermug Strikes,* with animal sounds and an instant energy, has a rumbling Glam sound akin to the hypno-thud proto-Glam Rock of John Kongos—only lots more giddy. Jim Corbett's unrelenting bass vibrates as the heightened drums and percussion of Ed Pranskus meld with the guitar. The whole album feels very much alive—it is crunchy peanut butter. And jelly. *Strikes* has a rather unique sound, recorded live off the floor apart from the vocals and one overdubbed guitar. "There's only two guitars on that record. Most of the time, guys will put on the rhythm tracks and then the lead will go on top of that. No, when we played the songs, like when we recorded 'Africa' and all that stuff or any of the songs off the first album, I played the leads and overdubbed the rhythms, if you can believe that."

Never underestimate the almost andro-smooth tongue of de Angelis joyously hitting the roof of his mouth, followed by an "Ahhh ahhh" group response, with de Angelis alternatively more than capable of bringing up a strained howling grit. Oh, and he throws in a kazoo solo on "Africa." Huh? When de Angelis first suggested it, Durst said, "A kazoo, are you serious? Try it!" Now Durst reflects, "The unfortunate part was that Joe could actually pull it off. That's the unfortunate part. So he did a kind of 'Yakety Sax' solo really is what it is. I don't know where the fuck he ever got the idea for the melody—actually, Joe doesn't have to worry about melodies, they just pop out. Open your mouth, Joe, and out comes a melody—he's a melody maker."

If "Africa" were to be used as a tourism jingle, Canada would be emptier than it already is. Was it a hit? It hit the charts, sure—more so than their first single, a cover of the Kinks' "You Really Got Me." The rest of side one is a medley, shifting around with all its moving parts locked in, followed by a whole other side filled with some lovely little self-contained gems.

The album was produced by Greg Hambleton and released on his Axe Records label, whose roster was all over the place: they had a soft-pop hit with the gorgeous "Could You Ever Love Me Again?" by Gary and Dave, an unlikely duo who looked like rugby players turned stockbrokers, and later released the primo stoner rock of Starchild, whose guitarist would much later go on the Christian chat show *100 Huntley Street* still playing guitar with his hair long in the back, though now short in the front to show his born-again face.

Strikes was recorded at Toronto Sound by its manager and engineer, Terry Brown, faintly fresh from England, having worked there on "The Doughnut in Granny's Greenhouse" by the Bonzo Dog Doo-Dah Band (a masterpiece) and Donovan's "Mellow Yellow" (which later became a butter jingle for the Dairy Board of Canada). In Canada, Brown immersed himself in the studio working with April Wine, Pagliaro, Stampeders, and Max Webster.

Front cover and opened cover of *Orbit* by Thundermug (Axe Records, 1973). Author's collection.

U.S. release front cover of *Ta-daa!* by Thundermug (Mercury, 1975). Author's collection.

The album's bigness is represented by the album cover. Durst claims that this was the first airbrushed album cover in Canada. It's a perfect example of Glam aesthetics and airbrush art. Set on top of a cloud against a white background, a lone match strikes itself on a book of matches creating a curved lightning bolt. What does it all mean? It just looks cool, all hyper-sleek and cartoony. Roger Hill won a design award for the eye-catching cover. Although this was the only work that he would do for them, Hill's artwork set the tone for subsequent Thundermug albums.

Thundermug Strikes is not a misnomer or a fluke. They put it in a bottle and let it strike again in a different place, in 1973: the second album, *Orbit*. Their name is in faux gold chrome, and clouds part for a black fold-over sleeve revealing not only planets but a long-playing record as well. Does lightning strike in space? The science is hard, too hard: please don't challenge the energy being channeled, spare the rod. But don't expect more of the same. Durst bemoans a lack of consistency negatively impacting commercial success for the band. They reached for the stars, but it doesn't sound like a cash grab. *Orbit*, recorded at Manta Sound, is loaded with hits. In music industry terms, there were no hits—well, the title track cracked the Top 40. In my own personal relationship to the album, it's all hits. I am not alone in this: decades on, it has become more sought after by people who know best, whose eardrums have highly evolved taste buds—especially in the region known as sweet. Yum yum.

On *Orbit,* Thundermug try on various styles, going from one to the next, find they all fit quite nicely, well-tailored to suit. This diversity makes for dynamics. The lead-off single, "Orbit," bursts into cosmic themes of the other, feeling different: "I don't look like them, nor them like me . . . I'm far from home, won't you be my friend." Then the bizarro acoustic and heavily moisturised skin slapping "Molly-O," culminating in chanting and incanting. The electrified classical-style guitar instrumental "Victoria Muse" is Durst in perpetual overdub, nary a flub (why would there be?). "Mickey Mouse Club" never caught the ears of Disney sadly, nor their lawyers thankfully; for something so cartoony, they do a couple of time changes smacking two disparate parts together for fantastic fan fiction, rocking so hard your mouse ears fall off, then a slow-mo fist pump on a dime, pausing for Corbett's bass to distort beautifully, some fuzz guitar, Pranskus's drums doing a million things—all of them just right. "Come on, everybody!" The side closes with the satisfyingly spy-themed riffer "The Investigator." Side two opens with steady bass—the sparks from Durst's guitar and the hits from Pranskus's drums ricochet around each other; when de Angelis comes in it turns into a perfectly melodic crunchy confection betwixt pop and rock. "Garden Green" is all over the place, never straying from sweet surprises. And the record continues sweetly. And even a bit goofily (with a string section). Then a heavy heavy monster, "Bad Guy," that just screams heavy! Ending short and sweet with "To Tell the Truth," a beautiful group sing for weddings and other such occasions that really only require about half a minute.

The American release of their third album, 1974's *Ta-daa!,* not only contains one or two different songs from the Canadian version but also has different cover art, showing what looks to be a hastily airbrushed bedpan (half-full or half-empty—volume is undetermined) struck by bolts of lightning . . . in space. The back-cover photo of the band is in murky black-and-white, not giving the full effect of their new outfits, which are full-color front-and-center on the Canadian release.

These brand-new custom-made outfits, though quite striking, did not fly. As a nod to the matching striped suits of earlier Toronto blue-eyed soul shakers like the Mandala, Thundermug went for the exceptionally vibrant red and white color combo jumpsuit option. Durst remembers (and will never forget), "I think we played in a club on Yonge Street in Toronto downstairs. I can't remember the name of it, but it was a well-known bar. And the moment we entered the room with the outfits on, there was talk of Kentucky Fried Chicken outlets. Yeah, it was embarrassing. It was terrible. But these things happen. We played at the

Thundermug concert ad, Leisure Lodge Tavern, Preston, Ontario. Image courtesy of *Waterloo Region Record*, June 9, 1975.

Forum in Ontario Place; somebody from the *Toronto Star* said it was what looked like a pyjama party gone wild. That was the best, most complimentary thing that was said about those outfits. Whose idea was it? No idea." I thought they looked like hip ice-cream men selling a bright array of razzle-dazzle ice-cream flavors from a tricked-out van playing fuzzed-out melodies. The Netherlands single of "Jeanine"—one of the album's highlights—shows a photo of them on stage in these outfits and they look (and sound) very junkshop Glam.

The photographer Gérard Gentil took full advantage of the outfits for the superior, Canadian *Ta-daa!* sleeve. Dressed all in black with his shaved head and French—possibly Haitian—accent, Gentil got Thundermug into posing for the camera, telling them to "Poosh it! Poosh it!" while making them stand very, very still. Thundermug is literally making a full-body gesture going, "Ta-daa!", mouths all agape. Then, using the flash full-on, Gentil made a painting with a bar of lights, red and white stripes swirling around behind them composing an album cover that was spectacularly sublime and ridiculous. This Canadian sleeve also shows off an awesome new band logo, their name vibrating in repeating yellow lines, a cartoony bolt of lightning underneath. This logo was so good that the Calgary Glam band Buick McKane nicked it as a sly homage.

Moving back to Toronto Sound, *Ta-daa!* had a different engineer who really held back on the dynamics, not as punchy or crunchy or full sounding as their previous albums. Durst says the record company gave it "minor effort," with no overdubs as the label owner and producer, Greg Hambleton, wanted a type of delay guitar so that "you didn't need a second rhythm guitar. And of course, that's cheesy beyond fucking belief." It was also hockey play-off season and because of this Durst says that the engineer "was watching TV while we were recording." Not that he had much of a rock pedigree in the first place; apart from Thundermug, his fingers had controlled the knobs of some very flaccid stuff (even if the Carlton Showband is your cup of tea, you'd probably agree). This was combined with Hambleton wanting the band to write "Beatle hits." They did indeed cover "Drive My Car," while their more exploratory efforts went completely unreleased. *Ta-daa!* is a fun enough record, sounding deflated by the pressure of making a hit. By the time Mercury Records came on board for the American release, Thundermug was done with the business.

In Axe Records' hunt for a hit, Thundermug did a single version of Neil Sedaka's "Breaking Up Is Hard to Do" in 1975, with a vocal so snotty it bears striking similarities to the Turtles'

Canadian release front cover of *Ta-daa!* by Thundermug (Axe Records, 1975). Author's collection.

"Eleanor," which the Turtles cynically recorded as a rebuff to their label's request for a hit—except that "Eleanor" actually became a hit. In Thundermug's case, Sedaka released his slow version around the same time and they didn't stand a chance. Durst quips, "If you hang your hat on commercialism, man, that's what you get." In 1976, Thundermug released a serviceable cover of the then-current Euro-Glam stomper "Clap Your Hands and Stomp Your Feet."

He elaborates, "That band was destroyed by capitalism. It was destroyed by the hollowness of just get a hit, get a hit, and then also the hollowness of the radio industry at the time. The reason we got a record deal one time was because Clive Davis got fired from CBS and the guy under him liked us. And when he moved up, we got a deal. Great, eh? We really just wanted to do art, through the music, and be good. It's nice to have a hit but, you know . . . ehhh. We never got along well with the business that way and, in the end, it blew out our morale and took us down."

Since these experiences, Durst has devoted his life to ending oligarchic capitalism and is a firm believer in co-operatives. In the '90s there were Thundermug reunions and a couple of successful independent albums, but de Angelis was not involved. Then, in 2003, after the death of his brother Paul de Angelis, he gave Durst a call. They decided to make some music and have since collaborated on five CDs. In 2006 came Thundermug's induction into the London Music Hall of Fame, with the original lineup performing "Africa"—without the red and white striped suits, but with the mandatory kazoo solo—and they sounded great!

Durst still tours extensively as a blues artist. 2020 was a very intense year for him. His wife Susan passed away in February. Then, one month later, he received a phone call from a young man telling him that he was his son. And he is. On his website, www.billdurst.com, Durst notes, "Many people say they feel the hand of Susan in this situation. What do you think . . . ?" Upon meeting his son and his son's family for the first time, it turns out—surprise surprise—that they are all quite musical—so musical, in fact, that they even have a family band.

FLUDD

IF FLUDD HAD LEFT OFF with just their first album, a pleasant enough, gently milque-toasted album tapping a soft vein close to Crosby, Stills, and Nash (no Young), then they would not merit much—if any—inclusion in this book. However, the very next year, in '72, they got their ya-yas out and recorded the single "Get Up, Get Out, and Move On," the title itself a call to action, found in recent years on Euro–Glam Rock compilations of dubious origins. What happened? Wah-wah happened. A whole lotta wah-wah pushing it open. The guitar just wah-wahs so harrrd! Known for what Greg Godovitz calls having a "backwards sounding phasing technique," it was the short-lived Fludd guitarist Mick Hopkins's only vinyl appearance with them.

The main crux of Fludd consisted of two British immigrant brothers, Brian and Edmund Pilling, on guitars and vocals; Greg Godovitz as mischief-making bassist Greg Godovitz; and John Andersen on drums. Fludd's sartorial splendors knew no limits; oceans couldn't keep them away from such finery: they even took proper transatlantic flights for fancy apparel. Coffee, tea, satin, velvet, a peacock plume, or me? *C'est moi*. Ha ha.

In the September 1, 1973, issue of *RPM Magazine,* Peter Taylor writes, "I guess you could call Fludd Canada's glitter band. When they hit the stage your eyes are assaulted by the flash of sequins, glitter make-up, satin duds, feathers and five guys who don't believe in standing still while they rock. At the same time, your ears are soaking up some of that good old high volume music."

Their second album, . . . *On!,* looks like an imported box of bonbons all red and golden shiny—so many chocolates to choose from—gingerly pluck one with deft fingers and note that they are filled with creamy syrups laced with . . . ? Mellotron moves on in and moves on up

Inner gatefold and front cover of ... *On!* by Fludd (Daffodil Records, 1972). Author's collection.

Sleeve of "Always Be Thinking of You" single by Fludd (Daffodil Records, 1972).
Courtesy collection of Ed Pilling.

and it's not a letdown by far. Fludd made a real beaut. This album was originally to be called *Cock On* . . . but, without a word to anyone in the band, the label wiped the first word away.

After taking me for fish and chips, Godovitz and Ed Pilling sat down with me, opening up the album to reveal band photos, with Godovitz commenting, "That's possibly one of the more embarrassing photographs of me. It's that little teardrop made of stars."

Ed noted, "Brian, of course, is in the limo." A limo? "Half of your energy is created by what you create with your imagery—performance or what people perceive you be. It's like show business. To drop a nice, classy limousine, they think you're doing alright. Showing up in a high school was pretty impressive."

Plus, adds Godovitz, "It was always easy to pull chicks." He pauses to point at the album gatefold band photos. "The guy in the middle, Peter Csanky, was the guy with the first Mellotron in Canada, but we knew we were going to get rid of him so he ended up in the fold-in crease." And yet . . . *On!* is awash with spacey Mellotron. Inspired by the Beatles, this switch from the first album's real strings to fake strings made it easier for stage performance. "Alas," Ed explains, "the problem was with the cold weather because they're tape-loops. There were a lot of problems. It wasn't practical. We were the first band to have one." Ohhh, chilly chilly Canada. To stay warm one has to rock and Fludd wanted this album to represent that, yes, they rocked, partly from the influence of the Move: the Pilling brothers even knew the great Roy Wood as they had lived in Birmingham, England, for a spell. Says Godovitz, "You can hear the Move influences in the end of 'Down Down Down,' the long 'Brontosaurus' thing going on and on."

Godovitz also often visited England: "I went to England on my own when the whole Glam thing was just starting. I remember I came back with incredible fucking clothes and my hair dyed silver on the tips and Ed and Brian went, 'Fuck!' I think it was about two weeks later

Fludd at the Manor, Shipton-on-Cherwell, England, 1973. Courtesy Ed Pilling.

we were back on a plane to go shopping." Where did you go shopping? "In London: Granny Takes a Trip, Alkasura, Biba, I Was Lord Kitchener's Valet." And, of course, Mr. Freedom.

Ed describes, "I was thinking about this today because I used to wear these feathers tied in my hair. Big feathers. At the end of the day trying to get them out was a nightmare. Trying to get them undone. There was a bloke that I met that lived in my building that was a London hairdresser. It was brilliant, this was. He put a really white streak in my hair where I used to put the feathers, then he colored it in with magic markers. And it looked like feathers. I could wash it out and change it."

Godovitz responds, "I saw a chick in London who had blue hair. I stopped her and said, 'I'm with a rock band. Where did you get that done?' And she told me. I had a lot of hair back then. So they gave me a shag cut but they dyed an inch like one of those Theda Bara hats, so that when you shook it, it moved and it was silver. Remember the time I came back from another trip on my own? You picked me up from the airport and we played that high school. And I wore the one suit on stage. Then the kids from the school ripped off all the fucking clothes. I don't know why we never followed up on that. It was in Alliston. Someone's going to notice a guy walking around in a velvet toreador outfit in fucking Alliston. I just remember crying all the way home because all my clothes were gone." Alliston is a town in Ontario known primarily for potatoes.

In 1973, Fludd went to England to do what was known as "environmental recording" at the Manor, the estate of the billionaire (now Sir) Richard Branson, the owner of Virgin Records. The band were drinking quite heavily. These sessions went unreleased, including an unfinished Bowie tribute, "English Spaceman," that Godovitz describes in his memoir as "perhaps the most stupid thing that I have ever written." Much mayhem ensued at the Manor, including Godovitz burning the sheet music for *Tubular Bells* for kindling as its serious prog composer, Mike Oldfield, rushed to stop him, expressing a horror unparalleled by *The Exorcist*.

Fludd's keyboardist, Peter Rochon, was fair game for fashion. Ed explains: "He used to wear white ladies' evening gloves. He painted his face up, his hair was all wild."

Says Godovitz, "That raccoon thing he did with his face."

"He just looked bizarre," Ed added, "and we loved him!"

"I think it's safe to say," Godovitz went on, "that Peter and I had a pretty good competition as to who would be the wildest dresser. When we went back to the Manor, we all disappeared to our rooms to have a little fashion show as to what we bought. I had no idea that he had a dress. I bought this phenomenal red and white vertical satin suit. Amazing fucking rock gear. I come down there, Jack the lad. He comes down in a dress with evening gloves. You win, pal. There's no way I am wearing a fucking dress. You win." Godovitz adds, "I do recall wearing hot pants shorts with glitter on them, but I didn't have the legs for it."

They were all trying to outdo each other in attire. Godovitz candidly asides, "The chicks loved it! I used to use my lipstick on the girls when they were sucking my cock and my cock would look like a barber pole."

Top: Fludd live: brothers Ed and Brian Pilling, c. 1972. Courtesy Ed Pilling. Bottom: Ad for Goddo at Montebello Inn with Exotic Dancer, 1977. Courtesy of the *Standard*.

Ed explains, "One of the things that I learned when Brian and I were in England and one of the things I loved about the British bands is that they all made an effort to look like something. The Canadian musicians and groups were pretty flat. And even the American bands, there was not much going ... the Brits had it down, you know. They would just get into it. I always thought of it like the theater: you go to the theater, you don't want to see people on the stage that look like you. It's showbiz! That's where it really came from. I thought it was your job to entertain and make people feel that they have gone out of their own skin seeing something they can't do or walk around in. We were just having fun and felt it was our responsibility to look like you were trying to entertain people and brighten things up a bit. It was great that the girls liked it. That's another thing, I think: a lot of men in this country were fearful of feeling feminine, but we didn't give a damn. It was a freeing feeling, wasn't it? It always bothered me that men never had the opportunity to look as colorful as women."

Godovitz says, "We walked around in public like that. One of the things I liked about it because he told you he was wearing ballet shoes? I was almost as tall as him in those days, with eight-inch platforms."

"It levels out," notes Ed. Godovitz describes one incident during their ballet slipper period where they were staying at a hotel in a northern town on a Super Bowl sports weekend that had riled up the locals. "So, I'm walking down the hall, black crushed velvet pants with mirrors down the sides of the leg, full makeup in the afternoon, and these two guys come out. This guy grabs me and throws me up against the wall and goes, 'What the fuck is it?' to his friend." Luckily Ed showed up at just the right time to save Godovitz. Upon seeing him, one of the guys said, "Oh, fuck, check out Goldilocks here," Ed clocked the guy—BANG!—and it was over. Of Ed's efficient technique, Godovitz notes, "I never saw many fights with him go past one punch."

His right hook came in handy. Ed explains, "It was a dangerous place for that. We came against this a lot. I was trying to save my life. Believe me, I'm not a bully, I'm not a scrapper. I hate bullies anyways. If anyone started to intimidate us, they weren't going to get away with it. It was basically a survival thing. You get into a position where you have got no choice."

Godovitz asks, "What was that place called? Lancers, that night in St. Catharines? The whole restaurant had a barroom brawl because of us. I was just sitting there and the wrong guy said the wrong thing to Ed and the next thing there were tables flying. I was already in the van crying."

Even just having long hair back then Godovitz says, "You couldn't go anywhere." Add makeup, colored hair, women's clothing ... both on stage and off, even to the grocery store. Godovitz says, "We were doing it for real. And we thought we were the only band in the country, I didn't see another one at first, so we went and saw the Wackers ... I remember Bob Segarini never looked good in makeup. I'll say that to his face, and what a face! He and Randy Bishop did that 'Night and Day' thing, super Glam, super gay. We were astounded that there was another band in the country that was doing what we were doing and the same sort of pop music as well."

Fludd got all decked out for the Maple Music Junket. This event was put together by the rock journalists Ritchie Yorke and Pierre Juneau, flying over the cream of London and Europe's rock press—including Nick Kent and Chris Charlesworth and various *Melody Maker* writers—to show them what eastern Canada had to offer. Open to the public, it cost three dollars and fifty cents in 1972 to see Crowbar, Lighthouse, Fludd, Mashmakhan, and April Wine play Massey Hall in Toronto. Ed had a bright yellow custom made "Big Bird" ensemble with wings and wizard sleeves, while Godovitz's outfit mostly came from Long John's in Toronto: "a pink velvet suit like a tuxedo made with brocade binding and hand-painted Beatrix Potter shoes." Fludd delivered the goods musically to match. Alas, the all-important overseas rock press got so drunk on the free booze that they never even bothered to see them play.

Though buying new clothes was all-important, Fludd couldn't always dash over to London. This was where the local clothing store Long John's did in a pinch. Godovitz explains, "John was a Londoner . . . John was great because you're standing in front of the mirror checking yourself out, you know, a Jack the Lad and he's standing there like this going, 'Greg Goddo, exactly what is it you see when you look in the mirror?' He's insulting you! I said, 'Oh wow, this is great, Oscar Wilde is my fucking haberdasher.' John was like, he was so far ahead of it."

Ed describes, "I gotta tell you, I'm sure we had the biggest dry-cleaning bill in a rock band in the country, because our manager used to tell us that. And we would change every night because you have to, we sweat so much. You couldn't wear it again. So, we were playing three or four nights you know, quite a lot, and he'd take all the cleaning and it was like hundreds and hundreds of dollars each week just to keep our clothes dry cleaned. There's no way we could perform any night without sweating because everybody worked hard."

Godovitz left Fludd before their third and final album, *Great Expectations,* which has a few Glam ditties: the dynamic trumpet blasting epic "What an Animal," the shooby-dooing "I Held Out," and the Brian and Edmund Pilling tropical rum-drunk vacation episode "Brother and Me." In 1978, Brian Pilling died from cancer, much too young.

The power trio that Godovitz formed in 1975 was called Goddo, with Gino Scarpelli, a former member of Walter Zwol's band Brutus, and Doug Inglis, who replaced Marty Morin, before recording their debut album. The second Goddo album, *Who Cares,* is an audacious Glam masterpiece from 1978, full of coy punk ribbings, confident dynamics amidst the male bravado—album title self-effacing in appropriate, gleaming silver epic scale and font. Godovitz put the book *Subliminal Seduction* to his own use by using two mics for the song "Sweet Thing": one for his vocals, another for a young woman who was fellating him as he sang. "Cock On," a song connecting to the equally grand second Fludd album, was also included, making Ed glad. Written while Godovitz was still in Fludd, it refers to the times Ed's pants split on stage, letting it all hang out. This didn't stop him.

On one such occasion Godovitz sashayed over, standing in front of him to let him know. Ed merely responded, "I know. Get—the—fuck—out—of—my—way."

Another song, "Oh Carole (Kiss My Whip)," was about Carole Pope from Rough Trade, a band Godovitz loved. "I wrote it because, you know, first time I saw her she was at the Gasworks upstairs and she had black leather on, she had a riding crop and she was, like, smacking her leg and her ass with it. So, I just went home and wrote the song." Ed describes an occasion encountering Pope: "She came downstairs, we were playing the Gasworks and she was playing upstairs with Rough Trade. I thought she was great. She came down and sat beside me. I said, "Hi Carole," because she'd never seen us nor met me or anything. She says to me, 'You're a pretty good singer for a man.' I said, 'Thank you.'"

With Goddo, Godovitz never toned down; he still dressed up in girl's blouses and velvet. He says, "Even with Goddo, my sensibilities about always looking good on stage, I never went through that when everybody else started doing that, the spandex thing and stuff. I was always wearing fucking canary yellow suits. You know, leather jackets designed with different colors and I went for a whole year wearing silk pajamas in public—a whole fucking year I spent wearing them, which was fucking bizarre, everywhere I went: restaurants, shopping." Both Ed and Godovitz continue to dress impeccably today. For the interview, Godovitz wore velvet, and Ed was in a parrot-patterned shirt.

ROUGH TRADE

GROUNDBREAKING, TRAILBLAZING, ahead of their time: those are just a few of the adjectives that accurately describe Rough Trade. The name "Rough Trade" itself does not mean, as an example, someone trading gold bouillion for tinfoil, as I initially thought with face-value naïveté.[7] Although we, as listeners, are greatly rewarded with such an exchange: we come out ahead with musical riches.

Meeting at a band audition in 1968, Carole Pope and Kevan Staples soon formed a musical trio called O, with, on keys, Clive Smith, who was later known for his animation work directing the monumental *Rock & Rule*. Pope met Staples while she was painting cels for *Rocket Robin Hood* at the studio where Smith was an animator. This cartoon took the Robin Hood legend and blasted it into space, making a TV show that was legendary for its shoddiness.

Even early on, their music's subject matter often had sexual elements. Their band name, O, came from *The Story of O*, a legendary erotic novel of female submission written by a completely mysterious author. Most people believed that the book was written by a man. Decades later, the French novelist and journalist Anne Desclos revealed that she

---

7 "Rough trade" is gay slang for a casual male companion with an element of danger.

Rough Trade band photo, 1975. Image courtesy of the *Toronto Star*, September 20, 1975.

wrote it after her lover, the writer and critic Jean Paulhan, casually told her that a woman couldn't write an erotic novel like those of the Marquis de Sade. She proved him wrong and he sent the book to a publisher, pretending, in the book's preface, not to know who wrote it.

Pope's lyrics have a literary sensibility, often sharp and audacious. She notes, "I/we were influenced by writers, theatre, multi-media artists, and fashion designers and we brought that into our work. I was an avid reader and was blown away by Henry Miller, Violet Luduc, Susan Sontag, Joan Didion, William Burroughs, and the *Story of O*. I got into fashion in the '60s when I was still a kid. My mom started taking me to the theater when I was a baby, so that was always an influence. I tried to recreate looks I'd seen in fashion mags and loved Mary Quant and Vidal Sassoon and always loved camp movie stars, and that came to fruition when we got to work with Divine. So all of that influenced my writing process and fashion sense." Staples provided the appropriate music to her smart lyrics. "That's what drew me to her in the first place," he told me, "was that she was writing these songs where, like, nobody's ever said that in a song! I'd never heard somebody use 'fallopian tube' in a song."

Staples describes his own influences: "High fashion was definitely part of our background. My father was a couturier and dress designer and also a costume designer for years, so fashion in our house was something I grew up with from age zero. Carole was always interested in fashion and so it was always a part of our lives and a part of the 'fabric' that makes up what created Rough Trade. But in those early days, if you look at everybody—in fact, I was still wearing a satin jacket in some of the early shots. I don't know if I was wearing velvet or not, but definitely came out of that late '60s, early '70s, everybody gave up the hippie thing and they got into a little bit more style-conscious clothing."

Restless Underwear show ad. Image courtesy of the *Toronto Star*, December 19, 1977.

With Rough Trade still far away on the horizon, O was very much late '60s. Smith states, "We were very serious. We were going to be rock and roll stars. We wore silk shirts and bell bottom trousers, it was the real thing—scarves—I guess we were sort of hippie-ish. We played quite a few gigs." Kevan says, "We played a couple of folk clubs. We tried to get into the Mariposa Folk Festival. I mean, they must have just thought we were like the weirdest thing in the world. We had two acoustic guitars and an electric piano. And we thought we were a folk act, so we thought we should go play the Folk Festival." O also appeared in the animator Gerald Potterton's[8] National Film Board short *Super Bus*. Made for Expo '70 in Osaka, Japan, the film features a multi-colored Super Bus zooming across Canada in countless rapid cuts, trying to fit the whole country into six minutes, pausing for breath in Ottawa as O performs on top of it.

After Smith left to help form the Nelvana animation studio, Pope and Staples entered the 1970s performing as a duo under another sexually tinged moniker: the Bullwhip Brothers. Later on, Pope would whip Staples on stage during "True Confessions." So, there was that fascination. Staples recalled, "Oh, yes. Sadomasochistic. Definitely, because it's funny. For us, it's the humor and also sexuality, especially for Carole, was always so interesting. And again, my background—my mother was an interior designer. So you can imagine my mother's friends. And my dad was a dress designer—you can imagine his friends. I grew up in a world that was for a large part mostly gay, and I thought straight people were

---

8   Potterton had an extensive career, including directing the 1967 NFB short *The Railrodder*, starring Buster Keaton, and the 1981 animated feature *Heavy Metal*, as well as working on 1968's *Yellow Submarine*.

Super Bus. Image courtesy of the *Ottawa Journal*, February 15, 1969.

weird, even though I was one of them—you know, like they were an odd bunch. I think it was when Carole and I got together that, again, all that input was there, the fascination with that world and also the fascination with the humor of that, of sexuality, the humor of ambiguity, androgyny—I think that really interested us. And certainly, we were that in a way. I mean, I wasn't like your guy guy and she wasn't like your girl girl, right? So it was a match made in heaven." The importance of Rough Trade goes beyond Canada. Rough Trade were trailblazers in so many ways, opening the door for so many who followed, with openly same-sex lyrical themes early on in a time when it certainly was much harder to do so.

In the forward to her autobiography *Anti-Diva*, an absolute must-read that really delivers, Pope writes, "When Kevan Staples and I created our band, Rough Trade, we just wanted to play. We didn't expect anything except the thrill of getting the songs out there. We ended up pushing musical and sexual envelopes. We morphed androgyny, humor and various musical genres into one twisted freakish phenomenon. . . . As a writer, I've been obsessed with sex simply because it's so funny. It's nature's perverse joke, and a never-ending source of material for me. We're all slaves to urges we have no control over and some of us are utterly guilt-ridden when those urges surface. I love that."

Pope and Staples' very first show after switching their name to Rough Trade happened at the Global Village Theatre, named after the Marshall McLuhan term "global village" (you know, like, connectivity). Founded in 1969, the Global Village Theatre was an experimental theater, very open-minded; they welcomed drag shows, normally held in bars, giving space

Front cover of *Avoid Freud* by Rough Trade (True North, 1980). Author's collection.

for the elaborate production *Façade*. Rough Trade's first performance was at Platform, a regular late-evening event at the theater. A newspaper ad had Rough Trade listed as playing Platform in 1973, though they may have performed there earlier. Pascal, the gender non-conforming chanteuse performer who often collaborated with the art collective General Idea, would perform, as well as the comedy duo of Danny Aykroyd and Valri Bromfield. Many in the burgeoning sketch comedy scene were involved with Platform, with Marcus O'Hara, Catherine O'Hara's brother, and Gilda Radner both working there. Rough Trade quickly befriended future members of the Second City comedy troupe, many of whom would go on to the ground-breaking and brilliant *SCTV*. Staples elaborates: "When they first opened Second City here, those were like the people that we hung out with; we tended to hang out with theater people more often. Theater people, dancers, drag queens, more so than hanging out in the music world, say." Not that there really were any original bands playing the clubs at the time—punk hadn't even arrived yet.

After adding a bassist, a conga player, and then a drummer, Rough Trade's debut as a full band was in 1973 at the Original 99 Cent Roxy, a movie theater that was an early supporter of John Waters' movies, including regular midnight screenings of *Pink Flamingos* starring the incomparable Divine. Rough Trade's midnight show also saw their old friend and bandmate Clive Smith guesting on piano. It was not a traditional live venue, as Staples recalls: "We lined up on a stage that was literally three feet deep and forty feet wide. There was no proscenium. So if you step forward, you'd fall off the stage. And I think we played for maybe a half an hour and cleared the place out. I think the only people left were like the six people that came with us. The sound was terrible because this was a big empty room—it's not the best room to be playing in. And you're a novice band, so you don't really know what you're doing." The noted Roxy booker Gary Topp remembers the show as being very loud. Staples adds, "And there was a running gag because Gary had loaned us money to rent the PA and we never paid him back. And I think the last time I saw him he said, 'You know, you still owe me twenty bucks.'"

With Pope and Staples as the constants, the band lineup would continually shift and, at times, expand throughout its history. Staples explains, "I mean, some of the early bands—there was the seven-piece—it was four women and three men and I always really liked that we for the most part always had women in the band other than Carole, and I really liked that combination, having that mixture." The band built a following; they were great, funky musicians. You could go to their shows and you could dance, you could let go.

Their first album, *Rough Trade Live*, was recorded direct-to-disc, meaning that it was carefully recorded straight to master tape, no overdubs, resulting in less noise—a clean, precise sound. The band had to be honed, and even though they were, it took a lot of takes for everything to be just right for this unique process. I remember hanging out at the late Ty Scammell's record stall at the Vancouver Flea Market seeing audiophiles from Japan come in specifically to buy that album for its sound quality. *Rough Trade Live* has atmosphere. It's an energetic and soulful groover. No Prog. Soul. Theatrical, too. It reminds me musically and otherwise of Jobriath—not intentionally, also audaciously, with Pope's voice in a category with Shirley Bassey's. But Rough Trade are doing their own thing. Distinctive. Singing with a full voice, purposefully lingering on a word or two with intent. She sings absolutely everything with conviction. Often with candor. Provocative, sultry, and autonomous.

The opener, "Birds of a Feather," is an anthem for the ages. With a chorus about flocking together, the verses surprise with lyrics like, "Come into my cage—I mean, my room." It's not just recorded perfectly, it is perfect. So much so that in 1978 Tim Curry of *Rocky Horror Show* fame recorded it for his first solo album, *Read My Lips,* produced by Bob Ezrin, who had worked with Alice Cooper, Lou Reed (*Berlin*), and KISS (*The Elder*). Ezrin had known Pope and Staples prior to Rough Trade, and all were trying to get an album going together. It was Ezrin who suggested "Birds of a Feather" to Curry, as well as their song "Grade B Movie," which he also recorded. The latter sadly remains unreleased—a shame, as it is a perfect choice, being so torrid and torchy and tongue-in-cheek. But he renders "Birds of a Feather" with gusto. Like "Don't Dream It, Be It," it is a mandate. Staples reveals that Curry was not the first choice: "Originally Bob oddly was going to get Dr. John to do 'Birds of a Feather,' but Dr. John couldn't sing all the words, it was too many words for him. Because Dr. John is kind of a simplistic song singer, right? And there were just far too many words. I mean, that song is nothing but words just coming at you anyway." Thank goodness that didn't happen because we don't want to miss a thing. Staples adds, "Tim is just a wonderful, wonderful guy and a great performer. And he and Carole became really good friends." Rough Trade and Curry even played a show together. Pope says, "Tim is very sweet and intelligent. He was great to work with and a font of fabulous gossip. I got to sit in on a session he did at the old Columbia studios with a full orchestra."

This first Rough Trade album was a one-off. The band did not have a record deal, yet there were numerous TV appearances, including more than one spot on the CBC-TV show *90 Minutes Live*. The show name was later changed to *Canada After Dark,*[9] a more adult-sounding reference to what is often thought of as the country that always sleeps, it probably got some laughs at the network's planning committee meeting then silence, then a shrug and greenlit

---

9 Though, as my co-worker at the warehouse has noted, "After dark? Isn't that just sunrise?"

before the lights went dim. *90 Minutes Live* was hosted by Peter Gzowski, better known and suited for radio, folksy with his salt-and-pepper beard just full enough to show a chuckle or two. But if Canada ever needed anyone after dark to guide them along, it was Rough Trade, upsetting warm glasses of milk across the land's nightstands. Canada is a very repressed nation and Rough Trade was the tingling balm. For their first appearance, they performed "Dyke by Default," an unreleased song that Pope sang with Jo-Ann Brooks, who was with the band for three years and is all over the first album. With this number, they simultaneously list and take down clichés and stereotypes, then make another list of famous people, including Tallulah Bankhead, Gertrude Stein, and Lauren Bacall.

Between the two Gzowski appearances, the viewer sees a fashion transformation with the band—looking great each time, but with a different vibe. The first has them dressed in vintage '30s and '40s, most likely from the shop Amelia Earhart, befitting the names dropped in "Dyke by Default." With the next appearance, they're sleeker, more befitting their band name. Pope and Staples are dressed all in black, harkening bondage overtones and punk foreshadowings. Pope kindly gave Gzowski a t-shirt that said 'FETISH.' She explains, "The FETISH was designed by General Idea. We were all into S&M. I wish I still had mine." One can envision this host sheepishly trying it on under his corduroy blazer.

Rough Trade did get plenty of press attention. Reviewing a show in a 1975 issue of the very Canadian news magazine *Maclean's,* Marci McDonald describes the crowd: "Out in the darkened depths of the nightclub, teen glitter queens were living out the lyrics. They slid their arms tighter around the girls they danced with, pelvis to pelvis. The Happy Hooker herself[10] took up the message, clutched a slim hipped guy to her, locked her lips to his in a solid five-minute star turn of her own. The entire hermaphroditic hip underground was there for the occasion, but there were straights too jamming the doorways, beckoned by a word-of-mouth blitz and the posters outside promising a band called Rough Trade ('Repulsive yet fascinating'). And when they weren't hanging on each other, they were hanging on lead singer Carole Pope's every word."

Though aired on national television, such songs as "Dyke by Default" made the record companies balk. Staples elaborates: "I mean, we couldn't—literally couldn't—get anybody to sign us. And we were already a top act in Toronto. I think it was a hard thing to sell for sure. Nobody knew what to do with it. And I don't blame them but, at the same time, it's like, wow. Sometimes I think in hindsight that if we'd been in London, England, or New York City we might have had a better chance of climbing out of that." And, being so urbane, there weren't a lot of places for Rough Trade to live in Canada. "We weren't really confident that we would do well in the rural community with what we were doing. So, we tended to stay in the city and really just developed an audience that was supportive enough that made it viable for us to play. They followed us around wherever we went in the city, which was great."

---

10 Xaviera Hollander, a.k.a. the Happy Hooker, was living in Toronto at the time, making a fascinatingly unwatchable movie, *My Pleasure Is My Business.*

Here's a little tidbit about the British label and shop also named Rough Trade, highly regarded for its smart roster of punk and post-punk, founded by Geoff Travis in 1978 and flourishing today. No less a reliable source than the Toronto publisher and music critic Robert Charles-Dunne was told by Travis that on a visit to Toronto he saw a poster advertising a Rough Trade show at the Gasworks (or perhaps the show itself—sources are reliable, but memories are hazy). Travis subsequently nicked the name for his label upon his return from the colonies. So there.

"We were more like a cabaret act because there's so much at play with a Rough Trade show that has to do with humor and theater," says Staples. And that most certainly is in keeping with some of the acts they played with, including a show with the drag queen Momma Cooper in the Meat Market, the basement venue of the Colonial Tavern. Martin Short had a disastrous stand-up comedy set opening for Rough Trade, starting and finishing that element of his notable career. The Clichettes (Louise Garfield, Johanna Householder, and Janice Hladki), a feminist performance art collective, would often open, doing elaborate high-concept lip-synchs (they won the 1984 National Lip-Sync Championships in Houston, Texas), involving choreography and costumes. Rough Trade also took part in a key General Idea event doing the music for the Miss General Idea 1984 pageant, which, as General Idea was often wont to do, did not take place in 1984.

Rough Trade made music for people looking for something new that wasn't "bro rock." Both Staples and Pope loved musicals. And Cole Porter. Staples elaborates: "It's the city. Urban, gay, social, glamorous. That's been around for a long time—nobody invented that recently. And you're just a voice for that culture. That was our connection with Divine, too, because Carole and I would go to New York and then we'd go and see Divine on stage doing these crazy women behind bars and these crazy shows, plays—they're not musicals, they're plays—and they were off off off Broadway and they were hysterical and fantastic. It's like Charles Ludlam and the Theater of the Ridiculous. Those influences were there—those were the things that we loved. And even here in Toronto that was our crowd. And that's all about glamor. I mean, drag—it's very glamorous."

Women Behind Bars was a live theater parody of '50s women-in-prison movies, starring Divine as the matron (a necessary requirement of the genre) and directed by Ron Link; it was so successful that it ran for a year in New York. In 1977, Rough Trade created their own musical, *Restless Underwear*, and brought Link and Divine along for the ride, first renting and then packing Massey Hall. When it came to drag, Divine was a game-changer, total next level, moving beyond conventions such as body types and, well, beyond everything else really. Pope wrote the script for *Restless Underwear* with her sister Elaine, who later won a comedy writing Emmy for *Seinfeld*. When I asked Pope about the script, she replied, "It was trashy cabaret. Elaine and I wrote a series of skits for Divine and I. One was Truck-Stop Girl, another was about a lesbian tenement. Very 1950 noir craziness. Oh, there was one about a singer named Crass Elliot who was based on the wonderful Cass." Of the show, Staples notes, "We just did it for one night on a shoestring budget and I think the reviews of the show are less than favorable but the audience and we had fun, so it doesn't matter, right?" Many of the songs, including "Lipstick on Your Dipstick," which Rough Trade had already been performing for a couple of years, went unrecorded. Not long after that, Divine started recording pivotal dancefloor sides with the producer Bobby Orlando. "Divi really was so fun to be with," Staples recalls fondly.

Three years later, they revived *Restless Underwear* in New York and it was disastrous. The poster made it appear to be a Divine show when, in actuality, Divine performed just a handful of songs this time around. Plus, a poor sound system made the audience's booing more audible than the production itself. Staples candidly admits, "They expected a full Divine show with a band and they got a band with Divine, so it didn't go over very well and it was sold out. It was unfortunate to have two thousand people booing at you, but it was a very good learning experience. So that was the end of that show. We had visions of taking it on the road but they didn't pan out."

Much was happening already, though—so many triumphs. Even very early on, Rough Trade had headlined El Mocambo. They had the opening slot for Roxy Music at Massey Hall in the '70s and later on for David Bowie on the Canadian leg of his massive 1983 *Serious Moonlight* tour: these musical artists embodied, transcended, and moved beyond Glam—as did Rough Trade. Lou Reed was a fan; two of their members even toured with him. Rough Trade was a band that moved forward. As well, they wrote and recorded the hard-driving "Shakedown" for the controversial 1980 movie *Cruising*.

The Junos were (hmm, I guess they still are) a Canadian award show for the music industry—more industry than music, aimed at glad-handing the troubling egos of Bruce Allen and David Foster and their like-minded list of Rolodex contacts. Pope states, "We were asked to perform 'High School' on the Junos. We had a friend, the late great Sparkle, dress up in drag and sashay around the stage. They asked me not to grab my crotch … I did. It was live TV and I knew they couldn't stop me. I loved our look. Leather and eyeliner on everyone. I miss the days when straight men wore makeup and eyeliner. Super sexy." The future number-one hit "High School Confidential" hadn't even been released yet; that crotch gesture strategically happened on the lyric "she makes me cream my jeans," and this provocative performance on national TV worked wonders. Staples explains, "That was when Bernie must have decided that, 'I better sign these people because nobody else is.'" With the ink barely dried, their album *Avoid Freud* was released on Bernie Finkelstein's large independent label True North Records, with distribution by CBS. The Junos appearance was in April of 1980, and the album was recorded and released the same year.

Rough Trade appeared on *SCTV,* the greatest television show of all time, with their talented friends in the cast playing preteen characters to perfection during the "Pre-Teen World" segment, asking Rough Trade awkward questions including "How late are you allowed to stay up at night?" During their performance of "High School Confidential,"

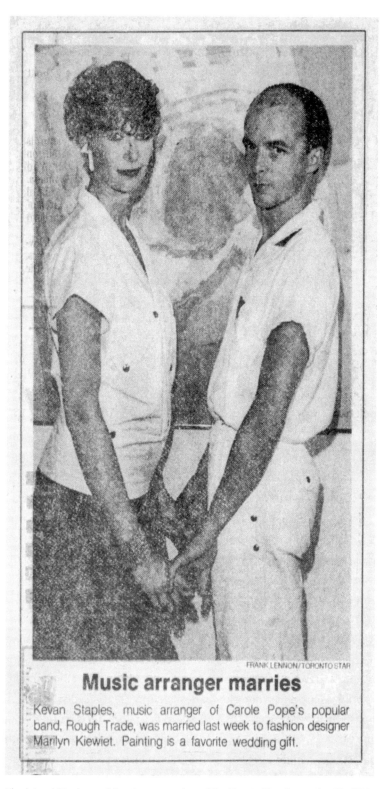

Kiewiet and Staples wedding. Image courtesy of the *Toronto Star*, September 12, 1983.

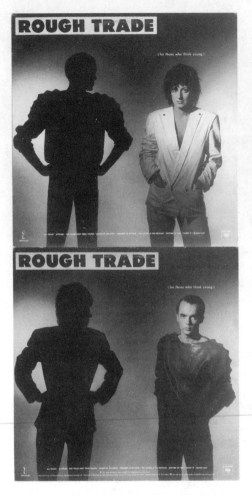

Front and back cover of *For Those Who Think Young* by Rough Trade (True North, 1981). Author's collection.

just one word was bleeped out and that word was "cream." The word was just too creamy. It certainly was pesky; to get airplay, the band had to record an altered "safe" version for CHUM-FM, putting a damper on the entire line.

In "High School Confidential," every line is a *bon mot* cementing it as a gay-bar karaoke staple. This is no mere teahouse tray of pastries—this is a full buffet of *bons mots*! Oh yes, there's much more: the sultry "Lie Back, Let Me Do Everything"; "What's the Furor about the Führer," about how Fascism has a stranglehold on the modern world (true!); "Grade B Movie," an incredible piece of camp melodrama, a perfect album closer with its refrain, "Don't stop Johnny, don't stop Johnny . . . " *Avoid Freud* is at turns candid—provoking an arched eyebrow—and camp. Pent-up struts. Yet ever so sleekly ushering in the '80s with openness.

Much had changed in that long stretch between albums. Besides guitar and piano, Staples added synths. As he told me, "Technology changed, so, for me, I got interested in the technology, and when MIDI first started out in computers and all that it was a natural progression through my interest in buttons and knobs. And again, for Carole and I, it was always about the songs—our whole purpose was just that we were songwriters and the band was a vehicle for that output, so it was always changing—you know, what are we going to do for the next song? What can we do? And we wanted to pick and choose from everywhere. We liked '30s cabaret music, but we also like musicals and we like hard rock and we like funk, and so our songwriting was all over the place. We were not very consistent in our songwriting because we were pulling from so many different sources."

Avoid Freud's black-and-white sleeve, designed by General Idea, was stunningly refined: dramatically lit portraits of Pope on one side, Staples on the other. Pope explains, "We were in awe of GI and big fans of their Dada aesthetic. The album covers they created for us were works of art and I can't believe they haven't been part of any General Idea show. I loved Jorge Zontal, who photographed us and really captured our essence." It also reflected their changing interest in fashion. "I was a starving artist and vintage was affordable, but I loved leather, and when we started making some money I got into that. We were huge fans of Claude Montana and Thierry Mugler. On our first trip to Paris we got to rummage through a box of leather jackets in Claude Montana's warehouse while he looked on a little disdainfully. The jackets we wore on the *Avoid Freud* album were by Thierry Mugler. We got them at the Room in Simpsons. That was the best store in Toronto for avant-garde [style] '80s designer [clothing]. We'd wait until stuff went on sale and grab it." The song "Fashion Victim" fit perfectly—name-dropping designer labels, casually throwing them off like nobody's business. When asked about Mugler, Pope says, "Kevan and I both loved his work. The sharp lines, the beautifully tailored suits. I loved how his creations were powerful. I met him in the '90s. He came to one of my gigs in L.A. with Iman. I yelled at him from the stage, saying, 'I wore your suit on one of my album covers!'" Alas, Pope no longer owns the Mugler: "Sadly, I did a designer purge which I was sorry for after the fact."

My friend Madge has been deeply inspired by Pope, stating that her fashion and style contribute to the idea of a powerful woman and not being confined to a certain type. I asked Pope, on behalf of Madge, about the power that comes with owning your sexuality versus flaunting it, and she responded, "I don't know, I'm just me. I'm secure with myself and my image and really don't give a fuck. I think it's a lot of work to flaunt your sexuality and it really should be effortless. I wish I could afford to wear Rick Owens clothing because to me that's the next level. Brutalist chic."

Rough Trade also wore very striking custom-made outfits. These were designed by Marilyn Kiewiet. Originally from Detroit, Kiewiet moved to Toronto after working in fashion in Amsterdam. She was soon working for Sandy Stagg at Amelia Earhart repairing, redesigning, and repurposing elegant and unique items of vintage clothing. This shop was a hub for artist types who were her kind of people, really. She then started a successful line of loosely worn, patterned knitwear called Blitz that was sold for several years across North America. Kiewiet and Staples were dating, so it was only natural for her to collaborate with the band on styling. Kiewiet says, "I would be very involved in putting together the look, even creating some of the outfits. Both Kevan and Carole have a very good, strong sense of fashion and they like things that are a bit over the top, daring—pushing the envelope, so to speak. It was always a very creative time to create these looks with them. I would have ideas and I would talk them over with Kevan and Carole or I would get all the Italian and French fashion magazines and we'd go through and see what we thought was cool and the kind of looks we wanted to go through with. It wasn't really in Canada at the time, you couldn't really buy it here, so we made it." On tour in Europe the three of them would hit the stores.

Both Staples and Pope had a preference for leather, be it outfits or jackets, with Kiewiet designing the striking pink leather outfit that Pope wore for the infamous Junos appearance. Certain performances cried out for their outfits to be appropriately outré, like a dare. When they opened for the Tubes, an American act infamous for its stage show, Kiewiet designed something very memorable for Pope. Starting with a pair of pants, Kiewiet recalls, "the bum was just cut out and then a piece of clear vinyl put in. And they were very fitted, obviously." Pope added, "We wanted to look shocking. It was actually chaps. The clear plastic ass would steam up on stage."

Elaborating further on Rough Trade's aesthetics, Kiewiet states, "There was a lot of boundaries being pushed and we often would try to do that with the clothing as well. We did a lot of outfits that were S&M-based, bondage-based outfits. And it was always tongue-in-cheek. But I think a lot of the things that they wore back then underscored what they were also saying in their lyrics. There's a freedom of expression in a sense: don't be ashamed of your sexuality. Don't be ashamed of your body. Don't be ashamed of your sexual preferences. Just be yourself. I think it was pushing boundaries that way, too. I mean, Carole was doing that before Madonna was even born. I think that was another element to what we would come up with for looks." When Staples and Kiewiet married in 1983, Kiewiet wore Mugler and Staples wore Parachute. As Staples put it, "The groom wore white." Pope was best man and wore black.

Rough Trade's third album, *For Those Who Think Young* (1981), was again strikingly designed by Jorge Zontal for General Idea, using spots and silhouettes dynamically highlighting their fashion. Staples' outline is most intriguing: flip the cover over and we get the full, unique effect. Kiewiet had designed him a gray leather suit with silver studded stegosaurus tips running down the three-quarter-length sleeves. She recalls, "I just liked the idea of basically, instead of a suit, kind of a sweatshirt look, a leather sweatshirt. I think that was the starting point. And he looks good in a boat neck, he has a really nice neck, so I wanted to emphasize that."

With Staples as co-producer, the album opens with the phenomenal single "All Touch," simultaneously tense and catchy. "Baptism of Fire" is emotionally hypnotic, the music weaving a spell with "I was choking on cheap cuisine with this traitor turn tricks in latrines, I was screaming about my lifestyle, say they want to kick you like the underdog" as just one choice smattering of the smart lyrics. Dusty Springfield sang backing vocals on the album. Rough Trade would also write and produce the vulnerable closing ballad "Soft Core" for Springfield's 1982 album *White Heat*, her voice accompanied by Staples on grand piano.

Rough Trade's album *Shaking the Foundations* followed in 1982 with an even darker mood and an even more synth-pop sound, opening with the erotic thriller "Crimes of Passion," a story-song that is both sweaty and bloody. The video acts it out literally with both the straight and the gay couples from each verse lit by pulsating swaths of neon red in this bedroom melodrama. "Endless Night" follows with lyrics about having to repress being gay in not-so-permissive straight society. The album is not without torrid wit, climaxing with "Fire Down Below" and "Kiss Me Deadly," which contains the amazing line, "You caught me between silicone injections." The iconic Nona Hendryx of the influential American soul-rock (and space Glam) trio Labelle sang back-up vocals for this and the following album. Rough Trade also wrote songs with Hendryx, including the hypnotic single "Transformation" which was featured in the very '80s TV series *Miami Vice* and the 2024 movie *Love Lies Bleeding*. Rough Trade's rhythm section changed midway through recording *Shaking the Foundations*. Two more Rough Trade albums—the diverse *Weapons* and *O Tempora! O Mores!*—followed in 1983 and 1984.

Says Staples, "I think the last album that we did was really a big departure in some ways and that was the least well received record and that for us was, 'Okay, we're done.' We couldn't keep fighting the system anymore. And we couldn't get out of Canada. We couldn't get our records released anywhere else. Both times that we had an American record company involved in releasing our product they went out of business almost as soon as they signed us for whatever reason, and that had nothing to do with our records, but they just were not good companies in the first place. And maybe they were grasping at straws. Who knows? So we had bad luck, I think. And the fact that the press was starting to be kind of nasty, and we just thought, 'We've had our fun, let's get out now and move on.' And in some ways, when I look back now, I think maybe we should have just hung on because I think within a year the whole industry here changed. It was also the beginning of the CD era. It was a lot easier for Canadian acts to get American releases." As a proper send-off, Rough Trade held a series of farewell concerts attended by their numerous fans and friends.

Beginning in the '80s, the horrible tragedies of AIDS hit home with many loved ones dying way too soon. Staples states, "These are the people that you admire, and those are the people that admire you. So unfortunately, so many of these people were lost during the AIDS era, which is sad. I mean, how many friends have we lost from that? Creative people, bright lights?"

Rough Trade were cherished by so many for expressing what other bands did not or could not dare to. They were beloved—they needed to exist, to give much-needed voice at the unique musical intersection of so many shining worlds. After the band broke up, Pope moved to L.A. and made several solo albums. Staples moved into soundtrack, sound design, and audio work for TV and film. Staples concludes, "The whole Rough Trade was just the best time, the time of our lives for both Pope and we were blessed, we were lucky. We had really great fans and we had a really great run and I have no complaints. I just sometimes have regrets that we didn't stick it out. But, you know, the truth is at the time we don't think we could have, we just had enough, we needed a break." Naturally, Rough Trade have done several reunion concerts since. They never really left. Pope is developing a Rough Trade musical. Pope's website states, "It follows the true story of Howard Pope, Carole's real life brother who was a guitarist (indie rock god) and one of the original members of the ACTUP movement who fought to get AIDS drugs released to the people who needed them and raise awareness about the need for research and advocacy. He died of AIDS in 1996 and his story is emblematic of the stories of so many amazing young men who lived, loved, fought for their community and paved the way for LGBTQ+ rights today."

STREET LIFE AND TOBY SWANN

WHAT QUALIFIES? A MID-'70S Toronto band naming themselves after the song that kicks off the third Roxy Music album would most certainly qualify as Canadian Glam. One hundred and a bunch percent. Lots of sax, at that. And, by kicks, Roxy Music gave us plenty with this song, fingers snapping amidst coaxed sounds, a sensuous rocker so obsessively alluring that if one isn't going to produce a child to name after it, then form a band.

Street Life the band is scarcely remembered—even by the band members themselves. Like an ancient blip all gauzy and hazy. There apparently weren't any photos, and they never made any recordings; now we can only have faith in the powers of the mind going back over decades of time. Street Life was formed by Toby Swann and Howard Zephyr, a.k.a. Howard Szafer. I reached Swann somewhere far away and warm. Much as he likes Canada and the people there, Swann is done with the cold. He seemed adrift on a boat when I rang him. Perhaps he was on Antigua in the Lesser Antilles, after playing in bands in a hotel bar in Mexico and with his girlfriend in the beautiful country of Guatemala going up the river to play in a frontier town where "your life was worth about fifty bucks." The phone connection was lousy, but I will strive to do my level best to tell the story properly.

Growing up in Oxford, England, Swann moved to Canada at the age of seventeen, landing first in Montreal, then on to Toronto. He recalls, "I had a job with a carpet company there up in Dufferin and Finch. I could work mornings and then I could go check out music in the afternoons and evenings. It was quite good. In one way, it was very impressive because the bands that were playing in the clubs were a lot more professional than most bands in Toronto. But their ideas—they were just completely, they were like fifteen years in the past. They were really proficient players. They played Doobie Brothers. They were not playing their own stuff." There wasn't much else, save Rough Trade, who were around doing their own thing.

Zephyr came along when Swann needed a roommate. Their rather different musical tastes converged. Explains Swann, "I was more into the Glam. I was very into the kind of Bryan Ferry, Lou Reed, David Bowie type thing at the time. And Howard was more into R&B, jazz. I told him what I was

> Howard Szafer, 15, is doing his studying in a corridor at Toronto's Bathurst Heights Secondary School. The principal banished the honors student from his classroom until the boy gets a haircut. But Howard is determined to let the hair reach shoulder length. He says the long hair has increased his social life.
> —CP Wirephoto

Teenage Howard Szafer grows his hair in 1966. Image courtesy of the *Standard*, October 3, 1966.

into. I said, 'Either way, you can fit in on the saxophone. Take it wherever you want to go with it.' We put together this band. We didn't play too much. We played on the art gallery circuit, like A Space." A Space is one of Canada's oldest artist-run centers and was fully into crossing disciplines outside of the mainstream. Zephyr adds, "A week-long engagement at the Chimney upstairs from the Gasworks is one I recall. A week at Grossman's as well, I think."

Apart from galleries, there wasn't much in the way of venues for original music then, and most of Street Life's songs were originals. The interdisciplinary artist Andrew Paterson recalls them covering "Sea Cruise" and Roxy Music's "Editions of You," because if you're called Street Life you might as well fly close to the source. Roxy Music fans were a loyal but way too small bunch, a crowd so "in" as to be ignored. For example, at the Original 99 Cent Roxy movie theater, Gary Topp would give out copies of the first two Roxy Music albums during screenings and they were always left behind at the end of the night. Shocking, I know. Just the album covers alone—who would turn that down???

Toby Swann. Image courtesy of *The Kingston-Whig Standard*, December 18, 1980.

Zephyr found Patrick Gooding, a drummer fresh from London, Ontario, who had some training from Jim Norman, the rather proficient drummer who was playing in Rough Trade at the time. Says Gooding, "And, even though I'm a rock drummer, I've got a jazz and classical music background. So, it swang. It wasn't just pounding, you know, rigid four-four—it had funk to it. The whole point is to make it swing, so people wanted to move to it."

Most likely forming in 1974, Street Life was a co-ed band: besides the three men, there were two women on bass and piano. Gooding remembers, "The bass player and I played really well together. Liz, the piano player, was a classically trained jazz pianist. What was her last name? She used to play piano with a flautist at the really super expensive hotel in Yorkville—all the movie stars used to stay at the Windsor Arms." Unfortunately, no one can remember the bassist's name or Liz's full name. It can be hazy when some random pops up to ask you about some forty to fifty years ago. If you were in the band, please drop us a line. We would most certainly love to hear from you; we'll add your name in lights somehow.

Gooding describes Zephyr: "We called him 'Howeird.' Howard was a star. He was like the best frontman ever. And he played really good saxophone. He was a very unusual guy and had a great voice. And you know what? He's got a face like Jagger. Howard was a natural-born frontman. He wrote some pretty cool songs. Howard was also a big ladies' man. He drew a lot of ladies out to the scene. You know, he's got those outrageous features, the big lips, and Howard knew how to move on stage. He would keep people entertained. And Toby, all the girls were crazy about Toby and being a guitar player and because he was young and cute. And he's got a baby face, too. Let's face it, when the girls are coming out, it's going to do well, because the girls showing up means the guys are gonna show up."

Much of the songwriting was split between the lead vocalists, Zephyr and Swann, with Liz making some contributions. Says Gooding, "Toby and Howard and Liz had a great sense of melody." Besides each member's own unique influences, together they had synergy—they were tight.

Swann took the Roxy Music love into his stage attire. As he puts it, "I just wore a white tux, Salvation Army, second-hand stores. I liked to wear tuxedoes. It was fun. Especially the old Glam . . . what are they, the old brocades? The Liberace kind of shit. It was fun. Whatever was cool that I could find would be the rags I'd wear. Howie and I, we had a lot of fun with it. Howie got into his flowing garbs. He had a dashing Italian look. Howard's a very unique person, in any case. He just was Howie times ten for the stage." Gooding notes, "Howard could wear anything. Howard was a wild man. And there'd be nobody in the club dressed like Howard on stage. You get these bands and they're wearing what their audience is wearing. But not Howard and not Toby. Toby would look like, you know, the Glam guitar player every eighteen-year-old girl would want to sleep with, and Howard would end up with the strippers. There was only one Howard Zephyr. He was an unbelievably unique performer. He was a true performer." The whole band looked good and they all loved fashion. Gooding would later co-own a vintage clothing store in the '80s.

Playing in the city, the response was usually good. Gooding recalls, "Promoters were looking for another Rough Trade type thing because Rough Trade was doing so well. We were the perfect fill-in band for Rough Trade because we would appeal enough to the Rough Trade crowd that we'd be like a B version of Rough Trade, so we'd keep their crowd coming the next week when Rough Trade was taking a week off. So we started to get very successful. We worked every week at the Yonge Station. We played a lot on the second floor of the Gasworks, upstairs, where Rough Trade played. We were doing the rounds of all the clubs." But Swann notes, "Sometimes if we were out of downtown Toronto playing somewhere, basically the reaction was quite confused. The record companies thought we were a bit too weird, an English sound in Toronto. We didn't get any offers, I'll put it that way. It was a good group."

Gooding left Street Life to join a well-funded progressive rock trio. By early 1976 Swann and Zephyr were the only original members left, now with drummer Imrey de-John, keyboardist Jenny Gitan, and bassist Gord Best. The band split up not long after. Zephyr would later play in the '80s funky post-punk bands Rent Boys Inc. and the Garbagemen.

As for Swann, "There's quite a period after Street Life fell apart I decided I wanted to make a living just playing the guitar. I basically answered any of the 'guitar player wanted' ads. I'd play for anybody who paid me." One country band, Divided Fines, had a country drummer and a reggae bassist from Jamaica. Swann was doing a stint in the Bobby Sky Band, a pub band playing in a dingy bar with a beer-saturated carpet near the mental hospital, when he gave his two weeks' notice to join his girlfriend at the time in India where she was doing doctorate fieldwork studying the Holy Women there. Cut off completely from the Western world living in a monastery, he got a flash of inspiration. He explains, "I knew exactly what I wanted to do and it was put together a really simple, loud, fucking rock 'n' roll band." The band was called Battered Wives. Shocking. Well, the name was. (It really was. People protested.) This lineup didn't last, so Toby formed an entirely new lineup of Battered Wives. The band recorded an album, succumbed to management pressure, and changed their name to the Wives for another album, then changed their name back for a live album.

Robert Charles-Dunne was hired as the publicist for El Mocambo, bringing in an array of bands, including Devo, Blondie, Duran Duran, and the Ramones. Impressed by how well this was doing, the club's owners started a label with him, thinking that this would be a success, too. Charles-Dunne sums it up: "Nightmare." Though they did have an impressive roster with the El Mocambo neon palm-tree sign as the logo—a Toronto landmark.

He continues, "When I was a publicist, but before working with the El Mocambo, I was hired to promote a band called Battered Wives. Decent band, good records (mostly), an engaging live act. I won't go on and on about what a drag that name was, because without that drag I doubt most people would have heard of them. When they splintered, I had started El Mocambo Records and had put out some pretty good records. Toby came by with a demo for some really nice hard poppy songs. I signed him for a solo album, but I don't think any of those songs were on the album I ended up paying for."

That album was the impeccable *Lullabyes in Razorland*. If you ever find yourself in Toronto getting chills from the stony faces in the financial district, located next to the sports district, threatening to consume everything, pull up your wide trenchcoat collar and make haste into the safety of a record shop where you will probably find a gently used copy of this album for a song—it has a lot of songs, actually, and all of them are great! Every single one. Dud-free.

This is absolute Glammy synth-rock: plenty of synths and the band rocks, a perfect melding. Swann remembers, "Back then I was living with a lady named Trish Cullen who was one of the top keyboard session [players] and composers in Toronto. She was writing film scores. And she was doing a lot of sessions as a synthesizer player." Cullen had also done a stint in Rough Trade and co-wrote one of the songs on their first album. The synths are very, very prominent on *Lullabyes in Razorland*. "Yeah, that's her," Swann recalls. "Who else did we have in there? Terry Wilkins was playing bass, I believe." Wilkins, who was in Rough Trade

Back cover of *Lullabyes in Razorland* by Toby Swann (El Mocambo, 1980). Author's collection.

for their *Avoid Freud* and *For Those Who Think Young* albums, also produced *Lullabyes in Razorland*. Cleave Anderson played drums and played them wonderfully.

The keyboards sparkle appropriately for "Diamond World," the opener. The rollicking rock band setting the tone with the instructions, "Rule number one says you GOTTA HAVE FUN" (the printed lyric sheet hammers the point home using all caps). Next is their cover of "Somewhere over the Rainbow" from *The Wizard of Oz*. This is an even more camp song selection than Sparks covering "Do Re Mi" from *The Sound of Music*. The choice is left-field perfection, Toby doing it because "I just liked the song and I was a big fan of Pete Townshend and the Who, his guitar playing. That intro is a big, crunchy guitar chord." With his alluringly exotic British accent, Swann sings it straight, yelling "Dorothy!" in the tornado midsection as Cullen's synths wind round and round then bring up the chorus in an unearthly Sonovox-like voice, Anderson hitting the drums oh so right. Released as a single, the sleeve has a photo of Swann falling past a giant rainbow. CFNY put "Somewhere over the Rainbow" into heavy rotation. It may have also been spun in some gay clubs. Swann notes, "I'd been told that I came very close to getting a deal in the U.S. with that song."

Next up, "Hey Doc" is sung in a side-mouth drawl like Devo on that year's "Whip It," or the way Russell Mael of Sparks later would on "Eaten by the Monster of Love." While visiting a doctor, Swann lists such maladies as "I got lost in a guitar solo, fell off the stage, sure I broke my elbow," eventually working to the chorus of "Hey Doc—I need the medication, not now—right now." Were his pleas answered? In the next song, a jaunty one, Swann talks to the moon: "Hello, moon, do you feel like rocking tonight?" And the moon talks back. They duet. "We'll show them flash, we'll show them style." Side one closes with the title track, coiled, more drum fills, driving, with an air of menace—not just having a laugh. The best relief is to listen to side two. Troubling bubbles come up, a song about working-class drudgery: "I sell my days but the night is my time to share with . . . secret friends." Personal power in a private land, sweet release and comfort, changing work clothes into "colors so bright they startle the eye . . . urban superstar." And then into "Magic," which is exactly that, attainably so: "It's magic!" he screams excitedly. Listening to the rest, this album just never falters nor misfires. I just want more please. He yells, "No more!" and that's it, album over.

Released in 1980, Toby Swann notes, "I thought it was a good record. Maybe it was a little too soon. Maybe it was in the wrong time. I don't know." Charles-Dunne states, "But without a touring act helping to promote it, the LP sank with little fanfare."

The March 1981 episode of the CITY-TV show *The New Music*—a very Canadian newwave episode with Blue Peter, the Sharks, and Drastic Measures—opens with Swann in concert performing songs from *Lullabyes in Razorland*. He gives a terrifically sweaty, half-buttoned-tux-shirt performance. Cullen is on keys in a red leather jacket. On "You're Wrong," eyes agog, Swann does a call-and-response "Yes, it is!" "No, it isn't!" "Yes, it is!" with the two back-up singers smartly dressed in khaki-coloured military-style garb hearkening back to the back-up singers on that 1975 Roxy Music tour.

Swann accidentally wound up playing on the greatest animated rock movie ever made, *Rock & Rule* (1983), for the epic finale with Cheap Trick and Blondie. Cullen wrote the score and Swann played on the demo in Toronto. The demo was a success. Going off of that, Blondie recorded their parts in New York and Cheap Trick recorded theirs in Chicago. Swann recalls, "And they couldn't get a certain guitar phrase. They were here for three hours. I wasn't supposed to be playing on it at all. Trish was down in New York and I was up in our place in Toronto. The phone went off and it was, 'I've got tickets for you down at the airport, come down and help us.'"

Swann did record another album, with a band called Gamma Gamma backing him up. For this album, Jan Haust put him in the studio with Chris Spedding. Listing all of

Spedding's accomplishments is an impossible task, but, besides a long career playing in numerous bands and solo—including his Glam single "Motor Bikin'"—he played on pivotal albums by John Cale, Harry Nilsson, Bryan Ferry, Brian Eno, etc., etc., etc. Spedding came up from New York to produce. Swann recalls, "He'd come up with ideas for guitar lines. He's a really interesting guy. It's pretty good." The album was never released.

DISHES/DRASTIC MEASURES

WHAT IS INCREDIBLE? The Dishes' televised concert on the TVOntario program *Nightmusic* is incredible. Well-coiffed, soft-colored outfits, sleeveless tops in salmons and pinks and yellows, chic with clasps—oh, this one looks like a Marilyn Kiewiet design. Some of the other clothing was vintage, clearly selected and mixed together with discerning eyes, pushing it all fashion forward in time. Saxophone and keyboards to the fore. Drummer dressed loosely—but not too loosely—in Union Jacks announcing "A Tale of Two Plates," saying the inspiration was Charles Dickens and *Ladies' Home Journal*. The unique singer out front, nasal warbling, "You're so clean, I can see myself in you"—blue mascara, mic-clutching with conviction, swaying his hips. Bowl-cut bassist in form-fitting fatigues announcing the song he wrote titled "Chef's Surprise," about what happens when a Parisian chef gets fired. It is suitably dramatic. One verse is sung in French. The guitarist is quiet in shades wearing black criss-crosses on an otherwise pristine white dress shirt. Who are these guys? I love them. Then another song by the bassist, "Beginning with Breakfast," with its Roxy Music–style intro and synth fader play, altogether more ramshackle than Roxy—no no, not all their songs are food-themed, ha. But they are a frenzy of flavors, each song presented like a fresh course. The audience is dressed: a Hawaiian shirt, a sailor suit, a bottle blond in leopard print—farther back is more casual, the curious. Thanks to technology, years later, a sum total of eight of these TVOntario concert clips were uploaded to the Dishes' YouTube channel for people to watch at their own leisure. This special originally aired across the entire province and was replayed numerous times, back when TVOntario used to program exciting new, regional music.

Similarly, the beginnings of the Dishes were made with a cathode connection. Regional television, particularly public access television, put technology into the hands of the people. Anyone could come into the channel's studio to do a show about practically anything—you name it: cooking, current affairs, staring directly at the camera for thirty minutes, gardening, frothy religious rants—it was all rather egalitarian and flourished from the '70s on into the '90s and beyond. I would exclaim that the Dishes are my favorite Toronto band, but someone out there may tut-tut me and tell me that they weren't exactly from Toronto.

Thornhill is a suburb touching just north of Toronto. Every Friday night, young Tony Malone would watch and call in to a cable TV show featuring a DJ spinning records and

Early Dishes ad in *FILE Magazine*. Image courtesy of *FILE Magazine,* Spring, 1976.

cutting jokes, broadcasting live from a small Richmond Hill station transmitting at least as far as Malone's television set in Thornhill, the next suburb over. That DJ was Steven Davey, and he and Malone lived just a few blocks away from each other. Soon Malone started guesting on Davey's show, leading to a show of his very own. Being a few years older, Davey eventually moved from the family home to downtown Toronto. Malone met another musician named Scott at his high school who, as it turned out, was Davey's younger brother—what a small, interconnected Thornhill world. Scott Davey and Malone started playing music together in 1974. Applying for university, Scott wasn't sure if his schedule would allow for a band. Malone says, "I got him to promise that if he didn't get accepted we would have a band. Apparently, his application got sent to the wrong place and then it got there too late and so he missed his opportunity to get in. So I got him for a band. Heh heh."

Tony explains that Murray Ball really wanted to join the band as singer, but Scott was initially against it: "Scott wanted him and me to be able to sing the songs we wrote. And he didn't want a singer there, but I pushed for it. After a little while I convinced myself that Murray's voice and presence would be just weird enough: I could direct it, if I could keep it in the weird territory . . . " They made the right choice: Murray was dynamic and unique.

One day Malone walked into the high school band room and saw Michael LaCroix—they'd known each other since childhood—with a saxophone. Wheels turned. LaCroix says, "Fall of 1975 (I believe), I got a call from friends from high school (Tony and Murray) who were forming a band. They wanted me to play sax. I was working as a farmhand on a sheep farm, and rock and roll seemed a better idea. So I came back to Thornhill." Why sax? LaCroix explains: "We were all big fans of Roxy Music, therefore the sax." Besides Roxy Music, there was also a profound love of Sparks along with the earlier twee British group the Idle Race.

Malone says, "Scott was the songwriter, basically, and I was just starting to write songs. I was nowhere near as good as Scott yet, but my arrangements really inspired him, my ideas of where a song should go. So we were collaborating in that sense. And Mike just loved it. He just loved having someone to play with. He's one of those guys who's totally positive—if you bring him into a project, he's just so into it, he loves it. And he brings in all that energy that makes you want to go even further."

After hearing a tape that Steven Davey had made with Martha Johnson (later of Martha and the Muffins), Malone convinced him to be the drummer, though he notes that Steven tellingly replied at first, "Oh, but I'm not a drummer. I'd rather be the band's manager." No matter—he was in. They then asked their close friend Ken Farr, a guitarist, to learn bass, which he did and became quite skilled at it. They had a coy band name—the Dishes—and a motto to go with it: "Already a household word."

There wasn't much happening in Thornhill. Much the same could be said of Toronto. Steven had been making connections downtown and booked the Dishes' first show at an unknown loft in late 1975. One of the very few—if any—regular venues for original music was the Beverley; well, the Dishes pretty much made it a venue for original music, located near the

Ontario College of Art (OCA) where the art students dwelled. Attendance was so sparse that one night they had an audience of one: their friend John Corbett. Malone says, "He watched the entire three sets. Loved it, applauded after every song." Consistency helped build a following. Malone notes, "1976, by the end of that year, we were packing the place. Every time we played, every night, it was overflowing, full, people on the stairs, people standing. We had the most interesting audience. One night there were a bunch of bikers at one table and a bunch of really gay guys at another table and a bunch of people from OCA at another table and it just was so interesting the kind of people that we're all bringing down to see our band and it made the whole thing more colorful." Members of the Dishes would also go see Rough Trade—both bands overlapping numerous scenes—and vice versa, even playing on bills together. Soon, other bands began to spring up and play the Beverley, including Flivva and Martha and the Muffins, who also used synths and sax, albeit in a more new-wave manner.

Malone played his final show with the Dishes in February 1977. LaCroix says, "It was Tony's band, his concept, his ambition—he pulled it all together and wrote the first songs. He left because he felt he had lost creative control, and he had, to some degree. Steven had assumed control of our image and management, using his contacts in the art and music community. At the time he was a journalist writing about music; he had a lot of contacts and he lived downtown. The rest of us were much younger and still living at our parents' homes in Thornhill. Tony and Scott were co-writing, which wasn't a problem, but the friction between Tony and Steven was unresolved and led to Tony leaving. I would have preferred Tony stay. His arrangements gave us our peculiar sound. We became more mainstream after he left."

The new keyboardist, Glenn Schellenberg, affirms this, saying, "There were two songwriters. Scott was poppier. Tony was kinda crazier. I don't know. Tony wanted to call the shots. He's extremely talented." Schellenberg was already a Dishes fan before he joined, always seeing their shows at the Beverley. Plus, he conveniently lived just around the corner. He explained, "I went to the same high school as Scott and Murray and Tony, just two or three grades after them. Everyone knew I played piano because I was taking classical lessons." Malone says, "I just wanted out, because we were fighting too much. I left them in the best possible shape I could and I even found them a new keyboard player two months before I told them I was leaving."

In fact, Malone still went to their shows, including one pivotal show at the Crash and Burn in June. Malone had already formed and then broke up a band called the Streets after just one show—a dry run really—when How'rd Pope approached him. Pope was the little brother of Carole Pope of Rough Trade and a fan of the Dishes. Malone says, "We hit it off right away. He was surprised that I was at a Dishes gig and cheering for them. But they were actually putting on an excellent show. They sounded absolutely fantastic. And they were playing really well. And I was glad that they had been able to pull it together without me, but they still fought constantly and eventually broke up because of it. So I was right

The Dishes in the *Toronto Star.* Image courtesy of the *Toronto Star*, April 16, 1977.

about that. But anyway, that's how I met How'rd. I said, 'Well, I need a new band, man, want to play?'" Pope responded with, "Absolutely." The new band, Drastic Measures, was formed then and there and were playing shows by the end of the year.

The Dishes wrote the song "Summer Reaction (Crash & Burn)" about that place and time and said as such in the intro to their TVOntario performance of it on August 30, 1977. When I exclaimed to Schellenberg how unfortunate it was that the Dishes hadn't released an album, he replied, "The TVO thing was like that." A video album—how very forward thinking.

The TVO special had a smoother sound than their first single, which they recorded and paid for themselves, again helping to pave the way for the more DIY sensibilities of the soon-to-come Toronto punk singles. When I told Schellenberg how they really kicked the doors open, he says, "Murray's voice is really a challenge. Steven was hopeless on drums: if you listen, the kick is never on the downbeat, it's always on two-four—he didn't know how to play the drums." I prefer to use the word "charming." Schellenberg continues, "The weird thing was that punk came along, then we got assimilated a little bit because it made more sense than anything else, but actually we were Glam."

That first single—really a 7-inch EP of sorts, titled *Fashion Plates,* released in 1977—is such a delightful cacophony—everything rubbing against everything else like petting multiple candy-colored cats the wrong way—but no one minds; it's working, it's carbonated! Glorious melody lines spring out, pushing the smart, smart lyrics along. Hammered keys and sax ever present—wails, squeals, and skronk. Opening with the swoony "Monopolies Are Made at Night," then the warm companionship of CB radio culture with "Walky-

Talky." "Police Band" has TV-cop-show chase-theme runs on the keys, flowing effortlessly into an ode to Fred Victor's Mission near the Beverley, "I wonder what is in this food … oh, whoa, somehow it doesn't taste religious."

The sleeve for *Fashion Plates* looks like a lost Bonzo Dog Band photo shoot, all of them dressed in costumes related to occupations: parking attendant, surgeon, uhhhh . . . other jobs that people work at. The art direction was by the late, great artist David Buchan, described by Schellenberg as "kind of like the fourth member of General Idea." Extending beyond the sleeve, LaCroix notes, "David Buchan was trying to coordinate a fashion look for us, but organizing a band is like herding cats." That same year in May, the Dishes did a full set for Buchan's Toronto performance of his *Geek/Chic* show in the lavish Crystal Ballroom at the King Edward Hotel, which combined Buchan's extensive interest in fashion with his art practice.

Members of the Dishes later took part in Buchan's *LaMonte del Monte's Fruit Cocktails*, a video variety show featuring the debut of Buchan's character LaMonte del Monte, named after the chief manufacturer of fruit cocktail canned preserves in thick syrup; Buchan would later expand and extend this character into an entire family tree casting familiar faces from the scene. Also noteworthy was the Clichettes' much-raved-about performance of "You Don't Own Me." Like something from a floor show below New York's Club 57, *Fruit Cocktails* was co-written by Steven Davey, who looked curiously identical to the show's emcee, Red Sublime. So much brightly colored artifice in the air. Del Monte wore a bright day-glo orange ensemble designed by Marilyn Kiewiet. She also designed Murray Ball's outfit—the same as his TVO apparel—as he lip-synched to "Privilege" surrounded by adoring fans crouched on the floor.

Much of the Dishes' clothing was purchased at a jam-packed Queen Street store run by an elderly Polish man. LaCroix explains, "He had had a fire at one point and had water and smoke damage. Rather than clean out the damaged stock, he put up new racks in front of the old stock and hung new stuff. I discovered that if you burrowed in deep, there was all kinds of good stuff, vintage stuff from the '50s, which I loaded up on. I made the mistake of telling GI [General Idea] and they cleaned the place out. Their (and my) fabulous '50s look came from that store. The Sally Anne [Canadian slang for Salvation Army thrift stores] was also good for '50s vintage stuff too. I bought a spectacular orange suit and cashmere overcoats there. I also invented my favorite outfit, my 'patient wakes up mid surgery and runs away from hospital trailing tubes and scalpels' outfit, which had a large piece of liver in a pocket on my chest. 'Schism now' shirt was also mine."

The Dishes left the province for the one and only time in October of 1977. It wasn't so much a tour as a direct flight for General Idea's *Hot Property* art event at the Winnipeg Art Gallery. Schellenberg says, "It was Steven's first flight. I sat beside him on the plane. Steven was saying, 'What's that? What's that?' Steven—for all his worldliness and cosmopolitan charm, I don't think he ever left downtown Toronto. He was totally nervous on the flight."

This particular event was one of the art series of audience rehearsals that General Idea did for the 1984 Miss General Idea Pageant (an earlier audience rehearsal in Toronto had Rough Trade provide the music), conceived as an audience fire drill for when the 1984 Miss General Idea Pavilion would burn down. This pavilion was never built, but its conception and destruction were elaborately planned. With copious government grant dollars to spare, General Idea jet-setted the Dishes out to perform just one song and one song only with the event's name, "Hot Property," as its title, opening with the lyrics, "Gee, it's hot in here, is it me?" One tour, one show, one song. The art for their subsequent seven-inch *Hot Property*, from 1978, was by General Idea, black and white and red all over, abstract flames surround a newspaper headline. It's an art object, but let's not get precious—this is a semi-permanent guest for the turntable, playing over and over and over again, never wearing out its welcome.

With this second 45, some of the harsh edges get ironed and pressed and folded but not too much—it's a look, it's a choice, it's top notch. Piano sounds got switched out for synth. All of the songs are by Scott Davey, including the perfect theme "Summer Reaction (Crash & Burn)" with its resonant chords chiming in at the get go.

In many ways, General Idea presented themselves as a band with hyper-glossy images of the three members, even writing in the Summer 1978 issue of their own *FILE Magazine*, "We posed for photos that could grace album covers." Ball and LaCroix would often meet Felix Partz of General Idea for beers at the Parkside; Ball had done not only modelling for GI's *S/HE* series of photos but also renovation work on their loft. The Dishes did appear in the pages of *FILE Magazine* early on in an ad from the Spring 1976 issue, still with Malone, all looking sharp, billed as "the nation's newest hit-makers," and later in the 1977 "Punk" issue, which featured a *fumetti*[11] shoot (akin to the ones in New York's *Punk* magazine) conceived by Steven Davey and Buchan. Titled "I Love Lucasta," this *I Love Lucy* parody with the Dishes bursting in featured Lucasta Rochas from the 'B' Girls and Ball, with an appearance by Buchan and Anya Varda, head of the Dishes Fun Club. Of that fan—er, fun—club, Schellenberg notes, "Steven's just making stuff up," but did say that the glamorous Varda often participated on stage in Dishes shows, holding up a "NO!" sign during their song "Farrah No!"

For the Hot Property era, the Dishes switched to wearing red and black outfits. When they opened for Talking Heads, Schellenberg recalls that Tina Weymouth told them, "Oh, I like the waiter outfits."

The Dishes had great wit. Although all of the songs on the seven-inches were by Scott Davey (apart from a co-write with the third Davey brother, Mark), some of the other members contributed. Farr's songs from the TVO special were strong and clever, a real delight, with Malone and Scott Davey's "Ghidra" as the perfect closer, embodying the carnage he hath wrought, a monster movie, flames added in post. LaCroix noted that the Dishes' songs

---

11 Comics done with photos.

Sleeve of *Fashion Plates* seven-inch by the Dishes (Regular Records, 1977). Author's collection.

were "packed with puns"—indeed, one of Malone and Scott Davey's unreleased songs was titled "I Might as Well Be, Marcus Welby."

Unlike his younger brother Scott, Steven Davey didn't really have very many songs being played in the Dishes. John Catto of the Diodes remembers Steven Davey coming to one of their first rehearsals in late 1976, going, "Hey, I've got a song for you." Catto recalls that Davey also offered up career advice, saying, "And you should do this, you shouldn't do this." Catto adds, "I swear," and notes that Davey did the same thing a month later with the punk band the Viletones. He made a bit more headway with them writing "Rebel Unorthodox" for the Viletones' first single—although the band, who came off as more of a punk parody, did dumb it down for their own purposes. Catto continues, "And he was doing all of this stuff, he's kind of pushing everybody along, because I think he was sort of going, 'Well, I kind of want something to happen.'"

Of the Dishes, LaCroix says, "We were a band of guys who wanted fame and money. We were never political. As much as we have been called 'Toronto's first gay punk band,' I think it misses the mark. We were a band that had gay guys in it, but that wasn't the point of the band."

Seymour Stein, the co-founder of the major American label Sire Records, was a very important person, having signed the Ramones and Talking Heads, bringing their music to the greater masses. Thanks to Steven Davey, Stein also came to see the Dishes. However, since they weren't playing a show, Stein had to come out and down to Farr's suburban basement in Richmond Hill, where the band rehearsed. Schellenberg says, "I think that he liked it. I think maybe we were too queer or that Murray's singing was irritating or Steven was hopeless on drums. Or maybe he just didn't like it. He knew about us." I had to ask Schellenberg if Stein went to see any other Toronto bands at that time. His answer: "I don't think he went to anybody else's basement."

With that falling through, along with further fighting and less fun, it all sort of dissolved. When I ask Schellenberg why they broke up he remarks, "I can't remember if we ever broke up. We just kind of stopped doing it. Maybe we did break up. I don't know. We tried. The thing that was discouraging was we had a really neat product. Then the Ramones and Sex Pistols and everything started and we weren't really like that and we couldn't actually be like that. We were just in the wrong place at the wrong time and then we got kind of bitter." In 2001, a Dishes CD was released by Bullseye consisting mostly of the material on the vinyl and just the audio of the TVO concert. The members of the Dishes attended the CD release party held at the Beverley Tavern, the very venue from which they had energized into a scene just some years before.

For his next band, the Everglades, Steven Davey made sure not to be stuck behind a drum kit, moving out front to sing his own songs like "Rock 'n' Roll Cliché" with the Flivva guitarist (and future Brian Eno collaborator) Michael Brook totally shredding and with Schellenberg's bouncy keys. Even LaCroix joined for a while. Schellenberg's next band, TBA, was pure electronic pop. TBA were well regarded and got their picture on the cover of the Canadian gay monthly *The Body Politic*. Around that time, Schellenberg joined Martha and the Muffins since Martha Ladly, keyboardist and "second Martha," had left after their hit "Echo Beach": she had flown off to England to join Associates and then briefly Roxy Music, along with a couple of solo singles and an extensive design career. Schellenberg toured extensively with the Muffins for two years and played on their more experimental *This Is the Ice Age* and *Danseparc* albums from 1981 and 1983. He did the soundtrack for John Greyson's 1993 film *Zero Patience*, a musical comedy that addresses and dismantles myths about AIDS. Today Schellenberg is a professor emeritus of psychology at the University of Toronto Mississauga, known for his research on

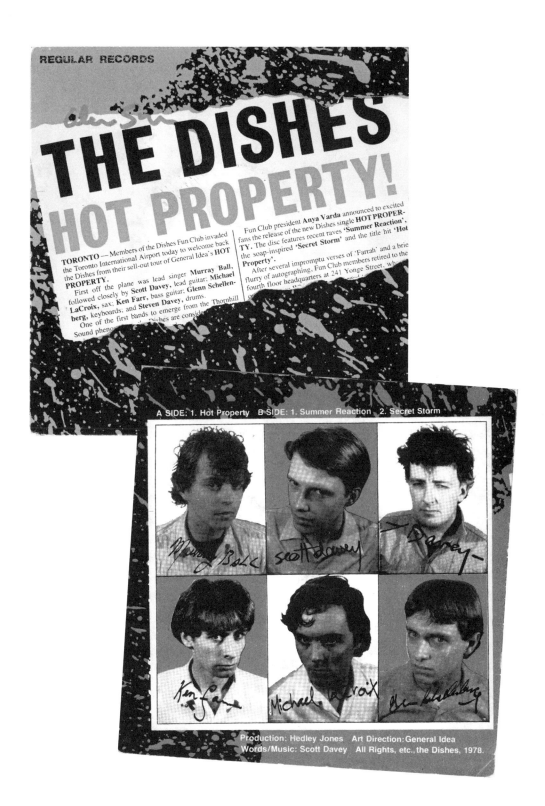

Front and back sleeve of *Hot Property!* seven-inch by the Dishes (Regular Records, 1978). Author's collection.

Front cover and inner sleeve of *Drastic Measures* by Drastic Measures (Columbia Records, 1980). Author's collection.

how music associates with non-musical abilities, basic music cognition, and perception.

LaCroix moved on to film, getting his first job and training through a Dishes fan: "I was there when he needed a last-minute helper. Just a fluke, really." After this job as boom operator on *The Last Chase*, an oddly anti-environmental (pro-car! big cars!) dystopian thriller from 1981 starring Burgess Meredith, LaCroix went on to work on David Cronenberg's *Videodrome*, *The Fly*, and *The Dead Zone* and a lot—quite a lot—more.

Ball was the cook and Scott Davey was a waiter at the hip Peter Pan restaurant, after the influential businesswoman Sandy Stagg and her partners bought it. Ball went on to run the Fiesta restaurant with Stagg, then other venues and clubs after that. Scott Davey moved into publishing. Steven Davey went on to be a well-loved food writer for *Now*, a Toronto free weekly newspaper. He died in 2014.

After the Dishes, Farr became Drastic Measures' bassist. The famed Toronto promoters Gary Topp and Gary Cormier loved Drastic Measures. When the Garys were let go from promoting legendary concerts at the Horseshoe, they put on the Last Pogo and the Last Bound-Up on December 1 and 2, 1978. By the time of the Last Pogo, the confines and dictates of "punk rock" were set well in place. This concert and the carnage that ensued have been well hashed out in a short film, a long film, regional punk books, think pieces, and bar arguments. Drastic Measures performed on the second night, the night that didn't fit, the more musically interesting night of the two, with Rough Trade, the reggae band Ishan People, and the Everglades. The Garys continued to regularly book them at their next venue, the Edge.

It was the Drastic Measures drummer Peter Novak who was friends with Nash the Slash, the mysterious, bandaged maker of avant-moody music treatments, often playing electric violin and looking like the Invisible Man but in fancy dress. Peter played Nash their music and he loved it. They, in turn, were blown away by his music. Malone elaborates, "He came down and we became instant friends. He loved the band. And a lot of it was that, you know, he was gay and really didn't have any gay friends at all and Peter was probably the only one he had, and here he was able to walk into a situation where there were a bunch of gay people and he could just be at ease with himself and I think he really, really enjoyed that. There's a lot of humor, there's a lot of laughter. He called himself Uncle Nash sometimes because he'd have to scold us and he goes, 'Okay, this is Uncle Nash talking now, guys.' He'd have to tell us when we fucked up a gig or when we were sounding like shit or not practicing enough." Nash became Drastic Measures' encouraging mentor. In their first year, he mixed their gigs, lent them his PA for rehearsal, and got them better equipment. Drastic Measures were soon signed to CBS Records . . . Canada.

For their self-titled album cover Drastic Measures favored white tuxedos (rented), pairing well with the tickled ivories. The album opens and closes with piano instrumentals right out of a haunted ballroom. They were occasionally called "Glam Punk," which has scruffier connotations, though their shirts were tucked in. It is far closer to what Malone was doing with the Dishes, just more refined yet still playful, waltzier, and utterly bedazzling. Hurdy-gurdying and bouncy.

Studio experimentation was key. The original drummer had quit twice, with the second drummer quitting in between; they both came back for the album sessions. On some songs, Malone got them to each play their parts, recording and leaving both in, even after the drummers said, "The parts don't line up!"—noticeably so on the song "Silk Stockings," where, along with saxophones acting like happy hornets discovering that they can make sweet honey too, it clashes quite well. Malone says, "I love it because there's so many people. There's so much stuff happening. It sounds huge, and it's fun, exciting, and really what I was going for was this big, orchestral pop band that was made up of lots of guitars and drummers and melodies happening all over the place. It's really a derivative of all the stuff I was listening to and that included Jelly Roll Morton from the '20s, movie music I was listening to from the '30s that I thought was really cool—I studied all the big bands of the '40s—don't like them but I studied their music, and the '50s was really interesting experimentation, like Patti Page doing five vocal harmonies on her records and stuff like that on old 78s, and Les Paul's experiments—all that stuff totally inspired me. So there was no one sound that I really had to reproduce." Plus, he became inspired by the musicians he was working with, bringing those elements into his compositions. A key influence on his vocal style was the close-mic crooners, singing sweetly like Rudy Vallée. "I just took it all as influence and inspiration but never wanted to sound like anybody else." And yet it was modern; it doesn't sound pastiche. Synths, synths, so much synth.

Whirling in stereo action. The song "Hotsy Totsy" has whistling. A disorienting delight.

Nash the Slash suggested they do some covers, convincing Malone that, with such an unfamiliar sound and songs, the audience needed something familiar to latch onto as an entry point. Tony suggested the children's song "The Teddy Bears' Picnic." Nash the Slash laughed: "That's not what I meant." Malone replied, "Well, I just always thought it would be a really cool thing to do for a rock band. My mother used to sing that song to me." Other covers were tried, but their version of Shirley Matthews' Canadian soul classic "Big Town Boy" was the only other one to make the album, complete with hand claps. "Teddy Bears' Picnic" had Malone's triple-track vocal up close and personal, Nash's violin coming in both channels, warm—at times it feels like riding a carousel—it was subversively whimsical, quite a big surprise and utterly disarming, a fantasy from childhood contemporacized, sung gently without irony. And people loved it. It became *the* single, and the free-form radio station CFNY played it plenty. The label originally pressed Drastic Measures' self-titled 1980 album on recycled vinyl (I'd like to think they used returned copies of Lou Reed's *Metal Machine Music* melted down and turned into these merry melodies). After the pressing of five thousand copies sold out, the label showed greater regard and pressed more, this time on new vinyl.

In terms of stage presentation, Malone says, "I learned a lot from Nash for my Drastic Measures decorations. He always taught me that the stage should be a dream place that you take people away to. He said, 'You've got to make it your own. You're not just up there to play some songs, you're there to take them into your own environment, your own space. You should decorate the place like that so that they feel brought into this, like a movie set.' And so, in some places, I would just go into the back rooms of the bar and find anything weird and interesting that I could drag out to the stage just to decorate it with. Sometimes it would be a matter of costumes, like when we did our live broadcast for CFNY: we all played in pyjamas and had teddy bears all over the stage." For another show, Malone bought black and silver balloons while the band wore red. The teenage comedian Mike Myers often opened. For a live CFNY broadcast, the lights came up to reveal Myers standing perfectly attired in sequins and top hat; he then tap-danced, told jokes, and introduced the band with his Don Kirshner impression. Myers' appearance in the Sparks documentary *The Sparks Brothers* shows, in my mind at least, the influence of Drastic Measures—as he has frequently acknowledged—on his teenaged brain and informed his future listening tastes, Sparks being a key influence on Malone's earlier band the Dishes. There's no denying the cross-over appeal. Drastic Measures may not make the algorithms, but if you love Sparks you'll find this band really makes it too.

Drastic Measures went through further lineup fluctuations—a whole new lineup, apart from eternal Malone. The album cover shows two different bands—the main album players Kenneth Farr and How'rd Pope only appearing crunched in an elevator on the inner sleeve, and Peter Novak nowhere to be found. How'rd left and went on to join the Biffs.

With their saxophone, the Biffs had similarities to the Dishes, just more of a herky-jerky sock-hop sound.

In 1981 Nash the Slash's own Cut-Throat Records label released a Drastic Measures single. "Modern Heart" is perky and swoony, with vocal-group harmonies expecting arms outstretched in unison, belying the scrappy, black and white, even punk-looking art.

On the March 1981 episode of the CITY-TV show *The New Music*, Drastic Measures follows Toby Swann—what a one-two punch. Malone with curly mullet in a long tuxedo jacket overtop of a yellow t-shirt, leopard print synth front and center, sounding like a calliope as he sings, "Saucer eyes oh saucer eyes" . . . guitar doing riffs dreamed out of *The Arabian Nights*. Do they perform "Teddy Bears' Picnic"? You bet they do! In the audience, a bespectacled young woman beams, dancing up and down, covering her mouth once she notices that she has been caught by the camera lens. The numbers keep on coming, swiftly speeding in and out.

Their second album, *Wild Boys,* was more stripped down than the previous album (what isn't?) but still strong. It was recorded in 1981 and remains unreleased. They had no management. Labels weren't interested. CBS (Canada) didn't feel like an option anymore due to label politics that went beyond the band. And speaking of stripped down, they even posed for an album cover: all of these young men standing in a rock quarry in attack formations wearing only brightly colored loincloths.

Exhausted, frustrated, and depressed, Malone broke up the band. A couple of years later he reformed it with a new lineup who went the more experimental route, and this lasted a little while. In 1990, he wanted to make a completely new sound, but people insisted it be Drastic Measures, and it didn't last long.

Nash the Slash and Malone provided the atmospheric score to Bruce McDonald's 1991 movie *Highway 61*, a road comedy about a man, a woman, and a drug-filled corpse on their way to New Orleans with Satan on their trail. Their collaboration was released in a small run on Nash's label Cut-Throat and is not to be confused with the movie soundtrack album, which is more Toronto roots rock focused—Toronto got deeper and deeper into roots rock, waning along with the 1980's, wearing on.

The CD *Drastic Measures 1979-92* goes all over the map of pop experimentation and differing lineups. Does it have the hit "Teddy Bears' Picnic"? Yes, it does. Much of the rest contains previously unreleased material, including songs from *Wild Boys*. The CD compilation just gives us a hint of Drastic Measures' recordings; we are told that there is more in the vault. The liner notes, by Nancy Drew of *Teendick Magazine* (sounds legit), state, "Every song here says something interesting, and most of them won't turn you into a devil-worshipper."

The later songs bring Captain Beefheart influences more and more to the fore. This interest led to Malone's much more recent ensemble, Beefheart Project Toronto, which in the last few years undertook learning and recording the complicated, unique works of Captain Beefheart and His Magic Band.

Things can change over time. Malone's next band, Basketcase, alienated many a Drastic Measures fan by having more in common with aggressive sub-genres of metal. For the live experience, he would scream at everyone. This was quite cathartic for him. An album, *You People Are Sick,* came out in 1995. Malone says, "I was actually worried about it for a while because it's a portrait of a preacher who has gone insane; essentially he's become possessed. And he is sexually obsessed with everybody in his congregation. He tells them they're inhabited by the devil and he's got to have sex with them to get the devil out of them. And so, the songs are intentionally disgusting and weird and very dark. My stomach was turned by writing stuff like that. And I listened to the whole thing through recently because I wanted to see how it affected me now. It's been ages since I've listened and, like I said, I was always worried to play it for people because I didn't want them to think I was describing me. I'm taking on the character of this guy but I really didn't want anyone to think that I think this way and so I became a little worried about how the record would affect people." During our interview, Malone was rather eloquent: he moved smoothly from Basketcase into a rather curious tangent stating how there is an international Satanic child-trafficking cabal. Earlier on, he had told me how many of his old friends have distanced themselves from him the past few years due to his extreme political shift from the left. I later went on Tony's Facebook page and saw that his posts were often extreme and deeply unpleasant, of the QAnon variety. It is hard to reconcile this with the astute man I interviewed. Tony Malone died in 2022.

FLIVVA

THE MEMBERS OF THE BAND Flivva did not consider themselves Glam. How dare I defy them? Judging purely on the basis of their record album, the qualifiers and sound are there—I would absolutely place it as Glam. Please don't judge me as obstinate. If I didn't then they wouldn't be in this book and that would most certainly be a shame. Rock theater is in Flivva's very roots. They released a theatrical-sounding album recommended for fans of Armand Schaubroeck, John Cale, *Rocky Horror,* and Be-Bop Deluxe, and—as you shall find out—it has a tangible connection to Brian Eno.

The album art itself, though is devoid of color, stark and enigmatic, black and white, looking like a newspaper. The headline blares, "THE NAME IS SCHREIBMAN" with the album title *SYMPATHETIC EAR* underneath. Bold, all caps. The near-silhouette of a gumshoe walking away from us, past stacks of chairs, a venue in the off hours. This detective persona carried over into the liner notes written in hard-boiled first person, then listing the band members as the "cast of characters." But not so for the live show—there were no theatrics. The band's songwriter, Phillip Schreibman, himself says, "I remember one time we were unloading our equipment at the Beverley. And I was just who I am and wearing a t-shirt. And this guy came by who wanted to see the band and bought the album, and he was horrified that that's who I was, that I wasn't the guy—the private detective with the hat—that I didn't look like that. So, I never looked like that when we played. It was just for the concept of the album." Driving the point home, he offers up an anecdote about one of his influences: "I once did see the Velvets. They came to Toronto in '69. There was something called the Toronto Pop Festival. And they just stood and played. They didn't do anything."

Our story begins at Rochdale College in Toronto, a student-run co-operative, an alternative free college that only lasted a few years before it all fell apart (drugs). But from out of Rochdale's idealism flowered a few still existing institutions. Theatre Passe Muraille was one of them, having been founded there early on, in 1968. Their name translates as "theatre beyond walls": they believed that plays could be staged anywhere. This experimental theater company was founded by the visionary Jim Garrard, who was the artistic director for just a brief period from 1968 to 1969. Later productions featured the very first work of the distinctively Newfoundland comedy group CODCO in 1973. Theatre Passe Muraille's 1975 production *I Love You Baby Blue* was based on the soft-core porn programming that the fledgling network CityTV would air, which also inspired David Cronenberg to make *Videodrome.*

Schreibman grew up in Orillia, Ontario, playing in bands in high school, then relocated to nearby Toronto to attend university, from which he eventually desired an escape hatch. Musical theater provided that opportunity and beckoned him, promising to make proper use of his talents and interests. When Theatre Passe Muraille mounted their very first production, *Tom Paine*, Schreibman was there, composing all of the songs. He speaks glowingly of Garrard, saying, "He was a really wonderful director and mind-screwer-upper." A couple of

Front cover of *The Name Is Schreibman—Sympathetic Ear* by Flivva (Dog Records, 1977). Author's collection.

the songs for *Tom Paine* were also used for Theatre Passe Muraille's next play, *Futz*, about a farmer who falls in love with his pig. Its nudity and themes of bestiality were relatively mild, yet the police morality squad routinely charged them with indecency. Oh, that's bad. However, this gave them loads of media attention and was a boon to ticket sales. Oh, that's good.

Garrard envisioned Theatre Passe Muraille's Summer 1969 production of Jean Genet's *The Maids* as a full evening event to immerse the audience in. Keeping to the context of the material, the theater was transformed into a cabaret bar named the Golden Mink. Waiters clad in gold jockstraps and nothing else took care of the hungry and thirsty attendees who were left with just one place to leave a gratuity. The set and limited edition show poster (featuring the scantily clad characters Mimos, Divine, and Darling—and no show information) were designed by members of General Idea. Foreshadowing Flivva, Schreibman put together a house band called the Lady's Black Glove, with the actors from the play performing, often in drag, the songs that he wrote for them. There were a drummer and guitarist but no bassist: "I think I kind of just did bass with the lower keys of the electric piano. And then the play itself would be put on as the main entertainment of the evening. And I did an underscoring of the entire play, kind of improvised underneath that. I had an electric piano and pedals attached to it."

Schreibman's involvement with Theatre Passe Muraille led to work in London, England, on the 1972 play *Pilk's Madhouse,* by the unorthodox British writer and director Ken Campbell under the pseudonym Henry Pilk. Campbell is simply too expansive for summation. He was heavily involved in the ventriloquism community, wrote and directed science-fiction stage adaptations of the *Illuminatus!* trilogy and *The Hitchhiker's Guide to the Galaxy*, acted in Derek Jarman's film *The Tempest,* and ventured to Canada often. *Pilk's Madhouse* was first presented in Toronto at Passe Muraille, with Schreibman doing the score. Not long after, Andy Jones—later of CODCO—performed it in England at the Royal Court Theatre Upstairs, the same theater where *The Rocky Horror Show* would have its premiere the following year. While there, Schreibman was able to play a few solo music shows. In 1973 he returned to Europe on a grant to study music and theater and visited different electronic music studios and the Berliner Ensemble, the legendary East Berlin theater company established by Bertolt Brecht and Helene Weigel. Thanks to another grant in 1976, he was able to work with Campbell again. Besides Passe Muraille, Schreibman later worked with more mainstream theater companies, including the Manitoba Theatre Centre and the National Theatre School of Canada in Montreal.

Schreibman and Flivva's drummer, Mary Jane Card, both came from Orillia; they were high-school sweethearts. An early incarnation of Flivva played at Kafé Kafka at the University of Toronto Playhouse. This coffeehouse was run by Garrard, who was now teaching at the university. Garrard was a real connector and it was through him at Kafé Kafka that Schreibman met Andrew Paterson. Garrard also introduced Paterson to the playwright Michael Hollingsworth, who wanted to do rock theater. I'll attempt to explain this multi-disciplinary muddle. Paterson, Michael Brook, and Card worked with Hollingsworth on his play *Strawberry Fields* in the basement of the artist-run center A Space. Within that play, the performance art group the Hummer Sisters (Marien Lewis, Bobbe Besold, Janet Burke, and Deanne Taylor) started what Paterson describes as an "intermission insert" that expanded into a full show of its own called *The Patty Rehearst Story* (with music by Paterson and Brook). *Strawberry Fields* and *The Patty Rehearst Story* were the first productions of VideoCabaret, a multi-media art and theater company that used both pre-recorded and live video in their shows, often with banks of televisions on stage. Paterson states, "I was an orphan who played guitar . . . they needed a band. Flivva didn't have a bass player and Michael Brook was playing guitar at a higher level than I did, so I joined as a bass player. I did not play with Flivva prior to their involvement with VideoCabaret."

Pilk's Madhouse ad in the Toronto Star. Image courtesy of the Toronto Star, December 12, 1972.

Schreibman candidly says, "I had left Canada for a while and while I was away the Hummers absconded with my band, which was the drummer Mary Jane Card and the guitar player Michael Brook, and Andy. And so they were working for them, and then when I came back we kind of split the performance so that I had my band back for the beginning of the show and they took them for the latter half, which was their own show." Paterson notes, "Phil didn't play behind the Hummers. I think they thought he would as he was a highly regarded theater composer."

Schreibman regarded Flivva very much as a band. In terms of performance, he says, "I tried to sing the songs theatrically. And I tried to imbue the songs with certain characters—that each one was a different character in a different storyline to it—and tried to sing it as if it was whoever I imagined writing the song. Later songs became, I think, more personal. They're not as much on the album."

Flivva and VideoCabaret soon moved on from A Space to an upstairs Queen Street venue called Frank's Place, where Flivva's *The Name Is Schreibman—Sympathetic Ear* album was recorded live on "11-12-76." And, oh my, what an album. Opening on a single piano note repeated, Cale-like in its repetition, then switch. Everything comes in: the shaky, contorted vocal describing squalor, the guitar warbled in its detailed finesse. Asking what sparked this song, "Bedroom of Flies," Schreibman answers, "It came out of a person I knew who had made a suicide attempt and when we came to his room there were so many flies, because there was blood all over the place. And it was just filled with flies attracted by the blood. And so, it was like a bedroom of flies. And then I was thinking that the whole world is—I mean, it's just flies fucking in the world. And that we're all just in this bedroom of flies."

Applause. What is the guitar doing now? Staccato hiccups menacing, then pure prowess, an ode to "Northern Girls," cabaret on the keys. "Sailor," a swoony ballad about sailors sung by Marien Lewis—with Schreibman's harmonies they combine like Meat Loaf (but don't tell them that, they may take it the wrong way).

Then shit gets dank and nasty and lewd, with a grinding guitar riff to match. Someone squeals. "The Ritz" does not sound ritzy; it is pure lust that does not inspire lust, it does the reverse. As the song ends, one can vaguely make out unpleasant homophobic slurs bellered from someone in the audience who sounds far coarser, far less witty than the song itself. They had to combine two different performances of "The Maids" on the album because this heckler was so disruptive. Schreibman explains, "Anyway, he was an absolute jerk, and he kept on yelling out in the middle of our songs. I mean, it wasn't that anyone was worried, but it was just spoiling the recording. So finally I got really mad and I tore off the boom off my microphone and I went storming down, and he was sitting there with his foot up and I kicked his foot so hard his shoe flew off. Then he stood up and I had the mic boom—I was gonna smash his fucking head in. And these people jumped up and prevented me and then

An Evening With the Maids 1969 poster designed by General Idea. Courtesy of Theatre Passe Muraille.

PHILLIP SCHREIBMAN

MICHAEL BROOK

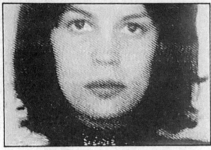
MARY JANE CARD

ANDY PATERSON

Band portraits from the back cover of *The Name Is Schreibman—Sympathetic Ear* by Flivva (Dog Records, 1977). Author's collection. Thanks to Phillip Schreibman.

he was kicked out of the space. And the guy who did the recording, the engineer, Jimmy Bungard—great guy, and it was his recording equipment and everything—it was done on a four track—and so he shut the machines down and picked up a pipe wrench thinking that it was going to get even worse, but anyway it settled down and we finished the recording." Others did find this heckler upsetting.

Decades later this heckler, David Gilmour (not the same-named musician), became an established CanLit writer of the kind of books you give a boring, old relative for Christmas. As a teacher, he was quoted by the CBC saying that he taught a canon of "serious, heterosexual guys," adding, "I'm not interested in teaching books by women." Some people never really change.

Originally written for the Theatre Passe Muraille production of the same name, "The Maids" opens with haunting cries from the guitar, then,

> "Some lace from grace late fallen lay,
> 'Neath a hairbrush on the vanity.
> The hairbrush bristles turning grey,
> The vanity insanit'ry[12]

12 Yes, it was clearly pronounced as "insanitry", a word that connotes both "insanity" and "sanitary."

The green clock tick talks
To the telephone
Who waits to be answered.
The powdered question stands alone,
such a rouge would be absurd.
The Maids, the Maids are serving us tonight,
The Maids, the Maids are waiting on us tonight.
The Maids, the Maids are waiting, are waiting for each other, for Madame . . . "[13]

"Jack," about Kerouac, was originally another Theatre Passe Muraille song for the 1972 collaborative "survival theatre" production *The Black Queen Is Going to Eat You All Up.* "Jack" wears its Lou Reed influence all over, head to toe, one of the wistful faded glamor numbers. "All the stars I used know, the ones I hoped to be . . . It's going to be alright." The song "Man in Black" was written for a musical that Schreibman wrote, *The Ballad of Jack of Diamonds,* about a mythical cowboy. "Streetcar Hearse" is a rock procession tracking a personal, urban descent—"You've just got to remember when things couldn't get much worse, it'll be Canada 3 A.M. December, and you'll be riding that streetcar hearse." Cymbal washes, rapid bass patterns. The song was written from the perspective of a man living in his mother's basement in Ottawa who had murdered someone: a true story, no less. Schreibman explains, "And it was just in the way that you think about how does a person get to that state? How do you get to the point where you have to commit that kind of act?"

To take us out is "Nobody Knows You When You're Down and Out," the 1923 Jimmie Cox blues standard, a real end-of-the-night number, a staggered slow dance, a self-deprecating laugh. The kind of song that has a long cigarette ash hanging from it. Guitar!

Self-released on Dog Records, the album received a positive review from Peter Goddard, the rock critic for the *Toronto Star,* calling it "a stunning work" and "classy and controlled decadence."[14] A thousand copies were pressed, but many were destroyed due to a most unfortunate infestation of termites. Schreibman recalls, "And they just ate the covers off them and left the termite goo over the records."

Some copies of the album have a sticker saying "Flivva" slapped on the front. This was done after the fact, correcting the coercion of a wannabe manager who had told Schreibman, "Oh, no, don't use Flivva. You should use your name." However, this suggestion led Schreibman to come up with a private-detective concept to link it all together, with *The Name Is Schreibman* as a take-off on *The Name Is Archer*, the first in the series of Ross Macdonald's Lew Archer detective fiction books. Schreibman says, "And also the ironic thing which is it's such a terrible name to remember or spell or anything. So that was the irony of it, but I'm sorry now that I didn't just call it Flivva because the actuality of it was

---

[13] Music and lyrics © 1969 Phillip Schreibman. Thanks to Phillip Schreibman for allowing us to print them.

[14] Quotes are from his review in *Shades*, no. 5.

that it was Flivva, and it's just an easier thing to do. If I had to do over again, I would have just called it Flivva."

Paterson says, "I remember Steven Davey [of the Dishes] thought Flivva were interesting because they sounded like Bryan Ferry covering Wilson Pickett songs. Later on, Roxy Music did cover 'Midnight Hour,' so there we go." Naturally, Davey remarked on this while Flivva were on stage doing a Wilson Pickett number. Much of Flivva's repertoire were originals by Schreibman—though they did play "Nancy Boys," an unrecorded Paterson original.

Changes were afoot for Flivva. Paterson notes, "I left in February 1977 after the Hummer Sisters warmed up for John Cale at the New Yorker." Paterson moved back to guitar for his own band, the Government, which became the house band for VideoCabaret until 1979. VideoCabaret is still around as a very different entity. The Government primarily existed autonomously, releasing a few recordings. Today, Paterson is a video artist and writer. His current musical act, Derwatt, is more electronic, with Paterson's wry, witty vocals.

Michael Brook's brother Greg became the new bassist for Flivva. Gwynneth Mann joined on sax, but left the band in 1979. Flivva started playing the Beverley Tavern regularly. The Beverley was an early shining light of Queen Street, with its mingling of the art and music scenes—the Dishes and Martha and the Muffins were mainstays. Schreibman's Rhodes piano sounded full-toned and warm but, being a Rhodes, it was heavy and cumbersome; transporting it upstairs to the Beverley was an unenviable task.

Flivva had no manager and there weren't a lot of venue options. "And we began to lose Mike, and Mike started going and playing with Martha and the Muffins and the Everglades." Flivva never played outside of Toronto simply because they didn't know what was out there. Schreibman recalls the closest thing to touring was one outdoor show with Paterson still on bass at the University of Toronto.

The movie *Scanners* has one of the most visceral and indelible images of the body horror that its director, David Cronenberg, is reputed for. Michael Ironside's character uses his telekinetic powers to cause Louis Del Grande's bald, bespectacled, mustachioed head to explode. And it makes a big mess. This has since become a popular meme. Both telekinesis and retrocognitive abilities are unexplained powers of the mind. Related and less known today, the 1980s Canadian television program *Seeing Things* was co-created by and starred Del Grande as a bumbling newspaper reporter who uses his extrasensory powers of retrocognition to solve murders; since he is too high strung to drive, he often begs his ex-wife to give him rides. Unlike many shows, *Seeing Things* isn't easy to describe in an elevator pitch, what with its rapid tonal shifts from comedy to suspense. When the visions come, the camera fixates on Del Grande's throbbing, non-exploding head. Eerie, droning, unfathomable sounds accompany the flashes. These sounds, along with the rest of the soundtrack, were done by Schreibman using synth and acoustic piano. To make the eerie sounds for the visions, Schreibman explains, "It was a combination of violin, guitar heavily pedaled, and a bicycle wheel going around and getting rattled by a piece of cardboard, I

Flivva, 1979 lineup, left to right: Gwynneth Mann, sax; Phillip Schreibman, keyboards & vocals; Greg Brook, bass; Mary Jane Card, drums; Michael Brook, guitar. Courtesy of Phillip Schreibman.

Louis Del Grande in Canadian television's *Seeing Things*. Image courtesy of the *Winnipeg Sun*, February 14, 1985.

think." Del Grande knew Schreibman from Passe Muraille, where he had been a writer and director; a couple of Del Grande's productions there had music by Schreibman.

Seeing Things had a very catchy theme song, one of the greatest in Canadian TV and one of the greatest in all of television, in a Randy Newman vein: "I'm seeing things, believe me, I've never seen before, little things deceive me, like when you threw me out the door! I couldn't believe my eyes"—and then some scat. I was quite surprised to find out that this theme song, credited to Schreibman, was done by most of Flivva, with Mary Jane Card on drums and Michael Brook on guitar.

Brook played in the initial lineup of the Everglades in 1978 with former members of the Dishes, then went on to be a tour guitarist for Martha and the Muffins. He later came up with the "infinite guitar"—a guitar modified with electronics. Starting in the '80s, he began to work extensively with Brian Eno—no longer the ostrich-feather, bespoke, skulleted Glam head-of-state Eno but now the more chill, ambient innovator Eno, ever tasteful.

With Card, Schreibman released a most delightful single in the early '80s as the duo Big Red—two songs of synth pop, singing of heartbreak: "Sad but true, I can't think bad of you, I wish I could, it would do me good, give me lies to remember you by." Following Flivva, this was the second release on Dog Records. In 1996, Schreibman recorded a most unique meditation CD under the name the Slow Peepers, using the manipulation of nature. Starting as a field recording of the spring peeper frogs where he lives, each consecutive track is slowed down to half-speed. He explains, "And it's just then when you get it down to the sixth level of slowing it down, just cutting the speed in half each stage. It's this amazing, pure sine tone that's coming out of their mouths. And it just sounds brilliant."

Another Dog Records release was a cassette by the late musician Richard Carstens. In the '90s Carstens and Schreibman had an original instrumental band with the former Flivva members Card and Greg Brook called the Rex Rabbit All Stars that Schreibman describes as "Zen R&B." This band's main claim to fame was recording the theme for *The Sunday Night Sex Show* with the sex educator Sue Johanson, a live call-in show where people could phone up and get frank, honest on-air information from Sue; the show regularly featured a sex-toy review segment.

In 1998 Schreibman published his incredibly moving and sensitive memoir *My Cat Saved My Life,* about how his cat Alice saved him from depression. After Alice died, he focused on writing about this human-to-cat relationship; he had also been processing the death of his parents in the years previous. Schreibman says, "And so the book is about basically dealing with death and dealing with an animal and how an animal opens you up to experiencing the physical world and life itself."

Flivva did go on to record another album in a 24-track studio with Greg Brook on bass. It was never released. One song, "Whirlwind," from 1979, exists as a rough mix on YouTube. This is a softer Rhodes organ song and quite lyrical: "but then silence attracts me . . . "— building dramatically. Of this album Schreibman says, "And they're good songs. I didn't like my voice on them. And I don't know. I just kind of gave up. But I think there's some good songs there." By this time the band was breaking up. Later, however, Schreibman says, "In 1985, I went to London to try to get a recording deal for Flivva's second album but failed miserably. It was the wrong time for us. The fashionable snare sound was all gated-reverb, and we were not into effects. And our musical and lyrical style was not the current one. I was so depressed and embarrassed that I contemplated not returning to Canada."

Schreibman concludes, "I guess I'm sorry that Flivva didn't pursue itself more. I wish it had. But I had some wonderful times playing live and from being in a band. What a fantastic rush that is. It's just the greatest thing. I'm glad that I lived my life in such a way that I was able to play in a rock band, which, in my estimation is one of the great inventions of the twentieth century. I just think it's an amazing thing altogether as a form of communication, as a way of transmission, as the conglomerate of it—you know, when you listen to all that music, early rock stuff and surf music and rockabilly and just all the stuff that would have been on K-Tel Records and everything, it's just fantastic, all of it, just the sound of everybody playing together. You know 'Louie Louie' by the Kingsmen? You know how shitty that recording is? Apparently, it was done with one microphone, and the singer stood under the microphone on a box and sang up. There's so many of those stories of stuff recorded every which way. And it lives. You know, it still lives and it has that incredible energy. So I just say if there's anything I want to say about Flivva, I wish we played more. I'm glad that it happened."

THE CLICHETTES

THE CLICHETTES TOOK LIP-SYNC TO NEW, ambitious levels. It's an art form. Many lip-synchers are merely content to mimic the pop stars, parroting with pathos, a budget replication of idol worship, to create an approximation focused on the singer and not the song. The Clichettes used the material and subverted it to their own ends, adding layers of meaning.

I looked up "lip-sync." The internet dictionary says, "move the lips silently in synchronization with a pre-recorded soundtrack." The Clichettes more than ran with that. Their name reads like a blend of two different things. The word cliché means "an expression, idea, or action that has been overused to the point of seeming worn out, stale, ineffective, or meaningless." The Clichettes clearly used older material as a jumping-off point, but their name is self-deprecating to the hilt: they put fresh spins on this material. The suffix "-ettes" had long been used in popular all-woman vocal and dance groups. Of lip-synching, the Clichettes member Johanna Householder says, "We wanted to be rock stars, but none of us could play an instrument or sing, so it was the most expedient way to be a musician."

In 1978, David Buchan invited the Clichettes to be a part of *Fruit Cocktails*, his lip-sync performance evening, which also involved Murray Ball and Steven Davey of the Dishes. Although it was live-to-tape direct from Toronto's Masonic Temple, *Fruit Cocktails* was a segment of a national video art conference that had several names, take your pick: the Fifth Network, Cinquiéme Réseau, Teleperformance. Oh, that last one's good—I like that one, feels appropriate, the festival had plenty of performance—video and performance often intersected.

For *Fruit Cocktails* the Clichettes consisted of Householder, Louise Garfield, Janice Hladki, and Elizabeth Chitty, whose studio they rehearsed at. They performed a song made famous by Lesley Gore in the early '60s, "You Don't Own Me," which Garfield describes as "an outright feminist *cri du cœur*." Against the brightly colored backdrop, they stand in a line, all wearing individual outfits personally selected and ready to wear from each of their own closets, with their eyes—those gateways to the soul—completely covered by white sunglasses. Miming finger snapping in unison, they move to point accusatorily at the audience, then turn their backs for a prolonged moment and casually turn back, a succession of synchronized poses and gestures, some shimmies. As the song escalates, their hands get clenched and they rapidly pound their fists on the stage. It was a hit! The "APPLAUSE" sign was all aglow, but the audience needed no such prompting; they could think for themselves. The Clichettes were a sensation! Next stop: Toronto (where they already were).

Similarly, a few years earlier in the zeitgeist but across the Atlantic Ocean in the U.K., the Moodies, five women and one man on piano—all from a fine arts background—took a variety of mostly older songs, including girl-group classics like the Shangri-Las' "Remember (Walking in the Sand)" and covered them from a performance-art point of view. The Clichettes took this post-modern approach further by taking old songs and *not* covering them, leaving the audio part as is through lip-sync, though really they didn't simply let these songs be. Both the Moodies and the Clichettes were not doing nostalgic replications. There was much, much more going on.

The Clichettes all met through Toronto's contemporary-dance community. Garfield started dancing at a rather young age after initially being enthralled by *The Nutcracker*, taking classes at the Canadian Junior Ballet Company at the age of seven. Then, later at

The Clichettes in the *Toronto Star*, 1978. Image courtesy of the *Toronto Star*, December 28, 1978.

SEED, Toronto's first alternative high school, she was taught by Gail Mazur Handley. Garfield states, "Gail was a superb, inspirational teacher and encouraged my budding choreographic talents. She taught Nikolais technique, improvisation and composition which was not being taught in Canada at the time [Gail came from the U.S.] and I found it really well suited to my body and discovered an interest, passion, and talent for dance composition. It was intellectually challenging as well as physically hard. Alwin Nikolais's work was also visually stunning and original which really appealed to me. Eventually I travelled to New York City to study briefly with Nikolais and his partner Murray Louis."

Householder was born in the United States. She told me, "I left the U.S. when Nixon was elected for the second time. I politically exiled myself, then went to England. I ended up going to the London School of Contemporary Dance, and that's where I met some Canadians, some Torontonians, and so then I came to Toronto, because I didn't want to go back to the States." She attended York University to complete her B.F.A. in Dance: "I was much more interested in performance art. I didn't actually go into dance in order to be a dancer. I wasn't interested in being part of a company or anything like that. That was also a feminist stance—like the hierarchical nature of dance companies that would usually have male choreographers at the top. So, there was a big, independent choreographers' movement. Big. God knows how many—maybe there were a dozen of us, I don't know—it was huge and people were just really exploring different ways to look at movement." Householder and others from York were drawn to a place called 15 Dance Lab, which she says was "run by a couple of refugees from the National Ballet—they left the National Ballet the way I left the U.S. They were company dancers, but they had had it with the politics of ballet and had started this space with a collective of fifteen dancers." Householder says the founders of 15 Dance Lab, a married couple named Miriam and Lawrence Adams, "were great radical thinkers and they really supported all of us twenty-somethings coming out of university who really were passionate about making work." Householder met Garfield, Hladki, and Chitty after some of the original fifteen dancers had moved on. 15 Dance Lab was very experimental and multi-disciplinary, with Lawrence Adams pushing the dancers to incorporate the new medium of video, at one point even attempting to start an artists' television studio. Of significant influence, Miriam Adams's own work often involved humor.

Garfield says, "I spent one semester at York University Dance department but dropped out, unhappy and unsuited to Graham technique and fed up with the long haul up to York U. But while I was there I met Carolyn Shaffer. Together she and I created an evening of work at 15 Dance Lab and improvised regularly at the Music Gallery. This led to a world of possibility and collaboration with the many other, primarily women dance artists who burst into this scene of cross-disciplinary collaboration."

And from all that came the Clichettes. None of them can remember how they came up with the name. Garfield thinks that it might have been the "collective wig/brain." When I asked her about the Clichettes' inspirations and influences she replied, "A shared experience of '50s and '60s comedy and TV, pop music, Motown choreography, anti-war politics, counterculture, and feminism."

Through the Clichettes they were able to implement their backgrounds in dance and performance. Householder adds, "And our politics as well. So, you know, you're pushing that, unpacking the girl groups' ethos of hurtin' and cheatin' and aching and bleeding and all of those things and turning them on their heads." Garfield states, "Everything we did was put through a feminist lens. The music we chose to perform had to fulfill our ability to bring a feminist analysis to it. If we couldn't find a way to reveal the embedded misogyny in a song, we would drop it. Ultimately, creating context through narrative was the only way we could continue to lip-sync with a clear feminist message."

Chitty wasn't in the group for long. Householder says, "Yeah, it wasn't her thing. She was in a few performances. And then she was like, nah. She's a more serious artist, I guess I would have to say. She didn't want to humiliate herself the way we did. We were all about humiliating ourselves—somebody had to do it."

So the Clichettes became a trio. They were very consciously a collective, often being called difficult because they were three women who didn't have a leader; they made collective decisions. Of lip-synching Householder says, "I was very committed to the fact that this was an art form, even if a very debased and degraded one. I often refer to lip-sync as the people's art form."

This was long before the truncated, digital TikTok era. The only people doing lip-sync before the Clichettes were drag-show performers. Some of the Clichettes' drag queen friends would give them stage makeup tutorials. Householder adds, "And then trying to get our wigs done, which was always a nightmare"—those wigs were larger than life, too—"they were much larger than life and then they became even larger."

The Clichettes were expert record trawlers. Householder says, "You can't not love the Shangri-Las' whole catalogue." Besides putting new contextual spins on girl-group classics, they were expert at lip-synching spoken-word recordings, such as late-night Romantic-poetry come-on albums by Renzo the Continental and Alan Burke's seemingly stream-of-consciousness album *My Naked Soul,* that they found on intensive used-record-store searches, often visiting KOPS Records on Queen Street, going through all of the 45s looking for anything with an odd title, then listening to find out if it measured up to the name to become fodder for the work. Connecting further to the Queen Street art, fashion, and music scene, all of the Clichettes worked together at the Parrot Restaurant, Greg Couillard and Andrew Milne-Allan's innovative fine-dining hub.

The Clichettes performed at countless benefits. Householder says that they were "benefit queens," adding, "We performed at benefits for everything—for abortion rights, for medical aid for Nicaragua, for women's shelters, for fundraisers for artists who'd been evicted. You name it, we performed in the benefit for it. And including the anti-NAFTA, anti-free-trade thing, you know—that was towards the end of our career." At one of the

The Clichettes: Left to right; Janice Hladki, Johanna Householder and Louise Garfield can be seen in unusual show at the Horseshoe Tavern through Saturday.

The Clichettes, 1980. Image courtesy of the *Toronto Star*, May 21, 1980.

first Pride events they did "Puff the Magic Dragon," revealing that it was not, in fact, about smoking marijuana but was actually a coded gay love story.

Humor was ever present and important. When I asked Garfield how the audiences reacted, she replies, "Laughing their guts out and being very loyal fans. This was deeply satisfying, validating, and fun!" The Clichettes' first proper paying gig was at the comedy club Yuk-Yuks, resulting in a review that described them as a good-time nostalgia act. Householder says, "Nostalgia was not our intention at all—it was anti-nostalgia—it was, like, this stuff is a load of bullshit. Although we did unearth some of the more feminist songs of the '50s and '60s, like 'Too Many Fish in the Sea.'"

As a result, the Clichettes decided to bring in a writer to work with them and write stories around the songs to further bring the points across. The Clichettes now embarked on ambitious, full-scale productions—all with different themes, all elaborate and presented in theaters. When I try to fathom all the preparation involved, Garfield exclaims, "You said it, brother! . . . We learned on our feet about script development, dramaturgy, costume, set, lighting, and prop design. Sound design was fundamental and fascinating to integrate lip sync, background sound, and interstitial connections to scenes. Not to mention producers, stage managers, dressers, graphic designers, and publicists." There were countless costume changes. A million of them, some right on stage in the middle of a song.

Half Human Half Heartache was their first stage show, at the dawn of the 1980s. The humor writer Marni Jackson worked with the Clichettes for five years on this and their next production, *She-Devils of Niagara*. Jackson's website states, "*Half Human* established the premise (the Clichettes as space aliens who must learn feminine behavior to disguise themselves as earth girls), and the cabaret show was a big hit in Toronto, with productions that followed in Ottawa and Vancouver. Our next endeavour, *She-Devils of Niagara*, was a more ambitious stage show in a regular theatre. The Clichettes were cast in a dystopian future where gender was strictly regulated, and history had been banished to the basement of a wax museum in Niagara Falls."[15]

---

15 https://marnijackson.com/personal-history/.

The Clichettes' *"Up Against the Wallpaper."* Image courtesy of the *Toronto Star*, March 17, 1989.

From being space aliens in their first production to Mock-Men in the second (as well as a turtle), the next stage of evolution for the Clichettes was to become the set, to become the furniture. Their third production, 1988's *Up Against the Wallpaper*, was written with Kate Lushington, who at that time was the artistic director of Nightwood Theatre, Canada's oldest professional women's theatre. The artist Renée Van Halm designed lightweight Styrofoam costume walls. The fruit bowl on top of the dresser which Householder played was rendered in the style of *Bacchus*, the painting by the Baroque master Caravaggio. "We were able to move around in them. But I was eight months pregnant at the time, so Renée made the drawers stick out a little bit for my baby. And then Louise's was a fireplace and Janice's was a bookshelf." There were again numerous costume changes. Householder also played a shag rug. She recalls, "I was a very lumpy shag rug. Janice was a vacuum cleaner. And Louise was a table with a lamp, but then it had a phone on it so she could call people and listen to the answering machine." The media artist Frances Leeming designed a beanbag chair costume for Hladki. Inspired by the increasingly relevant housing crisis, *Up Against the Wallpaper*'s theme was Toronto's last affordable house. As the show went on, they had to increase the house's cost from $450,000 to $750,000. And if it were to happen today? Well . . . that house would cost much, much more. Besides playing the furniture, they were also real estate agents and the evicted tenants. The songs included

The Clichettes – *Go to Hell*. Photographer David Hlynsky. The male bodysuits were designed and built by Vera Schubert-Laurence. Photo courtesy of Johanna Householder.

Lene Lovich's "Home Is Where the Heart Is" and Shirley Bassey's "I Who Have Nothing." Spoiler alert (where are you going to find out what happens in this live production from the late '80s?): in the end, the furniture winds up in the city dump, lip-synching "Stayin' Alive." A message of hope.

The Clichettes' final production had a most strikingly memorable name: *Out for Blood*. How could you not want to see that? It's just so visceral. Wait for it—the full, original title was *Out for Blood, Back in Five Minutes*. Householder explains, "*Out for Blood* was really about female monstrousness. We wanted to be monstrous females. Louise was Medusa, Janice was Bernardine Dohrn, the leader of the Weather Underground, and I was the Bad Seed." Dressed as Patty McCormack's evil child character Rhoda Penmark wearing pigtails, Householder lip-synched Peggy Lee's "Is That All There Is?" They opened with

Eartha Kitt's "I Want to Be Evil" and dressed as cops for "My Generation." The show had an elaborate, interweaving plot where somehow Medusa's head winds up at a riot against the Vietnam War, with Penmark and Dohrn. Garfield co-produced *Out for Blood* and would later go on to produce films, including John Greyson's ground-breaking *Zero Patience*, a musical about the AIDS epidemic.

A notable stand-alone Clichettes performance had the three of them in buff, male bodysuits with removable male appendages. They hired a costume designer, classically trained in the European costume tradition, named Vera Schubert-Lawrence. When the Clichettes first met with her to describe what they needed, Householder says, "She opened her handbag and she took out this piece of flesh-colored net that she had embroidered hair—pubic hair—I mean, it looked like pubic hair—she just brought out this piece of skin with pubic hair on it basically, and we went, 'That's it! That's it!' They were beautifully done. They were quilted and she embroidered the armpit hair and the chest hair and the pubic hair and the muscles were all quilted. And then I remember going over to her house one day because we're trying to look for the right material to be the balls, and we're going through—it's one of those kitchens that's got all the jars with beans and lentils and barley . . . " Pantry type stuff? "Yeah, pantry type stuff. And so we were trying everything and I think we finally settled on wheat germ. We were tempted to have barley—like, that just seemed like it could be good—but it was too heavy, actually. They needed to have the right weight—heft—texture—weight. So Vera did those and, yeah, fabulous, fabulous job."

They now needed to find just the right heavy metal number to accompany this bodysuit performance, so they went to Sam the Record Man and asked the man (not Sam; he was busy doing other shit) behind the counter for a recommendation. He replied, "Motörhead—that's what they're listening to in the trenches." Householder explains, "You have to go to the experts." They chose "Go to Hell."

There were mishaps. Garfield recounts the first performance in the costumes: "My detachable penis on my naked-man suit fell off backstage when we were warming up, which would have ruined the surprise ending of the song, so the costume designer quickly sewed it securely on. It didn't fall off. But when it came time to rip it off at the end of the song—I couldn't remove it. That got my heart racing and I had to pull *very very* hard to finally achieve the effect." Another malfunction involved a performance in her fringe bikini bottom. She explains, "I thought the shorts were too long, so I proceed to cut them shorter. Little did I know that, by doing that, I was decreasing the width of the crotch. And when it came time in the choreography to go the ground and spread our legs open in a second position, my bikini was *much* too revealing!"

Gail Singer's 1991 National Film Board of Canada documentary *Wisecracks,* about women in comedy—including Phyllis Diller, Whoopi Goldberg, Paula Poundstone, and Ellen DeGeneres—also features live footage of the Clichettes. James Brown's "This Is a Man's World" plays while the Clichettes, in their male bodysuits, triumphantly hold Canadian-flag-emblazoned fake flying-V guitars; however, their machismo leads to confusion as they try to find a place to put their penises, like pinning the tail on the donkey. Once placed, they unzip the outfits, trade the hair-metal wigs in for massive beehives, and don schoolgirl outfits to lip-sync the Shangri-Las' "I Can Never Go Home Anymore." Cut to the Clichettes in their street clothes being interviewed, with Hladki stating how, because they don't fit into a "mainstream, male idea of theater," they are often disregarded and diminished as a result, but if men were doing this they'd be regarded as innovative and "furthering the form."[16]

In the 1980s lip-syncs entered the mainstream. Countless contests were held in school gymnasiums, church halls, and bars across North America. In 1984, the Clichettes entered the National Lip Sync Contest in Houston, Texas. They won; I mean, no need for build-up: it was a cinch, really. The contest was held at a bar called Cooters, known for having massive drinks called Betcha Can't and the longest bar in Houston, somehow fitting into its strip-mall location. After a successful fundraiser—"Send These Lips to Houston"—held at the Rivoli, with performances by many in the Queen Street scene, the Clichettes flew to Texas with their costumes and their carefully selected entry, a recording of the German schlager song "Sailor, Your Home Is the Sea." Most famously sung in German by Lolita, this American hit version added an English-language section in the middle recited with a slight lisp, adding a layer of visual linguistic absurdity to the lip-sync. Donning sailor hats, the Clichettes wore matching full boat costumes, giving the impression that they were actually in little boats—ruffled blue skirts doubling as waves of water, legs sticking out to goose-step, all tightly choreographed and funny as all get-out. They stood out from the competition, a sea of cheap celebrity imitators: Princes, Kennys, Dollys, and the like. The judges loved the Clichettes. "Much to the chagrin of the organizers because they were hoping, I think, to put together a kind of stable of look-alike performers to open shopping malls and that kind of thing," adds Householder.

Another highlight was on a New Year's Eve opening for Rough Trade—who brought out their special guest Dusty Springfield. Of Springfield, Householder recollects, "She was very gracious and thought we were fun. She had amazing fingernails. I do remember that. Talk about Glam. This was before nails became what they have become today. But she was the first person I knew who had major artificial nails like that."

After the last Clichettes production of *Out for Blood* in 1992, Hladki went on to a Ph.D. and to teach film and women's studies at McMaster University. Garfield was producing feature film and Householder began teaching at the Ontario College of Art. Both Garfield and Householder continued to perform, sometimes together, having lip-synched Carl Reiner and Mel Brooks's *2000 Year Old Man* comedy routine for friends' birthday parties, Garfield also performed Eddie Lawrence's "The Old Philosopher." She says she was drawn

---

16 Clichettes interview, *Wisecracks*, directed by Gail Singer (1991), National Film Board of Canada.

The Clichettes in the boat costumes. Image courtesy of the *Vancouver Sun*, December 31, 1980.

to this routine by "the bizarre and hilarious lyrics about being down on your luck, along with a strong, vivid personality coming through in the performance. His wacky voice." Spoken word material is tricky, but the Clichettes had a mastery of subtly capturing the movements and expressions perfectly. Garfield doesn't perform as much anymore. For fourteen years she was executive director of Arts Etobicoke, bringing arts closer to the community, including developing the urbanNoise art training program and QMAP (Queer Media Arts Program) for youth in the region. She received the Urban Hero award in 2017 for her work and Arts Etobicoke at Nightwood Theatre has named a scholarship award after her for the development of new plays by later-in-life feminist artists.

Johanna Householder more recently performed Peggy Lee's "Is That All There Is" for a karaoke-video-by-artists project organized by the artists Luke Painter and Meera Singh. Being immersed in the world of academia and art as a professor at the Ontario College of Art and Design, she lip-synched a lecture given by the philosopher Alain Badiou, "On the Subject of Art." Besides being interested in the philosophical content and the particular tropes of the philosophical language (e.g., "We have to begin at the beginning, and what is the beginning? What do we mean when we say something *is*?"), Householder was also interested in the role that the moderator Josefina Ayerza, an editor of *Lacanian Ink*, played in the lecture. She explains, "She performs, as women so often do, listening. So, she's performing listening while Badiou is performing philosophizing. I was really, really struck with her performance of listening. It's a two-part piece and I play both roles in which Badiou is lip-synched live, and she's on video next to him listening."

At the end of our interview, Householder said, "Although I don't feel like the Clichettes are over, we had a very precise twelve-year career as performers, but, as you noted, both Louise and I continued to perform lip-sync. So it's like you can take the girl out of the Clichettes, but you can't take the Clichettes out of the girl." It never ends! "It never ends, the eternal humiliation."

CHIKKIN

THERE WAS A TIME NOT SO LONG AGO when you would find sealed, still-in-shrinkwrap copies of *Which Came First?* by Chikkin everywhere for a dollar, in every Toronto record store. This album will be impossible to find one day. Some fucking tastemaker is inches away from latching onto it. Don't be fooled—it comes off like gold, a treasure.

Like the album title itself, finding out about Chikkin provides no easy answers. Scratch and scratch that skull, crack it. It was released on Egg Records???? Of course it was. This label seemingly didn't release anything else and yet was able to spare no expense on the lavish packaging. The band's futuristic logo is rendered in reflective silver foil laid over a photograph of a golden egg cradled in purple velvet. The record itself is pressed on white vinyl with a yellow yolk center: an egg. You read it right; they took this whole Chikkin thing too far—so far that they turned a joke into an *objet d'art*. Put the album on the turntable and it ain't no rubber chicken. It's an egg of alien origin. The back cover says, "Hello from the future, soon you will understand." This statement is accurate.

The effete power-pop opener "Replicas" makes you feel kinda funny but also kinda squiggly, kinda good? Play-Doh Beatles rubbed in Pixy Stix candy powder, non-threateningly commanding, "Give me your love baby, I don't want to marry you, but you're welcome to make love to me . . . just a replica of two of us." The guitars are really squelching. Bobb Trimble–like vocals. "Up This Close" is a lullaby creeper, a ballad of soft, slightly trepidatious vocal melodies but a band rocking, pumping, and sizzling drums, synths almost become horns and start edging, it's almost too much to bear! And oh, those synths. How many times have I listened to this thing? Fifty? One can't keep track of time. And I still don't know where it's going to go, just that the colors are changing and this shape-shifting band of Jerry Corneliuses always plays it catchy. Hell, there's even a jazzy instrumental showing that, yes, we got this! And the lyrics? Check out a line or two from the nuanced melodic epic "Not a Sin": "'I'm not a sin' was engraved on her eyelids, though from looking there wasn't a single trace, she must have wanted hard for a finger-tip Love, to convince even God to re-engrave her face." WOW! Then follows a Bizarro World folk song, drumrolls please, they're going to rock. Is this the most lucid album ever made by *Homo sapiens*? It's not abrupt. Half this album was recorded on tippy toes, and when that sweet sweet stuff teetered and fell from the high shelf we all got our desserts. Who were they?

The April 22, 1979, *Toronto Star* reports, "Billed as Canada's youngest recorded group, Chikkin involves three middle-class, suburban Toronto kids who have been playing together for six years and are now all 18 or 19 years old: David Tomlinson, Eddy Valiquette and Greg Evans. . . . Chikkin is prepared to hatch its second album. Later this year, the boys will provide musical accompaniment while the federal government's Egg Marketing Agency fries the largest omelet in history, in the world's largest frypan, in Guelph, Ontario." Don't know about that omelet, but the second album never happened. Three weeks later, the *Toronto Star* printed a letter from one of the album's fans (Jane Messica, Willowdale) wanting to know more about Chikkin. She begged the newspaper to print a photo, so they did. The black-and-white newsprint photo was murky and tiny.

Which Came First? was a mystery. Other than its existence, I could find next to nothing. Tracking down band members was utterly futile. Finally, as a last-ditch effort, I called the sculptor of the cover's

Front cover, white vinyl and yellow, and inner sleeve of *Which Came First?* by Chikkin (Egg Records, 1978). Author's collection.

golden egg and cracked the case. Not only is David Eastwood still sculpting today, but he was an original member of Chikkin, playing the first of what may have been just two shows: Chikkin probably played twice and that's it. Wearing extremely tight, brightly colored shirts they opened for the similarly provocatively named Teenage Head in Hamilton due to both bands' managers being friends. They also opened for Goddo.

Still in high school, Tomlinson studied music at the conservatory and played percussion for African dance classes. Eastwood believes, "He's probably still playing music." Whereas Valiquette "wrote most of the interesting songs." The clever ones. The album erroneously credits only three band members. "I didn't even play bass when I joined the band," Eastwood told me. "I tried to learn. Yes, we had two bass players at one point. I think there's a bunch of different bass players on various tracks. I recorded a few tracks, but they probably ended up as outtakes." Two of the album's songs were written by Ben Hanes, the rhythm guitarist in the first lineup who may have sung on all the album's songs, uncredited save for a thank-you. It took a year for the album to come out. Eastwood left early to play with Richard Carstens, an early Toronto punk musician who had played with members of Flivva.

As for influences, "We were listening to the alternative rock that was coming out of CFNY, a lot of British stuff: Steve Harley. Eddy was from Montreal, too. He was into the Montreal scene." Harley, a romantic Glammer with decadent, evocative lyrics, makes sense as an influence. And CFNY Radio was key. After Chikkin, Eddy became a DJ on CFNY with a show devoted to Québécois music. As radio stations became more and more corporate in the '70s, CFNY was pivotal, a more free-form alternative. The legendary DJ David Marsden joined CFNY in 1978 and became program director.

Back in the early '60s, when Marsden was Dave Mickie, he was a star DJ when the radio DJ was King. Marsden told me, "Some of us were Queen. The DJ was the center of everything through that '60s period on AM and then, with FM progressive radio where the DJ played and said what he or she wanted, the DJ also played a pretty strong role at that time as well." Marsden dressed like the star he was, in gold lamé, electric blue mohair suits, and a blond pompadour. His patter was so manic and mile-a-minute that Marshall McLuhan quoted it verbatim, devoting a chapter of *Understanding Media* to him. Oh, and Marsden had very good taste. "At CHUM-FM I played what I wanted to play. Ultimately that's why I left, because they brought in a playlist."

Marsden was the one behind Chikkin. When I asked Eastwood if Marsden was the Svengali, he replied, "I think Svengali was the right word except that there isn't really a sinister, taking-advantage connotation with David. He was in the background. Eddy and Dave and Ben were at school together. They needed a place to rehearse. That ended up being Dave Marsden's basement." Marsden named the band. Without its creative spelling, "chicken" is also gay sexual slang for a young man. When I asked Marsden about the name, he replied, "I don't know, but it was probably my own little joke."

Front and back covers of *Nuclear War 1984?* by Robin Armstrong (Kangi Records, 1976). Author's collection.

Dave Mickie Club 11 Dance Party radio show ad. Image courtesy of the *Toronto Star*, March 27, 1965.

Marsden believed in Chikkin and made the album happen. Eastwood states, "It was Dave Marsden's brainchild. He put his life savings into it, hoping it would go somewhere." He produced it and came up with all of the ideas for the packaging. It's not clear how many copies were pressed (some say a thousand), but Marsden's name is nowhere to be found on the album. Eastwood says, "The only thing that he didn't do was promote the album itself. He thought it was an unfair advantage. He was the God in the underground radio scene. Which is kind of a shame as it ended up going nowhere. I think it's like a self-published novel."

Marsden explains, "As I think back on it, I thought that because radio was always really, really serious and very safe about such things as payola and all that crap. That's kind of like the reason that Rush doesn't refer to CFNY in the song "Spirit of Radio" when in fact it's all about CFNY, because if I put my name on it other radio stations would have looked the other way and went, 'No, we can't do that. He's our competition.' That would be the only reason I could think of that I wouldn't have put my name on it."

As well as releasing the album, he was the one who most likely secured distribution for A&M Records. There was even further interest. Marsden notes, "A large label—I can't remember what the label was called. Clive Davis, I think, owned it. They were very interested in the band. We never signed a deal. There were a few things they wanted so the deal never got signed. Who knows, if I had signed the deal they could have been huge, I don't know." Marsden saw the album as ahead of its time, comparing Chikkin to the band Japan.

What happened to the members of Chikkin? Even after talking with their collaborators, it is uncertain if the lads on the cover are alive or dead. Does the spirit reside after death? Their music sounds as if it could have been recorded in the last few years, or last week. They could have their 1978 songs slipped into a modern avant-pop album or something yet to come and it'd work. Some older folks gave it casually dismissive reviews; a more scathing review in the *Saskatoon Star-Phoenix* deemed it "absolute garbage." It's meant for open ears, and it keeps getting better with age—fresher and fresher eggs. Not only is the chicken a well-worn tool in comedy, the chicken is sacred in many cultures, the chicken's egg being a symbol of resurrection and renewal.

Addendum: another curiosity that Marsden was involved with was the *Nuclear War 1984?* album by the astrologer Robin Armstrong, one side being "The Signs of the Zodiac Interpreted" and the other side being about the days to come in 1984 when there will be global catastrophe! The front cover's trippy cosmos is offset with jarring words in yellow all caps proclaiming, "WORLD ECONOMY COLLAPSES, FUTURE SHOCK! WITHIN THE COMING DECADE." The back cover features "Robin Armstrong, Professional Astrologer," with mustache and maroon cravat, surrounded by astrological scale models. On the album Marsden's voice commands, bringing to life Armstrong's predictions, as somebody's elbow hits the reverb button at dramatic moments. This album was done through Marsden's company Lip Service Studio Productions, which normally created radio commercial spots. A pretty much unknown album to synth enthusiasts, it is notable in that John Mills-Cockell of Syrinx did all of the intense music. When asked about it, Mills-Cockell laughed and said, "I don't recall doing it, but I know that it exists."

Nuclear War 1984? was catalog number 101 on a label named Kangi. I asked Marsden about this mysterious label. He replied, "The guy who owned that I think was an airline pilot who was interested in music and stuff. I don't know what else they ever put out." Armstrong later went on to create a large musical instrument called the Celestial Harp, designed to heal and play a person's horoscope.

LYNX

IF THERE IS AN EPITOME of a hard-hitting Canadian Glam Rock album, it would have to be 1976's *Missing* by Lynx. Missing Lynx. It's a strain of wordplay, very strained and unrestraining—unless ordered. Look at the photos on the back cover: all five band members have golden, luminescent lynx eyes!!!

Of all of the Lynx family, the Canada lynx may be the smallest but, as domestic as it is to Canada, it still cannot be domesticated. Lynx can't be tamed! These nocturnal animals got teeth and they leap right out of the speakers as soon as needle catches vinyl. Flanged and fuzzed rock, overfed, and distorted Goldtop guitar. The singer has such 'tude, boasting in an anti-capitalist sneer, "You know I don't like money much. In fact, it makes me sick!!!" The other mates chant, "Dollarrrrrrs!" Keyboards getting rinky-dink, as in a low-budget Canadian kids'-show montage, then later on transforming into wailing sirens! Guitars winding around each other, cowbell clopping. "You know, I told you once that I'm the best you ever had!"[17]

---

17 Imagine a scenario where teenage Vince Neil was taking copious singing notes when his kissing Canadian cousin dropped by his Hollywood home with this record in 1976 (pure and utter speculation on my part with zero basis in fact—let me state that it is not a great leap from this to Mötley Crüe's premature-ejaculation concept album *Too Fast for Love*—except *Missing* is not only earlier, it's far better).

Front cover and top third of back cover of *Missing* by Lynx (Quality, 1976). Author's collection.

Two of their songs are explicitly about rock, schooling us with "Goodbye Education, Hello Rock & Roll," punctuating high-pitched "Ya-ta da-da-da-da!" like Vaseline on a chalkboard and "Rock All Day, Roll All Night," which is all about learning to keep those two things (rock, roll) on separate schedules. In stoner rock circles, a song called "Lucifer" would run about ten minutes. Lynx does it all for us in three—too fast for Satan, echo cranked up full tilt. Total fucking classic.

The Swartz brothers, Mike and Rob, were the real throttle of Lynx as chief songwriters with their very lead vocals and guitar and post-pubescent mustaches. But soon enough they were gone. Bassist and drummer too. Everyone was gone from Lynx! *POOF!* Is this a classic record label racket story? They were signed to Quality Records, but the contract might not have stated what kind of quality—the first album is top notch.

I reached out to the keyboardist curiously credited as playing keys on this debut album and more extensively involved in subsequent Lynx albums (more on *that* later). He is currently playing resorts in Spain, but he intimated that he wanted thousands of dollars ("Dollars! Dollars!") for an interview. I looked in my pocket and all I had was a handwritten note reading "SELF WORTH." He didn't see Lynx as Glam at all, implying that they were closer to punk. Punk don't strut. Punk don't bloat either, and the second album goes straight for the bloat, a late-night, pompy "drugs are wearing off" bridge party mix of Styx and Deep Purple—cuz what keyboardist doesn't love Deep Purple? (eyes light up behind the synth racks at music stores across the land). What happened?

Luckily, I was eventually able to get the full record company swindle story from the guitarist, Rob Swartz. Obsessed with music since he was a little boy, dreaming of becoming a musician, his life changed when a door-to-door guitar salesman came knocking: his parents opened that door and bought that guitar and enrolled him in guitar lessons at the age of ten for a brief spell, but it was enough: dreams do come true. As a teen, Rob played in a peculiar band that he describes as having "a mish-mash of certain styles and very strange weirdness—a lot of wah-wah—I was using a lot of wah-wah—I can't even tell you the name of the band I was in. I don't think we knew. We did all instrumental tunes. I was very, very young." With the bold promise of fun ("It'll be fun"), his older brother Mike convinced him to join his more pop-oriented band Black Wheat, in much need of a new guitarist. A plethora of church-hall and school dances followed: "We started playing junior highs. And then we finally made our way up to high schools. Rush would come. We'd play our high school the week after Rush had finished. So, Rush was just up and coming. They weren't massive yet, they were Rush."

Black Wheat's next order of business was a name-change to something less befuddling, more befitting, out of the fields and into the forest. "We just wanted a word that would grab people. We were just throwing words around. We were looking at dictionaries—some of the guys were looking at sentences. But I just thought a word, just one word would stick in your head more than a sentence. Thank God, no one was named Lynx back then." Today there are a multitude of different musical acts called Lynx who, even with Google name searches and other modern search methods at their immediate disposal, simply can't be bothered. Just remember: this Lynx was first and foremost.

Let us now take a moment to sing the praises of cool parents everywhere. Not the lax kind (not cool) but the Lynx kind, like the Swartz parents, cool parents who help to foster creativity. The drummer Rick Haberman's cool parents let the band rehearse half the night away in the basement rec room of their wealthy York Mills home. Haberman's mom even encouraged it, she owned a variety store with the regionally astute name the York Miller, replete with a record store in back. She soon told her store's record distributor, Steve Taylor of Taylor Records (a family business), about the merits of Lynx, and that was when Taylor decided to get into band management, sending the boys into the studio to record a demo at the Mercey Brothers' recording studio in Elmira, Ontario. Taylor plopped down three grand or so and drove the four members of Lynx to Elmira, where they recorded six songs, of which Taylor chose three, and Lynx recorded those three again. These songs showed off their versatility: a Poppy Family–style pop song, a ballad, and a hard rocker called "Lucifer." No major record companies in the area expressed any interest until the Summer of '76: seasons changed, and Taylor brought the tape to Quality Records, who listened to "Lucifer" (the song—okay, maybe the guy, too) and went, to quote Rob, "Ohhhh, we're looking for a hard rock band that can be the Canadian KISS, and this band seems like they can rival KISS in Canada." Quality was already KISS's label in Canada, so naturally Lynx were excited. With his parents' permission, Rob signed a recording contract with Quality Records at the age of seventeen.

Lynx started prolifically writing in that vein, rockers and ballads, coming up with twenty songs in three months. Cut that in half and you have cut an album. These songs were augmented with some expressively versatile keyboards by Glenn Morrow of the band Chester (known for the soft-rock single "Make My Life a Little Bit Brighter"). Rob notes Quality's next move: "And then they said, 'You guys need a keyboard player because he's not joining your band. He's a studio musician. So we're going to get you a keyboard player.' And then boom! like a genie in a bottle Tony Caputo shows up. Tony is ten years older than us. Tony's an accomplished musician." Deep in the album credits Glenn Morrow receives a "special thanks" while Caputo's photo is up top with the original four members.

Quality provided Lynx with rehearsal space in an abandoned Philips electronics factory full of equipment fit for playing concerts at Massey Hall—a musician's delight with a massive PA system, lights, smoke-bombs, and flashpots. Ooh, it's like candy! They rehearsed diligently there for six months.

Make-over time! Accustomed to denim, the band was in for a shock. KISS became KISS after seeing what New York Dolls were doing, plus the girls that they were attracting. KISS kept away from all elements of gender play, added Alice Cooper–sized gallons of fake blood, and changed into cosmic bubble-gum superheroes, safe for Middle America. KISS

Lynx promo photo. Courtesy of Robert Swartz.

> **79** Movie
>
> **9:30**
>
> **6** **Caught in the Act** — Canadian glitter rock is the theme of tonight's music with the help of Mendelson Joe, songwriter, singer and guitarist and the up-and-coming group, Lynx. Joe performs, I Love You in C Major 7th, Do What You Do, and, Natural Resources. Lynx performs, Lucifer, Visions and, Break It Up
>
> **25** Scenario
>
> **29** The 700 Club

TV listing for Lynx on *Caught in the Act*. Image courtesy of the *Standard*, December 17, 1976.

were all about the costumes creating deep persona.[18] Quality Records' plans for Lynx were far less coherent, forcing them into looking like kinda-sorta Northern manbeasts. If a band called Lynx was going to be called "the Canadian KISS," then the wild animal was going to come out of its cage. Thrown into the salon chairs by the record company with scant warning from their manager, Lynx swiftly became tamed. And teased! Quality Records' A&R department hired Pat McDonagh and Vidal Sassoon Canada as costume and hair stylists. Prior to moving to Canada, McDonagh had done total mod styling, having helped discover Twiggy as a model and designing bondage-themed leather outfits for Diana Rigg as Emma Peel in *The Avengers*. Despite the stylists' pedigrees, Lynx's new look was an ill-conceived travesty of extreme awkwardness.

Rob sarcastically intones, "Okay, sure. This is your alternative, Canada, here you go, enjoy." He elaborates on Vidal Sassoon Canada's rather bold moves: "They did some very bad, bad things, they did bad things. Rick the drummer—oh my god, he actually came out in tears. They took his hair. They dyed it red. They cut off the long part. They made it short on the top, but they left tendrils of hair on the back, just tendrils, almost like a squid, like squid tentacles, and they dyed those tentacles. He was in tears coming out of that. He was freaked out. They took my brother, they dyed his hair blond, like a blond color. Luckily, they didn't cut it too much. And then they took Tony Caputo . . . Tony turned out like a skunk. They took his massive Afro and they put a streak here and a streak there that was light brown so he looked like a lynx. So when he went out in public he got chased a lot by people who didn't like the look of him." Rob got off easy: "They look at me and my hair was down to here. I didn't cut my hair for fifteen years. So, my bangs are down to where the rest of my hair was. They took a look at me and they went, 'Oh, okay, what we're gonna do is we'd like your hair the way it is. We're just going to put a henna rinse in. We're going to make it jet black with henna.' My hair became so black that under the lights it looked blue. So that's what they wanted. They want the lights to come on—the hair, the hair would look blue."

Their hair perfectly matched the sartorial terror that was thrust upon them: "My brother had a lynx pelt on his back with actual claws. He wore a lynx pelt which was attached

---

[18] Scant years later as a publicity move, KISS wiped off the makeup and bared their faces for over a decade until putting the makeup back on. It is my own personal dream to form "UNMASKED: The World's Only KISS-Without-Makeup Tribute Band," doing music strictly from that era.

to a black jumpsuit—claws coming out with the actual head. So that was pretty interesting. The tail kind of flopped around. The drummer had a wife-beater shirt on, but it was multi-colored, but they painted his nipples red. He got the absolute worst. I got the pleasure of wearing a suit that was made out of paper, and supposedly when paper is washed like a hundred times it becomes a hard material or something. And then there was the silver sewn into it. It was a vest. You couldn't close it, it's all open, so I had to watch what I ate. And then the pants were also made of paper and it was silver. So a silver suit with a vest with chains here with spikes sticking out about this big [gestures six inches]. And a necklace with a big spike on it and boots—oh, the boots were six-inch heels." Specially made by Master John's, these silver boots came up to the knee. Some of the band's platforms were drenched in fur. The entire band teetered around stage on them carefully moving like monsters. During one show, the bassist, Bob Walker—a name that was not going to help him—tripped and fell and took out the drum set. The record company also hired a makeup girl named Donna Weber, who Mike actually dated for two years. She applied loads of glitter.

KISS played stadiums. Lynx played bars. All over Ontario and Quebec and back again, in pulp-mill towns and deep into scary Scarborough. With bikers befriending and looking out for them in their ridiculous costumes, they never saw much trouble. The bikers liked their hard-rocking music. Quality Records also provided them with a massive sound and lighting system. "We saw a lot of things," Rob told me, "like, there were fights in the bars. We got outside one place—I think it was in Penetang, we were playing in Penetang—and that might have been one of the very early gigs and I remember it, I was pretty weary of these places—and coming up to the foot of this door, which was the Queens Hotel, which is what you would play up there, mainly the Queens because that's where the rock bands played—there was blood all over the door. What the hell—blood everywhere—and I walk in and I remember talking to the guy at the bar: 'What is that?' 'Well, it's okay, someone got knifed there last night, don't worry about it.' So, this is the kind of clientele. I remember once playing the Forge, which is downtown Toronto, all of a sudden there's a power failure, the lights go out, and all of a sudden, the lights go on, and the stage which was—we were actually looking down on the crowd—the stage was on another level. So you're looking down at the crowd—you're playing second story up, but looking down on the crowd after the power failure, which was ten seconds—there was a massive brawl that broke out—tables flying, chairs, people getting punched in the face—and it just went on and on and then it settled down and stopped, and then we played for another ten minutes—the power goes off again for ten seconds—all of a sudden, another brawl breaks out. But we were never involved in any of these, so we never got hurt. We were never threatened, we never felt threatened."

Mercifully for Lynx, the costumes didn't last too long, just enough for shows and a Canadian television appearance on the music show *Caught in the Act,* unfortunately lost

Front and back cover of *we are the people* by Lynx (Quality, 1979). Author's collection.

to the ages. This make-over wasn't even exploited on the sleeve of their album. It focused instead on their cadaverous faces and glowing animal eyes.

In one magazine ad for the album the band wasn't even shown. Instead it featured the scantily clad, buxom March 1973 *Penthouse* Pet Avril Lund provocatively holding the record between her legs. The Quality Records marketing department captioned it, "Best twelve inches she ever had." And the worst was yet to come.

Haberman, the drummer, was chronically late for rehearsal. Quality Records replaced him with the clockwise professional musician Ian McCorkle. Quality Records didn't like the way the bassist looked. They replaced him with a faceless professional musician. Quality Records then called a meeting with Rob and Caputo to tell them that Mike —Rob's own brother and the dynamic frontman of the group—was now out. Rob recalls, "I'm like, was I nineteen? Twenty? I had to make a decision whether to stay in this band, which I will probably not get a shot again for a recording contract like this, or leave and do what? Go back to school? Go in another band? I was so freaked out. I'm gonna have to stay. I've got no choice. I have to stay. I ended up staying. And they kept me because they liked my friggin' hair. And they liked the way I looked. I looked like a rock star. My hair down here."

Rob, the only original member, was now surrounded by older session musicians. The new Lynx started playing higher-profile concerts, opening for Triumph playing to ten thousand people at Ontario Place. Rob elaborates: "You just look out and see a sea of heads." With the lineup overhaul no one even noticed. "I had people come up and talk to me, but nobody ever said no, 'What happened to this guy?' Nobody ever said. It was like, 'Ah, great show, man. Can I have your autograph?' I was used to signing autographs all the time. I walk around now. I'm a sales guy for a living. Nobody ever knew what happened to me. I don't talk about it a lot, but it was very strange. But nobody ever cared, nobody noticed the band changed. We had fans. We had the same fans after. And I used to see the same people come to the shows. Girls called us coming to Toronto from Wawa. Same girls. 'Oh, we just came up from Toronto to see you.' That's another story."

Before the label fired them, a slew of high-powered rock 'n' roll songs were written by the original lineup of Lynx. These songs would have made for a great second album. It would have been fun! It was not to be.

Now helmed by the keyboardist, the band hit the studio. McCorkle and Caputo came to loggerheads. McCorkle walked, coming back a few days and a few thousand dollars in studio time later, and the fighting continued. Rob explains, "Everyone's fighting. I'm miserable as hell. So Ian said, 'That's it, I quit.' And I looked at Ian and I said, 'Yeah, I think I'm with you. I'm going to quit too. I can't do it. I can't do it. I can't play with strangers. I don't know these people. I don't want the arguments. It's not my band anymore.' It's like, that's not what I wanted to do." Although they fully played on the album, Rob and McCorkle are not listed in the band credits. Squinting towards the fine print, it reads like a sneer: "Special thanks to Rob Swartz and Ian McCorkle for their time and great talents."

If you loved the first album like I do, you will be very confounded by the second album, 1978's *Sneak Attack*—that's code for anonymous fart by the way. After breathing it in, it's not bad, I guess. The keyboardist moves up to the plaintive lead-vocal plate along with new guy Norm, who uses a drippy break-up ballad for an ice-breaker (this is a no-no on first dates but not so much for second albums). This incarnation of Lynx lets you know that they've been really inspired by those *Reader's Digest* classical-music box-sets. Expect lots of synth solos and a twelve-minute album closer. One song goes south of the border on a package resort tour, while another, "Crazy Lady," addresses the sensitive topic of mental illness with wolf whistles and giggling and stuff about how "We're gonna do it!" The album comes with a poster depicting a medium-resolution photo of a woman in a string bikini obliviously looking away, album hastily superimposed into her right hand. My poster was clearly once on someone's wall, then they learned shame, folded it up, and put it back inside the album.

The year was 1979 and, yet again, Lynx got another whole new lineup, again except for that keyboardist, plus: one lone Norm-penned left-over track. Featuring no original members whatsoever, this album sounds like bureaucratic paperwork, like they were contractually obligated to give the people a third album. What people? The album is called *we are the people* and this time it's personal, this time it's lower case. This band knows its audience. The band are the people. The album cover is mostly taken up by anonymous mannequins—the poodle-coiffed band members crudely cut and shuttled into the corner of the shot by ham-hock-sized fists trying to work their way around a pair of scissors and glue. On the back, not only are the band members naked, but the mannequins are too! Here's a secret about mannequins: they don't have genitals. A plain circular sticker declares, 'GREAT VALUE' for this five-gram vinyl. Many of these songs could have easily been used as segue music for mildly risqué lifestyle shows of the era, airing at 9 or even as late as 9:30 PM. Quality Records dumped hundreds of thousands of dollars into Lynx while making wrong-headed and cold-hearted decisions to drastically diminishing returns with this final album as the end result of their bureaucratic misguidance. Do you like synth trumpet? It all ends with the keyboardist doing some intricate runs of generic virtuosity and yelling, "Farewell!" like he actually means it. Eventually, fittingly, Quality Records dropped all of their acts, declared bankruptcy, and folded. Years later, a mysterious label called Uni-Disc started releasing many of Quality's back catalog of albums on CD without any of those bands' knowledge until they stumbled upon their own albums on the "New Releases" CD racks in the record stores.

After getting fired from his own band by the label, Mike Swartz wasted no time in forming a band called Wanderlust. It wasn't long after walking from Lynx that Rob joined. The album was half completed, then Rob's daughter was born. Today Rob has four grandchildren and still continues to play music. He released a CD in the '90s where he plays every instrument. Mike sings as great as he did with Lynx and is active in three cover bands. One of these, Mid-Life Crisis, has Rob and Mike playing together.

Despite all of the awfulness and awkwardness that they went through, the first Lynx album will last forever. It's solid!

JUSTIN PAIGE

WHEN I FIRST HEARD OF THE SINGER Justin Paige, my mind immediately went, "Canada's answer to Jobriath! He could have been Jobriath's more hirsute Canadian cousin!" Mm. It's not as simple as all that. Yes, Canada is known to be a country that reacts, often doing a Canadian version of whatever is already popular and pre-existing in the United States. Jobriath was the first openly gay Glam Rock superstar on a major label, with massive, provocative billboards up in New York City and Los Angeles. But here's the thing about Paige: he wasn't gay. But, here's the other thing: the creative forces involved with Paige were. Paige didn't write any of the songs that he sang. Those were all written by his bandmate Joey Miller. Miller explains, "Justin and I went to high school together. And he was a womanizer then. Loved all the girls—I liked all the guys, he liked all the girls. And when we did this album, you have to know that. I had to explain to him what the titles were because he was willing to do anything. For a career. He just liked singing the music. He tried many different styles of music. He did a nightclub act."

Prior to the album, Paige had a 1973 single on Capitol Records Canada with the not-a-bit-Glam-in-the-slightest "Stompin on the Bayou." Before too long, though, Paige would become known as "Canada's King of Rock and Rouge" and dubbed by *Now* magazine as "Canada's Lone Ranger of Sex."

Though it was called *The Everything Goes Show*, the host introduced Paige stating, "His act is so freaky that on our last show his entire song was bleeped." For this short-lived television variety show from 1974, Paige was only Glam in appearance, covering the Doobie Brothers yet sounding like burly Vegas lounge funk, due mostly to the *Everything Goes Show* house band. But what an appearance! Peroxide blonde, gold mustache, glitter everywhere, very generous portions of makeup including blue eyeshadow extending far beyond the eyes, gold and silver galore, topped off with both cape and scarf paired daringly together. Along for the ride were his omnipresent backup singers, a lesbian couple known as Franny and Zooey, themselves no less visual in sheer blue fishnet shirts, delicate chain-mail, matching make-up, and Ziggy Stardust–style mullets. There's no denying that the three of them belted it out. On another appearance, Paige wore ersatz-Egyptian-tinged garments while Franny and Zooey offset him dressed in evening finery performing an ecological ersatz-gospel Edgar Winter song that the host, Norm Crosby, described in one word as "Beautiful."

It was Paige and Miller's manager Frank Angelo who reintroduced them to each other. Miller describes Angelo as a genius, having started the Haircutting Place, a chain of unisex salons: "Oh, he loved Bowie and he loved Glam, the whole Glam scene, he loved all that music. He put Justin's act together, fixed Justin's hair. He did the whole thing." With Miller's strong musical theater background, a Glam Rock band seemed a natural fit.

Newspaper ad for Justin Paige's week-long engagement at Diamond Jim's. Image courtesy of the *Hamilton Spectator*, March 25, 1974.

Back and front cover of *Justin Paige* by Justin Paige (Capitol Records, 1974). Album front courtesy collection of Ian Marshall. Back cover, author's collection.

They loved working together. Miller found Paige to be not just a theatrical performer but also a terrific singer. A band was built, including Rik Emmett on guitar. Besides Miller's originals, they would cover Bowie and Lou Reed in their live shows.

Capitol Records Canada needed Canadian content. Seeing Paige, they knew that they could count on him to go out and promote the album—he was a performer. For Miller's record deal, he says, "Frank Angelo, the genius that he is, pulled up in his Cadillac, me sitting in the backseat, and the executives came up to meet me and they signed me."

The self-titled 1974 album opens with a reference to the Parkside Tavern, a popular yet dingy Toronto gay bar whose straight owners notoriously allowed plainclothes police to spy on the patrons in the washrooms, ready to make arrests at any sign of illicit activity. These were far riskier times. Softly and deceptively, Paige sings the intro, "Down at the Parkside you can get what you want," Faux-Ronsoning edging up and Paige is ready to unfurl, okay, this is a Glam Rock album, not an MOR

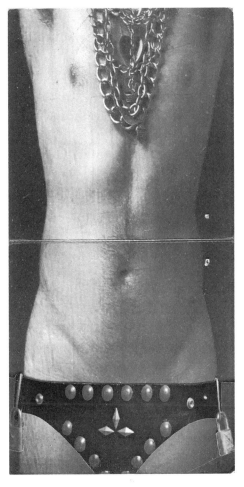

Inner gatefold cover of *Justin Paige* by Justin Paige (Capitol Records, 1974). Author's collection.

masquerade. "Rough Trade, never laid, keeps his banana in the palm of his hand!" No, not a literal banana. Red light and back seats, a jean queen—why, this is a full-on quest! The back-up singers Franny and Zooey, a.k.a. Fran Cheslo and Honora Doran, are integral, their tongues intoning, "Wah wah la la la la . . . " Wicked riff runs. Vocal delivery giving dramatic grit and gusto, at times even burly. The producer, Lee Decarlo, produced the second Fludd album as well as *Battle Axe* by Billion Dollar Babies,[19] but admittedly there are places where the production plods: for such outrageousness it can get banal, with some songs trying to be anthems, the fade-out button just slightly out of reach. But it has more than a few moments. "Prodigy" opens on an electrified keyboard doing elaborate classical runs. "Should Have Been Born a Lady" is a hand-on-hip statement on misogyny. Light-

---

19 Billion Dollar Babies was the Alice Cooper Band without Vincent Furnier after he went solo as Alice Cooper.

ers up, everyone—it's time for the closer, "You Win Some, You Loathe Some," an anti–"Little Help from My Friends" with "Piano Man"/"Rock 'n' Roll Suicide" nods to the onstage loneliness of the performer.

The album was Glam in its various themes of street decadence. Miller penned all of the songs on the album specifically for Paige to sing, approaching Paige as an image for them to create, a character for them to develop. However, Paige sings about other people, delivering profiles à la Lou Reed's "Walk on the Wild Side." Some of these character sketches contain a lot of coding. The song "Kaye Y. Kutie" is about a street prostitute, her name being a reference to K-Y Jelly, an affordable sexual lubricant. "Grease up the axle" is one lyric; another is, "Who keeps her basket full of fruit when the suit is made of cellophane." There are a few euphemisms for genitals throughout the album; besides "basket," there are also "root" and "banana." Did I already mention the banana? "Sugar Daddy" is about a john. With "Tea Room Tramp," "tea room" is lingo for restroom. "Steam Queen," ostensibly about someone in a steam bath, contains references to sailors and size kings.

Newspaper ad for the New Justin Paige Show at Cariboo Lounge, 1976. Image courtesy of *Waterloo Region Record*, June 19, 1976.

Miller explains, "The record company must have been very nervous. I'm just going to speculate that they were quite nervous about the lyrics. And the image that the lyrics portray ironically wasn't him (Justin). He was the music. He liked the music. Well, I think that Capitol Records was very concerned about it maybe being too gay—whatever that means. Because he was, he was himself, he loved women so that's what they were wanting to project. He didn't really care what people thought. He was overly gay-friendly, he just didn't care. He was seeing this. He was supporting the gay community. So that was Justin—he just wanted to have fun. Guys just want to have fun. He was like that. We went to Hamilton. He always did really well, he always packed the place. And on either side of the room there's big balconies and the stage below and he entered jumping off the balcony onto the stage and I never figured out, that was something he just wanted to do. It had nothing to do with gender or whatever, he just wanted to jump. He wanted to make an entrance and he liked to push the edge."

Canadian labels have a long-standing tradition of not taking risks, especially for the Canadian divisions of international major labels. And Capitol Records Canada was no less risk-averse. The one song on the album not written by Miller, "Rock and Roll Band," is exactly what you'd think it is and that was the label's safe choice as first and only single.

The album design itself was inventively wild. Painted-up cartoon depictions of the albums' characters are hanging out on the street—a hand peeping out from a manhole to dash the ash from a cigarette, a leather-clad man, gay and lesbian couples walking arm in arm, a steam bath, street worker Kaye Y. Kutie—this gaudily colored rendering takes away from how you might have imagined them. Leaving little to the imagination, the hazy back cover is the cover that really makes it—back should have been front—featuring a nearly nude Paige surrounded by Franny and Zooey in matching velvet chastity-belt jumpsuits, one of them covering his nether regions with what is either a shiny daisy-patterned purse— or maybe it's a toilet bowl lid?—other faces hazily peering out, everyone having a good time within the soft-focus photograph. Dig deeper and the real gimmick is just within the gatefold! Open it up and you get Paige's outstretched bare torso, the record itself nestling perfectly inside his leather undies. Now this is packaging—emphasis on package. The label clearly put a lot of money into the album itself but then . . .

For the live shows, Miller played keys dressed in a white tuxedo and top hat, conjuring up a bit of an Elton John appearance. In Dave Bidini's book *On a Cold Road: Tales of Adventure in Canadian Rock*, the guitarist Rik Emmett describes wearing a woman's black leotard, a fake white hand attached to the groin, and black lipstick; he then states, "I noticed folks in the crowd going, 'What the fuck?' and I realized what showbiz meant. That was a big thing, to be able to take my musicianship and subvert it to an entertainment venture."[20]

Miller invited his parents out for the hometown show in Montreal at Café l'Est, a large club filled with so much marijuana smoke that his parents got high just from the fumes. As fun as it was, there was no publicity and, once the smoke cleared away, it became readily apparent that there was hardly anyone there. Miller relates, "We came offstage and Rik said, 'I can't believe I'm doing this. I'm getting my own act. I'm going to have a bass player and I'm going to be one guitar and a drummer. We're going to have three people, have a band . . . ' and there they go. They became Triumph, I think maybe a year or two later, not much longer." Triumph went on to record sixteen albums. One of their back-up singers, Fran Cheslo, became the lead singer of a later incarnation of the bubble-gum band Chester.

When their manager Frank Angelo met Frank Toskan in the early '70s, they soon became a couple known as the Franks and later became business partners, launching MAC Cosmetics in 1984. One of Angelo's ideas was to get the drag icon RuPaul and the Alberta-born lesbian crooner icon k.d. lang to be MAC representatives. And his love of Glam strongly continued with Viva Glam lipstick, all sales of which went towards the MAC AIDS

---

20 Dave Bidini, *On a Cold Road: Tales of Adventure in Canadian Rock,* p. 117.

fund, raising millions to support people living with HIV/AIDS worldwide. One of the Viva Glam store ads had the word "AIDS" in it. Joey relates, "And there were places that said, 'I don't want that in my store,' and they said, 'No, it's gonna go in the store.' So the stores stood by them. It's very important. No, this is what we're doing, we're losing friends, we have friends who are HIV and also their makeup was helping a lot of female impersonators at Wigstock in New York—we went down for Wigstock. So they would go down and they gave makeup to a lot of drag queens. So they were way ahead of their time." Angelo died in 1997 following complications from surgery.

Miller had his first huge hit in 1978, writing the lyrics and music to the theatrical production *Eight to the Bar,* and has continued to write. He would later go on to cowrite a stage musical version of *Outrageous,* the important Canadian gay-themed film which included numerous female impersonations.

After getting dropped by Capitol Canada in 1975, Paige moved into the lounge scene, playing the Four Seasons and Harbourfront hotels before leaving music altogether, now living a different life.

ZWOL & BRUTUS

WITH ZWOL, WE ARE WELCOMED WITH A SOFT GLAM, a yacht Glam with an impressive voice, often compared to the vocal greats Elton John and Freddie Mercury. While the music explored the softer side, the live presentation, by contrast, was astonishingly unbridled. Zwol himself uses the whole stage, all over the place, energetic and eccentric, sexual. Not only that, but Zwol is the originator of Cueball Glam, with a head matching the sleek smoothness of his sound.

Born Walter Zwolinksi, he briefly became Wally Soul for the blue-eyed horn blast of "Funky Roller Skates," the first single by his band Brutus in 1969. Moving up the charts in Hamilton, Brutus performed it on Dave Mickie's CHCH-TV show *Mickie a Go Go* superimposed inside of a giant roller skate moving all around the studio, thanks to the advances of video technology.

As for his unique Cueball Glam look, youth and vanity combined to create innovation. Zwol explains, "Well, to be honest with you, I was twenty-one and I started losing my hair, and my mom said, 'Well let's do this, let's try olive oil every night and I'll massage the olive oil.' Before every gig I did this whole thing and then it just started getting worse and worse. I bought a toupee for $10,000 in 1971. But I just said to my mom, 'I think I'm gonna shave it. Mom, what do you think?' She said, 'You know what? I think your head looks okay so, let's do it.' So my mom and I shaved my head." At the time the only person known to do such a thing was the film actor Yul Brynner. "I remember looking at him—I thought, this is a really distinguished guy. I remember seeing him in *The King and I.* I went, 'Wow! I like this guy.' This really set it off for me. It was kind of a tribute to him." The opposite of Samson, yet it proved to be a strength, a virile trademark.

A couple more Brutus singles were followed by a hiatus and lineup upheaval and then the band came back full-on Glam, a new look and lineup for 1973. Zwol would apply his makeup a little differently every night, be it rainbows and rays over the eyes, face completely white like the influence mimes held over him, as well as performance artists and David Bowie.

This look could provoke the occasional adverse reaction from bikers at the bars in Brampton, Oshawa, and even Toronto. They would yell homophobic epithets and violent threats. One such man, standing six foot four, shouted, "You're dead. You're dead. After this gig, after your set, you're dead!" then did a neck-slicing gesture with his finger. Walking offstage into their dressing room, "the drummer's behind me, and there's the guy standing there with arms folded, looking right at me," Zwol recounts. "My drummer, unbeknownst to me, just grabs my shoulder, puts me out of the way, and goes wham! and just smashes the guy right in the nose, out cold. Just clocks him right out and I go, 'Holy shit, Danny. Wow. I didn't have the balls to do that.'" On more than one occasion, more than one of the drummers in the various Brutus band lineups took care of things.

One of Zwol's big influences was the transgressive, way-out, hallucinatory cinema of Alejandro Jodorowsky. Brutus grew closer to this aesthetic when the artist and inventor Don Norman came along to help inspire and carry out some of the wilder ideas. Norman made Zwol an ostrich-feather cape and then applied matching ostrich feathers to his custom purple snakeskin Master John boots. He then made outfits for the rest of the band. Alas, the cape kept slipping off Zwol's shoulders and was duly passed on to the mannequin. On stage, this mannequin was frequently the object of Zwol's affection. Norman would join them on stage and the two of them would make love to the mannequin.

Opening in 1971, the Ontario Place theme park looked into the future. Part of its architecture for the people included massive pods floating invitingly over the lake. When Brutus performed there, it was to a sold-out crowd, records were broken (not vinyl records, silly), and they were given a plaque by Premier Bill Davis.

Another aspect of the utopic Ontario Place was the Cinesphere, a full-on state-of-the-art IMAX theater in a massive geodesic dome. Ontario Place contacted Brutus by special request and asked them to be filmed partying for a segment of a new IMAX movie called *Energy*. Norman's massive warehouse space was the perfect venue for the party scene and they knew exactly who to put on the invitation list. Zwol explains, "Now at that time, I had a bunch of dwarf actors following Brutus around. They all wore makeup, they were all actors, and they had other actors that sort of came along, some beautiful model girls who were kind of asexual, they hung with these dwarf actors, and we invited them." Described as "Impressionistic images of power usage," *Energy* was first screened on May 17, 1975. With IMAX being larger than life, the film opens with a steam train coming right out atcha,

Brutus with Walter Zwol in rainbow facepaint, 1973. Courtesy of Walter Zwol.

then a six-story-tall Walter Zwol singing a new song appropriately called "Rock 'n' Zwol." At the IMAX afterparty, Pierre and Maggie Trudeau popped in—they had an invite. The gang convinced Prime Minister Trudeau to kiss Norman's tube and he did—Norman had a pierced ear with a tube coming out of it. The ever creative Norman designed and wore a pair of railroad spiked heels to the party.

Norman's warehouse contained many of his gigantic art pieces, some built to inflate. Ontario Place had hired him to make something for the kids, so he made a tube blown up with an exhaust fan for them all to run through. With another artist, he draped various large different-colored canvases over the Grand Canyon. But he designed costumes specifically just for Brutus to wear. For Zwol he made a vest that consisted entirely of zippers and a belt made up of thirty circular birth-control dial-pack dispensers. Yet it still wasn't wild enough. They needed to take it further. And one outfit in particular caused controversy.

"You know why we changed? Brutus had to change. What happened, we did an afternoon job at Seneca College. Seneca has the Minkler auditorium, two thousand kids. I wore this outfit—I had two holes cut in the ass and one right above my crotch—and girls swore that I pulled my dick out. They literally called the police. I was interviewed and they called me the devil—it came out in the *Sun*. And after that, I wore that outfit to a rural high school, and same thing: the kids all swore I had my penis out. I didn't, but I just had that hole cut above the crotch—and they pulled the curtain, the vice principal and principal came up and said, 'Get out, get out. We're taking you to court and we're taking you to the Toronto musician's union.' I had to pay a fine and we were not allowed to play in Toronto high schools anymore because that was our main . . . we would play literally five high schools a week, all southern Ontario. And then finally we had to go over and play northern Ontario. And that was the start of Quebec City. We went to Quebec City. I did the whole spiel. The French kids loved it!" notes Zwol. British Columbia loved it too, building a massive crowd, some of whom wore wild makeup. "We did some cover material. I would do one song by a group called Free called 'Woman.' And I'd do a half an hour where I raped myself. I literally went down to a G-string and put a dildo up my ass. I didn't put it right up, but I put it up and they just couldn't—I did it once in Vancouver, but it was a little too much. But Quebec—they loved it. They just loved it. There you go, talk about one-upmanship, but I could only do it there."

The superstar producer Bob Ezrin, who had a string of classic Alice Cooper albums under his belt along with Lou Reed's intense epic *Berlin*, approached Zwol after seeing and loving the newspaper article about his wardrobe mishap. Zwol elaborates: "He said, 'I'm not interested in 'Ooh Mama Mama' [the good-feeling lead-off track on their debut album *Brutus*]. I'm not interested in that stuff. I want you to get out there like Ozzy and just kick ass! You know, we'll write together. Yeah, I want you to do the heavy stuff. Go out there, do your makeup and just—I want the makeup a little more striking'—in other words, putting like evil things or whatever, right, you know, like a sword on my face or something. 'You're

Left: Brutus with mannequin, 1973. Walter Zwol, music, lyrics, vocals, keyboards; Dennis Pinhorn, bass; Lance Wright, drums; Gino Scarpelli, guitar. Photography: Gerrard Gentil. Courtesy of Walter Zwol.

very physical, so I want you to stop all the camp shit—I want you to just go out there and be mean, be brutal.' And I just said, 'Well, I still write those kinds of songs.'"

Here's a fun tidbit: Ezrin showed up again a few years later. When he was producing Lee Aaron he dropped by Attic Records and saw that Zwol was their A&R guy. He walked into Zwol's office and closed the door and told Zwol that he wanted him to audition for Black Sabbath. "So I flew down to L.A. on a Friday afternoon, got there, and sat there till Sunday afternoon. I said, 'Bob, what's going on?' He goes, 'The band's gonna break up for a little period. You might as well just go home.' It was like a free trip to L.A., sitting there scratching my head saying, 'What the hell is happening?' When Black Sabbath found their next singer, an unknown singer called Donny Donato, it was an accident, apparently due to *Kerrang!* magazine photographing the band during Donato's audition. Zwol was lucky, as that lineup only got so far as an Ezrin-produced demo, nixed by Ozzy Osbourne rejoining Black Sabbath for Live Aid in 1985.

Don Norman in his own custom-made outfit on stage with Brutus, 1973. Courtesy of Walter Zwol.

The notorious music business mogul Bruce Allen offered to manage Brutus on one condition: they had to move to British Columbia. However, Zwol's daughter had just been born. No can do.

With Zwol being the only original member of Brutus, his name was the only one on the equipment rentals and everything. Zwol was in debt. To get back to playing the lucrative southern Ontario market, Brutus needed to tone it down. Now, that isn't to say that they became boring—they just weren't pushing the envelope so fiercely. Zwol remained a frenetic, theatrical performer, expressively acting out the lyric. To quote the title of one of Zwol's own songs, he's still "A Little Bit Crazy." One time in Buffalo, he got so worked up that he passed right out on stage. His bandmate stood on his chest yelling, "Get up! Get up!" and Zwol came to, jumped up dizzy, and kept right on going. In 1975, Brutus opened for Sparks at Massey Hall in Toronto and all I can do is imagine what a show it must have been.

When Zwol wanted Brutus to expand musically, he found a new guitarist, Woody West. This meant that the hard rock guitarist Gino Scarpelli needed a new gig. Greg Godovitz was putting together his power trio Goddo and came to see Brutus, Zwol let him in on what was going on, telling him, "Gino and I are cool on it," and thus Goddo got Scarpelli on guitar. Everybody wins.

Brutus made an album so very pleasing that they called it *Brutus*—they named the album after a very good band—and it was released on the GRT label in 1976. *Brutus* goes down smooth, a li'l sassy with good vibes sent out, sway your hips, gentle up-lifter, ups-a-daisy, Zwol will belt it and throw in some coy oohs. He'll sing about doing a tango while the band pretends that they're the Band on an afternoon AM drive, not so much as a worry about the speed limit. "3.30 Came" is the eight-minute opus, an after-school memory book, with a flanged-out rooty tooty very old school, back of the barbershop quartet segment, then right out front and ready to strut that stuff, baby! That old school bell is a synth alarm! Wheeeee! Next up: a song that opens with a Gay Paree feel. Then we get a song about "Sailing" with no danger of hitting rocks and perishing—he sings that, if we wind up sailing into unknown places, those places will probably be good ones with the sun shining upon us; in comes a gentle wave of the marimba setting on the keyboard. On another track he is singing about feeling fine, making a motorboat sound on a lyric about a rock 'n' roll lady, but, ultimately, how they're doing it "For the People"—cue handclaps and cowbell and chants. On the album credits, beside everyone's real names, Zwol playfully gave everyone nicknames like Yazoo Bazoo the roadie, Hot Nick on lights, Pepe Del Grande on the keys, Woody West on guitar, Freddie Ferdowitch on drums, and Percival C. Eater on synths—who in actuality is Doni Underhill, who soon left to join up with Trooper.

Zwol was very loyal to Brutus. Island Records came calling from across the water. They said, "We're looking at three acts: Carole Pope, Nick Gilder, and you. . . . We're not interested in your band. We're interested in you." Zwol replied, "'I can't.' We'd been through an awful lot." They said, "You're making a mistake. Thank you very much." However, in the end, Island didn't sign any of them.

A variety of factors led to Zwol's eventual disillusionment with Brutus: the relentless touring and driving to key markets in Quebec City and all the way across the country in B.C.—along with rehearsals—also meant lineup changes from musician burn-out, with Zwol being the only constant, the sole original member and songwriter. It was almost like a solo project. Disastrous shows—such as opening for Peter Gabriel where the rest of the band froze up on stage—disheartened him. Flying over Lake Ontario, en route to London, he ruminated and felt like a dog chasing its own tail—the band was holding him back. Arriving there, for the first time he tasted Europe and wanted to go international. Zwol decided to fly solo. Showing his loyalty, he told the rest of Brutus that he would stay for a few months, from February to July, to give them a chance to get a new lead singer. What happened to Brutus after Zwol left is not known.

Zwol recorded his solo album from July up until September 1977, saved some money, then he and his manager, George Elmes, took it to London, New York, and L.A.: alas, no record deal came of it. Finally, Elmes decided to take it to Ralph Murphy, who had produced the Brutus album and was also a professional songwriter. With Roger Cook, they had a publishing company called Picalic. Cook was well known for his propensity for making countless hits and had helped write the Coke jingle "I'd Like to Teach the World to Sing." Picalic had pull. Two days later,

Inner cover of *Brutus* by Brutus (GRT, 1976). Author's collection.

Zwol got a call. It was Murphy: "Mate. What are you doing?" Zwol said, "Nothing." "We're flying you down, all expenses paid, we'll pay your rent. Come on down and write down here in Nashville." They cut more demos there and then jetted to L.A., with Picalic pitching the best of the Nashville and Toronto demos. Zwol continues, "Monday morning they started shopping. By Thursday a $100,000 check, certified check. Good god. I cried. I cried like a baby. I phoned my parents and said, 'You're not gonna believe this. I just got a deal, an American deal.' I have no Canadian deal. As far as I know, I was the first Canadian to ever have one with no Canadian deal. Right to America. Thanks in large part to Ralph and Roger." Together with Zwol, Cook and Murphy produced the album for the EMI label.

Back in 1976, David Bowie needed a guitarist for his *Station to Station* tour. Bowie got a tape. On the tape was the Windsor, Ontario, guitarist Stacy Heydon: the choice was made. Bowie told Heydon not to replicate the *Station to Station* album but to do his own thing. Ripping Telecaster leads were played; this then led to Heydon touring for a spell with Iggy Pop on his *Lust for Life* tour.

Zwol needed a guitarist for his 1978 *Zwol* album, named after Walter Zwol. They tried out a bunch of guys. Then they heard that Heydon was available, and Zwol loved Bowie: "I really admire Bowie, one of the greatest songwriters, as far I'm concerned, of all time, pop-wise." And, on Zwol's first solo album, Heydon's riffs come on strong but know when to ease on down. Just because Zwol makes Soft Glam doesn't mean he isn't diverse: the album sparkles and shines and literally, too—it's true, the cover has a neat gimmick. Zwol is wearing mirrored sunglasses so you can stare at him but you'd also be staring at a reflection of you to see if there's any spinach in your teeth. Using mirrors, the EMI promo team did giant versions of the cover in record-store windows and when the sun was shining just right, well, look out, traffic!

Front cover of *Zwol* by Zwol (EMI America, 1978). Author's collection.

"New York City" is a song that this municipality should be proud to own—hello, tourism board, got you a peppy song right here! France gave you the Statue of Liberty and Canada gives you the gift of Zwol. "New York City" is square, man! No, not the song, the actual single itself is square-shaped, and it was pressed on white vinyl. The song started to take off all the way over in England.

Zwol went on a wild, six-week EMI European package promo tour of TV stations and media outlets with Siouxsie and the Banshees, the reggae band Third World, and Kiki Dee and hit it off with the Glam Rock inspiration Jayne County, of whom Zwol says, "And I was drunk out of my brain and we're just kibbitzing around like crazy." Zwol had a troubling run-through in Munich, due to performing to track alone in front of a studio audience without a band; this was an entirely new experience that left him in a panic. Kiki Dee took

Zwol aside and gave him wonderful performance advice. It worked. The cameras captured his incredible performance of "New York City" on the German TV show *RockPop,* letting the TV audience experience the bravado charisma of Zwol, continuously moving but always in the spotlight—how does that spot keep up with tongue flashing, haute couture animal print hat, stylish, high-kicking Zwol? Zwol saw his performance's gay innuendoes as almost like a tribute to his friend Don Norman, who was now living in New York City. (On one visit Norman picked Zwol up at the airport and the New York authorities promptly took them down to the station: Norman was wearing a completely transparent outfit. A quick cover-up and they were ready to go out on the town.)

After finishing this European promo tour, the region of Holland was rather taken with Zwol's tongue-in-cheek song "The Southern Part of France", it was gaining traction there. They tracked Zwol down in Italy and flew him to Amsterdam for more TV and radio interviews. "The Southern Part of France" was written as Brutus was dissolving, on his first trip to Europe, sitting by a fountain in front of the big Monte Carlo Casino. Zwol reflects, "My mum used to sing a silly little song from the old days called 'In the southern part of France, where the ladies wear no pants.'" Over a dreamy groove, the lyrics evoke scenery leading up to this chorus of coy camp multiplied, with some moans and laughter thrown in for good measure. A film crew was put together and they flew to where it all took place, the southern part of France, to film a twenty-minute piece for Radio One in Amsterdam. "And we took a whole week down there. And just following a couple of prostitutes around and whatnot, because the song, you know, deals with a slice of life. I sang to track with them out there and the girls in the—you know, I guess they paid them, I don't know—and the girls walked around just following through the streets of Nice . . . or was it Cannes? How romantic, but it really was. It was a real fun time and then we went to the casino, shot some

Front and back fold over of "Cheerleader" single by Zwol (EMI America, 1979). Author's collection.

things there because I do name the casinos, the fountain on the other side flows like the fountain on the inside." Because of that song, Zwol still gets offers to play the Netherlands.

The American promo tour for *Zwol* lasted twenty-eight cities. Big money was going around—first stop, Boston, and the head of promo took him to a back room. Zwol describes what he saw: "I got there, I swear to God, there was a rock the size of a soccer ball. And I said, 'Who's paying for this?' 'You.' So I really made no money except for the signing bonus and signing on, but I mean nowadays you don't get a signing bonus like that. Not $100,000 U.S. I moved to L.A., bought myself a Porsche." Album sales were low, so Zwol sold the Porsche, then moved back to Toronto for a couple of weeks. Over in Paris was a DJ whose wealthy parents owned the largest TV and radio stations in France. Zwol explains, "She really loved music and she ran a radio show from twelve to four in the morning. 'The Southern Part of France' was the kick-off. She phoned the record company in L.A. They phoned me and they said, 'She wants to meet you.' So I flew over and I ended up staying and living with her for about three and a half months in Paris." While there, the director Jean-Jacques Beineix wanted to work with Zwol. He took some photos, but Zwol had to get back to Canada. There is a rather distinctively Zwol-looking character in Beineix's 1981 movie *Diva*, made not long after his France escapade.

When Heydon produced the second Teenage Head album, *Frantic City*, Zwol came in to play some synths on some tracks—alas, a tad buried in the mix. It was also around that time that Heydon rejoined Bowie for the unforgettable *Saturday Night Live* performance with Klaus Nomi and Joey Arias singing back-ups and carrying Bowie to the microphone.

With Zwol's next album, *Effective Immediately,* released a year later, it just continues to go down smooth. Not as 'Effective' as the first, scaling back to record in Toronto, the bravado's gone more mid-tempo but still giving pleasure with stand-outs like the pulse of "Shaka Shaka," designed to make you do just that, to shaka shaka, where treated real saxes almost sound like synths, melding with them into a real nice dip. There's some more coy, too—"Cheerleader" has some daring asides, like "Oooh, way up high!" and a spelling out of "C-H-E-E-R-L-E-A-D-E-R!" Greg Godovitz of Goddo pops in to chant along. The "Cheerleader" single features a realistic pencil drawing of cheerleaders spelling out ZWOL on their outfits, thronging him, based on a special L.A. promo photo shoot.

For the new label A&M, he released an album in 1981 as Walter Zwol and the Rage, a four-piece band doing heavier session rock. In the '90s there was a stint where Zwol had a weekly gig at a club called Berlin, which he kind of hated because he had to do covers. Luckily, he was able to change it up, let loose on stage. While talking music with Zwol, it was readily apparent that his tastes are diverse, he loves the music of Suede, Aphex Twin, Pulp, Van Halen, Thelonious Monk. The freedom of jazz has inspired him to write a bunch of new material. And it'd be so good to hear it. Please!

ROBBIE ROX

ROBBIE ROX'S MOST POPULAR ALBUM, *Raw,* was also his most uniquely unhinged. Called *Raw* because of the stripped-down rock band, it is—along with his previous album—quite musically complex. Challenging? Yes. Every song careens off into a million directions. Histrionics arguing for Ritalin. A vocal range that will break all the glasses in your summer cottage (don't have a cottage? break into one on the off season, now you have one, in a "property is theft" timeshare pinch). Jelly-spewing operatics: "Hold this note, I'm going in!" It is immersion, full-bodied baptism, your tub will never be the same, this music leaves rings.

Ring ring. "Hello, record store, do you have *Ethel Merman Sings Beefheart*? No? But you have *what*? Oh, what is *Raw*? I'll be there before you can say—" Another satisfied customer. Who wouldn't want to hear a song called "Bidet for a Donkey"? No one I want to know. "Hello Sandro" opens with Rox laughing like there are hula hoops caught in his throat, some Latin American style guitar solos thrown down with confidence. What is he on about? Something, absolutely—it shimmies away as soon as I put my finger on it—he sure knows how to grease up his recovered memories. This is a rock unit and nothing is straight ahead. The music gets epic and sweeping while he belts out with such contradiction, "It's a dime a dozen world!"—at one point intoning, "There's a pie in the background of everybody's mind," at another point singing like Frankie Valli, "Strong, girl, you've got to be strong, girl . . . "

The *Raw* lineup is known as the Catso, Porco, Rozzo Band—pseudonyms doled out to the stripped-down four-piece (Robbie Rox backed by Johnny Catso, Michael Rozzo, and Johnny Porco). A secret revealed: three of them are related. Apart from the drummer, John Hobbs, this is a talented band of literal brothers all sharing the surname Theodore: Michael, the bassist; Johnny, the keyboardist and guitarist; and Robbie, who also played guitar. Theodore? They aren't all Rox? Robbie Rox is a pseudonym too, a.k.a. Robert Theodore, a pseudonym that he has used since 1973 when his band was sitting around the band house trying to make a name for themselves via the brainstorming method. Robbie reflected back to the end of a romantic break-up when he walked away from the door of a bus station saying to himself, "I gotta be tough, this is killing me, I gotta be strong like a rock, like a rock, rock, rocks, rocks, rocks." He said to his bandmates, "Well, I don't know. How about Robbie Rocks?" They replied, "Yeah, but you got to spell it differently. It should be R-o-x, not R-o-c-k. So Rox." Rox summarizes, "And it stuck!"

Robert Theodore is a nice name but it doesn't sound Glammy. Robbie Rox is a hundred and a lots percent. The more starched out there may suggest that at least two of his albums are an argument for Canadian Glam to rein it in, that it's an acquired taste (here's another acquired taste: olives, delicious and worth swallowing the pits for), an absolute gem at certain occasions, including ridding your home of unwelcome guests (a Robbie Rox listening party is most welcome).

Rox is more than Glam. He's a freak! He plays freak rock! Indeed, he is also a client of that special club, Canadian Cueball Glam, his smooth pate taking up the album cover with *Raw* in red bold letters literally drawn across his forehead. The sleeve is strikingly unique. The photo flicker flashed with the lens wide open, Rox on repeat. Raw is how he eats it, a full steak hanging out of his mouth. Leaving the studio, the photographer John McKee said, "Aren't you going to take the steak with you? It's a good steak, it's Porterhouse." Living on and off with his mom and younger sister, he knew that it would be perfect for his sister's two great Danes—until his mother intervened, utterly unswayed by it already being slightly chewed. "So," Rox said, "she cooked a big beef stroganoff, and we're sitting at a table and my sister Lisa—I think she was like twenty-two, maybe twenty-three—she had a girlfriend there, and I said, 'Girls, this is a famous steak tonight. It's on an album cover' and she goes, 'What'd you do, put it on your head or something?' 'No, I had it in

Front cover of *Raw* by Robbie Rox (Bent Records, 1979). Author's collection.

my mouth.' And they're like, [sound of surprise and disgust] 'Aaaah!'"

Recorded at night at Phase One when studio time was cheap, but still no mean feat, the album was released on Rox's own Bent Records label in 1979. To quote Rox, "You are a serious artist, because you put this out. You're not gonna waste your time, right—some people want to buy a car." *Raw* was then distributed to record stores and sent out to college radio stations across Canada, receiving plenty of airplay. Getting it over the border into the USA, however, provided a new set of obstacles. His consistently fired and re-hired manager decided that they should take *Raw* to Akron, Ohio, home of Devo.

OPENINGS in commercial, all girl band: guitar, bass, sax, trumpet. Travel, read music, sing harmony. 929-9305. I

ORGANIST, vocals, essential for working R&B, soul band, Wayne, 484-6792. H

ORGANIST needed, (organ available). Ron, 532-6629. L

ROBBIE Rox are starving. Robbie Rox are an original 7 pce. union band, with a sound like you've never heard before. If you can help, please phone 244-8904 after 7. Ask for Robbie Rox. J

ROCK Bank needs female, keyboard also vocalist, 463-1101; 694-0975. I

SINGER Gay 90's available plus trio.

Classified ad placed by Robbie Rox, 1974. Image courtesy of the *Toronto Star*, January 8, 1974.

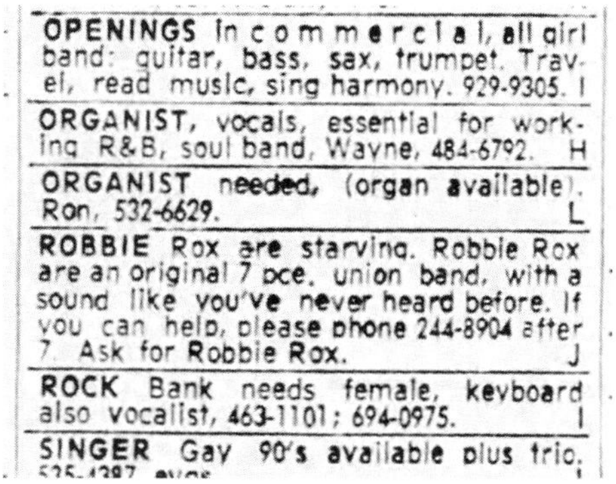

At the border, the guards pulled Rox, with his shaved head and recently grown beard, and manager over to inspect the van. Rox was put into a room with assorted freaks. The customs officers gathered around to look at a copy of *Raw* after one of them saw it and went, "Aaaah!" The stiffest of the lot approached Rox with it: "What's that?"

"Oh, that! Ah, that's a—"

"Is that you?"

"Yeah, that's me. And that's a porterhouse steak." The officers began to chuckle and laugh.

"What is this, your music?"

"Yeah, I write that music."

"Yeah? Sing some."

Rox broke into "Land of the Scared Starchos," singing, "I once knew these two guys Poster and Bruce Tabasco . . . "

"You call that a song?" The guards were now cracking up with laughter, but Rox and his manager were free to go. Over the border, his manager went into a phone booth and found a radio station in Erie, Pennsylvania. Boldly cold-calling them: "I'm here from Toronto. We just released an album."

"Oh yeah, come on up! We'll do an interview and we'll play a cut!"

After they arrived, the DJ randomly dropped the needle on "Bidet for a Donkey." Located in the Bible Belt, the radio station turned out to be Christian. *Raw* was clearly beyond the pale for them, deep into secular realms. In a panic, the manager yanked the record off the turntable before the song had a chance to finish.

* * *

Robbie Rox, 1974 Tour lineup. Courtesy of Robbie Rox.

Growing up in the suburbs of Ontario, Robert Theodore absorbed all kinds of music. He loved R&B. George Olliver of the Toronto '60s blue-eyed soul band Mandala was a key influence. He would see them and other R&B acts perform in Catholic school auditoriums. (For some reason, these shows always seemed to happen in Catholic school auditoriums.) Rox speaks glowingly of Mandala: "They were so energetic. They were—they were such a hot band. They were like the best band anywhere." At the age of fifteen, Rox performed his first gig at a party: "I was nervous as hell. The band decided to hire me based on a song that I was singing by Tiny Tim. It was 'Tiptoe Through the Tulips.'" This band included his brother John. Soon, they all donned white suits and were warming up for the R&B acts that they used to go see.

As the '60s waned, Rox's influences grew to include the Beatles and on into jazz and progressive rock. Humanities courses at university broadened his horizons further. His professor, Frank Zingrone, was taught by Marshall McLuhan. "Eric McCluhan, Marshall's son, was working with Frank right up until recently, until Frank passed away. So I stayed in touch with him. Marshall McLuhan is very fascinating. He's talking about subliminal seduction—and different things: the way that he was predicting the future, global village, and talking about urban corridors that would go from Toronto to Montreal, New York, Boston.

And in that way that was probably representative of the Internet." What Rox learned in the humanities later developed into lyrical themes for his songs.

Though the humanities stuck with him, Rox dropped out in his second year and moved to Quebec to work on a farm. He also invested in a gigantic Sentry IV speaker system: "So I started warming up bands that were coming to Quebec because I was the only guy that had equipment and also did a show. I was playing guitar. It was crazy shit. There are no words to it. I had this thirty-minute song where I'm using all these octaves and strumming like a maniac. And you can barely listen to it. You can listen to it for a little bit, then, 'Oh, okay, thirty minutes more of that.' Even though I knew there was a change in the thirty minutes—it did change gradually into something—nobody else would. But all those people that came out, that gave me the idea to want to express myself in a way, to kind of basically bring out—it was almost like an extraterrestrial explosion, so I had to let people know that I knew what the hell was going on in this world of a cookie-cutter society."

After moving back to Toronto, Rox placed an ad in the paper: "Singer with truck and sound system looking for work," or, as Rox succinctly puts it, "Man with truck." A drummer called and said, "Well, we got a band out here up in Mississauga in a barn." Rox came out with his sound system and started scat singing, hitting a whole lot of octaves. The drummer responded with, "You're hired, mate!" They played one gig at a high school and swiftly broke up. But members of that band became part of his horn band. With further newspaper ads, his circle grew.

Rox's voice came to him naturally. He'd already been singing the high tenor parts in his R&B acts. Riding around Quebec in his truck working delivery jobs to survive, Rox would sing along to his cassette deck: "I would just sing a lot. l would sing to different things and I could see it just open, change." Listening to the early Rox demo recordings, his voice is already fully formed, doing incredible things. Soon enough, a Theodore brother or two joined the band.

Their first gig as Robbie Rox was at Sunnybrook Hospital. The janitor working there booked them for the Annual Riverboat Dance at Warriors Hall, a clubhouse at the hospital for World War One army veterans. Being on the booking committee, the janitor told Rox, "Randy Russia is the guy that usually plays here, but he can't do it. Now, because you have the same initials, Robbie Rox, you mind calling yourself Randy Russia for the night?" Being a union contract, Rox replied, "Uhhh, okay." That very night they launched into their first number, "Reaming Me," a song about larger themes, of the higher power having it out for Rox. Beginning with a Latin rhythm, people got up to dance, then the time signatures changed—again—and again. They didn't finish the song. "They were so freaked out—janitors, army guys, they were all coming up to the stage—'Go home!' and everything—and they were trying to pull the plug. They were pounding my amp and everything. Next thing you know, they're climbing on the stage, they're chasing the band, the guys are running all over the hospital—the guys were running in and out of corridors—it was like a Bugs Bunny cartoon. I got out of the hospital, got in my truck, went to the phone booth at Bayview, and I called 911. I said, 'Help, the audience is attacking the band!' and she says, 'Isn't it usually the other way around?' 'No it's not, it's not a joke. Get cops here!' So, I go back to see what the guys are doing. I walk in the front of Warriors Hall and four vets jump on me and are punching me and I'm rope-a-doping it and covering myself. Then five cops walk in and all these guys stand up like they ate the canary or something and the cops come in—'What's going on here?' and all this. They kind of helped me up and they go, 'Do you want to lay charges?' I said, 'Look at these tired guys. No, they've been through enough. They fought for our freedom, right, guys?' And they're all kind of going, 'Yeah. Yeah.'" However, the hospital wasn't going to pay the band until the union stepped in for a meeting. "The union were behind us because they had booked us for what we do, which is just legitimate entertainment—it just happens to be very different."

The band got a gig early on warming up for the magician Doug Henning, with both acts sharing Rox's sound system. Rox yelled at Henning's tech guy for messing with the dials with Henning standing right there. "And now when I finally figured out who he was and how good he was, I figured that guy could have made me disappear that day. Right? Like I could just maybe disappear right on the spot!" Soon, the band found a booking agency and went on tour.

For the eastern tour, Rox shared vocals with a woman singer, performing at clubs looking for a little light entertainment. Kicking off in Thunder Bay, three sets a night for six nights, they were advertised on the radio as "Robbie Rox with girl singer doing Top 40 hits tonight at Finnegan's!" That night, a woman came up from the audience and said, "You're supposed to play Top 40." Rox shared no common ground with hit acts like the Eagles. After initially being freaked out, Thunder Bay eventually got into their show. As for the Holiday Inn in Kenora, Ontario? Not so much. That entire week the manager repeatedly called Rox into his office to say, "This isn't working." Brandon, Manitoba, however, was a hit. Rox describes the crowd: "They were students—they were all glue-sniffers or whatever. They just loved what we were doing. They were really remarkable partiers. They lined up to come see us. They loved it."

Rox's booking agent promised them a tour all the way to L.A. if it all went well. In Calgary, their show was cancelled because the promoter heard that they were different. Rox describes the next show, "We go up to Edmonton, Alberta. Fucking Alberta. I hate it just for that. We go up to this place in Edmonton and it turns out the curtains open and it's ballroom dancing. I think we did one song and the owner comes out and says, 'Get your band, get your kit, get the fuck out of here.' We lasted one song."

The booking agency gave them one more chance in Ponoka, Alberta. "You know Ponoka? Ponoka, Alberta, is a very very small, narrow-minded town. It's like a scene out of *Easy Rider*." The drunken bartender would repeatedly pull the plug on the band, and, though the staff of the nearby mental institution enjoyed and understood them, it wasn't enough to cut through the animosity of playing mostly to a roomful of cowboys. The next day the band went into the restaurant. It quickly became apparent that the townspeople had heard about them. "This real redneck lady came up. She goes, 'What'll it be?' I go, 'Oh, we're in

Robbie Rox and the '70s Horn Band, Toronto Star Trek '76 Convention, Bridge of the Enterprise replica set, July 25, 1976. Courtesy of Robbie Rox.

the band.' She goes, 'I know!' I said, 'Well, I'll have a clam chowder soup.' 'I'll give you a clam chowder, alright!' So I go, 'Guys, guys, let's get out of here.'

For their next tour they landed in Edmundston, New Brunswick, where the club was so freaked out by the band that the drunken, shifty owner wasn't going to pay them. Rox was so furious that his band tried to hold him down. He threw a table at the bar, clearing out the place—even the bouncers left. The cops were called, with the police chief understanding the situation. The band were escorted to the Quebec border by five police cars, each with its cherry lights turning.

This was all before Rox shaved his head. Zwol remembers Rox coming out to see him play, looking at Zwol's smooth skull, and asking, "Boy, do I have the guts to do it?" Back in university, Rox would look at Zwol on an album cover and think, "That's what I want to be like when I grow up. I want to look like him." Rox's hair was receding. Zwol and, especially, the April Wine drummer Jerry Mercer's fearlessly smooth heads inspired Rox to take razor-sharp action. After a few drinks at a party he mustered up the courage and, with a little help, his new look was born. Rox describes the strong reaction: "Friends would think you'd flipped. You'd go down the street with a shaved head, people would be yelling out the window, 'Hey, baldy. Hey, Curly. Hey, Telly. Hey, Kojak.' It was just non-stop. People—serious people—would go, 'Why did you do it? Why'd you do it, Rob? Why? Why?' 'Why did I do what?' 'Why did you kill that guy?'—nothing like that. 'Oh, shave the head? Because I hardly had any hair anyway. And I just wanted to clean it up and I just thought it'd be good for the show.' And, of course, at that time some women loved it! Some just thought you were creepy. So there was no middle to it."

Another part of the new look for the mid '70s was the custom-made tuxedoes, sometimes worn without a shirt—custom-made by an Italian tailor, M&M on Dufferin Street,

Front cover of *Construction Site* by Robbie Rox (Bent Records, 1978). Author's collection.

Toronto. I should note here that M&M had actually survived on into the twenty-first century, I'd often walk by and see their wild, old '70s clothes and wide-collared shirts with an M&M pattern fading after many years hanging in the window. M&M came recommended by Rox's booking agent, who said, "I got a tailor for you. You should dress differently if you're going to do something different." Being creative, M&M listened to what Rox wanted and delivered the goods: two colors with a zig-zag formation, curved collars, bell bottom trousers. He had a couple of different tuxedoes as well as other outfits. This is a man who would perform on local television with a t-shirt that read, "WE NEED BACKERS."

Their reputation as an incredible live band grew, along with their audience. The strobes and the super-fast duck walks and the push-ups—Rox is a consummate performer, conducting his band with bravado, sweat running down his bare, hairy chest. They were the talk of the *RPM* magazine showcase for talent-buyers. How could they not buy his talent? People often think that the Ramones' first Canadian concert, back in 1976, was the very first show at the New Yorker, a defining moment in the origins of the Toronto punk scene. These people are wrong. The promoter Gary Topp had booked Robbie Rox as the very first act to play the legendary New Yorker venue right after the stage was built, priming it for the big Ramones concert happening the following night or two. Topp loved Rox and booked him repeatedly at his venues.

There is certainly a very Toronto quality of wackiness and professional jazziness entwined in this music. Open-minded elements have overlap with the music of Max Webster, members of which used to come out to see them and vice versa. These envelope-pushers grew personally close with Rox, selling them his sound system. Both acts certainly had their Zappaisms, though Rox's voice was mercifully on another stratosphere. He was once tapped to warm up for Frank Zappa, until Zappa's manager decided Rox had too many similarities or too much energy . . . and excitement. Too much excitement.

Rox's first release was a single from 1976 on the short-lived Raunch Records label run by Paul Hoffert and Bruce Bell of the blown-out horn rock band Lighthouse, who were also in the managing and producing roles. The single stiffed, and Rox moved on to his on-again-off-again manager Jim McConnell. It's a great single. Punchy horns and thickly sweet jazz bass open it up as his voice alternates between high and higher as Rox dreams of being "Doomed to a Catchy Tune." It is exactly that. Nothing released on Raunch Records was actually raunchy: the very few other artist releases were light soul and funk. "World Thank You Please" was the B side—complex time changes give a multiplicity of moods, Jim Steinman as Rat Fink, horns doing hymnals, closing up with Rox repeating "Hawaiiiii" into "Why why why?" slowly sauntering out. Later, it was recorded as a punchier (yet longer) live version on his first album, *Construction Site*, giving it loads more stage swagger.

Released in 1978 but recorded two—and even four—years earlier, *Construction Site* wisely went the half-live half-studio route with a multi-piece horn section venturing into places most unexpected, even giving way to moments of space, amidst frenetics—the tigers are released and they're licking their butts. Starting the album with a song called "Reaming Me" is a practical choice, as is closing it with "I'll Be Fucked."

Unpredictable to the point of including the slow, dreamy number "Imagine This," with lyrics about Juicy Lucy and Louie Groovy. The title track asks, "Is there construction in your mind? Do you think we'll finish it on time?"—swiftly skewing into Faux-talian measures as his brother dazzles all over the keys, fuzzed-out guitars mimic the horns joined by falsetto ariarioheeoh. A loaded paper plate of jazz fusion cooking up some beans. Laser beans! Fully baked. A band of heavy hitters. John Theodore is an incredible jazz pianist, a real whiz. Yes, there's no question that Robbie is a tremendous performer, but his brother John's flying hands are also a joy to behold.

Some of this material was on an earlier demo tape put together and shopped around by his manager, Jim McConnell, at the Juno Awards as Robbie was led around to various tables of record company and other industry people, met Anne Murray, etc. The master tapes sat on a shelf in the recording studio for a year and a half until Rox yelled, "Fired!" at McConnell for the first of many times, got a bank loan to buy the tapes, and put it out himself as the first release on his own appropriately named Bent Records label. The photo collage cover features a giant Rox running amuck through the urban landscape of Toronto with only the newly built CN Tower beating him in height (and not by much). Continuously in Toronto, the sounds of construction must never stop—the whole city really is a *Construction Site*. The title track stems from his own experience as a summer laborer, lifting some of the workplace dialogue verbatim from his boss ("Here Joe, here are the wire cutters," "Shove them up your ass, I don't want them"). Rox actually gave a copy to his bosses' kids, who Robbie notes reacted accordingly: "They howled forever." The boss was proud—"but he didn't get what I said about him." With a thousand copies pressed, they launched it with a show upstairs at the El Mocambo to thunderous applause. The past couple of years of building an audience there and at the Edge had paid off: the album also received a lot of airplay by the free-thinking booster station CFNY—their live lightning captured by the live half of the album.

Ditching the horns and stripping it down, *Raw* followed a year later, in 1979, and, though *Raw* remains his most popular release, his next album, 1980's *Do What I Do*, his only release on Quality Records, had 10,000 copies pressed: ten times the number of *Raw*. Again managed by McConnell, who secured the deal with Quality Records, this album keeps to the lineup of the Catso Porco Rozzo band, but with a much more straight ahead, smooth, groove-oriented sound. Though slicker, it is also angrier; the songs are now much more lyrically direct, his vocals more reined in while his beard started growing out showing a darker mood. *Do What I Do* most explicitly shows Rox's studies in humanities with the song "Uncle Mcluhan," along with references to subliminal seduction and how "We're All Going to Die" from being so uptight. He also takes on both the psychiatry profession and the anti-psychiatry Scientology cult in "Doctor Collision." Rox elaborates: "Back then, I was cutting the crap out of just anything that was organized, any kind of organized society, secret society, society of secrets, organized religion—just anything that controlled people. I was so into freedom and not being controlled—there's too much of that." "Attack of the Van People" is a less rabid attack on the van subculture, which was a thing then—people were really into vans—inspired by Rox stumbling into a van convention full of vans and the people who were in them and really into them.

As the songs got more direct, they became more difficult, dealing with his rather sexually frustrated relations with women. "Ruin Your Night" was much more unfortunate, a misogynistic song about provocatively dressed women rejecting him. Rox describes the reaction: "It's a song that pissed off women so much that they wanted to kill me. They had

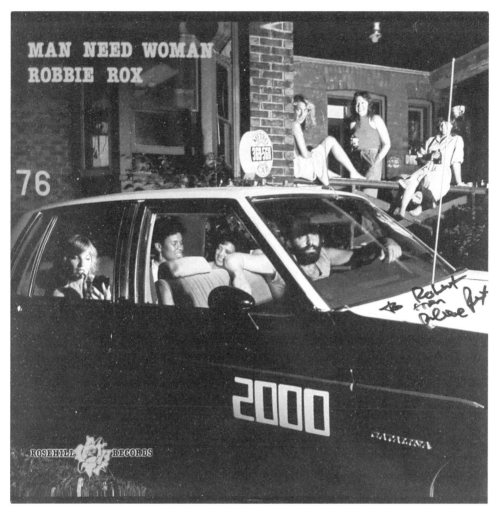

Front cover of *Man Need Woman* twelve-inch EP by Robbie Rox (Rosehill, 1981). Author's collection.

to hustle me out of the El Mocambo after we had a successful LP release, and the waitresses were so pissed off at me that they were waiting for me outside."

Known for his great smile, Rox covered it up with his now rather bushy black beard for his next two releases on his friend Wayne Scott's Rosehill label. Though there were lineup shifts, Rox's brothers John and Michael were still in the band. Both of these records contain a lot of anger.

At just four songs, *Man Need Woman,* from 1981, is the shorter and catchier of the two. The hard-rocking title track is about when women don't need men anymore. The cover features Rox as a cab driver amidst women paying absolutely no attention to him. His next album, 1982's *Ghost Culture,* was recorded by Dee Long of Klaatu at his studio and was Rox's slickest yet. It was also his most conventional. Inspired by the economic recession, this album also had themes of middle-class banalities involving conformity and peer pressure, including an ersatz reggae number about cottage life. On an utterly mid-tempo album, the stand-out track is "Miles," with its tripped-out synths and menacing rock riff helping to illustrate existential insomnia. This is the only song showcasing his high-pitched vocal prowess, this time multi-tracked—"I am free and I am me!"

In 1983, after finishing all of these albums, Rox decided that it was time to die. Or at least retire. It was a fake retirement. He planned to come back. "But we didn't do it right." The El Mocambo was packed. The final song, "Ever Been to Sea, Billy?", was all about leaving the music business. With a cordless mic, Rox crawled into a casket and the lid closed, him still singing as four large bouncer types carried him away. CFNY gave the event ample coverage. Rox came back. However, it was much too soon after and CFNY was miffed. "But eventually everybody forgot about it. Anyways, nobody cares." Thankfully his troubling beard was now gone and the mood shifted. The following year Rox formed the Monster Horn Band and performed extensively around Toronto until breaking up. In 2003, they reformed and released a CD. In the '90s, Rox released two CDs as Robbie Rox and the Rude Band. He still performs today.

In his career as an actor, Rox has appeared in numerous film and television productions, including playing the title character in the 1987 movie *Skull: A Night of Terror*, also known as *Don't Turn Out the Light,* and also as *Night of Retribution.* Yes, it was released under three different titles. As Skull, Robbie had both an eyepatch and a scar—back then facial disfigurement was used as shorthand for villainy, based on no factual research. This one-eyed psycho had a rather broad Achilles' heel: he was afraid of the dark. The movie opens with Skull in jail pulling the wings off of a fly. As a non-union production, this low-budget revenge thriller has lots of nudity, along with loads of reckless explosions and gunfire. This made for a few close calls on set: one actor's hair caught on fire. This movie is available on VHS under whichever title you have preference for.

Though they hailed from the same neighborhood, Zwol and Rox never really got to know each other until the mid-'70s, partly due to Zwol being five years older. The two grew close. Rox was a special musical guest on Zwol's live show in the '80s, with Zwol hosting and singing back-ups on Rox's songs. In 2017, I had the opportunity to see these two strong singers perform together, each with his own unique vocal styles and moves, two Cueball Canadian Glammers singing some old soul covers and having a ball. Let's hope they collaborate again. It was such a delight to see—they were such a joy.

CRACKERS

ONE DAY IN WATERLOO, ONTARIO, I found myself drifting up the stairs into Orange Monkey Records asking for some Canadian Glam and the owner said that he has got just the thing and pulled out a record by a band called Crackers, the cover photo showing nothing but an unruly sum of male asses in the recording studio, beaming towards microphones and at the camera, some hairier than others, boxes of crackers and stubby bottles in their wake, a real raspberry jam session. *Choice Cuts* it's called. Upon such a recommendation some customers would leave the store empty-handed in disgust, taking the mass mooning the wrong way—this book is not for those customers . . . yet one day they shall be ready, we are readying them. I laid my toonie[21] down immediately. In record-collector circles this is known as "low risk" at even quintuple the price—a sleeve like this, though, and the price will play nice. I wound up back at the record shop a week later wanting more Crackers.

Crackers. So many things come to mind. Biscuits. Or things that make a bang. A mild pejorative aimed at white folks. But most specifically, people who are cracking up. "Why, you're absolutely crackers!" Loco. Kooky. Bats in the belfry. Look at that back cover and all the funny faces of the band. One shot has the drummer writhing on the ground, a weird old masked sailor man, a chrome-domed three-legged flasher in a trenchcoat, and the bassist in evening dress on a chair with her incredibly long fake arms stretched several feet out. The songs, though manically going in multiple directions, are tight tight tight with heightened keyboards. They've been described as "lunatic rock" and as a cross between the filthy, hairy comedians MacLean and MacLean and the left-field musicianship of Max Webster.

Right off the bat on the first track, there's the first of many little musical jokes, a hockey-arena organ riff leads off "Crackers in Concert," recorded nose-thumbingly in-studio with dubbed-in audience applause, another musical joke. This song is a literal introduction, showcasing the instruments of every single member, introducing them one by one through a talk box. In case you don't already know, the talk box is an effects unit where the sound of the musical instrument (in this case, guitar) is modified directly through a tube coming from the human mouth, making it sound like the instrument itself is doing the talking. It's a real squelcher, I tell you, warmly welcoming the listener with an unearthly voice, a cyborg melding of human and musical instrument, intoning, "I'm going to introduce you to the band . . . " as the extraordinary talents of Patricia "Delicia" Warden on bass, Reg "Crazy Man" Denis on guitar, Monte "the Hose" Howze on keyboards, and George "the Hole" Holyoke on drums are each showcased and then brought all together along with a ripping guitar solo. Uh, wow, this record isn't just bizarre—they're really good.

---

21 Canadian two-dollar coin.

Promo pic of Crackers (Pizazz Presents, 1978). Author's collection, courtesy of Reg Denis and Patricia Warden.

How do you follow that up after getting knocked off your feet? Oh, just drop everything and plummet into some ersatz reggae about being destitute. And then into God knows where—you're just gone. This whole album takes so many tight twists and turns, you'll end up feeling side-swiped, elevated by a surplus of musical dynamics that throw on and off an overlapping cornucopia of musical styles and moods less easy to track. Modern synths and jazzy punctuations strangely mesh on the Western gun-fighting "Rio Bravo." "Gracie" is the college-radio hit dedicated "to uncle Al" and if you've ever had an Uncle Al then you were probably warned about him and the kind of dirty songs he'd sing three sheets to the wind (you can hear the bottles). It may just be one of the filthiest ditties ever recorded—next to "The Rodeo Song," at least—getting into bestiality, necrophilia, voyeurism, etc. It was the unexpected college-radio hit that program directors warned the DJs not to play. Initially the B side of their single from two or three years prior, distributed at truck stops and through CB radio, the record was flipped over to become so successful that it paid for this full-length 1978 album. Offsetting that bit of nastiness are "See You Tomorrow," a sweeping, uplifting cosmic ballad about the end of the world, and the unpredictable instrumental "Four Wheel Drive." The cackling, sax-bleating, bass-stuttering, drum-rolling, hot-flashing, circus-organ, Cossack-dancing song "Crazy Man" was inspired by the singer and guitarist Reg Denis's foregoing time-sensitive surgery for a brain aneurysm to fulfill his commitment to a four-month tour. Luckily, he survived, and two of the top neurosurgeons were there to operate on him once he returned home to Hamilton.

Hamilton is the city that is off from Toronto, with its own culture, thank you. Just look at the album's credits: engineered by Daniel Lanois, known mostly for his work recording the Hamilton heroes Simply Saucer's absolutely pivotal *Cyborgs Revisited* album, and produced by Steve Smith, who would later become known for his character Red Green—this fix-it guy in plaid is a "playing to the Prairies" institution with a very very very long-running Canadian TV sitcom followed by a movie.

Choice Cuts was released on the Pizazz label, one z short of the word "pizzazz" (definition: "an attractive combination of vitality and glamor"). Pizazz Productions managed showbands. Showbands were light lounge acts playing familiar covers that people could dance to, breaking it up with a funny skit or two. Some of the bands on Pizazz's roster included Great Rufus Road Machine, Terry Dee's Rock 'n' Roll Circus, Prime Tyme, and Jason, with Steve and Morag Smith, who included a '50s medley in their show. All of the Pizazz showband costumes were custom-made by an Italian tailor, probably Syd Silver Formals, fitting everyone with matching suits of dubious fibres. Pizazz's owner, Craig Nicholson, would also take the bands to massive warehouse rummage sales where they'd find oddities from all over the world to use in their acts. The Pizazz logo was bright red on yellow, lower-case "pizazz presents," with Canadian maple leaves located in the—uh—p holes. There were a handful of releases, including Great Rufus Road Machine's *Tribute to Canada* and Prime Tyme's *Live,* which featured a medley of mountain songs and the standard "Green, Green Grass of Home"

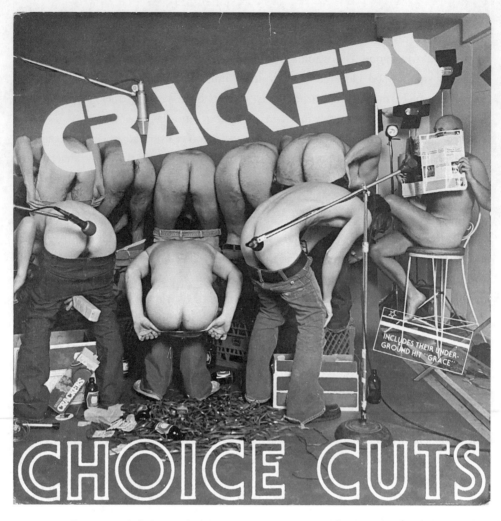

Front cover of *Choice Cuts* by Crackers (Pizazz Presents, 1978). Author's collection.

rendered as Italian dialect humor. After Steve Smith left Jason, he worked with Pizazz and brought Crackers into Lanois's parents' studio to record their single.

As much as these other Pizazz showbands played it pretty safe, Nicholson laughed his own ass off when he saw the photo of the bare asses. He took some liberties and, without the band's consent, used it for the cover of the album. An interesting choice. "You think? I had to show that to my grandmother," responds Warden. It is certainly visual, seared into many a retina with its un-tantalizing nudity, if one could see it at all. Record stores weren't exactly making window displays with it. Denis recalls, "They didn't show the cover, they'd show the back cover. When they advertised it in the magazines, it was just the brown bag. We got brown-bagged."

Even with their vast repertoire of songs, Crackers didn't really fit the showband mold. They weren't schmaltzy and they had their own original numbers and sound, but they were able to apply what they'd learned on the showband and Holiday Inn circuit to their show.

It's tough to pigeon-hole Crackers. Self-described as "the perverted personality rock show," when Crackers were writing songs they didn't even listen to music at all. If asked why they weren't playing the radio while going down the road, Denis would respond, "'Because we don't want to be influenced by anybody.' So we just would be writing—we'd always have a guitar going and Monte, even when we were going down the road, he would have this little Wurlitzer piano and he'd be writing all the time. We'd pick up people hitchhiking. We used to pick up Stompin' Tom Connors.[22] And I'd remember, we'd be driving down the Highway 17 or up on Highway 69 and we'd see him hitchhiking—this is before anybody knew who he was—and I pulled the bus over and picked him up one time. He sits down and the first thing that comes out of his mouth: 'Can I bum a couple of cigarettes?' 'Yeah, okay.' Then he'd go, 'Hey, can I have a beer?'—because we'd always had beer in the bus—we'd give him a beer and then we'd take him down the road and he'd shoot the shit with us and then we'd drop him off, go, 'Okay, we're turning off here.' And then my brother Rick would be driving the bus and we'd be coming home and there he is again hitchhiking, and I'd say, 'Pick up that Tom guy,' and my brother would go, 'I ain't picking up that fucking guy ever again.' I go, 'Why not?' 'He's nothing but a bum! He bums our smokes, he bums our beers, he never chips in for gas. Fuck him!' he'd say. I remember that, and it was so funny because I'd give my brother shit—I'd go, 'Oh, Rick, you shouldn't be like that.'"

Crackers clocked countless miles of road with a vast repertoire of 1,300 songs. This versatility worked in their favour. As Denis puts it, "We had a way with the crowd where we would size up the crowd right away and be able to give them what they wanted. We were able to play pretty near anything, but we always did good no matter where we went—you know, we never got chased out of town anywhere. We played everywhere—even Labrador, Newfoundland, then we'd go right across over to Vancouver and Vancouver Island and up the island and we did that for nineteen years." Warden adds, "We didn't have a home. We literally didn't have a home. We were just on the road."

Crackers would win over crowds with their strong sense of theatrical showmanship, mystifying them with Denis's three-legged-man routine or their silent-movie sketch with Howze's appropriate ye olde ragtime piano accompaniment. They'd start the sets safe and showy, "and then we'd get a little bit more risqué and, if that worked, then we'd say, okay, and we kept pushing the envelope. So then we had some undercover officers come in and watch the show. We did not know that they were there. And they ended up making us post something on the outside windows saying that 'this can be offensive, there's language' and stuff like that. But meanwhile they loved it," says Warden. For one show, at the University

---

22 A noted Canadian country music icon who recorded numerous songs about Canadian places, named Stompin' because of how he'd stomp his cowboy boot on a board as he played.

Front and back cover of *Hard on You* by Crackers (Lunatic Records, 1980). Author's collection.

"Grace" by Crackers (Pizazz Presents, circa 1977). Author's collection.

of New Brunswick, the crowd was so on board, making them do encore after encore, and Steve Smith was at this engagement exclaiming, "What are you going to do now? How the hell are you going to top this? You've done five encores, that should be it!" But they wanted more! So Crackers went out on stage fully naked.

Mostly Crackers dressed up, and not down, coordinating different outfits for each set and sometimes even during the set, changing behind the screen while Howze went wild on the Moog. This screen's prime use, though, was for the optic kinetic and commercial-grade slide projectors, with Denis noting, "And we made our own slides. We would go to the libraries during the day and go through all these books with pictures and we'd find the freakiest looking pictures that would suit the songs." The light man would change the slides and shoot the lasers and move the patterns of the kinetic projections. Flashpots would go off at key moments: during one set-up it even blew out the lightman's glasses. These quick screen changes were also important for their mask work. Donning one such mask for "Crazy Man," Denis would come out to a flashing strobe light, "and so everybody be watching me and I'd be marching with my guitar and with the strobe light look like a soldier, and then I picked up this thing that nobody would see—it was a great, big, giant looking fur thing. We called it the rat—it had a tail on it, and I'd be shaking that around, and then, when the song reached a certain point, this is when the lighting guys had to be right on the money, and then it would come to this big crescendo and then the drummer would go on his microphone and as he said, 'Got it!' then right instantly the strobe light died. This follow spot came on me, and at the same time I'd rip off this mask I had this look on my face, and everybody just . . ." Warden adds, "It was all timing." Using nigh-invisible fishing lines, Howze would pull on them, making instruments appear and move as if by magic, tambourines rising and shaking and violin bows that Denis would grab to play on guitar.

This is ingenious and fitting. Combining form and function, fashion innovation and bass-playing necessity, Warden came up with a signature look that was all her own: long evening gloves with the fingers cut off.

Denis's flashing Christmas-light coat was used year around—every Crackers show was a holiday, with their elaborate visual sensibility—they knew that people were there to see a show. Being difficult to find in Canada, a painter friend from California brought Crackers some luminescent paint and they used it to their advantage. All of a sudden, the lights would go out and the only thing the audience could see was Denis's glow-in-the-dark guitar.

The band played on red-carpeted risers, set straight across but at varying levels, with Howze leaping over his Hammond B3 to wave around the Theremin-like Moog ribbon. Holyoke often took his drum solo out into the crowd, descending upon them leaping and screaming. Howze elaborates: "He would start playing on all the tables, smashing ashtrays, playing on beer bottles and taking drinks—the bikers would put their helmets on, he'd play on their helmets, the chicks would lift up their tops and he'd play on their titties and stuff like that. So then he'd go around the whole room. And in the meantime, while that was going on, Monte would be on the vocoder saying, 'Come back, George. You're getting carried away again,' and then after that he would come back on the stage and walk across the stands on his hands then pick up the drumsticks and continue with the drum solo." Warden adds, "At one point he was going around on a unicycle drumming with his sticks, and when he was trying to learn how to ride that thing he had bruises all the way down his legs. They're really hard. We would all be trying it—we'd be going up and down the hotel hall."

The Hamilton TV station CHCH was quite visionary, with much more original programming than most other independent regional channels, thanks to the producer Lionel Shenken. They produced their own shot-on-video movie thrillers, *The Hilarious House of Frightenstein*, *Red Green* with Steve Smith, and music shows where Crackers got to strut their stuff! Over in radioland, Dr. Demento, the noted American novelty-song disc jockey, regularly spun Crackers on his show.

Name a Canadian university and Crackers has probably played it. Besides touring the halls of higher learning, Crackers played an entirely different kind of institution with its own kind of schooling, going out on the prison circuit. Because of Patti Warden's last name, she was nicknamed the Warden—which is what Denis called her when they performed at Stony Mountain Penitentiary in Winnipeg, a maximum-security prison. Warden describes it, "I was the only girl in there. It was pretty scary. And then I kept thinking: what if something happens? what if it gets carried away and everything? Then, after the fact, somebody decided to look this up when we were on the road, after we got out of prison, and he said, 'You didn't know this,' he said, 'but you had about thirty bodyguards on you.' I wish I had known that then, because I was really nervous."

Denis remembers, "One time we were playing in Montreal and we're playing on stage in this club and all of a sudden twenty cops with shotguns come in, surrounded everyone, shotguns cocked, stopped the band, turned off all the lights—'Don't anybody move!' They locked the doors. And then we found out, in the room watching our show was an escaped convict they were looking for. They hauled this guy out, chained him up. Talk about shooting down the momentum of the show, right?"

One early bill in Timmins, Ontario, they performed with the Glam comedy duo La Troupe Grotesque, who Crackers glowingly described as "out there." Denis elaborated: "People in the Timmins area, it was right over their heads—they're sitting there in lumber jackets and stuff and they're in skidoo suits and they're drinking beer and they're going "What the hell is—?""

To entertain themselves on the road they would put on their various masks and look out the windows freaking out the other passing cars. Patti even hitchhiked using the long prop arms, and Monte would put his portable cassette recorder to use. Explains Warden, "He used to go down and interview all the rubbies [alcoholic street people] down in the park, and he would ask them just different questions and all that kind of stuff, and they would feel really important because there's somebody interviewing them, so they would start talking to him about this or that and they all had interesting stories. That's just something that he used to do. His imagination was out there."

Howze used the tape recorder for "Little Johnny," recorded in Room 105 of the St. Vital Hotel, Winnipeg, Manitoba, on a "Big Ben" cassette, then enhanced in the studio for release on their second album, *Hard on You*. He must have recorded it on a dark and stormy night, a late one at that. This eerie keyboard song depicts a pure nightmare—it's an effective horror chamber piece, oohhh the chills.

Hard on You was released in 1980 on their own Lunatic Records, with Lanois engineering once again. The title track is a whirling gypsy fist-pumper about the school of "Hard on You." The synth-led instrumental "Visions" will give you just that—flute forgeries make for disappearing leprechauns amidst pulsing bass and vocoder cosmic monk chants, used in the live show for costume-change transitions. "The Shove" was a real dance that they performed, primarily using the groin. There's a pirate shanty and something called "The Tit Man." The limelight comes on for "Life Is Just a Stage," a perfectly maudlin showtune. The album cover, much more tasteful than their first, features a seedy hotel room, neon sign right out the window, with two of the actual hotel residents: a model clad in lingerie holding a barbell and handcuffs and, sitting in the background, a schlubby-looking man in woolly socks. Crackers are featured on the back. In 1987, Crackers released "Rok Attack," a swaggering single produced by Ian Thomas using some very 1987 touches (synth breaks) and have released two CDs since then.

I sat in Dennis and Warden's back yard in Hamilton, where I was granted just one hour; it expanded into more than three, with cookies, coffee, a look at their massive scrapbook, and a lot of laughs. I had to ask, "How did you both meet?" At last, the secret origin of Crackers.

It was the early '70s. Warden's mother, a keyboardist, was teaching at a conservatory for music. Denis's keyboardist bandmate, also at the conservatory, asked Warden's mother to come see them play and give some constructive criticism. After the show, she invited them all back for one of her regular basement jam sessions and it was then and there that Denis met Warden. After Denis's band folded, Crackers was formed, originally as a duo with Warden on keyboards. They did not remain a duo for long, as along came the unique keyboardist virtuoso Howze, who had previously played in a band with Denis. Warden made the switch from keyboards to bass: "So that's when I started playing it and I was liking it. I didn't think I would like it at all. And it worked. I stayed with it."

Crackers exists today as the duo of Denis and Warden, just like in the beginning. Denis has expanded into playing electric fiddle, mandolin, and some pedal steel, too. He is vice president of the Hamilton Musicians' Guild and Crackers are an active part of the Hamilton music community, playing numerous festivals. And they still hit the road, having played the Daytona Beach Bike Week for eight years as a result of their strong biker following, as well as a sweet working vacation at a high-end resort in La Cruz, Mexico.

After being together forty years and with both of them turning sixty, Warden said to Denis, "We should do something really special. What can we do?" They decided to get married. They waited a year for their Winnipeg priest friend to get healthy and conduct the ceremony, officially tying the knot in 2012.

TRIBE

A BLACK-AND-WHITE PHOTO RAN in the January 26, 1974, edition of the *Saskatoon Star-Phoenix* newspaper announcing a concert at the Red Lion Tavern. The ad featured an exuberant guitar-playing man, mouth wide open, in full makeup: white and another color, perhaps even a beauty mark below the eye—his hair may have even be dyed. The caption reads, "Peter D'Amico is the lead singer with Tribe, a band which emphasizes stage performance of a glittering nature in its appearances at the Red Lion this week. Pe-

Tribe: head to toe glitter

By CINDY KRIEG

Just what does the word tribe bring to mind for most people? In your mind there may appear the picture of a group living closely together. They may even be of common ancestry, but the outstanding factor which is most impressive is their wilfull sharing of what is theirs.

Well, the Tribe I'm about to speak of has all of the above mentioned qualities. These people live and work at close proximity to each other. Their founding and common ancestor is music and the creative co-existence that surrounds the entire Tribe experience is really remarkable.

On Oct. 24 at Ecole Algonquin Secondaire approximately 400 North Bayites had the opportunity to view a Tribe performance.

The first thing that drew attention was the appearance of the band. Peter D'Amico, who plays lead guitar as well as lead bass, which is itself unique as an upfront innovation, was dressed in an outfit that made him glitter from head to toe. This, added to the distinctive makeup which is used by Peter for the purpose of theatrical expression, made him eye catching.

Joe Wilderson, bassist, was dressed in a black costume for the final set. On his head he wore a large black hat with a hugh pink feather protruding from it and as the set got into full swing, both the feather and hat flopped about as Joe, grinning, moved up and down the neck of his bass with obvious ease and expertise.

FOUNDING MEMBERS

Peter and Joe are the founding members of Tribe and their uninhibited style as they work together contributes a great deal to the overall easy acceptance that the audience expresses for the group. Andy McLean, drummer, is the newest member of Tribe, though he is no newcomer to the Canadian music scene and has established himself as a fine drummer with several southern rock groups. His

Peter D'Amico lays it on.

ability allows him to blend into Tribe perfectly.

As was displayed, Tribe can handle any kind of music with no extra effort required. This may be attributed to the various musical backgrounds that have blended together in Tribe. These backgrounds move from folk to jazz though the music that Tribe puts down was described by Peter, who writes all the band's originals as "funky rock 'n' roll."

Tribe has recorded one record which, unfortunately for we Canadians, is only available in the United States. In January, the group plans to go back into the recording studio to put together a record that this time will be available in Canada.

For the past two years, Tribe has lived in New Liskeard. They chose to live in the North because they had found a certain warmth to radiate from the people they entertained for up there. As well, the land was beautiful and offered a peace that is hard to find for a touring rock group. It seemed the perfect place to be able to retreat when their hectic schedule allowed them to rest.

They are booked far into 1975 and primarily they will be playing in southern centres so they really have little opportunity to perform in the North now. But as was stated several times by the group, their formost concern is their audience and where people want them, they'll go. They are not only musicians but really true entertainers seeking to communicate with the people that make up their audience.

FUTURE PLANS

For the future, they have hopes of a studio and a production company whereby they can extend aid to upcoming musicians such as they themselves have received. Tribe realizes that this means more of the same ambitious determination that they have in the past four years displayed but they feel that it is all more than worth it.

In 1972, a Sudbury writer, Chris Johnson, said of Tribe, "they stand a good chance of making it big." Well, that was two years ago and today I'd say they stand more than a good chance of seeing their dreams come to life. True, it still will take time and effort but Tribe has a perseverence that is often lacking in bands and it is this will to persevere that is the binding factor prevailing over each Tribe endeavor.

Tribe is a group that not only works together but as well lives and dreams together. It is this common idea that will carry them through to the realization of all their work as they at least tear the lid off the Canadian music scene and enjoy their hard-earned moment of success, together.

Newspaper article on Tribe by Cindy Krieg. Image courtesy of *North Bay Nugget*, November 8, 1974.

Newspaper ad for Tribe at Sheraton Summit Inn. Image courtesy of *Calgary Herald*, February 22, 1974.

ter wears radiant pink glittered top, fur-trimmed pants, and the make-up is indicative of light-hearted pantomime approach." The following month an ad in the February 20 edition of the *Calgary Herald* announces Tribe's limited engagement at the Sheraton Summit Inn with "GROUP 'TRIBE' HAS UNIQUE SOUND AND LOOK." This time, along with the D'Amico photo, an awesome photo of the drummer is also included, stating, "sequined, black Louis Laguan in leopard skins and a platinum wig smashes out a rhythm on the drums." The ad also notes D'Amico's face paint, along with other hype.

On the phone from his recording studio in Calgary, D'Amico explains, "Looking at that picture and the outfits that I was wearing, yes, I did have glitter on my eyelids. So, well, you got glitter on your eyelids and it walks like a duck and it talks like a duck. Like, come on, dude. What are you talking about? My managers sent me for mime lessons. I was sent to study mime."

Oh! Who did you study under?

"Well, it was a weekend thing with Marcel Marceau—can it get any better?"

This Montreal seminar with the world's most famous mime immensely helped D'Amico's stagecraft and focus. Not long after that, he started wearing his half–*commedia dell'arte* mime mask on stage. But why did his manager send him to study mime?

"I can answer that with the first review we got in *Beetle* magazine, by Karen Hepburn. I mean, it was such a stunning review. I remember her name. I remember she was really pretty. That's not material here anyway. What she wrote was, 'A guitar in D'Amico's hands is a weapon. If you can communicate without sound, how much more deadly can you be with sound?' And that was the impetus for me to wear makeup. That's why the whole band didn't wear it. And I was wearing it for like two years before KISS, I was wearing it before Marc Bolan and T. Rex. With it, again, this idea of communication and soon as the whole Glam Rock thing came about, my manager came along and said, 'Gone!' and my face got washed. That's the truth. Now, does it look like Glam Rock? You're damn rights. Did everybody think it was? Sure! That's what we were doing without realizing what the rest of the world was doing because we were in this Toronto bubble."

Feeling my way through the mire of time, it can be difficult to find exact dates to latch onto. The air gets laden with not only the fog of memory but also grains of salt extracted from the rocks of Canada where surely Tribe toured—they toured a lot. It's uncertain exactly when that review of Tribe may have appeared. The first issue of *Beetle* magazine was cover-dated December 21, 1970, and the magazine continued until 1975. Bolan appeared on the March 10, 1971, episode of the television show *Top of the Pops* with glitter on his face, Glam going into full swing right after. The words "early" and "hyperbole" both qualify. D'Amico's make-up and mask period was brief but, according to the ads, still happening in 1974.

After forming in Toronto in 1969, Tribe moved to Sutton, then up to an old farmhouse in New Liskeard in northern Ontario. Where's that? Peter answers, "New Liskeard is far enough north that sixty miles . . . keep on going, all of the water flows into the Arctic Basin. We were far enough north. And that whole north country became our playground, and then, from there, we did the seven cross-Canada tours. If it had an indoor toilet, we played it. We played a couple of hotels that had outdoor toilets. It was the '70s. We did eight tours of Newfoundland."

Tribe would do two ninety-minute sets a night, instead of four short sets. "What was that first ninety-minute set, Robert? It was nothing but '50s rock and roll. And it was never a full song. There'd be a verse and a chorus if you're lucky. And I would just pop it off the top of my head. I was going to dances in 1957 when I was seven years old. I was Peter Traynor's roadie when I was ten years old.[23] I heard all those tunes by the live bands. They're stuck in my head. So now the guys in my band didn't know these tunes but, come on, they're three chords, four chords at most. So I would just start babbling and changing keys and doing this and the band would chase after me. I would pick

---

23 Peter Traynor was co-founder of Traynor Amps and a Toronto-based bassist in early-'60s bands.

up and away we went. And so that the ninety-minute 'rock and roll' first set was never the same way twice because I didn't know what the hell I was doing. Here's a thousand songs—pick one."

Sometimes a whole set comprised just "You Are My Sunshine" done in an array of styles: Hendrix, Zeppelin etc. . . . Peter exclaims, "And the audience would be, 'These guys are fucking crazy!' And we're sober."

Sober?

"No drinking allowed, dude. Well, we had a tough manager. Yes, it was a self-imposed rule. She came to us in the very beginning, literally in the first couple of days, in the era when one seed of marijuana would put you in jail for twenty-five years. She said, 'If you've got a bottle of Chivas Regal open in the backseat of the car, the cops will say you can't do that. It's an open bottle. Thank you very much, boys. And they'll take it but they're not going to bust you. Better good scotch than bad dope.'"

Okay, but you didn't drink?

"Come on dude, we only played for four hours, what the hell do you think would happen afterwards? Work with me here."

Tribe performed a set at the Rock Acres Peace Festival with April Wine, Fludd, and many other bands before the Satan's Choice motorcycle club caused the event to end a bit earlier than expected.

The December 8, 1973, issue of *RPM* describes Tribe's dual bass attack as being something "that has the walls shaking and the floor boards rumbling. The music hits you directly in the guts and moves out from there until your whole body is moving with the good rock. They dish out concert hall excitement in a bar atmosphere." Yes, there were two basses: D'Amico and Joe Wilderson, the two constants, with Attila Ambrus on guitar and Lew LaGuan on drums as the lineup at that time. They were not a First Nations rock band from Calgary, Alberta, as some internet sources such as Discogs have erroneously stated. D'Amico says that this inaccuracy may have been because of their name describing

TRIBUTE TO MAX WEBSTER'S *HIGH CLASS IN BORROWED SHOES* ALBUM COVER

Here's a subgenre that isn't so much sub as a "little more off the top" and quite the switch in the bouffant lane of Glam, specific to the Canadian regions: Cueball Glam. In terms of "vibe," Zwol's smooth pate had saucy swagger while Robbie Rox and Rex of Crackers' chrome domes continued where the testosterone left off.

Kim Mitchell wouldn't relinquish the hair 'til eons passed and even took to ball-capping in his early solo days. When he was in Max Webster though, he had a skullet to rival that of Brian Eno. Look at him on the cover of the evocatively titled *High Class in Borrowed Shoes*—was there ever a Glammier album name? Like a dirty tiara it is—Glam album title 100%. He's scrutinizing his nails wondering if the manicure did the trick, other hand on exposed slender waist, tights, earth tone lava lamp tights under sheer shorts, much of the band lifting themselves up in clunky brown platform heels. The well-trimmed bearded bassist Mike Tilka in white with baby blue sash looks like a former racecar driver turned Québécois sex cult leader teaching us the benefits of UFO cloning through deep-tissue erotic massage (bassists are dextrous), whereas the keyboardist Terry Watkinson goes watercolor Pierrot in tight pants by way of Hermés. And the drummer? He is the drummer. Sleeveless top. Dammit, even he kind of works.

1977's *High Class in Borrowed Shoes* is an epitome. Max Webster's self-titled 1976 debut album had

Front cover of *High Class in Borrowed Shoes* by Max Webster (Anthem, 1977). Author's collection.

too many ripped-off Frank Zappa vocalisms. Zappa, like Prog, is head music, yet that deep aloof sardonic voice is congested head music: too head-cool to excite. Listen to early live boots and Max Webster are explosive. This was a band that early on would cover Zappa, yes, but also Bowie.[1] Alas, no one from Max Webster wanted to talk to me, no Bowie talk in sound or vision, no talk of anything—my liver is far too chopped for their liking, but no onions—my breath sparkles—come hither, Max Webster. Aw, let's face it, they have had plenty of ink spilled to cry tears of joy over. An entire book by Martin Popoff has been written about them. No Bowie in that book either, but it states that they were influenced by the Sensational Alex Harvey Band with the blistering mime guitarist. This album cover is starting to make much more sense. Found in dollar bins from coast to coast of Canada.

 . Dave Bidini of the Rheostatics and the book *On a Cold Road* (about Canadian rock n' roll road horror stories) casually dropped that to me in a café one mid-afternoon a few years ago, hardly expecting me to cement it in print. It was only recently that I found confirmation of Max Webster covering Bowie.

their longest lineup: "I'm Italian, Joe being the bass player was German American, Lewis was a black American drummer, and Sonny Wingate, he liked to tell people he was an Eskimo [Inuit, as we would now say]. And that was the Tribe, the four guys being totally different." Further confusion may stem from decades later when D'Amico won two Aboriginal People's Choice Awards—one in 2007 and one in 2008—for albums that he produced and engineered for Dallas Arcand, a.k.a. Kray Z Kree.

D'Amico saw Tribe's talents shining as a live band. His skills in the studio were still years to come. In 1976, Big Harold's Records released an album by Tribe, but it wasn't their first album: "We did three albums. The two albums didn't get released due to record contract problems and the third album—which unfortunately was released. The guy released it with ghost vocals and we never approved it, and he had somebody else come in and finished playing on it, and it was released under our name. We got fucked over sideways."

Big Harold's Records seemed to have used this same tactic on at least one other band. Formed by a former Halifax showband frontman and booking agent with the nickname Big Harold, this label only released a few things, then vanished; aspersions were cast on independent financing from unsavory organizations, with tragic results. The Tribe album *Female Trouble* has been described as a concept album, but the name and concept were by the label owner. It appears to bear no relation to the 1974 John Waters movie.

Back in the 1970s people took part in an activity known as hitchhiking. The cover of *Female Trouble* is a photo of a woman engaged in this activity. She is standing on the side of the highway in jean shorts with her thumb out. The liner notes state, "We're telling it from our point of view. The ladies that we treasure, and the ones we let get away." *Female Trouble* is a mix of original songs credited to D'Amico, with names like "Young Girls" (about groupies) and "Rock and Roll Queen" (about a groupie), along with covers of "Groovin'" and "Hey Good Lookin'." Their version of "Hit the Road, Jack" starts off loungey but with vocal phasing—then the road goes very off to far-away lands into Middle Eastern–sounding guitar and organ solos.

But what happened to the recordings of the first two albums? D'Amico explains, "When we were on tour in Newfoundland, the local kids broke into the house, set the shed on fire, and all our recordings and copies of the first two albums and everything else went up in flames. Everything just . . . went away. I like to say God's got a sense of humor."

Eventually Tribe became the duo of D'Amico and Wilderson, changing their name to the Pair Extrordinaire (*sic*; not to be confused with the '60s soul lounge act the Pair Extraordinaire). Apart from D'Amico and Wilderson, Tribe had already gone through a lot of band members in its career. D'Amico loosely quotes the manager of the Keddy Motor Hotel in Saint John, New Brunswick: "Listen, Peter and Joe are basically an act. The other guys might as well be sticks." This manager offered the two of them more money than they would get as a band, plus Keddy's was one of the largest hotel chains in the Maritimes, so, with their showmanship, this meant steady bookings and good money for the two of them with their "idiot drummer" (i.e., a drum machine from an organ) along for the ride.

Internet information can be spotty but Discogs says that the infamous *Female Trouble* album was re-released by Big Harold's with a pasted-on cover as the Pair Extrordinaire, with a goofy cartoon drawing of D'Amico and Wilderson in shades and a floppy hat. D'Amico replies, "I hate to tell ya, brother—I don't know what you're talking about. I had no idea that was even in existence."

The Pair Extrodinaire's 1978 album *Live from the Maritimes* consisted of cover tunes recorded at Keddy's

Take the record out of the country—though you'll never take the countr[y] out of the record—and tell people a[ll] over the world that it is a lost classi[c] and they'll believe you. It is. A classi[c] I'm lost. I once posted the albu[m] cover to social media and said, " just love the Frogs" (and I do). Ki[m] Mitchell and Jimmy Flemion coul[d] alternate, Eno skullets and all. Thro[w] Flemion's angel wings on Mitche[ll] and one wouldn't blink. Of course Max Webster had the Frogs beat b[y] a few years or so. There ain't nothin[g] like 'em.

The guitars on *High Clas*[s] sound so raw—maybe not as in stantly noticeable when mixed wit[h] the wax finish of the shiny synths These synths really do the trick o[n] "Diamonds, Diamonds," a song s[o] bloody luminous it turns on all th[e] limelights wherever it plays, co quettish as can be, a stripper coo[l] down number on the downtow[n] East Side. Did I mention that th[e] album title was evocative? All of th[e] lyrics are evocative, too: "Oh wa[r] it's been done before, that's wha[t] they say." Have you ever heard a[n] anti-war song so casually blasé? Ye[t] oomphing it on after some nast[y] stutter riffs, a greasy bag bum[p] 'n' grind. They make Pye Dubois' skewed lyrics work. There's eve[n] payoffs, though the music isn't a straight arrow either—the listene[r] keeps coming back for more o[f] this puzzle, not necessarily know ing what "America's Veins" is o[n] about, unpredictable riffs comin[g] in and out, drums bashing, synth calculating the risks. How are thei[r] subsequent albums? I love *A Mil lion Vacations*. Even the last one 1980's *Universal Juveniles*, wher[e] Mitchell shuffles the lineup an[d] Watkinson (who could be depend ed upon to write a great song o[r] two per album: "Let Go the Line will make you weep as you cruis[e] past all the locked cabins along th[e] lake) is gone, is worth it. It's not lik[e] it's going to break the bank.

Motor Inn, with engineering by Traynor. The cover photo makes the two of them look like they are flying—Wilderson in a top hat and D'Amico in a bright red British military jacket brandishing a sword (easy now). The album was released on D'Amico's own Black Bear Records, a label that is still very active releasing all kinds of albums recorded at D'Amico's studio in Calgary, where he relocated in 1981. Though no longer playing together as a duo, both D'Amico and Wilderson are working in this studio to this day.

LAURICE

MANY GLAM LOVERS JUST LOVE THE SINGLE "I'm Gonna Smash Your Face In" by Grudge. It shoulda been a smash hit. After that, Laurice, a.k.a. Laurie Marshall, had a career as a Canadian disco diva singing about flying saucers and now lives in Kelowna, B.C., with his partner making music and videos.

Laurice's glammiest songs were recorded in England. The 1973 single "I'm Gonna Smash Your Face In," with Laurice recording with his best friend Simon Potter as Grudge, bears an unmistakeable *Transformer*-era Lou Reed influence à la "Vicious" but, instead of hitting with a flower, there ain't none—it's a bare fist! The violence is quelled with its soft vocal delivery, pop hooks, and a camp Elvis imitation. However, the violence continues audaciously on the other side, opening with a loud cackle on "When Christine Comes Around." There's a rather peppy verse about her eyeball: "I think I'll rip it out and put it in my pocket." A horrified response exclaims, "You wouldn't do that!" and then a Mae West imitation not too far off from the Elvis imitation purrs, "Come up and see me sometime." We are in the audacious *Whatever Happened to Baby Jane?* territory of camp melodrama.

This single was released on the mysterious Black Label owned by the eponymous Cyril Black, the black sheep of his family. Laurice explains, "He knew, believe it or not, an heiress, Prudence, who lived in the south of London in this beautiful mansion, and she heard the song and she loved it. The next thing I know, we were in the studio and produced the whole thing. It was banned immediately, of course, by the BBC, so of course it became an instant cult classic. Cyril was so bad that, I think because of taxes, he fled to Canada. Now I don't know what happened to him after that. I tried to track him down. But I never heard what happened. So I don't know."

There were more Glam 45s. Under the moniker Paul St. John, Laurice did a very unique UFO-themed single for Pye in 1972. Both songs are hypnotic, almost like rock sambas, with Laurice's incredible voice flying up to the higher range. "Flying Saucers Have Landed" contains a fuzzed-out riff and space effects as lyrics refer to the book *Chariots of the Gods?* by Erich von Däniken, which theorizes that aliens visited earth thousands of years ago. Laurice notes, "My own father was absolutely riveted by his theories, so I subsequently decided to write and record 'Flying Saucers Have Landed' based on von Däniken's books."

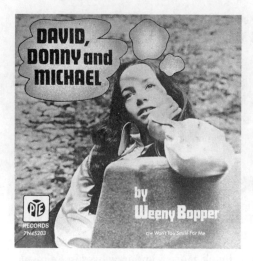

Sleeve to "David, Donny and Michael" single by WeenyBopper (Pye Records, 1972). Author's collection.

The flip side, "Spaceship Lover," takes us on a romantic journey through the cosmos.

Laurice wrote and produced Glam singles for other artists, including the exuberant junkshop stomper "Beautiful Child" (1973) for the band Spiv, on Pye, and the teen idol ode "David, Donny and Michael" by WeenyBopper (1972). Says Laurice, "I did a lot of session singing in London—Abbey Road and various other places. I worked with some people you may have heard of, Kiki Dee, and people like that. Anyway, I was recording my demos at Apple Records and George Harrison walks in, he congratulated me—I could kick myself; I should have asked him, 'Do you have any names I can go to, can you recommend anybody in the States?' But I didn't. So I lost an opportunity there. He seemed very nice."

Backed by a full band or even with just a piano player, Laurice would perform in the working-men's pubs singing Andy Williams ballads, rock songs, smooth jazz, you name it. It was a smorgasbord of songs, pastiche for the pubs, not done so much as a gesture of art but to please the range of young and old who would gather at this local meeting place, as is British custom.

Besides Lou Reed, there is the unmistakable influence of Dusty Springfield, the flamboyant icon of blue-eyed soul. Laurice says, "Dusty Springfield was my big hero. I mean, I loved Dusty. I saw her twice." Her mezzo-soprano voice with its range was versatile. You can clearly hear the breathy accents in Laurice's voice. He would take deep breathing to extremes on his disco tracks.

Laurice notes in one of his videos, "I can claim the mantle of being a founding member of the music genre Gay Rock." Recorded before leaving England, these catchy pop nuggets are all Glammy stunners with overtly gay themes. There's "Rock Hard," a pulsing rocker with a gargle solo; "He's My Guy," a dreamy ode done in epic girl-group style; and the S&M-themed "Born to Serve," which uses kazoo in a way that makes one shimmy. Not only is "Wild Sugar" energetic fun, it is a total bridge between Glam and disco, foreshadowing the next stage of Laurice's career. When I asked if those songs saw release in the '70s, Laurice exclaimed, "No! No! They wouldn't release them! Are you kidding? Are you kidding? These people today have no concept of how uptight it was then. I mean, they're uptight now, you know, but I mean, then it was—I had a terrible time. I mean, I had an awful time, because I was a gay artist and don't say I didn't have the talent. I did. The thing is they didn't want to know."

Sadly, these songs were shelved for decades, finally seeing release these past few years on the indispensable *Best of Laurice,* volumes 1 and 2, released by Mighty Mouth Records. Both albums are packed with should-have-been pop hits from a better, alternate universe.

Laurice grew frustrated with the British record industry. As he puts it, "I mean, I turned down seven recording contracts in one year because I knew they wanted to bury me. They did that with any artists they felt. In fact, they still do it. Did you know that in those days, they expected you to sign a seven-year contract? And also, they would sign you up because a big record company in those days—I don't know about today—only needed two successful artists on their label. And all the other artists on the label just carry that—they're all tax losses. So, they don't promote them. They do nothing. That's the truth!"

When Laurice moved to Canada the musical shift to Glam Disco made sense. Laurice explains, "I was inspired by disco and, going back a few years, in the early '70s in London, there was a drag club that I used to go to with an Indian friend of mine. And every time they put on Stevie Wonder's 'Signed, Sealed, Delivered' we beat a path to the dancefloor because we loved that song and I wished it could go on and on and on. And when 'Get Down Tonight' by KC and the Sunshine Band came on, I flipped—I just loved that song. It was the synthesizer line in it that really did it. It was just a great, great record."

"When I came to Canada, I was looking for a recording contract and I tried New York, and that didn't work because nobody there wanted to take a chance on an unknown British singer, even though I had some great demos with me. Wonderful demos. But that was it. Well, a Canadian record company[24] signed me up to do a disco single with my producer, who lived in Nashville, and we recorded '(All Day and All Night) We Will Make Love,' which was recorded actually in New York, and it became a big Canadian hit and then a massive international hit. But not in America, not in England—they would not release it. Well, they did actually—a little Buffalo company. What was the name of it? I can't remember,[25] but anyway, they released the single three times, even though it was topping the charts with the rest of the world, but the DJs refused to play it. The problem was that in Canada and in America, the rockers there hated disco. They hated disco because they thought it was too black and too gay."

"I mean, the music establishment in Canada hated me. They made no bones about it. But I was persona non grata as far as they were concerned, and it didn't matter how nice I was to them. They didn't want to know—I'm not including the disco pools. And talking about the actual music establishment in Canada, it was very conservative, very straight. In fact, the people in charge were very senior, if you want the truth. I think that they were still living in the '50s and that's how it was in Canada at that time. I think French Canada was a bit freer. But they have the Catholic Church, you know, putting their, you know, boots on them."

The May 22, 1976, issue of *RPM Weekly* writes about Laurice (recording then as Laurie

---

24 Hardcore Records, a subsidiary of GRT Records.
25 Amherst Records.

Marshall), "How do you break a sexy, new disco record in stuffy Southern Ontario? One way to find out is to do it yourself; that's what Laurie Marshall is doing. Marshall, who recently came here from Britain and is a landed immigrant, cut All Day and All Night with producer Ralph Murphy and licenced the disc to GRT, who pressed it on their label. The moment it came off the press he was running it around to many of the hundreds of discos and disco record stores from Toronto to Detroit before the official May 7 release date. Marshall, a music publisher and producer in Britain (a staff producer with Pye for a time), left the Isles because he was 'depressed with British Radio.' He wrote All Day and tracked it in New York."

In the following week's edition, *RPM* writes, "Laurie Marshall advises that his GRT disco single All Day, All Night, is taking off in Montreal as well as Toronto, even though the official release date was delayed. He sold 700 singles in a week in Montreal and he's going to remake the song into an eight minute 12" disco disc. He's off to New York to produce an album to be mixed by Gotham's disco king Tom Moulton."

A few months later, the November 6, 1976, issue of *RPM Weekly* ran a column about just how behind the times the Canadian industry was with disco, describing how Canadian record labels didn't want to make disco twelve-inches, that a major unnamed Toronto record store won't stock them—though they were selling like wildfire in the USA and at Disco Sound in Toronto. The piece was written by Peter Frost of Disco Sound, a record store catering to disco. A later article in the April 21, 1979, issue of *Billboard* states, "Peter Frost, co-owner along with Fred Goshine of Disco Sound, claims that Toronto stations have shown an unfavorable bias against black music, and that the acceptance of disco and r & b by radio in this market is only just starting to surface." Disco Sound would buy advertising on a radio station just over the border in Buffalo, New York. The article goes on to note that Disco Sound opened in 1975 to fill a need, as there was a lack of interest in disco and R&B from other record stores in Toronto.

In 1975 Laurice worked at the record store Sam the Record Man on Yonge Street. He recalls, "I was put in charge of the disco section because all the other guys in the shop hated *hated* disco! They were all rockers. I mean, I liked both, but I was the only person there who liked disco and they never heard of it before. The manager of the shop only allowed me to play one hour of disco records from 5 PM to 6 PM in the evening and he was very reluctant to do it, but they *were* a record store [laughing], so they had to play some of it. Customers kept coming in and asking for the new Donna Summer album—her first as it happens, *Love to Love You Baby*. Nobody had heard of it. One Friday evening a box of the Donna Summer album hit the store. I impatiently waited for the five o'clock hour. The store was packed with customers looking through the stacks of records in the store. I took an album out of the box and put it on the record player. As soon as the needle hit the record the siren strains of 'Ah love to love you baby . . . ' drifted through the store. What happened next I will never forget. It was so astonishing. I watched in sheer disbelief as everyone in that big store, including the staff, froze. It was as if someone had stopped time.

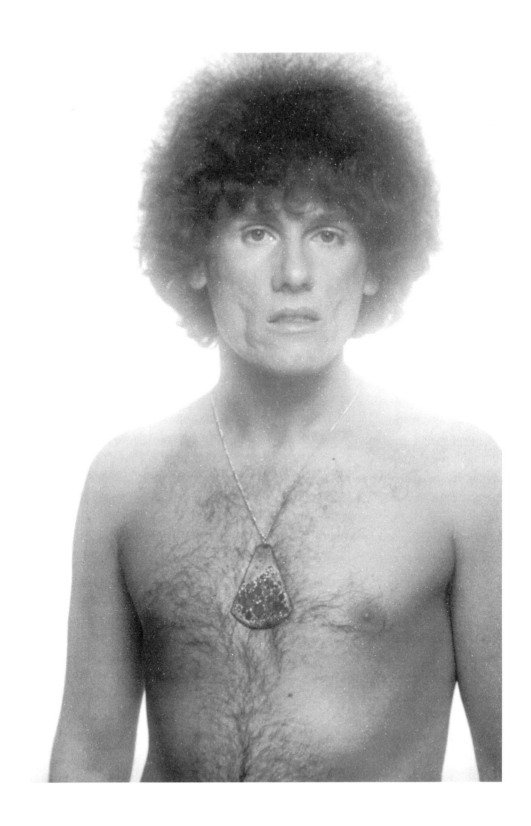

Laurice, 1976. Courtesy of Laurice.

Everyone remained motionless for about six to eight seconds, paralyzed by the sound of that beautiful voice. Then a mad rush to my counter and the box of Donna Summer records was gone in a flash. The manager's jaw nearly dropped on the ground. He had never seen anything like this. Neither had I, and I know I will never see something quite like this again. I turned to the manager and said, rather wryly, 'I think you better order some more.' The manager nodded, shocked out of his mind. After that, slowly but surely, disco began to sell in the store and I managed to push disco a bit more. This was good because when my records came out they sold very well. Of course, I had long left the store by then."

1976's "(All Day and All Night) We Will Make Love" was produced by Ralph Murphy, who was more known for producing acts like Zwol and April Wine. However, it was mixed by Tom Moulton—yes, *the* Tom Moulton who originated remixes—this was an early record for him. There were even French and Spanish versions, all featuring copious moaning, going beyond language.

Montreal was a disco hub. There Laurice performed the sensual song on *Feel Like Dancin'*, a TV show taped in a discotheque, often featuring guest performers such as Grace Jones and René Simard and audience dance segments. With the audience sashaying along, Laurice was attired in a silver lamé robe that looked like a haute couture emergency blanket and a natural afro generously sprinkled with what looked like glitter but really was danger. As he puts it, "I had diamond dust in it, and that was very dangerous because at the time the sparkle—diamond dust was like ground glass—if it got in your eyes you were in trouble, but I wore it."

Laurice's next record, 1977's "Disco Spaceship," had a pumping disco sound and cosmic themes, a celebration of our alien friends with their sexy moves, giving shout-outs to all of the planets, all races, all creeds. This song marked a return to Laurice's interest in UFOs. Laurice attended a lecture at the University of Toronto by Erich von Däniken and chatted with him after, letting him know about his UFO-themed music.

"Disco Spaceship" was released on Canada's Casino Records. They were not a disco label. Now if you sign to label with a name like say, Casino or Roulette, it's going to be a real gamble. When I told Laurice that I'd heard the label owner, Ray Pettinger, wasn't a nice man he replied, "He was not a nice man. That's an understatement. But what happened was, I recorded a whole album in New York at a very top studio in New York, and he didn't pay anybody for it, so we had to leave, and the result of that was—and this is jumping forward—my recording contract in Canada was suspended. I could not record in Canada anymore. That's why I left. It was horrible, and it was nothing to do with me. "

Asked further about the notorious Pettinger, Laurice replies, "I don't know what happened to him. If you want the truth, the very last time I ever saw him was when he was leaving on a plane, a small private plane, in Toronto, and I have to tell you, he said something nasty to me, and he walked away. And I have to tell you, Robert, I kind of felt sorry for the guy. I really felt sorry for him, even with the awful things he'd done. My producer had a nervous break-

Laurice performing "(All Day and All Night) We Will Make Love" on *Feel Like Dancin'*, 1976. Courtesy of Laurice.

down over this—everything—it almost ruined his career, and I just felt really sorry for the guy because I thought, you know, you've just got no compassion, no humility—very Donald Trumpish. A real sociopath, you know, and it was very, very sad."

It's quite clear that Laurice had no shortage of great songs, but the labels would not release them.[26] But why? To get some answers, Laurice went to his lawyer Bernard Solomon, a.k.a. "Bernie the Attorney, music lawyer to the stars." He was *the* music lawyer in Canada. Laurice explains, "And he said to me, 'Don't you know why this is happening?' and I said, 'Tell me.' He said, 'Because you're gay,' and he said, 'They don't like gays, and they don't like black music.' He said, 'You will never make it again here because they blackballed you.' And he knows! He was in the know. Everybody went to him. And I was shocked. But I refused to see it. I thought, 'I got to press on, no matter what.' And after the upset with Casino Records I flew to Los Angeles. I tried to make a living as a songwriter, and I started managing other artists and, let me tell you, that was such a headache in L.A.—these artists sitting by the pool waiting to be discovered. In the end I was so angry with all of them, I fired them all." Furthermore, Laurice told one of the artists, "Do not close your eyes." But did he listen? "I went to see him and he closed his eyes through the whole performance. You can't do that when you're performing before a crowd. If you look at my live performances on my YouTube channel, you see I always try and communicate with the audience. You don't turn them off."

---

26 The sweeping, classical-motifed "Love's Sweet Symphony" and "Rock Me thru the Night" were finally released years later on Laurice's *Dance Dance Dance* album from Mighty Mouth.

Top to bottom: Sleeve to "Hot Line" by Laurice (Stud Records, 1988). Courtesy of Laurice. Sleeve to *G.A.Y.D.A.R.* by Laurice (Mighty Mouth Music, 2015). Author's collection.

With this move to the USA, Laurie Marshall started doing music under the name Laurice. He explains, "I made it up for myself. I didn't even know there was such a name. And then people sort of took the name."

And what sparked the name Laurice?

"I wanted something that sounded French because I know that in America they're like, 'Ohhh, it's so nice,' so, let's do something sort of Frenchish, and Laurice was perfect. It suited me."

Laurice's twelve-inch "Hot Line" was released on Stud Records in 1988 and it sounds very '80s in a hi-NRG style. It's all about the phenomenon that was sweeping the continent at the time: phone sex. The audacious cover features a photo of Laurice in drag sucking on a banana. Laurice notes, "They refused to play it because they felt it was too gay. That's the truth. And yet everyone I played it to loved it."

Laurice performed "Hot Line" on the Hollywood TV show *Gaytalk*, at L.A. Pride in 1992, and at the first L.A. art exhibition of Tom of Finland; Laurice was also senior liaison for the Tom of Finland organization. He also helped the noted archivist Jim Kepner at ONE National Gay and Lesbian Archives taping stories about his life in Los Angeles in the '40s and '50s, noting, "It was quite depressing."

Laurice then moved to Fresno, California, where he met his partner Larry. At the time of our interview Laurice notes, "We've been together twenty-eight years." When they met it was the Bush (I) era and they were living in the fundamentalist heartland of California. "And the homophobia there was terrible, and people couldn't get jobs and everything was really, really bad there, and I decided that Larry needed to see a different country. We both went up to Vancouver and a girlfriend of mine in London had told me that Kelowna was a nice place to go. So we went and we loved it, and we thought, 'Oh, this is great.' We went back to Fresno …" Now the mayor of Fresno, Alan Autry, a born-again Christian, was notorious. Laurice explains, "And within three days of our getting back, he called this huge rally there—anti-gay and save-the-family rally with this reverend there who sounded like somebody from Hitler's Nazi era, and he was just horrible, and there we were demonstrating, about a couple hundred of us on the other side of the road, and there were five thousand people surrounding the town hall, which by the way, was completely illegal, and I looked at Larry and he looked at me and I said, 'I've had enough of this, we're getting out.' And so I was able to sponsor Larry to get into Canada—it took three years—and we had a lesbian lawyer, who's quite well known, barbara findlay [she spells her name in lowercase], in Vancouver, and she got us in, but she was the one who—you know, they banned the gay parade here, Gay Pride, and she came and won the case here in Kelowna against the mayor at the time. That's why we came to Kelowna, and I'll tell you what, I'm glad we did when we did."

In recent years Laurice has performed in New York, Brooklyn, Philadelphia, Calgary, and Vancouver, as well as at Kelowna Pride three times in a row and at the now sadly closed Milk Crate Records, where you could buy Laurice's albums. Laurice continues to record. 2015's *G.A.Y.D.A.R.* is Laurice's first new album in almost twenty years, and with songs like "Big Boy," "Fantasy Man," and a very moany version of "Sugar Sugar" (really just Laurice singing overtop of the original Archies song) it is a lot of X-rated catchy synth-pop fun. My copy included a random page from an old gay porn magazine. There's also *Balladeer* and the soothing sounds of *Echoes*. Laurice's latest project, *Tribute,* features odes to Motown, zydeco, reggae, and artists like Grace Jones, UB40, and Janet Jackson. With Larry's help, Laurice is making brand new videos for his YouTube channel—there may even be a new one posted right now.

NEIL MERRYWEATHER

NEIL MERRYWEATHER RECORDED TWO albums full of shimmery, spacy Glitter Rock, making spaceship cruising music through the twinkling expanse full of stars. The first album, *Space Rangers,* begins on earth with the gritty "Hollywood Boulevard," opening up on a cartoon soundscape of horns and voices and revving motorbikes. Canada sure is a long way from Hollywood, let alone space. Before all that, Merryweather was a part of the integral building blocks of Canadian rock history.

He wasn't always Neil Merryweather. Born Robert Neilson Lillie in Winnipeg, his family left for Ontario when he was just a couple of months old. He played in bands that kept changing their names—one band briefly went by the Ookpiks after the popular Inuit stuffed toy—while he was changing his own stage names. After playing bass in the Toronto heavy psych band the Tripp, he left in 1967 to join a version of the Mynah Birds with Rick James—who was not yet the "Super Freak" funk icon—he wasn't even Rick James yet. The Mynah Birds certainly had some interesting people pass through their ranks. Merryweather joined after the Mynah Birds members Bruce Palmer and Neil Young left the band to find fame in L.A.

Front cover, front and back inserts to *Space Rangers* by Neil Merryweather (Mercury, 1974). Author's collection.

This latest lineup of the Mynah Birds fell apart while they were recording at Motown in Detroit, so both the yet-to-be Merryweather and James went back to Toronto to reform the band—not knowing that James was about to get busted on breaking and entering a fancy-dress shop in Yorkville Village. Merryweather explains, "And that's when I got Bruce Cockburn as the guitar player in the band, but then Rick gets popped because of one of the waitresses at the local coffee shop, the Night Owl—the cops had gone around all over the Village looking for him, like a month or so before, and when we were sitting out there having coffee when we got back to Toronto thinking about who we're going to get for the band, the waitress turned him in. So then he was in jail in Toronto for a couple of months before they finally sent him back to Buffalo where he was a draft dodger. That's the real reason he came to Toronto when he was younger in the first place. He was draft-dodging the Navy."

The new band, without James alas, was now dubbed the Flying Circus—this was before Monty Python, mind you—and landed some rather high-profile gigs opening for Wilson Pickett and Roy Orbison. That band wouldn't last long, as Merryweather explains: "I didn't dig Bruce Cockburn's folky kind of writing and we didn't really hit it off as people either, and so I left, and that's when I formed the band and wound up going to L.A."

Of his roots, Merryweather says, "I'm a Toronto boy. The Toronto sound and all the bands that wound up getting involved with everybody from Bob Dylan to Alice Cooper to you name it—we just had a thing going on in Toronto at the time—and I'm still proud of being in the early stages of it back then. But, you know, unfortunately, the label business wasn't there yet." Los Angeles has a reputation as the entertainment capital of the world with a great many Canadians residing there.

The seed to leave was planted in Merryweather's head by the former Mynah Bird and Buffalo Springfield member Bruce Palmer, now back in Canada. Palmer convinced him that he simply had to go to L.A. But if L.A. was so great and all that, then why wasn't Palmer still there? Merryweather answers, "He got busted. He was driving a Corvette in Topanga Canyon, and he had a shoebox full of weed on the dash, and I guess he was a little high and he miscalculated the road and wound up in a ditch and the dope went all over him. The grass went all over him and a cop came along and they busted him, and then they found out that he didn't have legal papers to even be there, so they deported him. We ran into him at his brother's place near the Village in Toronto. We went to see him and there was also a girl that was the secretary for the head of Warner/Reprise there and they were followers of that Moon guy." By Moon, he means the Moonies cult leader the Rev. Sun Myung Moon. Instead of running off to join the Moonies cult, Merryweather and his best friend, the former Tripp frontman Jimmy Livingston, formed a new band, then followed the flight pattern of those other Mynah Birds south to L.A. No, they didn't fly—they piled into the drummer's brother's Chevy Impala and drove nonstop for two and a half days, arriving in L.A. in the summer of '68.

Merryweather wasted no time. Within a few months they were signed by Capitol Records, doing two albums of heavy blues-rock for them. After that band fell apart, Merryweather recorded more albums for more labels. He was prolific. RCA signed him and his then girlfriend, the singer Lynn Carey, because of their harmonies—both of them being incredible vocalists with a dynamic range—and released the 1971 album *Vacuum Cleaner*. The album cover features Merryweather and Carey looking quite glamourous, with Merryweather in a Russian fur hat and Carey decked out in a huge afro wig made out of French hair. They looked so good that to announce the album a giant mural was painted of it covering the entire side of the Whisky a Go Go on Sunset Boulevard. Side two of the album opens with an introduction by Kim Fowley before the band kicks into a cover of the Miracles' Motown hit "Shop Around."

It was Merryweather who got Fowley signed to RCA. Says Merryweather, "I'd run into Kim in places and so I got him signed. I went to the A&R guys there, and I got him signed to RCA with the promise that I thought he could do some good work because he had done 'Alley Oop' and he had done other records in the past, and he was a character and I thought it would work out. So I went to the first session, and he was with Kate Taylor, James Taylor's sister. He was hanging out with her and a whole crowd of his freaky people. And here we are in an RCA studio, and I thought he'd come in with something planned, and it was just pandemonium! He had nothing going except crazy lyrics and you know, 'Play this beat!' and I didn't have the time to try and organize the freak show, you know what I mean? So I told him to do it himself, and I told them [RCA] that Kim was going to do it himself, and obviously it didn't work out."

The director Russ Meyer's 1970 proto–Glam Freak Rock blockbuster melodrama *Beyond the Valley of the Dolls,* about a woman rock group, is heralded today as a jaw-dropping camp classic—deluxe Criterion release and all. Carey sang and co-wrote a couple of the songs on the soundtrack, which is full of memorable songs that a few smart and fun bands such as Redd Kross have covered over the years. Many an obsessive record collector gazing at her album covers has stated that Carey really should have been in the movie. Merryweather explains, "She got offered one of the roles, but we had made an agreement with each other that we wouldn't pursue any other side things. Actually, when I was at Capitol in the lobby one day talking to the receptionist, these guys in suits walked in, and the guy looked at me and walked over with this little four-guy group of suited men. He comes over and he gives me his card and he says, 'You would be great in my new movie,' and I just laughed. I thought, 'Well, geez, thanks,' and the chick at the reception, she went crazy because it was the guy that produced *Dirty Harry,* and I guess the guy thought I would be the perfect killer guy in *Dirty Harry*, but I didn't even pursue it because Lynn and I had a deal that—you know, she was an actress too. She's done TV work and movies in her teen years, and we made a pact that we were going to stick together and just work on music. So when she got offered the acting job in the movie, that was one thing, but she also got offered to do all the lead singing." Merryweather showed up at a couple of sessions and went with her to the film premiere: "It was exciting, and I was happy that Lynn was doing it."

Stu Philips, who produced the *Beyond the Valley of the Dolls* soundtrack, also did Meyer's next movie, *The Seven Minutes*, a courtroom drama based on an Irving Wallace novel, the kind of book you'd buy in an airport if Jacqueline Susann's novels are a bit too much content-wise, you know: borrrrring. Not only was this Meyer's least outrageous film, it was also his last major studio movie. As the bright spot shining out from all of the subdued earth tones, Merryweather and Carey perform in a discotheque scene, singing "Midnight Tricks," mentioning incense, no peppermints. Even more albums followed, two of them with the band Mama Lion, prominently featuring Carey.

> **HELD OVER**
> TONIGHT 'TIL SUNDAY
> **"FLYING CIRCUS"**
> featuring Bruce Cocburn
> FRI. AND SAT. AFTER HOURS
> WITH "FLYING CIRCUS"
> **LE HIBOU**
> 521 Sussex Dr.   233 - 0712

Newspaper ad for Flying Circus with Bruce Cockburn's name spelled wrong. Image courtesy of the *Ottawa Citizen*, February 8, 1968.

Not long after Merryweather left Mama Lion, the road manager, Robbie Randal, said, "You got to see Bowie, man. I got tickets. I want to take you to see Bowie. You got to see this guy." It was the Hollywood Palladium stop of the *Ziggy Stardust and the Spiders from Mars* tour on March 12, 1973. The show notably affected Merryweather: "Blew my mind. I just freakin' loved it. I just thought it was just magical. And you know, the costume changes, the way it was staged, the musicianship. It was just a great show." The very next day Randal came over to Merryweather's place suggesting, "Why don't you write something like that?" Merryweather replied, "You mean like this?" The first song, "Hollywood Boulevard," was written in five minutes.

Merryweather continues, "And he shit his pants. But that was the beginning of the Space Rangers. So I put an ad in a local rag, *Music Connection,* looking for a guitar player, and I had Timmy for drums [Tim McGovern already had a heavy rock pedigree, having previously drummed on Randy California's *Kapt. Kopter and the (Fabulous) Twirly Birds* album] and a guitar player I found, Timo Laine. He came over to audition among other people that came over, but he had an Echoplex, and he really had a command over the Echoplex and wah-wah with his Les Paul in a Twin Reverb, and it just blasted me out of the room with the sound."

That's right, *Ziggy Stardust* so inspired Merryweather that he made not one but two albums—one in 1974, the other in 1975. The first, *Space Rangers,* opens with "Hollywood Boulevard," a paean to ex-pats, the allure dragging us away from the frosty climes—a motorbike revs up as a voice sings, "Hollywood . . . la dee da da . . . ," then the juiciest guitar, like a giant blueberry, the everlasting gobstopper of guitar sounds panning through eardrums connecting the salivatory glands as tarnished clouds of glitter grit poof. And just as those clouds of glitter poof start to dissolve, they poof again . . . Merryweather's fantastic voice singing, "High-heeled boys everywhere, Bowie-like babies with angels' hair, like Disneyland, quite insane . . . you'll all come to see the queens on Hollywood Boulevard . . . yeahhhh yeahhhh . . . " And what is that other sound way up in the mix, ever-present all through this shining pair of albums? The Chamberlin, of course.[27] The Chamberlin on *Space Rangers* was played by Laine's friend, the former violinist Bob Silvert. This unique musical instrument is played like a keyboard, very analog—beams from space, new alien emotions. It's kind of like an early sampler but with tape loops of various instruments and effects—including the human voice. One song ends in a Chamberlin choir fading out, then up, then out again. Merryweather is absolutely a Bass Guitar God, but this is also very much a Chamberlin album.[28] Late nights in the cosmos. Stranger in a strange land—I hear it's called Hollyweird.

The heavily altered covers make sense: "Eight Miles High" is not about drugs, it's about space; and then there's a Glam thank you to Donovan for his ode to the great superhero "Sunshine Superman," bringing on the sneaky bass strut.[29]

Unlike much Glam doling out three-minute singles as snacks, there are tracks that stretch out, like the proto-doom rocker "Road to Hades/High Altitude Hide and Seek" and the eight-minute Space Rock closer "Sole Survivor," with air raid sirens and screams, ending into a distorted trumpet moaning out "Taps" going kaput. This effect was done very literally, as Merryweather explains: "I pulled the plug. When we were making the actual transfer from the sixteen-track to the two-track for the master I wanted it to die like that. So I unplugged the machine, the twenty-four track, so it was still feeding as it was dying." Death is not really the end. There's a whole other album.

Space Rangers was recorded quickly. They went in to the studio and within an hour cut "Hollywood Boulevard." However, Merryweather says that the band was not to last, apart from drummer McGovern, "They all disappeared on me. Bob sold the Chamberlin and went back to the Midwest somewhere to go back to school. Timo disappeared—I couldn't find him—and I had been giving him money that I had left over from Mama Lion to pay their rent and doing everything and then they just deserted me. But the tapes—I already had done the tapes—I'd already taken them into the studio and recorded, basically, that album. And Robbie Randal again comes around and he had the tape and he took it over to play for Skip Taylor, who used to produce Canned Heat, and the guy's brother was there and he went crazy for it and asked if he could manage me and I was, like, starving all of a sudden again, because I'd given all the money to these guys that bailed. And he had gotten a deal, a cheap deal, to buy the master from Mercury. But it gave me enough money to actually put this second version together with Mike Willis, and Timmy was still with me and we got Jamie Herndon, and I bought a Chamberlin from Sonny and Cher that was up for sale because

---

27 Some of you may be more familiar with the Mellotron, but it was actually a modified rip-off of the Chamberlin. You read it right—the Chamberlin was first! Its inventor, Harry Chamberlin, got ripped off by his employee Bill Franson, who ran off to England with it where Chamberlin's patent couldn't reach him.

28 Another legendary album using the Chamberlin is *The Cycle Is Complete,* by the aforementioned former Mynah Bird Bruce Palmer—this zonked out piece of psych has the former Merryweather bandmate Ed Roth credited for organ and Rick James providing vocals and percussion etc.

29 Donovan in turn replied to Glam with his album *Cosmic Wheels* and a star turn across the hallway on Alice Cooper's *Billion Dollar Babies.*

they had broken up and they were dissolving all the stuff they had for their act, and so I got that and continued the Space Rangers sound and then wrote the second album and we went into the Village Recorder and within four days we came up with that album, and that was the story of the Space Rangers." Of this new merry band of Space Rangers, the keyboardist and guitarist Jamie Herndon was only a couple of years away from playing in the Canadian Glammer Nick Gilder's band—including playing on Gilder's hit single "Hot Child in the City."

The credits for the first, eponymous Space Rangers album read a little murky due to a bit of band drama. When Laine heard the news about the record deal, he finally reappeared... after the new lineup was formed. Wanting to keep everybody happy, Merryweather offered Laine a place as second guitarist, expanding the lineup to a five-piece. This was not to be. Merryweather notes that Laine wanted fifty percent of everything: "I never got much for the record, but I'm willing to share it equally—that's how I ran the band—and he wouldn't go for it, so it didn't work." Laine, representing himself and Silvert, continued to cause trouble. Things got so heated that Merryweather says Laine's mom even called him, imploring, "Why do you do this to my boy, Timo?" Merryweather really felt bad about the album credits, but he was left with no other recourse—he couldn't use their names. The guitar was credited only to Mike Willis, who played on a couple of tracks, while the Chamberlin and synthesizer were credited to the mysterious Edgemont—in actuality the nickname of his friend Linda Edgemont, who was able to come in and fix a couple of bum synth notes on the album.

For both albums the whole process was organic and exciting: one-take wonders recording the energy of great musicians where there was complete creative control. Merryweather describes, "If I had an idea, about, you know, King of Mars, we just went in and we just cut it, and it always had to be the way I formed the melody and put the song together and arranged the song. Both albums went together that way. It was magical to have guys that were good enough to actually play what I could think of in my head at the time and jam it out." Right from the opening struts and poses of the second album, *Kryptonite*, it's a full-on band. The Chamberlin sounds stage-ready with wind machine aimed directly at it. The album's back end gets the Glammiest: "The Groove" is a total "Bowie fauxie" in quivery intonation, structure, piano, and rock 'n' roll star subject matter. High-pitched vocals and guitars swagger on "Always Be with You," then the synths get to swagger and squiggle for "You Know Where I'd Rather Be," moaning about making poor decisions as a middle-aged businessman. "Let Us Be the Dawn" is a lift-off song, floating away from the awful people of earth, yet it sounds much more like the discovery of a new planet.

Around that same time Merryweather produced a project called Band of Angels, a girl group for the '70s space-rock era. The Space Rangers were basically the band for this project, with McGovern on drums and Herndon on synths, Chamberlin, and guitar. Strictly a studio project, the members of Band of Angels were Merryweather's almost-then-wife Devereaux Kirnsey, Barbara Frye, and Herndon's then-girlfriend Donna La Maire. They mostly sang in unison, with Devereaux doing the lead on a gone groovy and cosmic version of the Shirelles' stunner "Will You Love Me Tomorrow." Two singles were released. They gave the Zombies' "She's Not There" a gender switcheroo to "He's Not There," with all softness and jazziness removed, yet cosmic and also fiery. A couple of B sides were originals: "Every Minute," written by Merryweather and Devereaux, and "So Hard Livin' Without You." A version of "Nights in White Satin" was recorded but remains unreleased.

Now Merryweather knew that to be Glam Rock one needs to look Glam Rock. The inner sleeve for *Space Rangers* shows him skin-tight in a custom hand-painted leather jacket, flames on the front, a phoenix rising out on the back. For the second album, *Kryptonite*, the band were drawn as comic-book superheroes by the veteran *Captain America* artist Don Rico, and now these sunshine supermen needed to be all decked out in real life. So Merryweather picked out some material with flair, then visited the tailor in the back of Trashy Lingerie on La Cienega Boulevard in Los Angeles. Purple satin, gold lamé—Herndon flies the 'fro and got blue leggings under purple satin short-shorts; McGovern the drummer's head to toe in pink; stars applied all up and down Michael Willis's arms and legs; Merryweather's blond bangs properly aligned. Huddled together they were band-photo-ready with their backs against a planet.

They really didn't get much of a chance to wear these outfits on stage with their live shows pretty much limited to a week at the Whisky a Go Go and a week at the Starwood in L.A., but their biggest show was for the KSHE Radio birthday party held at the Kiel Auditorium in St. Louis on November 1, 1974. Also on the bill were KISS and T. Rex. Merryweather says, "And we did incredible. I mean, people were just—they went crazy, and J.R., the road manager for KISS, thought I was the best vocalist he ever heard in his life, and that night, actually, when we got to town to play the gig, they had us booked in a nice hotel close to the Kiel and I opened up my bass case and somebody had stomped it at the airport, so there was a sneaker imprint on the case and they broke the neck on my bass, so I didn't have a bass. I had to use Gene Simmons' black Fender Precision and it had fake blood all over it, and my young girlfriend at the time had to clean it all up before we went on stage. It was funny, but we kicked ass that night. I mean, it was just a magical night and that that act should have gone on to break all the norms because, for a four-piece act, we sounded like an orchestra."

T. Rex's Marc Bolan loved their set. Merryweather recounts, "What happened was he freaked out. He thought that was the best act he ever heard in his life, and he came running into the change room. He was crying. I mean, he was so fucking blown away by the set we played, and Gloria Jones was with him, his girlfriend, and they hung around for a long time. He gave me his number and he said, if you ever come to England, please call me. So, when I had to dissolve the band, I went straight to England and I was going to call him to help resurrect it before everybody got other gigs. And I waited one day too long." Marc Bolan was dead.

As for the break-up of the band, Merryweather says, "I did that second album, *Kryptonite*, within, I think five months after I signed and had the first one out. I delivered the master for the next one and they loved it. So they gave me the money. I had the same stinking deal, but that kept the second band alive and then when that ran out, I couldn't

Back cover, front cover and inner sleeve to *Kryptonite* by Neil Merryweather (Mercury, 1975). Author's collection.

even keep the band alive. I had to sell the Marshall stacks and, you know, the equipment I had—I had to let it go. I had to sell it to stay alive myself. So bad, lousy management and a shitty label deal caused the death of the best band I ever had in my life."

In 1976, he produced the Glam Rock band the Hollywood Stars. This was long after Fowley, their manager, had left; Fowley had put this band together, in fact, and placed a couple of their songs with KISS ("King of the Nighttime World") and Alice Cooper ("Escape"). The Hollywood Stars singer Mark Anthony used the resulting album that Merryweather produced to land a deal with Clive Davis at Arista, but Merryweather says, "Clive Davis never bought albums. He always got an act off of a demo or an actual finished product. But he had always wanted to do it again so he could have his name on it. He never took a finished album and just said, 'Okay, we're putting it out.' He always had to somehow maneuver to have it redone under his regime, so to speak. I got along with Clive, so he liked the album so much he asked me to produce it. But Mark Anthony continued stabbing me in the back, and they went with some engineer that worked with Bowie. And they put it out and it bombed. And most of the guys in the band thought what I did with them was better." Some years after Anthony's passing, the rest of the Hollywood Stars reunited and Merryweather sent them the old tapes with the album finally seeing release as *Sound City* in 2019, named after the studio it was recorded in, opening appropriately with "Sunrise on Sunset."

While at Sound City Studios, Merryweather produced the singer-songwriter Kyle a.k.a. KYLE—it seems everyone was on a first name basis with this stranger, but not much is known about this artist or this album. Merryweather got a heavy friend from his Toronto days, William "Smitty" Smith of the Canadian soul group Motherlode—known for their hit "When I Die"—to do all the keyboards. It's uncertain if this album was ever released. Merryweather recorded his own solo album *Differences* at Sound City as well; the songs get more introspective singer-songwriter, with the glitter not fully dusted and brushed away.

Of this wild, wild time Merryweather says, "There was a whole scene going on when I was doing my album where one of the Band of Angels, Devereaux, became my wife. We were all high at a party at my house and I got married with her on my knee on a rocking chair, because one of the people we knew—through the mail he became a minister. Here was the highlight of the party: we got married. Anyway. I was always—as George Harrison once called himself—a cocksman. I never was able to stay loyal very long to anybody. So there was a whole mess of stuff involving a bunch of people when I was doing that *Differences* album at Sound City. Eventually I went to Europe and I split up with her."

Differences was released in Europe, where he lived, and he produced various musical projects for a few years. After returning from Europe, Merryweather had a very bad experience with Lita Ford from the Runaways, producing and playing on her first solo album, which included the drummer Dusty Watson. Merryweather got ripped off by Ford and her management big time. Now completely soured, Merryweather gave up music and took a job with the City of Los Angeles. "Then the computer age hit. My wife says, 'You're all over the internet,' and it was always this Space Rangers, that all the albums are popping up, and my wife gets me excited, and we built this little studio in the back of this house we're living in." After reuniting with Herndon and Watson, they started recording and releasing music under the name Hundred Watt Head. When I talked with Merryweather, he was working on a new Space Rangers album, *Space Rangers 3*, with Watson and Peter Reveen,[30] which is being planned for release. Merryweather had also been making massive, colorful paintings and was excited for the elaborate reissues of the first two Space Rangers albums. They came out in July 2021. Sadly, Neil Merryweather passed away on March 28, 2021.

BONUS TRACKS!

OH THOSE PANTS!

Oh Those Pants! were an Ontario Art College band who primarily played there starting around 1974. They only did oldies, with a large rotating lineup including two sax players (one in a sailor suit), two drummers, and two singers slathered in glitter wrestling each other amidst countless costume changes. One singer named Lord Lust would sing "Runaway." The other was Eddy LaGrande. Other members were Cerise Suavage and Miss Micheline. Martha Johnson of Martha and the Muffins started here on organ. They posted a full concert to YouTube but didn't release anything.

WENZDAY

Wednesday hailed from Oshawa, which sounds a lot like Ottawa, the nation's capital, but softer: the nashun's capishul Oshawa. Their first album was filled with the teen-tragedy '50s oldies "Teen Angel" and "Last Kiss," dusted off and refurbished for the '70s. making multiple appearances on K-Tel compilations as a means of fulfilling their obligation to their country. Soon enough they got over the soft hump, changed their name to Wenzday, released their third album, *Nearly Made It* (oop, so close), in 1977, and won the Nashunal Capishal Spelling Bee. Wenzday got a cool logo where the Z is a swooping lightning bolt.

Back cover of *Nearly Made It* by Wenzday (Skyline Records, 1977), Author's collection.

---

30 The son of "The Man They Call Reveen," the famed "impossibilist."

To my thirsty ears it sounds more like late-era Mud or Glitter Band after the glitter was showered off but still gathered in the navel. They cover "Fancy Pants," by the Glam boy-band other-rans Kenny.[31] Wenzday's version of "Ruby Baby" is transformed into a handclap heavy rocker. Yeah, it's pretty Glam and there's some Bowieisms on the track "Dream Queen."

LENNEX/PERFECT AFFAIR

Lennex started out as a Glam-Rock-loving cover band from Niagara Falls criss-crossing Canada playing T. Rex, Mott the Hoople, and the more crowd-pleasing Bowie numbers such as "Rebel Rebel" and "Suffragette City," along with some Rolling Stones standards etc. After opening for their hero the Glam guitar God Mick Ronson's band in Connecticut, Lennex were ecstatic to have him produce some demos. One song successfully landed on a 1982 Q107 radio-contest compilation album and the other was a flexi-disc[32] that came with an issue of *Music Express*.[33] They were initially a two-frontman band, with Rick Rose and Johnny Dee, a.k.a. John DeGluili, who left to form Honeymoon Suite; then Greg Fraser joined the band for a year before going on to form Brighton Rock.

Lennex's album with Ronson, *Midnight in Niagara*, a straight-out rock album, was recorded, then shelved. The label Attic Records wanted something more new wave. Now called Perfect Affair, they went back to the studio, with Ronson producing basic tracks, then the Canadian Cueball Glammer Walter Zwol producing the rest—pushing synths to the front, guitars meld into synths, gated drums, everything processed, a totally treated studio project. Some songs stemmed from

---

31 The contractually messy act run by unpleasant Bay City Rollers management.

32 Flexi-discs were flexible, thin vinyl that many magazines, including *Breakfast Without Meat* and *Mad*, would insert in their issues.

33 The name sounds like *New Musical Express* but this was not the *NME*—no *New*—this was a Canadian music mag.

THE HOLLYWOOD BRATS

New York Dolls were from New York. From around the same time, the Hollywood Brats were not from Hollywood. Formed in London, England, a couple of members came over there from Canada in the early '70s. Andrew Matheson's tawdry, thorough, and very entertaining quippy memoir *Sick on You*, named after their best song, gets deep into the deets through a rapid-fire barrage of quips ever so eloquently strung together. It is for the best that you read it. If you have no interest in music (why are you here?), you can read it for the numerous accounts of petty theft—they'd practically be urchins if they weren't so vain—along with anecdotes of Peter Wyngarde at the Speakeasy, watching *Cabaret* on a loop, etc.

But what does he write of Canada? Before he details his escape to London, Matheson quickly bypasses and dispatches Canada with a devastating description of his blue-collar job: "In the shower I lather up in terror as usual, eyes wide open and stinging from soap. Keeping a sharp lookout because these Canadian nickel miners are a tribe of knuckle-dragging, grunting violent troglodytes. They know it's my last day and they've been making noises about cutting my hair." He makes no mention of having any sort of musical career there. Canada is a blank spot that

Promotional photo of the Hollywood Brats, c. 1974.

gets a mention in hindsight later upon his arrival in Great Britain: "I haven't been in London since my parents kidnapped me as a child, dragging me, kicking and screaming in a sack, to Northern Ontario."

Matheson then found just the right drummer, Lou Sparks—it turns out he was Canadian and of Micmac heritage. In 1971, with the keyboard player Casino Steel and the guitarist Eunan Brady, the Hollywood Brats formed. Teased, coiffed, got ruby red lips. Spending their allotments at Mr. Fish, leader of the "Peacock Revolution" and designer of "man-dresses" worn by Bowie. Pink feather boas so long they graze the floor—even in heels. Ruffles have ridges. Stonesy and snotty. Good, raucous fun. Tight pants with the Lennex days—you can hear it under that total '80s sheen as Rose sings in his rock voice, "New York, L.A., and Detroit, she's out there to exploit, Paris, Montreal, merci . . . "—but it's more than sheen, it seeps into all the cracks. AOR, ok? This self-titled 1983 album is like a workout-mix montage from a movie about a down-on-his-luck kid who makes the grade and gets the girl. That movie could be named after any song here: "On the Edge" (about "danger zones"), "Hard Fight," "Crazy," and, oooh get that gating on the Jiffy Pop, I want to watch "Queen of the Night"! A few years later, Ronson came back to produce a solo single for Rose.

LPS AND 45S:

JUSTIN THOMAS—*HOW I OVERCAME MY FEAR OF* . . . LP (BOOT RECORDS, 1976)

This is a double album that also doubles as a therapy session in the form of a rock musical. Stemming from a stage show and later a book, there are countless spoken interludes in this 1976 musical autobiography and special guests include "the Happy Hooker," Xaviera Hollander. *RPM*'s review describes Justin Thomas as "a former extreme psychiatric case." With a large photo of Thomas, the sleeve lists "How I Overcame My Fear of . . . Whores, Royalty, Gays, Teachers, Hippies, Psychiatrists, Athletes, Transvestites, Clergymen, Police, Children," . . . and on and on . . . ending with "Myself." Expect a lot of discomfort. But they say that from discomfort comes growth. In the gatefold are photos, including one of Thomas as a mime-like joker and one of him in drag, corresponding to his song about dressing as a saucy woman named

mixing-board arrows leaning all the way over to the right, in the red. It's a grower. Smart dumb energy. They know better than to heteronormalize the girl-group classic "Then He Kissed Me" by the Crystals, respecting the song while the guitar sounds like all the strings are going to sproing off. It's an utterly great album that never lags. Alas, it only saw release in the Netherlands after the band broke up. However, the nascent London punks were able to find it and lodge it into their genetic make-up.

Lou Sparks returned to Canada (Halifax, Nova Scotia, to be precise) in 1974 but the whole band got back together in London in 1980 to record a raucous version of "Little Old Wine Drinker Me." It was around this time that their album finally saw release in England by Cherry Red Records.

Matheson made a rather good solo album (*Monterey Shoes*, 1979) of well written mid-tempo rock songs for Ariola, one of the more evocatively named record labels, then when he returned to Canada for a few years in the '90s recorded a CD called *Night of the Bastard Moon*, the sound of hitting your forties, produced by Casino Steel. *Sick on You* received glowing book reviews in 2015, causing Matheson to reunite with Brady and Steel. Sparks is spoken of warmly on Matheson's Facebook page but is mysteriously absent, presumably still somewhere in Canada.

Front cover to *How I Overcame My Fear of* . . . LP by Justin Thomas (Boot Records, 1976). Author's collection.

Flaming Mamie in his summer-camp floor show—he sings the song in the Flaming Mamie character's voice. My copy was autographed with a note, "Here's to clarity and the love that follows." Thomas (not his real name) was active in his philosophy of "label liberation," rightfully believing that labels can imprison us, even giving out LLDs—label liberation degrees—stating, "I'm a PERSON 1st."

FORGOTTEN REBELS—*THIS AIN'T HOLLYWOOD* LP (1982, STAR RECORDS)

The Forgotten Rebels were known for feather-ruffling. They were edgelords before there was a name for such thing. There's something unsavory about this band. Their *Tomorrow Belongs to Us* EP (paraphrased from the song the Nazis sing in the movie *Cabaret*) has the frontman, Mickey Sadist, singing, "I want to be a Nazi." Sadist has said, "Racism is stupid," and that the lyrics are facetious. The Forgotten Rebels do get left out of the history books, probably for the song "3rd Homosexual Murder"—satirical shock value? CFNY refused to play them because of it. Another of their songs is called "AIDS"—the less said the better. Maybe they were trying to be joke punks, but it's such a bad joke. They wanted to be Glam, but Punk was easier for them to play (yet some people went Glam because prog was too hard to play). With their second album, *This Ain't Hollywood,* from 1982, the Forgotten Rebels finally caught up too late to their Glam dreams, opening with a cover of Gary Glitter's "Hello," setting the template for the rest of the album, not relenting at a steady clip, leaving behind all that unpleasant shock value—though they do throw in the added pummel of their most popular song, "Surfin' on Heroin," plus a couple '50s-style ballads. If only they had just done this and this alone. Their hometown of Hamilton named a noted rock venue after this album.

THE VILLAGE S.T.O.P.—"NORTH COUNTRY"/"VIBRATION" 7" (RUBY RECORDS, 1969)

Proto-Glam from 1969, the B side is total freak beat from out of Hamilton, Ontario. Eerie synths, glob chomping bass, everything moving in and out of sync, vocals going off and echoing, drums thumping away at it to the ever-living end—it's too much! It's too much!!!! The Village S.T.O.P. only released one single but were heavily into live theatrics. According to the website Museum of Canadian Music, after they got into covering "Help, I'm a Rock" from *Freak Out* by the Mothers they did black and white facepaint, looking like low-budget *Star Trek* aliens, then pushed further into full day-glo body paint lit up by black light and strobes. They even moved beyond skivvies! (naked) and moved to New York for a spell. According to John Mars's interview with the singer Fraser Loveman for *Blitz* magazine, he was warned off joining the band in New York City by various burlesque dancers as the Village S.T.O.P. were just so freaky (painted balls), but he joined anyways. They then did a half-hour live freak-out where they'd come out in robes that they'd doff. A couple of members joined the Kasenetz-Katz Super Circus, the leaders in the proto-Glam field of bubble-gum music.

ANTIQUE FAIR—"FUDDLE-DUDDLE" 7" (TUESDAY RECORDS, 1971)

When the Canadian prime minister Pierre Trudeau was confronted about mouthing "fuck you" in the House of Commons in 1971, he called it "fuddle duddle." Soon, everyone was talking "fuddle duddle." With a prompting from noted Stampeders manager Mel Shaw, Greg Hambleton (Thundermug's producer and Stompin' Tom's plywood-board provider) quickly recorded a song about it the very next day in the studio. With its hand claps and '50s-isms, it sounds like a lesser Mud song crossed with a Life Savers jingle. Would you believe that there was actually more than one "Fuddle Duddle" song about the incident? The House of Commons' "Do the Fuddle Duddle" was released on the GRT label. According to the April 10 edition of the *Hamilton Spectator*, both groups got their songs to the record stores just eight days after Trudeau said those very words.

SHINE—"STREAKING LEFT, STREAKING RIGHT" 7" (ORION, 1974)

Opening with a reverb-drenched chant of "Streaking!", it's got the Glam thud and crunchy guitars. Shine seems to be a one-off group taking on the streaking trend—people would basically run naked in public. "If this is show and tell, it sure is going well . . . " There were a few Glam streaking numbers; however, this one was written and sung by the dancehall reggae artist Lloyd Lovindeer during his '70s stint in Canada. Like much of Lovindeer's material, it is funny! This one-off was released on the Stampeders manager Mel Shaw's Orion label. Lovindeer tells me, "I don't recall much about Shine, but this is what I can tell you: I was a member of a four-man song-and-dance group called the Fabulous Flames, with Glen Ricketts as the lead singer. When he left, we were then being managed by Mel Shaw and it was at that time we did the streaking song. Under his management we linked up with a four-piece band of white musicians so I *think* that's how Shine came about. I am not certain

ERSATZ '50s

A wave of '50s covers bands ensued all over the place in the '70s. In Canada this wave was less predicated by the important Rock 'n' Roll Revival concert in Toronto than by the ersatz nostalgia of Sha Na Na in the USA. The transcendent innovator Jimi Hendrix got these theater kids to play before his set at Woodstock in 1969 and then Sha Na Na were on practically every TV variety show in the '70s—including their own—decked out in gold lamé performing covers of '50s rock 'n roll. Dispensing with futurism—no future, no present production techniques even, not even the past with all its trauma, this is an idealised rubberneck flashback. These are good-time oldies.

In Vancouver, the most popular band on Barry Samuels' roster—more than Heart, more than Sweeney Todd—were Teen Angel and the Rockin' Rebels, formed in 1970, early on in the nostalgia game. They took it far—no other retro-'50s act in Canada could hold a candle to them, nor could many of these acts outside of Canada. They inexplicably had three albums of mostly covers, with the first album selling over 20,000 copies (unsure if this number included the "FREE ALBUMS" advertised on their show posters and haphazardly thrown out to the crowd), partly because they tirelessly toured across North America. These records were meant as mementos of the live experience. What little original material they did have was arranged in a '50s style. People find comfort in the familiar. Even today cover bands are very popular—everyone can sing along to their memories. Live, there is no denying that Teen Angel and the Rockin' Rebels schtick had raw energy and got people dancing—it was a rough and ready Xerox, sometimes with

Bolt Upright and the Erections. Image courtesy of *The Ottawa Citizen*, February 2, 1973.

ten or eleven band members. According to the excellent PNW Bands site, they went through thirty-five musicians before breaking up in 1980. They would crown one lucky audience member "greaser of the night"—cannily sponsored by Brylcreem. In 1975, they did a commercial for the A&W fast-food restaurant chain to celebrate National Teen Burger Week; festivities included twenty-five cents off every Teen Burger. The PNW Bands site says that the frontman, Peter Dean, still performs as Teen Angel, and in recent years he's incorporated a Kenny Rogers (of Kenny Rogers Roasters fast food chicken restaurant fame) imitation into his act.

Out of Ontario, the Greaseball Boogie Band had a double album of '50s covers. They then dropped that and developed a new gimmick, dressing up Mafia style in suits, and changed their name to Shooter. They'd come out shooting at the crowd, not with real bullets—that could negatively impact their crowd size—but with harmless corn feed. Shooter's music was not hard-hitting either, being pleasant soft-rock covers of Leo Sayer and his milksop ilk. In Ottawa, Ontario, Bolt Upright and the Erections put on a show with tough guy posturings.

From Saskatoon, Rik and the Ravens only wore the '50s outfits for a show or two, slicking their long hair

because the linkup of the Flames and the musicians was quite short." According to the March 23, 1974, issue of *RPM Weekly*, Shaw was the one who brought the band of "transplanted Jamaicans" into the studio. He then played it for Quality Records, who signed them, then started the Orion subsidiary label all on the same day. The B Side, "If You Can't Make It, Fake It," has a Sly and the Family Stone groove.

CHOYA—"LET THE CHILDREN BOOGIE" 7" (CUE, 1973)

Paul Clinch had been part of the Cycle, who released a highly regarded yet quite rare psych album. Less sought after is Clinch's work with the band Choya, who released a lite-AM disco album on the bubble-gum label Buddha and a single on the exclusive Radio Shack label.[34] A couple of years before they were embroiled with Radio Shack, Choya had a single called "Let the Children Boogie," and they weren't using the "boogie" lightly, loosely tipping a top hat to T. Rex. T. Rex loved to say "boogie," more than once declaring "I Love to Boogie" and "Born to Boogie," a strong intent at such a very young age. Bolan even told his chum Ringo Starr to "Back Off Booga-

---

[34] Radio Shack was not a shack made of radios. Radio Shack was the common mall electronics franchise where you could try to upgrade your Quadrophonic 8-track CB radio system or get the pudgy-shirted store employee to hungrily up his commission by selling you a Flavoradio, the last AM-only radio on the market, for the kids. I recommend getting a Flavoradio in avocado—barring that, vanilla: after licking one, it has been determined that these flavors were merely colors, they didn't even have a scent—even if you are tripping the Flavoradios are odorless and flavorless. Radio Shack still exists in a fairly dormant multi-national state after a couple bankruptcies and bypass surgeries. The Radio Shack label does not. Their primary act was the Peaches, a sister act from Brampton whose gimmick was that they were sisters looking all community-hall-bridesmaid fresh in identical evening gowns, which really seems more like a contract stipulation than anything else; they probably also had a box of After Eight mints on their rider, gingerly following the product's rule by only eating these individually wrapped slender mints after 8 PM, culminating in their 11 PM curfew. The Peaches sang other people's middle-of-the-road hits, often as medleys in supper clubs; in those gowns they probably hit a few weddings too pulling double duty on the front lines of the ceremony itself by catching a few bouquets and getting paid to sing.

Teen Angel and the Rockin' Rebels.
Image courtesy of *The Ottawa Citizen*, March 3, 1974.

up into ducktails, but, unlike many revival acts, they did their own material with their own twangy humor, putting a rootsy rockabilly spin on the lightly naughty number "Back Seat Boogie," the soulful "Hummingbird," and "I Just Threw Away the Welcome Mat."

There was no shortage of show bands trafficking in nostalgia on the lounge circuit. One such act, named Bananas, released one album of mostly standards, including "At the Hop" and a couple of originals. Bananas also played car shows. With the album named *Come and Get It,* they willfully chose to use a close-up photo of a woman eating a banana.

loo," and guess what? Ringo wrote a song called just that. And over in Canada in 1973, Choya were telling everyone to "Let the Children Boogie" not once but twice! On side one they're belting it out gruff and barroom with some crazy old synths swooshing along to the band's sashay. Flip it over and—just like Gary Glitter's influential "Rock and Roll," parts one and two—it's "Let the Children Boogie, Part 2," and the synths have taken over! Cool!

BOND—"BACK SEAT DRIVER" 7" (CBS, 1975)

On their album, the Ontario band Bond would get more treacly, Rollers-style, all cozy in their sweater vests—support slot for Stampeders. This 1975 single-only track goes Glam pop like Wings' "Helen Wheels." Another single, "Dancin' on a Saturday Night," is a more amped-up cover of the soft-Glammer Lynsey De Paul.

SPACE PATROL—"BURNING LOVE" 7" (UNITED ARTISTS, 1975)

A honky-tonk stomper it is, with hands a-clapping along. One band member, Jimi Bertucci, was involved in a long string of projects, most notably Abraham's Children, but this band only did a little bit of touring and this 1975 single.

WILLI—"PISTOLERO"/"MOTHER" 7" AND "THINGS THAT GO BUMP IN THE NIGHT" 7" (RCA, 1975)

Willi is the disco producers Willi Morrison and Ian Guenther—known for producing Thor's *Keep the Dogs Away* and the KISS-related Skatt Brothers' Glam Disco leather-club staple "Walk the Night"—doing a couple of 1975 oddity singles. "Mother" is a Glam and country hybrid with screaming vocals gone slap-happy on the slap-back effect.

CHAPTER 6
QUEBEC

MACK

THE VAST, DESOLATE STRETCHES of Canadian highway have broken many a band rendering rock 'n' roll dreams into the landscape equivalent of a long, hard look in the mirror. Being in a band can be like being in a relationship with multiple people, with the barren expanses between shows testing the mettle, bringing out assorted dysfunctional elements. However, in the case of Mack, reputed to be the first Glam band from the province of Quebec, a band with plans and dreams, this was not existential—no, this was physical. A highway accident resulted in the tragic death of their keyboardist, David Kazinetz, at the age of twenty-seven. Mack continued on but they were never the same, the Glam was gone.

Mack played over two hundred shows in their first year and a half alone. They clocked countless hours on the road, thousands of klicks in a week, disorganized managers and booking agents sending them rolling along from one distant town to the next, sometimes in the middle of snowstorms, too busy to ever see their peers or influences perform. They were to open for New York Dolls at L'Araignée (French for "the spider"), a small basement club in Montreal, really the only venue for those kinds of bands, but New York Dolls were not allowed across the border. A second attempt into the country proved successful for the Dolls; however, Mack by that point were most likely on stage in another town. Their Alice Cooper–inspired spider eyes, polka-dot suits, and platform shoes certainly provoked the ire of less liberal-minded townspeople. Nick Catalano, the drummer for Mack, notes, "We were actually escorted out of town by the SQ [Sûreté de Québec, the provincial police] because the guys wanted to beat us up—the girls loved us, but the guys hated us."

Catalano was a drummer who always marched to his own beat in life. With little provocation from his friend, a permanent Psychology student, Nick would wear makeup out and about on the streets in 1971. Catalano says about his friend, "He's never done anything but study. So, he used to study the effects that it had on people to have outrageous behavior. He would do things like put a dog collar on me and we'd walk around St. Lawrence and St. Catherine with me on a leash barking at people—this was before the band. But the band, when they asked me to join I said, 'I'll only join if we can do *that* kind of thing, some outrageous stuff.'" Alas Catalano didn't name the band; he didn't like the generic-sounding name with its unfortunate connotations of large trucks barreling down the highway steamrolling everybody. Mack, as a band, were anything but burly; there was nothing tough about them. "Literally nothing . . . I never thought it was representative of what we did at all," said Catalano.

I interviewed Catalano in his store Beatnick Records (est. 1999), the record albums pleasantly surrounding and engulfing us. Although Mack were the very first to do Glam in Quebec, Catalano fully acknowledges the regional roots of rock showmanship in the '60s garage scene with Les Classells dyed all blond decked out in matching white suits and Les Excentriques completely pink from their pink hair all the way down to their little pink toes. Catalano elaborates: "There's garage bands from the '60s in Quebec that

GAGNEZ UN SOUPER AVEC VOTRE MEMBRE PRÉFÉRÉ DU GROUPE DE ROCK'N ROLL MACK ET DEUX BILLETS POUR ALLER LES VOIR AVEC PAG ET LES ROCKERS À LA PLACE LAURIER

UNE AUTRE INITIATIVE DE POP ROCK POUR MIEUX FAIRE CONNAÎTRE LES GROUPES QUÉBÉCOIS

Tout ce que vous avez à faire, c'est envoyer votre nom, adresse, numéro de téléphone et votre choix du musicien préféré de MACK à Pop Rock, 8381 Haut d'Anjou, Montréal, Qué., H1J 1T8.

Passez une ASSEZ bonne soirée avec le musicien de Mack que vous aurez choisi, ils sont tous à votre disposition. Nous vous. Un seul détail: nous vous demandons de nous dire en quelques lignes ce que vous pensez du retour du rock'n'roll. C'est l'occasion pour Mack de tâter le pouls de leur public et de vous faire un petit cadeau.

Nous donnerons le nom de la gagnante dans la prochaine édition.

Nicky Calino   André Deguire   David Kazinetz   Luc Giroux

avons déjà fait des reportages sur le plaisir que l'on peut avoir avec ce groupe. Faites-en l'expérience vous-même. Il va sans dire que ce concours est ouvert principalement aux jeunes filles mais toutes les entrées seront acceptées. Vous pourrez même emmener une amie avec

Et surtout, ne manquez pas Pag et les Rockers, avec Mack en première partie, le 27 novembre à la Place Laurier, 1371 Laurier est. Information: 524-1179, réservations: 844-7515.

Note: De préférence des gens de Montréal et des alentours...

Pop Rock magazine's Win a Dream Date with Mack Contest, c. 1974. Courtesy Yves Monast, *Pop Rock* magazine chief archivist and administrator.

Mack in *Pop Rock* magazine, c. 1974. Courtesy Nick Catalano.

did some really good records, whether it's Les Lutins, Les Misérables, the Sinners. So, there's the '60s scene which is not that far removed. I mean, it might not be Glam, but the Sinners used to do fucking outrageous things on stage. Also, bands like the Rabble used to go on stage and they'd all stop in the middle of the song and get on their hands and knees and play with dinky toys and stuff and go boom boom all over the stage and get back on instruments and continue their song and everyone went, 'What the fuck was that?' You know? The '60s scene was better than the '70s scene." And those Rabble albums are some of the wildest things pressed onto vinyl, akin to the Godz and *The Moray Eels Eat the Holy Modal Rounders* in pure freak quotient. So, what happened? Drippy folky prog music happened, with guys wearing plaid shirts and girls in granny dresses.

In late 1972, Catalano was drumming in a Top 40 bar band when another musician named André Deguire walked in wanting him for a new rock band he was putting together. Catalano had one condition: it had to be Glam. He told them, "We can't be just another t-shirt and jeans band. We're not the Doobie Brothers." With David Kazinetz, a keyboardist from New York City, he found someone who shared his Glam vision, stating that "David and I were like the taste barometers." Oscillating away on the first mini-Moog in Quebec, Kazinetz wore an American flag on stage, jokingly flaunting his home country. With no budget and plenty of enthusiasm, Mack had bad smoke machines and a paint-can light show. Catalano describes the hijinks: "We brought strippers on stage who would turn around—they didn't do a complete strip because we could have gotten in a lot of trouble—they'd pull down their pants and have 'MACK' written around the back of their asses. We were doing that kind of stuff. We did it in Bordeaux Jail and Archambault Prison; we played there for the prisoners. It's the weirdest feeling when you're playing on stage and there's girls all around us and there's guys with machine guns up there. We had to do 'Jailhouse Rock'—which is one of our finishing tunes—probably ten times as an encore. They were also going ballistic that we brought women strippers with us."

Apart from hitting the prison circuit, a mainstay for many bands at the time, Mack mostly played high schools and CEGEPs (in Quebec, bridging schools after high school that are mandatory for university admission). At these schools no one knew who they were;

the kids just knew there was a show and they'd go because what the fuck else are you going to do? A rock show was an event! And Mack gave a show. Mack would sow confusion, but every so often with their verve and showmanship they would win them over. When they played Macdonald College the girls were screaming and pulling their hair out and rushing the stage, causing Catalano to wonder to this day if it was all a set-up. But Mack had the goods. "We were the best live rock band, we weren't the best musicians." At one of these CEGEPs they deeply inspired the future members of Danger, Quebec's second Glam band. The Montreal guitar god Walter Rossi brought Mack out for a five-night arena stint to open for his heavy rock band Charlee, whose stoner-rock album had recently hit the streets. After the first night Mack brought the house down, Rossi told them that they had to go on last after Charlee for the rest of the run. Sit-down gigs such as those opening for the very prog Mahogany Rush fared less well: Mack wanted the audience out of their seats and participating in the show, but the Mahogany Rush audience wanted to sit, scratch their chins, and quietly judge them.

A magazine called *Pop Rock* covered Mack extensively, showing them before and after haircuts along with running a "Win a Dream Date with a Member of Mack" contest which Catalano describes as a "nightmare date contest." "Somebody went on a date with me. It was okay. I had to bring the two brothers along, but it was okay. And then the fact that nobody showed up to film it: what is the point? I'm in a restaurant with a girl and her two brothers and there's nobody to take photos of it to say, 'Well, this is a girl that won the contest.'"

Mack had big plans. Kazinetz's parents owned some real estate in New York City and the whole band was going to move there and try to make it. "We were tired of getting chased out of town." These plans went awry en route to Trois-Rivières as a last-minute replacement for a band called Apocalypse. They'd had road trouble before, but this time it proved fatal. Kazinetz died two days after the accident on August 1, 1974.

The colors fade, the makeup melts away, yet the band marches on minus one key member. With the vision dissipated, Mack became a conventional rock trio and headed into the studio to record their first and only album *Rock & Becs*. This is an album born of tragic compromise. Before the album, all of Mack's songs had uniquely wild lyrics by Catalano. "The Clearasil Kid" sounds like "Jim Dandy" but was about teenagers getting zits, with the lyrics, "Zowie Powie, he comes to the rescue, changes his costume in a telephone booth, Clearasil Kid to the rescue." Catalano elaborates, "I wrote all the English lyrics but then we did it in French. The bass player wrote the lyrics *and* whatever meaning the songs had in English they didn't have it anymore. Our manager was this guy Alain who truly and still is a separatist—although not a staunch one, but still enough to say, 'You're in Quebec, you should do a French rock album and then we'll put it out in English after.' That never happened. It came out in French but it never came out in English." With the lyrics forcibly changed Catalano received only one song-writing credit on the album, a co-writing credit at that. Which is just as well: the new lyrics were abysmal, piss-poor. Catalano says that a

Front cover of *Rock & Becs* by Mack (Les Disques Zodiaque, 1975). Author's collection.

recording of the whole English language version of the album exists!

After laying down his drum tracks, the band and management team kicked Catalano out of the studio for being opinionated. The album was recorded and mixed during the off hours with a first-time engineer who later went on to work with Mahogany Rush. As soon as it was all completed and mixed, they brought Catalano in to hear the entire finished album and asked him what he thought. "Worst piece of shit I've ever fucking heard," he said. "I don't want my name on it. It sucks. It's fucking terrible. Never mind how we're playing, that has nothing to do with it. It just sounds bad. Like there's no fucking . . . when we recorded the tracks, the bed tracks, there was a lot of balls, a lot of fucking dynamics. Now it's like echo and the piano sounds like it is underwater. It's just fucking awful."

And the album cover? It truly is one of the shoddiest drawings I have ever seen of a fox, the perpetrator having completely forgotten that foxes have tails! The fox has no tail! The artist tried to class it up by giving the fox a tuxedo, failing completely by working exclusively in what seems to be the medium of felt markers and scrap paper. The album art isn't even in full color: black and white with yellow thrown in as an after-thought to symbolize "yield." Okay, now I'm just being mean. That's not fair. Mack wound up selling the album at their shows for five bucks a pop before breaking up. A couple of members, including Catalano, then formed a straight-ahead rock band called Fighter. And as for the Mack record itself? It's totally fine. Oh, but if only for what might have been.

DANGER

DANGER OFTEN GET PIN-POINTED AS PUNK, and not just any ole punk: the first punk band from Quebec. Sure, we can call them that, give them a medal, a gold Participaction[1] patch even, however, this is Glam! Punk? Glam? Hey, you could just call it rock 'n' roll! No, we are here for Glam. Gimme Danger. It never ceases to crack me up how those dusty old rock history books (pre-1999 mostly) tidily positioned punk as a reaction against progressive rock and all the old rock dinosaurs (my favorite dinosaur is the triceratops because it just looks cool)—professorial critics on high caught sweeping Glam Rock under the rug. Nice theory, buddy, keep it presbyterian, see you in the trades brrrrrap . . . . I give you the grade of "class dismissed."

Danger does best exemplify the slippy-slide open bleed from Glam to Punk as Quebec's second Glam band and then, subsequently, Quebec's first—or, perhaps, second—punk band, depending upon where you wanted to place the Quebec punk band the 222s, who played with Danger in 1976. Honestly, making grand pronouncements on who was first -or even second- is generally not altogether sound. Who said life was tidy?

Before Danger, their guitarist Polo Belmar had a grade-school band with his school chum Pierre LaFortune called the Punx in 1972. Punk as a genre hadn't popped yet, and the Punx had the longest hair in school, trailing down the halls like a comet's tail behind them. Belmar was into Glam since its inception with T. Rex's "Hot Love" being spun on Montreal's CHOM-FM by the soft-spoken and forward-thinking Doug Pringle, a DJ who came direct from England launching a radio format upheaval with the strains of "Also sprach Zarathustra" à la the giant monolith from *2001* advancing humanity to the next stage. Pringle himself even had a single of his own around 1973, produced by The Wacker's Randy Bishop, and it was *en français*: "C'est pas le jeu," on the esteemed Quebec label Gam-

---

[1] Participaction was a Government elementary school fitness program where a variety of competitions were held and patches were awarded: gold, silver, bronze, and then the one just for participating: that's the one I got. I was with my family at Centre Dining ("Chinese & Western cuisine") when I saw a totally inebriated guy with a silver Participaction badge on his trucker hat. My pious, child self became angry at this drunk. How did he win it?

ma. This mellow single wasn't totally Glam per se, but it sure had the beat and the claps.

It wasn't just Bolan and Bowie that hooked Belmar. He exclaims, "And then Alice Cooper came! That would change it all around because he's the one to take Glam Rock and do Shock Rock, Theater Rock. The basis was Glam too --but crazy Glam with attitude, kind of entering into punk rock. He had a lot of attitude, although it was all staging, it was all theatrical stuff. He had everything. Everything. Every performance. I saw Alice Cooper maybe five times in the '70s. I saw him in '71, '72, '73, '74." When Slade played Montreal to five hundred people, mostly teens and a few of the older avant-garde crowd in the know, Belmar was there and enthusiastically relates, "I remember everything. And I applied everything that Noddy Holder did on my shows. Having the audience participate to every fucking single song." Nick Catalano told me strictly off the record when I was buying the lone Danger record at his Montreal shop Beatnick Records (hot tip: good store!) that they were also influenced by his own band Mack, reputed as the first Glam band in Quebec. Indeed, as Belmar states, "Because every time they played, we went to see them."

But it was New York Dolls, neighbors to the south waking us Canucks up with their Yanqui Glam, that caused Danger to form. Belmar was one of fewer than a hundred people attending New York Dolls' Montreal show on September 27, 1974. His brother Pierre P. Belmar bought him a brand-new Goldtop Les Paul which looked glittery and sounded gritty, as Glammy a guitar as there was; Belmar later had it changed to candy-apple red with pink trimmings. Mere weeks later Belmar joined Pierre's instrumental prog band Melly'on and completely overhauled their sound, wisely moving the energetic and charismatic Pierre to lead vocals. The following month they did a six-week stint in a town called Lac St. Jean, six hundred miles away, playing Stones, Dolls, T. Rex and Bowie covers. By the third week they packed the place, performing for bikers and the bikers' pals and the bikers' pals' pals and so on and so on. And so on.

During this stint, their manager dropped in to say hello, get the monies owed, and share a tidbit of flaccid inspiration. Belmar regales, "After three weeks we are playing, he is still waiting for us to send the money, his cut, and we're spending everything. We're new in the business, so we don't know about that. So, he comes just to get the money and at the same time he says, 'I have a plan for you guys. I have a name for you. Let me tell you this. The first week, you send that tomato to the radio station.' Okay, send the tomato to the radio station. Okay. 'Second week, you send a whole bag of tomatoes to the radio station.' Oh, okay. I'm not sure I'm following you, but go on. 'Third week, you send a bottle of ketchup.' And then we go, 'What the fuck is wrong with this guy? What's the name?' He says, 'There it is.' 'What?' 'Ketchup.' He wanted to call us Ketchup. So, we look at him like, 'You are fucking out of your mind, man,' and we turn around and there's this door that's broken and it's written DANGER on the door so I say, 'I'd rather be called whatever, Danger, than that . . . Danger? Yeah, Danger, that's a good name!' So, he goes 'Okay.' So we adopted Danger right there and went like, 'Hell, man! Ketchup? Are you fucking crazy?' That's a real story, man."

Danger promo shot, c. 1977. Courtesy Polo Belmar.

Danger consisted of two sets of brothers -Pierre and Polo Belmar, Johnny and Gino Gervais- along with a fifth member, René Pronovost Jr., who later became a step-brother to Pierre and Polo after his mother married their father. Describing Danger as a real family band, though accurate, still seems wrong somehow; they never cashed in on that like the DeFrancos or the Osmonds did—this is a food-fighting, beer-can-gripping band of brothers. Polo did his best to force both his brother Pierre and René, the bassist René, to shave off their mustaches, yet strong traces of an upper lip wisp are apparent on their album jacket (the bassist). Danger went against much of the music happening in Quebec at that time, what Polo describes as "*rock agricole,*" farmer music, plaid-shirt stuff.

Polo would devour every issue, cover to cover, of *Rock Scene,* along with *Punk Magazine,* where he saw a kinship between John Holmstrom's art style and his own—best exemplified by his drawing in the Danger album gatefold of a maniacal, slobbering cartoon superhero punching through a brick wall. *Rock Scene* magazine was a very Glammy publication from New York City jam-packed with photos of the wildest bands, accentuating the enticing possibilities of what rock could be. Glam inspiration Jayne County wrote an advice column for *Rock Scene*. In regard to the fashion tips, Polo took that advice and

Danger live in 1975. Courtesy Polo Belmar.

transposed it to Montreal. Soon they would hit the sales, rummaging through boxes in the Eaton's department store basement pulling out gold lamé, evening gloves, big hats, platforms, and all manner of frilly things. Danger's fans began to dress like them, men and women, with no difference between—androgynously, a blurry flurry.

As the hype man, Polo and Pierre's brother Dédé Belmar would go out and prime the crowds, screaming, "Are you brave enough? Are you really brave enough for Danger?" and the girls, oh, everyone, would go into a frenzy. Danger would strangle rubber chickens, shoot Pierre with electricity, and make him a martyr to the song "Défence et fin du monde" while messing around with their mom's crucifix—returning it to her after the concert stained in booze and blood. Polo sighs, "Poor Mom."

Like Mack and other acts, Danger played the prisons. They went over rather well at the Christmas party for the Archambault Institute, a maximum security prison. "I remember I innocently carved on a wooden table, 'Rock 'n' Roll is freedom,' unaware that there were cameras all around—well, they had told us but I felt it was a good message, silly me! I remember a huge guy grabbing the Marshall cabinets one by one lifting them on his shoulders as if they were mere pillows! We thought he would make an excellent roadie! When we played the concert (which was videotaped—we have a copy of that) we noticed that everyone was high as fuck and you could smell the marijuana scent mixed with the sexual smell of semen and sweat … iiiiiiish. At one point during the show, my brother Pierre said, 'This next one is dedicated to all of you who are missing their wives.' And in the front row someone yelled, 'Don't bother, here's my wife!' intertwining a young inmate, his left hand in his poor young 'wife's' pants! We all laughed at my brother's stunned face. . . . But, all in all, they absolutely loved us and we were booked there two more times. . . . Before we departed last time we went there, we met with the prisoner committee's president, a guy whom I thought was fully rehabilitated, at least in my opinion, and a few of the 'less dangerous' jailbirds, and we had a great discussion about freedom, the confinement, the day-to-day life in prison, and spiritual things. … I was sure this guy would be out by next year (they're all lifers), but just two weeks after that we learned he'd killed an inmate with an ice pick (thirty-three shots or so)!"

Danger toured across Quebec and Ontario and on into the most decidedly un-Glam regions of Nova Scotia and Newfoundland and New Brunswick, where—in the town of Oromocto—they were threatened by a man with a twelve-gauge shotgun exclaiming, "Man, you're not playing tonight! You're too loud!" The club quickly threw the overly indignant customer out. Fights broke out throughout these small towns. When in such situations, from the stage Danger would pause, then break into "Sympathy for the Devil."

Makeup artists just love the carte blanche option. Black lips and swaths of red—that's what happened when Danger first appeared on the Quebec television show *Et ça tourne*, returning for two more appearances, including an episode honoring the death of Elvis.

How did Danger easily fit into punk? "Because after the tour and all that, all that beautiful clothing and Glam stuff is all ripped up and it's all dirty and, plus, you get the attitude, because the pay is not always so good. And the reception is not always so good. The places aren't always so good and the food isn't always so good. And so you get the attitude and all the torn shirts and stuff. So you're a punk rocker. That's the next step."

After a couple of years and then some, it was more than time to make an album. Danger creepy-crawled into the top-notch Le Studio during Nazareth's two-week vacation from their next subpar effort. Nazareth were none the wiser to Danger; maybe Nazareth should have been in the know so that they could up their game—no candles for Nazareth to hold. Having the same soft-separatist manager as Mack, Danger also had to change their English lyrics into French. Unlike Mack, Pierre rewrote his lyrics carefully, taking five months to do so before cutting the vocals, keeping the intent. Polo's song "Violence Dance" became "Du Côté de la Démence" on the album. A couple of songs went unrecorded while a couple of new ones were created in the heat of the studio moment.

What an album! '50s revival slop with blazing hard rock solos. Reduced, reused, and re-recycled Chuck Berry riffs and hoots and screams and a barking dog and whistles with delay and other cool '70s effects dripped on—set phasers on fun! A motorbike revs its engine. Alvin (of *Alvin and the Chipmunks* fame) once sang, "I Wish I Could Speak French," and that's where I'm at, a shamed Canadian who wants to go back in time to shake sleepy seven-year-old me in French class awake! The singer has such "going for it" conviction, here's your goods fully delivered in record time, it's a kick! I need a translator. I wish I knew what the singer was on about.

Side two opens with the out-of-the-gates show-stopping show opener "La Balade bentale," curiously never performed live by Danger, a dynamic instrumental overture—layered guitar, big climactic drums, and a little Québécois twang as if choreographed by professionally trained wild horses. If they were called Dangerous, that'd be stupid, they're not. They have a sprinkle of an element of danger that draws in those with a penchant for same—unpredictable, energetic, a little bit goofy. Front and back cover featuring the band photographed in playful recklessness. The album closer "Metal Rock" isn't Metal so much as metallic. Speaking of Chipmunks, that song is manic paced, whooo ooohs, chanted heys, and handclaps with an amphetamine solo that ain't noodly so much as being completely comprised of noodles, harmonizer working overtime. And they're done! Bravo. More! More! Alas. At first Danger themselves found it too slick, even though everyone else loved it—this album has the perfect amount of polish, a glistening spit shine, saliva bubbling.

Danger album launch show, October 28, 1977 (note: same date as Sex Pistols album release). Courtesy Polo Belmar.

Front cover of *Danger* by Danger (Telson, 1977). Author's collection.

When it comes to Danger, all we have is one album, short and candy sweet. Hell, it's a great legacy. Thanks to RCA, the album was even released in France. The single "L'Amour dans l'métro," a midtempo '50s-style ballad, received a bunch of airplay, and more than five hundred people showed up at their record launch. With the death of Sid Vicious and other events, Danger decided the whole punk thing was dead and broke up shortly after the release of their album.

Danger didn't really see themselves as punk. "Even by then, we weren't calling ourselves punks," Polo Belmar told me. "We were calling our music garage; we were a garage band. That's how we described us because, first of all, we all worked in a garage. They were painting cars, me and my brother were pumping gas. The greasy stuff, you know, the real greasy stuff. So, it wasn't really punk, but then it came out like that, the punk rock scene. Yeah, why not?"

After Danger broke up, Polo had a stint in the 222s as lead singer. Since then, he has made albums going all over the musical map, involving himself in rap, reggae, and trucker music. More recently he has returned to Glam with his covers act the Jeepsters, named after the T. Rex song. They have been known to open their shows with Danger's instrumental overture "La Balade bentale." And the crowd loves it.

ANGELO FINALDI

TALKING TO ANGELO FINALDI, he can be so self-effacing, yet he permeates so much of Montreal music history. Recording with Richard Tate as Angelo & Eighteen, they were a rarity in that they were Canadians on RAK, a pivotal U.K. label in the grand scheme of Glam. RAK was the noted producer Mickie Most's label, releasing massive top-tier Glam Top Tens by Suzi Quatro and Mud—plus the Arrows, Kenny, Hot Chocolate, and more. Angelo & Eighteen's sought-after 1972 single came early on in the scene. The A side, "Midnight Flight," is a soft groover with Glam guitar riff intervals that's perfect for, yes, surprise, midnight flights into the arms of a loved one—"I'm yours," organ swells, pulsing codes tapped on guitar tones with the ending getting very percussive—flip the single over and the percussion continues, the rumble deepens, lifting off with "Flight 2," which is a trip all its own, a near-instrumental, Finaldi chanting away and grunting, drums à la John Kongos. This is a primal ritual of yearning devotion—"Heyyyy I'm yours! Uh! Uh!"—sending signals out to the future, where much more recent listeners and taste-makers can't believe it was released way back in 1972—affordable jet-setting can cause distortion in the timeline. How unsurprising that the single is about off-hour air travel—just look at Finaldi's itineraries: it's truth!

Finaldi moved to Quebec from Naples in 1959: "Listen, my father he took us here. My father was from a wealthy Italian family. He never worked a day in his life. But he was in conflict with his father. He had a hotel in the '50s in Caracas [Venezuela], I was living in Caracas for a while. And then we came here, but we never starved. You know what I mean? It was rough. We became immigrants—from bankers to immigrants in Canada. In Montreal there's snowstorms. I'd never seen snow. Maybe once in '56, one morning it snowed and we were collecting it with plates and putting lemon and sugar on it—southern Italy, there's no snow, there's no such thing." Of Naples, Finaldi says, "Naples is an incredible fuckin' city, man. It was the home of art; they invented the *castrati*. Naples, very heavy."

In 1964, Finaldi was barely a teenager playing in an Italian wedding band in Quebec. He noted, "It's too bad, I would have loved to have been around jazz, let's say you grow around Miles Davis, it's better than a fucking Italian band, we're not talking the same language here, but it doesn't matter because if you got a bit of brain you catch up with things in a way. You don't stay in an Italian wedding band." Then the Beatles hit: "There was a lot of talent in Montreal, but it wasn't the time for Quebec. Britain, they were way ahead of the

Front and back covers of *Angie* by Angelo Finaldi (Deram, 1974). Author's collection.

game, but when the British came up with all the bands, obviously everybody—the whole world followed, there were bands everywhere, you should have seen it. They never sold that many fucking guitars like in 1964, '65. Think about it—the Beatles came out on Ed Sullivan; the following week in America everybody started to grow their hair, kids would be wearing high heeled boots. Brits are shrewd, they were able to sell American music to Americans with high heels and long hair because they did all the Little Richard and Bo Diddley and Chuck Berry. And blues—the Rolling Stones were doing Muddy Waters, John Lee Hooker, and then eventually they started doing their own songs, but mainly they broke with American music, thanks to African Americans again. It all comes from there."

Moving ahead to 1967, the music impresario Donald K. Donald enters the picture. Finaldi notes, "I was living at his place for a little while. I wasn't getting along with my old man. And he started to book the Forum. And I remember opening up for the Who with this band I was with who were nothing to write home about." Oh, what were you called? "The Montreal Philharmonic Holocaust. It was like a cheap Mothers of Invention band, but cheap."

Expo 67 was the World's Fair in Montreal. Through a mysterious decision-making process (perhaps straws were drawn), in 1967 the world came to Montreal. Finaldi elaborates, "So that year, Montreal went on the map as a city worldwide, people started to notice Montreal." Expo 67 highlighted idealized, near avant-garde architecture of the future—no harsh edges, throw in a geodesic dome. Some of this architecture was to decay a few years later and become the setting to Robert Altman's post-apocalyptic Ice Age '70s downer film *Quintet*.

As incredible as Expo 67 was, its official opening was fairly exclusive—so exclusive that it isn't remembered. The unofficial opening of Expo 67, however, was an all-night Super Party ("dress very optional" read the posters) put on by the artist and designer François Dallegret at Place Bonaventure. Living in Montreal to do design on Expo 67, Dallegret's architecture had a fantastic hyper-style; he also designed a drugstore to become a curvilinear white smooth, very smooth, concrete grotto named Le Drug with two levels, drugstore on top and restaurant below, with a Pop Art gallery in the back showing Warhol and pals.

Proceeds from the two-dollar admission to the Super Party went towards Expo 67 tickets for welfare recipients. This admission included buffet-style food and drink and performances by the wildest acts Dallegret could find, including Finaldi's band the Philharmonic Holocaust, the Rabble, Suzanne Verdal performing riding across the venue on a bicycle attached with massive balloons lifting her up and away, Lothar and the Hand People, and Tiny Tim, of whom Finaldi says, "He wasn't even known, man, Tiny Tim. I was sitting in the dressing room and in walked this fucking giant with a raincoat and a grocery bag. He had carrots in it, some vegetables, and he's listening to a transistor radio. He walked in, I was alone with him. So I went, 'Hi.' He goes, 'Hi,' with that high voice. I said, 'What do you do?' He says, 'I sing.' Okay. He was listening to the hockey game. He loved hockey. Then he went on stage. I think he went on around two o'clock in the morning. And after one song they started to throw bottles at him, oh my God, and he was blowing kisses to the audience and they had to get him off the stage because they were going to kill him."

Donald K. Donald's music empire started growing with the opening of a club called Snoopy's. Finaldi says, "So one Sunday afternoon, we were playing in his place and there was a band called Les Sinners playing there. And Richard Tate was subbing for their drummer who was like—he wasn't much of a drummer. So, when I saw Richard Tate play with them because they were all friends, I was floored. Richard Tate was a brilliant fucking drummer, man, brilliant! I mean, he had guys like Alan White, Jeff Porcaro, and Carmine Appice really going, 'Wow!' but he didn't want to play drums. He wanted to play guitar when he was with me. Crazy motherfucker. I was crazier than him. That's what Mickie Most said one day. He says, 'I thought Jeff Beck was crazy, but you're crazier than them.' I really am—psychological fucking issues. I'm okay now, man, because I do what I do, but I was very suicidal all the time. Don't forget, back then, man, I'm from Italy, it doesn't matter anymore, but back then, you have an accent, like, it wasn't the same. You understand? It wasn't the same, being an immigrant, it wasn't the same. Now there's no more of that."

Les Sinners went through a dizzying confusion of lineup changes. Georges Marchand left to join Les Mersey's wearing a very trendy miniskirt on stage (Tate was the drummer for Les Mersey's). Marchand was replaced by Ernie Rock from the similarly named Mersey Makers, who had an English-language single, "C'mon." Putting Mersey in their band name was an unscrupulous way to fool the unsuspecting record-buying public into thinking that they were a British Invasion band. Les Mersey's were not trying to deceive; they just loved the Beatles. They had French lyrics and a more raw, garage-y sound. Likewise, for the more popular Les Sinners, whose first album is a real grinder—if you are a fuzz fiend, look no further! In 1967, following the release of Les Sinners' second album, Ernie Rock died suddenly of a brain hemorrhage while watching the former prime minister John Diefenbaker on television. Les Sinners continued on and the following year made *Vox Populi*, one of the great early concept albums bearing some similarities to *The Who Sell Out*. Their main songwriter, François Guy, a founding member, then left Les Sinners to form La Révolution Française, with two other former Sinners. Then, after one album, those two subsequently left to reform Les Sinners. Guy wanted to stay and keep La Révolution Française going. At the time, he was living with Finaldi and Tate, so they became a new version of La Révolution Française, with Tony Roman producing the singles that the three of them wrote together.

The tide in Quebec had turned with a strong push for sovereignty. La Révolution Française's song "Québécois" became very notable. Angelo explains, "At one point they were singing it every Saint-Jean-Baptiste,[2] but it never became like the official anthem, but still people would sing it. I mean, everybody remembers that fucking song, everybody knows it. But you know, that was an English song that I had called 'America.' It was against USA with Vietnam and all that. Then François did the French lyric. I had this little song on

---

2   A holiday politicized with the Quiet Revolution, a period of great change in Quebec starting in the 1960s, including an objective for sovereignty from Canada.

guitar. He recorded that and it became like a fucking huge success here in Quebec. You recall back in those days, there was no FM yet. And I remember a time I was in my girlfriend's car and it would be playing like on three stations, four stations at the same time. And the band was terrible, terrible fucking band, because we never practiced." They didn't gig often, but the shows were big, such as opening for the Doors at the Forum in 1969. With "Québécois" making a bit of money, vultures swooped in, it ended in shambles—a messy court case, really. Located off the coast of Spain, Ibiza was looking really good to Finaldi, the sun and the sand and the nightlife and—more alluringly—it was very affordable. Both Finaldi and Tate got away from the courtroom dramas and flew to Ibiza and there they stayed for a while.

Upon their eventual return to Quebec, they moved into a hotel with Michel Pagliaro's producer George Lagios. For Michel Pagliaro's massive English-language 1971 hit "Lovin' You Ain't Easy" Finaldi played rhythm and did the vocal arrangements. Pagliaro is quite simply *the* Quebec rock star and all that encompasses. He recorded in both French and English and was a rock star in Quebec and, to some extent, out of Quebec. Some of Pagliaro's output veers into straight-ahead rock—solid, some Stonesy nods. And many soft-rock hits to make the heart swell. Though Pagliaro encompasses so much more, he has his forays into Glam—his feet get wet.

Finaldi and Tate wrote the Glammy ass-kicker "Illusion" together for Pagliaro, released in 1972 as a B side to his version of the Beatles' "Revolution." Two years later the song was re-recorded bigger and *en français* for Les Rockers' album. Les Rockers were really just Pagliaro and his heavy friends doing good old rock 'n' roll—jukebox on the back cover showcasing lots of '50s covers (Chuck Berry and Eddie Cochrane) amidst some originals, sounding like Suzi Quatro in the way it gives it a big, modern production drive. They are rockers! Les Rockers!

Digging further into the Pagliaro back catalogue, the 1972 album *Pag,* with John Hagopian and Jack August, leans gently into Glam, then goes on a holiday dabble into "Rio Reggae." Look beyond the innocuous record sleeve of his self-titled 1974 album *Pagliaro*[3] and you will find Glam gold, including a few French-language versions of early Chuck Berry and Little Richard rock 'n' roll numbers and some great Walter Rossi (the man Bowie couldn't have) guitar work. A couple of Pag's own songs get super Glammy, including and especially "Viens danser": killer guitar riffin' into a flat falling chorus. An English-language version—without the extra blistering lead guitar—was released under the *nom de plume* Second Helping as "We're Dancing" and became a junkshop Glam treasure. Following a similar formula, his next album is also confusingly called *Pagliaro*—nearly as Glammy with even more searing Rossi guitar work. Whether Glam or not, Pagliaro's albums are well worth seeking out.[4]

---

3   One of many albums with that name. Pagliaro must have loved the name Pagliaro.

4   You can also find Pagliaro's music in Denys Arcand's arthouse Canuxploitation thriller *Gina* from 1974. This rape-revenge sub-genre movie features snowmobile chase sequences at a strip club in a rough-and-tumble Quebec town as the main setting, Pag on the jukebox. Besides the main character of Gina, who is there to work as a stripper for the week, there is an awkwardly placed plot of a documentary crew hanging out in the bar, also in town to film a factory's exploitation of its workers.

Front and back cover of *Rockers* by Les Rockers (RCA Victor, 1974). Album courtesy collection of Ian Marshall.

Front cover of *Pagliaro* by Michel Pagliaro (Much, 1971). Album courtesy collection of Ian Marshall.

Some websites state that Pagliaro also plays with Finaldi and Rossi on the *Patof Rock* album, but Finaldi says that, although he knew Patof, he had never recorded with Patof. Who played on this, the fifteenth of many albums recorded in the early '70s by Patof? Patof most certainly did. Patof was an incredibly popular television clown in Quebec. Becoming a clown made him one of the wealthiest men in Montreal. On *Patof Rock*, he sings "Rockers" in his burly clown voice, reshaping the lyrics to be about the goings-on in Patofville ("All Shook Up" becomes "Bonjour Patof") in full (clown) makeup and bright glittery attire, holding a guitar like he's never held one before. Finaldi lives in the late Patof's old building, often joking that it is haunted by the ghost of a clown.

Finaldi didn't just write one Quebec anthem, he wrote two. "Pepsi Forever," sung by Steve Fiset, had lyrics by the noted separatist Pierre Bourgault. This was not a soda-pop jingle, no no no. *Pepsi* was derogatory Anglo slang for a French Canadian. One explanation being that it came from economic classism, a poverty sneer, where it was oddly perceived that French Canadians drank Pepsi instead of Coca-Cola because it was cheaper. "Pepsi Forever" is a reclaimed song of pride.

The allure of Ibiza was strong. Finaldi and Tate flew back and there they met the music producer Lou Reizner, head of Mercury Records Europe and producer of Rod Stewart, and played him the songs they had written on their acoustic guitars. Reizner took the two young men to London, England, and there they stayed in Reizner's home, perhaps even cutting some demos with him. Finaldi had the producer Mickie Most on his mind, having seen him on TV back in Montreal. Most was incredibly successful, banking hits early on as a producer for the Animals and Herman's Hermits, sharing a production office with his long-time business partner, the notorious Led Zeppelin heavy Peter Grant, and then starting his own label, RAK Records.

"We were so fucking crazy. Oh my god, I'm embarrassed. I called Mickie Most from Lou's office in his house. He had a huge, huge house. I imagine Lou wasn't there. I paid all my karma, don't worry, man. I paid, I paid." Was there blowback? "No, I never saw Lou again after that. What happened is Mickie Most never answered the phone. He happened to pass by where the reception was, probably the girl Maureen—she used to date Robert Plant, because it was the same sort of office—and Maureen wasn't there and he picked up the phone. And he said, 'Hello?' And I said, 'Yeah, may I speak to Mickie Most?' And he says, 'It's me.' So, I said, 'Well, you know, my name is Angelo. I'm from Montreal, we got songs.' 'Come down now.' We took a cab. We went and we came up in his office and I remember tuning my fucking guitar with pliers and then after the second song he said, 'Stop, that's it. What do you want?' That's when you got something happening. I remember saying, 'Well, I'd like a pack of cigarettes,' because I wanted to smoke, right? And he sent the secretary downstairs to get us cigarettes. When we walked in there, she gave us an attitude, Maureen her name was and she had an attitude, like, 'Who the fuck are these guys?' but then it was okay, we became friends with her. The little things, you go through life without a camera or a phone taking pictures, subconscious pictures, either audio pictures or visual pictures, things you remember when you were six, things you heard when you were eight years old, like a situation, like forty seconds of something that happened—like that. I remember that. That moment we walked in his office because he called his brother Dave Most, it's like, 'Man, listen to this.'"

"So anyways, I was singing, I wasn't playing back then at that particular time because we had some decent songs, me and him, that we had done in Ibiza on two acoustic guitars. But we wanted to do it on electric. We would have had to be smart, do it acoustic with a bass player, a drummer, you know what I mean? But we had the fucking hang-up of Led Zeppelin where we wanted to turn all that into electric music. So, after a few months, quite a few months—because he put us up at the same hotel. He was paying

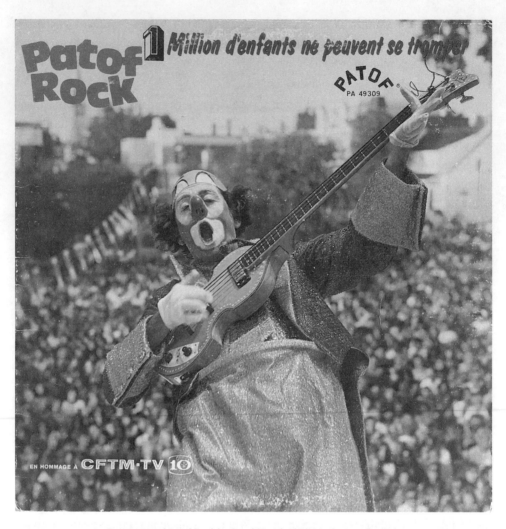

Front cover of *Patof Rock* by Patof (Patof, 1975). Author's collection.

us every week. He even called Ringo Starr to play at the session, I remember. He called George Martin to produce it. But George Martin, he was having a depression because he was in a divorce with his wife."

A few songs were recorded with Most but only the "Midnight Flight" single was released with session musicians that included Alan White (later in Yes) on drums and most likely Tetsu Yamauchi (later in Free and the Faces) on bass. A guitar volume pedal was flown in from New York. Finaldi and Tate also cut some of their songs with the bassist Herbie Flowers, known for his distinctive walking bass line on Lou Reed's "Take a Walk on the Wild Side," released that same year. Flowers loved them and told Most, "These two guys are like a diamond in a rock. You have to take away all the rock around it. It's a big job."

Carmine Appice wanted Finaldi to become the singer of what was to become the rock group Cactus but he had a thing going with Tate. At the Speakeasy, the exclusive rock-star hotspot where they all got a table after recording, Tate had a chance encounter with David Bowie's wandering eye (due to heterochromia, it could have been the blue one, could have been the brown one) in the men's room. Tate was a loose cannon and a little uptight. Luckily it didn't lead to anything bad; it didn't lead to anything at all. Finaldi was avoiding MC5, who were staying at the same hotel. He recalls, "Oh my god, those guys, man! They came to London to play, but they weren't making much money, that's for sure. So we became friends, like where the TV was downstairs there. But we sort of were thinking—like, I was scared because they were junkies and the drummer guy, he looked like the Phantom of the Opera and we were hiding from them because I was already having problems with Mickie Most."

When I asked Finaldi what happened with Most he said, "We blew it. He tried everything because we had some nice songs. I mean, don't get me wrong. We must have had some good songs for him to put us on a salary up in hotels and then he tried everything." Finaldi was depressed; he was going to doctors: "Mickie sent me there. I was crazy, I'd be in Hyde Park with the ducks, and I hadn't slept all night. You know what I think now that I realize? I knew that we were failing. Because Richard was too crazy." Finaldi went on, "I never thought I was good enough. I was very insecure all the time." One recording session went so poorly that when Most heard the results he fell down the stairs of his office.

Future RAK hit makers like Errol Brown of Hot Chocolate ("He was such a good guy!") and Suzi Quatro ("She wanted to jam, she wanted to hang around"—alas they were in no shape to) would often pop into the office. Finaldi adds, "And then they all succeeded, except us. I have no regrets. I'll show you something." At that, Finaldi shows me a photo of the cutest little grandkid, his daughter Titi's son.

They did leave behind a wild 1972 single, as Angelo & Eighteen, and wrote "Should I" for Peter Noone of Herman's Hermits, also produced by Most. Finaldi laughingly exclaims, "Everybody thought he was a little fucking saint, this guy, because I worked with him in London a bit. Peter Noone, Herman's Hermits. He was a fucking bum. Everybody thought he was a little clean-cut kid. He used to put cherry bombs in fucking toilet bowls and blow them up. Keith Moon copped everything from him. You wouldn't know, eh?"

Finaldi and Tate left London and returned to Montreal. Asking Finaldi to dig up all these memories can be a lot of laughs. It can also be painful. He suffered from severe depression but did the right thing years later and received treatment for it. Still, he is so hard on himself—I mean, look at where we are in the chapter. That's right, much more excitement ahead!

They weren't back in Montreal long before the Quebec singer Claude Dubois took Finaldi and Tate along to France to work with him. After that, they returned to London to work in the studio with France's own answer to Elvis, the megastar Johnny Hallyday. With endless reams of money to spend, Hallyday in 1973 used Peter Frampton and members of Spooky Tooth to make *Insolitudes*, an album more squarely in the '70s, dripping with forgettable MOR ballads, along with a French version of "Suspicious Minds." The Glammy rocker "Le Sorcier maudit" gives the album a very much needed boost of energy, with Hallyday belting it out accompanied by similar, steady undertones of raunchy sax and maniacal pedal steel by B. J. Cole. Michel Malory provided many of the album's lyrics, including "Le Sorcier maudit," about a rainmaker who talked to the wind; the music was by Finaldi and Tate, their sole song-writing contribution to the album. On his 1973 TV special with Sylvie Vartan, Hallyday performed it with gusto in a black satin jumpsuit, against erupting plumes of red smoke, acoustic guitar as useless prop.

While in London, Finaldi did see Most: "I just passed by the office. He was happy to see me. But he was disappointed because he was telling people he knew that he had found these two guys with these incredible tunes."

In Paris, Finaldi and Tate met Nanette Workman, a singer who was dating Hallyday at the time. They tried to put a band together with her. Workman originally came from Mississippi. Tony Roman had seen her on stage in New York and helped make her a star in Quebec. He produced a few albums for her, including a duet album with himself on it in 1968. Finaldi adds, "Well, at one point they were they were engaged to be married and Tony loved women and she caught him with two women and the two women ran naked out the back door in winter. So, she broke the engagement and Tony was left there nude with his high heel boots." In 1969, Workman was one of the memorable back-up singers on the Rolling Stones' "You Can't Always Get What You Want," and "Country Honk."

After Hallyday left Workman, she and Tate started dating. They both returned to Montreal while Finaldi stuck around Paris. One day, Tate rang him up saying, "Man, Nanette left me, come back, let's start a band." Finaldi elaborates, "Already I didn't know what to do in France anymore. I wasn't yet into my instrument. I was living with a fine person there, this girl really gave me a chance to—because you know, there's playing and playing, like, you can play an instrument but then you really have to play it. If you know what I mean. You have to study it."

For Tate's first solo album, *Tate à tête*, the whole Quebec crew is there: Pagliaro, Rossi, Workman, and, of course, Finaldi, who is credited as "Angie" on bass and co-writing. It's all produced by Roman. And look at that album cover! Literal *Tate à tête* as two Tates meet in the dark hazily—so hazy they overlap, even though the Richards are only smoking filtered cigarettes. Menthol? Maybe—the album does have a smoky, minty flavour. On the back of Tate's jean jacket is a bedazzled "Number One" (does the other Richard's say "Number Two"?) with a rainbow applique on his sleeve, no shirt, midriff peeping, and tight, white pants. This short and sweet 1974 LP has a multiplicity of moods all over the place. Lots of ripping guitar leads, funky at times too. Opening on a sweeping ballad and closing on a heavy thud groover. "Road Runner" is a wah-wah groove. The particularly Glammy "Bien dans ma peau" has crunchy guitar, T. Rex conga percussion, and high-pitched back-ups.

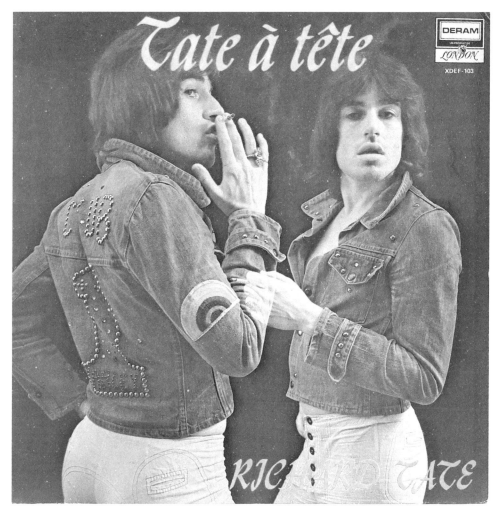

Front cover of *Tate à tête* by Richard Tate (Deram, 1974). Author's collection.

Spacious strings and horns appear on "Bien chez-nous." Guitar strikes thundering on "J'chu pogne"—translation: "I'm bummed." And a song about his place being infested with mice. Tate did a couple more solo albums after this. One at Muscle Shoals, then another at the Record Plant in L.A., full of session players. Of the third album, Finaldi remembers the company saying to Tate, "Here's your tapes. Get the fuck out of our offices."

Finaldi's solo album, *Angie* (1974), is of a pair with *Tate à tête*. Tate, Rossi, and Workman are here as well. When I asked how the album came about he replied, "I did it for a set of Ludwig drums and $1,000 in 1973." Asked further, he said, "I did it because my father was broke. I had to send him to Italy." This album's got some gritty heavy-duty guitar rockers, some swooners, and more, including a new version of "Le Sorcier maudit."

The song "Rose Bang" is the kind of Glam that weighs a ton. As Finaldi stated, "Fucking Richard, you could tell he was a good drummer, the fucking swing he had. And that's Wal-

Front cover of *Star Struck* by Moonquake (Aquarius, 1975). Author's collection.

ter playing guitar. We were playing loud! Wally had his Marshalls and the songs." I asked him if he ever performed this song. "Never—that song was never played live. That was the only time it was played." "Super Lady" is what you want it to be. The closing instrumental, "Carmen," is very much their "Maggot Brain," fading us along and away with it. Finaldi and Tate wrote the music—consummate musicians, not hung up on sticking to one thing. As Finaldi says, "Music is music." Many of these songs were what wooed Most. The Stonesy strut of "Sally Sue"—a song that Appice loved—became "Pas fou," with new French lyrics by Roman, who produced the album and provided many of its French lyrics, lyrics that Finaldi hated. Roman was an infamous character in the Quebec music industry, inspiring Finaldi to write a story titled "The High Heeled Giant," about Roman's Napoleon complex.

With the name "ANGIE" set above in a vibrational font, Angie himself smiles warmly and directly at the viewer from the album cover, dressed in jean jacket and red, low-cut shirt. The back cover is a full-body pose, red platforms hinted and blending into the warm red backdrop, Angie making a coy gesture, fingers on—or in—mouth, with his eyes in concentration and a thick, glorious mane of hair cascading down to his shoulders. This has the appearance of a teen idol album, if it weren't for the music inside—well, with the exception of one song, the single "I'm in Love," which Finaldi describes embarrassingly as "shooby-do." It's a butter-melter of a ballad in the classic '50s slow-dance ice-cream-social mode.

Finaldi wrote and recorded the "I'm in Love" single with John Hagopian, who was no stranger to Glam as a member of Moonquake, with Jack Geisinger, a.k.a. Jack August, on bass. Geisinger had done a lot of playing with Rossi in Influence and Charlee. Moonquake released a single, "Bang Bang Baby," a total Glam good-timer with handclaps way way up in the mix. This was the last thing Moonquake did, just after their two albums of gristly rock in 1973 and 1975. The second Moonquake album, *Star Struck,* looks like a Euro-Glam single with curved border framing the band in a posturing live shot—wide-open glitter shirt—. Its standout track, "Just Another Saturday Night" (this particular day and time is a popular Glam talking point; this one has got handclaps too), was covered and more Glammed out on a single by the German Glam band Giggles, who added siren sounds with their mouths and snapped their fingers. Besides playing in Pagliaro's band, Moonquake opened for April Wine a bunch. A side band of Moonquake was the Crescent Street Stompers, whose only Glam foray was a 1975 cover of the Sam Cooke song "Having a Party," which they turned into a stomper with the big drums and handclaps and guitar reverberations. Later, Hagopian and Geisinger would do highly coveted, atmospheric electronic space disco as Dogs of War.

Finaldi and Hagopian would collaborate together often, making disco music in the latter half of the '70s with groups like Bionic, Boule Noire, and Scum—who were more frothy than scummy. Montreal was one of the world's great disco hubs. Trying to smoosh the best of both worlds together, the Stone Revival Band, with Finaldi, Geisinger, and Hagopian, did a medley 45 called "Disco to the 50's." These people were playing all over each other's albums, moving from psych to heavy rock to Glam to funk to disco and—often, in Finaldi's case—wayyyy beyond . . .

With "I'm in Love" (1974), Finaldi and Hagopian knew that this was the radio-friendly number they needed to add to the *Angie* album, and they were right. A TV appearance had Finaldi in a burgundy top lip-synching "I'm in Love" to a studio audience, alone on a glazed maroon and yellow rococo festooned set. The single was zooming up the charts, and then it stalled and fell right off. Why? Finaldi gave me the backstory with Roman: "What happened, he had made enemies at this radio station because at one point he was a big-time sort of producer. And he would arrive there with a limo and all his crew and women. I mean, you should hear his voice, he had this fucking nasal—like if you scratch on a blackboard, that kind of voice? And they choked it because of Tony, because once you choke something, then there's no more." It was one DJ in particular who held great power: "He hated Tony Roman. I remember my mother was so disappointed because I was broke. I could have made a few dollars. She cursed him." Not long after that, this DJ was caught *in flagrante delicto* one evening in his car on the highway. Finaldi concludes, "And their car flipped and ever since he's paralyzed. Thanks to my mom. Then he became a fucking renowned television personality." By this time, Finaldi had already moved on.

1974 was quite a busy year for Angelo. He was now playing bass in Rossi's band Charlee, which opened for New York Dolls in Montreal. Rossi was greatly respected as a raw and exciting guitarist who had previously toured with Wilson Pickett and Buddy Miles. According to an interview Rossi gave to *It's Psychedelic Baby Magazine*, he even jammed with Hendrix. Rossi's psychedelic, freaky late-'60s rock band Influence left behind one fascinating album to be filed under the zany head-trip section of your *dépanneur*,[5] no prescription required—the Mothers being an obvious influence on Influence. Rossi's next band, Charlee, with his Influence bandmate Jack Geisinger, cut an album of heavy rock in 1972, a high-water mark for truants to intently nod along to. David Bowie (via one of his people) approached Rossi to come play guitar on the *Ziggy Stardust* tour. Rossi turned him down due to wanting to stay close to his ailing father. Finaldi explains, "I think Walter didn't want to leave his old father alone here in Montreal." It was Finaldi who got Rossi playing with Pagliaro.

New York Dolls and Charlee ad. Image courtesy of the *Montreal Star*, September 27, 1974.

Finaldi and Workman moved in together. Yves Martin, known for producing countless Patof albums and Tony Roman singles, entered the picture and became Finaldi's best friend. Martin approached Workman with a song called "Lady Marmalade." They cut it in one night: Workman on Hammond B3 and vocals, Finaldi on bass and arrangements, Tate, and Denis Le Page—who would later find success with the band Lime. Finaldi produced it with Martin. Martin used his pull in a problematic way. Says Finaldi, "He had so much power here in Quebec with the radio that they held back the Labelle version and they pushed Nanette's." Workman's version was sung entirely *en français,* not just the chorus; there is a long tradition of French-language versions of English pop hits released to Quebec markets. Over in

---

5 Corner store, in Canadian French.

the USA, with the rumblings of disco, Clive Davis wanted to release Workman's Quebec hit "Danser danser" and break it internationally with the French-language factor as a novelty. That factor made Finaldi say no; he was young and impulsive and didn't fully see that break then—which he speaks of with regret today: "In French her accent gave her a sensuality that she didn't have in English." Of "Danser danser" Finaldi says, "She wouldn't say '*danser danser,*' she would say '*dansayy dansayyy*'—that nuance."

The *Lady Marmalade* album (1976) was full of funky soul, as well as the evening moods of "Shame on You" building and intensifying with both Workman and Rossi letting loose, and a re-recorded version of "Pas fou" from the *Angie* album. An English-language album followed and then another album in French, both entirely written by Workman and Finaldi with a gatefold of them belting out vocals together in the studio. The album art showcases the warm grit of them all casually hanging out in the pub having a few laughs, Workman on the front and the lads on the back. She and Finaldi then did an album in L.A. with the American funk band Rufus backing them up. It flopped. Though the players were incredible, Finaldi believes that the poetry that they had had while recording in Montreal was lost. In 1977, Finaldi and Workman did "Kiss Me Goodbye," a disco duet single. Workman went on to make numerous albums. Reuniting professionally in the '80s, they did a more synth/electronic album, also self-titled *Nanette Workman*.

Nanette Workman. Image courtesy of the *Gazette*, August 30, 1978.

It's impossible to mention everything; Finaldi has just done so much. Where do I fit his cinematic production with the space-disco great Pat Desario (Dogs of War, Kebekelektrik) of the inexplicable "Hatchet Man" by B. B. Zee? Revenge genre but on the dancefloor. "Chop chop chop all the big ones down . . . I'm a hatchet man, I gotta cut 'em up . . ."

In the '80s, Finaldi worked on a rather unique album for the iconic star Diane Dufresne titled *Dioxine de carbone et son rayon rose* ("Carbon Dioxin and Its Pink Ray," an altogether accurate description of the album's contents). Dufresne truly did her own thing in the art-rock vein; she had been known to get Glammy herself in the '70s, strutting the stage in silver glitter thigh-high boots. Dufresne and Finaldi wrote and recorded demos of these songs together with just vocals, bass, and drum machine in the kitchen of Luc Plamondon, who had previously written the epic sci-fi rock opera *Starmania,* starring Dufresne. Finaldi did the music and Plamondon did the lyrics. "Plamondon eventually told me it sounded really good," Finaldi recalled, "like her voice and me, a bass and this drum machine—I'd program a beat and I'd play." This album was synthed way out. Dufresne lets her operatic voice go to unearthly plateaus, cascading and growling, uninhibited range, marching alien-robot hybrids behind her, stepping out for vocoder vignettes. At the time Finaldi was going through a severe depression, which he was eventually treated for in 2006; however, back then he simply couldn't make the album sessions and they recorded the album without him.

In 1992, Finaldi produced the first album by the Québécois hip-hop act Dédé Traké, featuring Polo Belmar from Danger and Polo's brother Dédé rapping over Polo's guitar riffs and samples of Pierre Henry's *musique concrète* classic "Psyché Rock." Finaldi won a Golden Sheaf award for best original music for the 1998 National Film Board documentary *Barbed Wire and Mandolins.* He composed "The Barber Song" for the popular 2004 animated film *Triplets of Belleville.* With the film's fourteen-piece band, Finaldi played jazz festivals and went to Portugal.

Of the countless songs that he has written and played on, the most records that Finaldi has sold came from a TV show called *Star Académie,* one of those generic "Some Region's Got Talent" music competition shows, with Nanette Workman's "Donne donne" being covered and dripping with 2004 production.

Forty years after "Midnight Flight," Finaldi's got travel on his mind again, still moving forward and every other direction. His 2012 album *Désoriented Voyage* is a travelogue beginning blindfolded and spun around many times. It goes all the way back to the age of powdered wigs covering the highest brows while using the technology of the future—a high-gloss digital "cartoon opera." A musical statement from the album's Bandcamp description: "Rome 1515, the greatest mind ever Leonardo Da Vinci anticipating today's slump in the music business, created another Divine Dante Alighieri in the form of a musical robot, naming him D. J. Ali D . . . " Multiple times/languages/places. A return to Naples, actually Little Italy, for some "Human Pasta" where the body shifts and noodles. Finaldi explains, "Actually, on the *Désoriented Voyage* album I do a voice that's like if René Angélil and Tony Roman were to have a child it would be that child—I'm doing the voice." *Désoriented Voyage* has a real café-culture quality with a mix of multilingual languages, meaning hey, this one's for everybody—especially if everybody speaks "open minded." His music from this era delves further into his Italian roots and includes contributions from his family: his daughter Coco sings on the album as the character "Stella."

Francoeur at the underground bar Le Conventum, 1972, just before the creation of Aut'Chose band.
Photographer: Danielle Arsenault. Photo courtesy of Lucien Francoeur.

Finaldi rapid-raps about Italian fare, tuba keeping the beat, using Dante's *Divine Comedy* as inspiration. It's a long way from "Midnight Flight" to *Désoriented Voyage*, yet they are so close they almost touch down. Finaldi looks younger than his years. In one of our conversations, I could hear him working intensively on harmonics. He is consummate.

AUT'CHOSE

PERHAPS IT IS BEST NOT TO DEMYSTIFY the Aut'Chose frontman Lucien Francoeur by detailing where he came from, how he came to be. He is a character, a strong one, archetypal, fully formed. He has strong presence, and it is hard to imagine an origin story. The details will be murky anyways, as the drinks had already been well poured by the time I arrived at the quaint Montreal pub to interview him. It was now afternoon; he had been drinking for some time. There was also a language barrier—oh, how I wished I could speak French. Thankfully, his friend and sometime bandmate Alan Lord is fluent in both French and English and was there to help.

The interview was already in progress when the tape recorder started recording, discussing the reappearance of a black-and-white 16-millimeter film thought long lost, made decades ago. The camera follows Francoeur and others walking, the camera then peers into rooms of naked people, people fixing, people rolling joints. Francoeur describes the scene: "Gloomy, it's gloomy, hard stuff." After being amazed by its archival quality, the film director Yves Simoneau transferred the footage, telling Francoeur that they should do something more: a documentary on Aut'Chose. Some of that footage did get used for a different documentary made by his daughter Virginie Francoeur, *Francoeur: On achève bien les rockers*, released in 2023.

Before Aut'Chose, Francoeur was already becoming an established poet, with five volumes of poetry under his belt. He had been performing his poetry on stage at La Casanous, often with Jazz Libre du Québec (known for their previous work backing the popular Quebec singer Robert Charlebois) playing behind him. Lucien describes the audience: "It was all hippies, you know? Not hippies—they were fucking granola, eh?" Showing up on stage in his leather jacket and motorcycle boots—like the ones his hero Jim Morrison wore—the crowd would react, "Jesus Christ, who's this bum coming to read his poetry?" To which Francoeur would say, "Why don't you go fuck yourself? Like Jim Morrison said, you're a bunch of fucking slaves. You're nothing." In dealing with these hecklers, Francoeur exclaims, "Pow! I would punch them."

Francoeur states that he met Pierre Gauthier through a friend who told him that he played like Pete Townshend. Gauthier's first band Genèse recorded just one single, in 1971: with Marie France Paquin and Liliane Gaucher on vocals, one side was heavy stoner rock and the other more folk rock. For reasons which will become apparent later, I interviewed Gauthier separately in his home. Hanging framed on Gauthier's living room wall is an Aut'Chose poster.

Front cover of *Prends une chance avec moé* by Aut'Chose (CBS, 1975). Author's collection.

Gauthier says that he met Francoeur at a party where he told him, "I'm a rock and roll poet." And Gauthier replied, "Yeah. Well, I'm a rock and roll guitar player." Gauthier continues, "Two weeks later he said, 'We have a show.' It was in that club in Montreal where all the artists were hanging out. And we came there with no songs." Who was playing in the band? "Just me and Lucien, that's all. The funny thing is he was reciting poetry. But really intense poetry, and I was improvising with my guitar in the back and all my influence playing a riff and rhythm and making spacey sounds. So, it turned out that in the crowd there was all the major artists of the day. Dubois, Charlebois, everybody was there. And I was improvising and I did this Bo Diddley beat, you know, bam bam bam bam . . . and here it became our first single called 'Ch't'aime pi ch't'en veux' . . . And from there it was the sky's the limit." The song title in English means, "I love you, but I'm mad at you."

Lucien Francoeur expressing "rock consciousness."

Francoeur of Aut'Chose live. Image courtesy of the *Montreal Star*, March 7, 1978.

That first Aut'Chose single from 1974, with its altered Bo Diddley shuffle and synths hitting the long notes, was recorded with a full band. Gauthier explains, "I formed the band with my brother—my brother was living in Gatineau near Ottawa. And I went there. I said, 'Come on down to Montreal. I'm starting a project.' He brought in his drummer. So, my brother Mick and the drummer and me—who else? Another guitar player from I don't know, I met him in a music store and I said, 'You want to join the band?' He said yes. And that was it. So, it became Aut'Chose." The guitarist Gauthier doesn't name was Jacques Racine, who would become a pivotal member. Gauthier notes that the band name came from that old Eddie Cochran rock 'n' roll burner "Something Else." Aut'Chose was born. They really were something else!

Francoeur had an unhealthy fixation on Jim Morrison—delving deep into the well, the total Dionysian, reaching back to the poetry of Rimbaud, a romanticization of the hard-knock life. "I was the first one in Quebec who had the Lou Reed album. I was the first one who had the David Bowie album in Quebec. People would come to my home and would say, 'Who the fuck is that?' 'Go fuck yourself.'" In his memoir, Lord describes Francoeur as the Lou Reed of Quebec—except Lou Reed was a strong musician. Francoeur is a poet and frontman. Certainly, Francoeur's ego is part of Aut'Chose's appeal—he has presence and conviction, he is committed. Let me be clear: Aut'Chose went beyond their diverse influences to create something strongly unique and special. I hesitate to describe Aut'Chose as gutter Glam, though to go that far down it becomes transcendent, lifting up, up, up. The albums are considered and intuitive, well crafted and produced, also raw. I remember the day I wandered into a Montreal record store asking for some regional Glam when the clerk turned me on to Aut'Chose. One of the records had tape holding the split sides together; I bought it anyway, being informed that most Aut'Chose albums often go through hard living and partying.[6]

---

6   I later came to know that clerk, Bernardino Femminielli, a consummate performer and musician himself; it is clear why he loves Aut'Chose so much. Hey, what's not to love?

With Gauthier credited for the music and Francoeur credited with the lyrics, the first album, *Prends une chance avec moé,* from 1975, opens with a somewhat regal riff, Francoeur's vocal comes in and he is riffing too. And screaming. Violins and a choir of artifice accompany Francoeur on "Pousse pas ta luck OK bébé," never holding him back—when it gets ornate, it never gets bloated or pompous. A groovy rock version of the instrumental *Godfather* movie theme—hey, it's the groovy Godfather! Kiss the ring? High five! Cowbell clopping by the former Genèse drummer Joe Marandola and back-up vocals from the former Genèse singers Mary France and Liliane for Aut'Chose's cover of Michel Polnareff's on-the-make number "Hey You Woman." This is the shaggy, visceral Quebec cousin to the ornate album masterpiece *Polnareffs*. An acoustic interlude, then "Le Freak de Montréal"—elaborate bass runs, big synths and cowbell, vocal effects on the strongly enunciated parts. The album culminates in the winding and ominous "Bar-B-Q Lady."

The faux hand-tinted cover photo shows a woman in a short, ass-revealing skirt reaching to put up an Aut'Chose poster on a cement wall, prominently showing Gauthier and Francoeur side by side. Smartly, the record came with a lyric booklet, as they are brilliant right to the marrow. The lyrics are almost all in French, but here is an English translation (thank you for translating, Alan Lord) of some of "Le Freak de Montréal (le Batman de l'Underground)" where Francoeur announces,

> "The head that's frozen
> The skull that's cracked
> I'm the Freak of Montreal
> I slapped wings on my suspenders
> A stereo in my brain
> The universe in my spoon
> I'm the toppest of top dogs"

When I asked Francoeur if he is the Freak of Montreal, he answered, "Are you for real? *Le freak de Montréal* is my alter ego, is a lost cause." Aut'Chose drew a diverse crowd of misfits—powerful motorcycle-club enthusiasts too. Lord says, "Bikers always like him. He had biker friends." Francoeur adds, "The waitresses from restaurants, they all loved me. I was liked by the street people, the working classes. And I was liked by the people that were deviants, they loved me. I was thirty years ahead of my fucking time."

In their 1975 concert film *Live au Jardin des Étoiles,* Aut'Chose is on a very large stage decorated with pop-art accoutrements such as a fake juke box and fake dancers, a real pinball machine that they're too busy to play right now (though there are pinball-art-style overlays flashing above them throughout), a giant red Coca-Cola logo appropriated for the band, implying: "Aut'Chose Is It." Gauthier on guitar creating Townshend-inspired windmills, not to tilt at, but full tilt. Clad in a velvet top, he has all the moves. The other guitarist, Jacques Racine, has tied his floral blouse bolero-style, the coy note-coaxer. Low bass nice and high in the mix, wearing his heart on his t-shirt. Red satin synth man. Drummer on a riser, hello. No one is the picture of health. They're all suitably shaggy, with a twist of limelight. Double your denim, double your pleasure, Francoeur is in the Canadian tuxedo, a perfect fit—who's your tailor? No shirt—the buttons undo themselves early on, revealing hirsuteness. A curly skullet, massive muttonchop sideburns unfurling, sunglasses so dark—did birds peck out his eyes? Shades removed to address the thrall—ah, there they are, phew! The words come, clutching the mic stand tightly punctuated with thrusts, a force when singing, stillness on solos, an occasional casual march in place. Play "Greensleeves"! And they do, for a moment, with Alice Cooper–style dramatic instrumentation. Always let them see you sweat, offer up the sweat for them to drink in, it's communion, that's quite the wafer you got there. "Ow! Ouch! Owwww!" Sometimes he "Ah"s like a snake full of sweet venom. This is intense. How long can this band last?

Of his attire, Francoeur explains, "I walk on the stage today as I'm coming out of the street, and by the way, I got to go on stage there, so I wear my same jeans, t-shirt Aut'Chose. I don't give a shit, I don't change, I don't wash, I'm on the stage and I love it and they love it. If they don't love it, they can go fuck themselves!" There was one time early on when he appeared wearing lingerie. He just did his thing and didn't know it was Glam yet. "I would go on stage with high leather boots, black pantyhose. I was weighing 130 pounds, I was slim. I was wearing a big hat. I was New York Dolls before they even fucking started." For another show, Francoeur came out in women's high heels: "I became the talk of the town." Adding a diss to a popular Quebec prog act—"Harmonium, they were wearing bird seeds." Francoeur wanted to go against the prog rock trend in Quebec.

When Lord found the music of Aut'Chose, it saved him: "Look, when I was in '72, '73, I was eighteen, nineteen—me, I was the only one who had *Aladdin Sane* and *For Your Pleasure*. I didn't know any other friends who had Glam records like I did. They all had Yes, E.L.P., fuckin' Jethro Tull, Gentle Giant, and all this shit, and then the Quebec answers to that which was Octobre, Harmonium, fucking Beau Dommage—man, we still fucking hate them. I'll tell you one thing: over here it was a prog bastion, there might be some underground Glam bands here and there, but you have to dig around. And then all of a sudden on the fucking radio I hear 'Nancy Beaudoin'—fucking Aut'Chose. Finally! Aut'Chose—especially the first two albums, Aut'Chose was the first fucking Quebec band that I was proud to put next to Roxy Music and Bowie, the first fucking band and that was this guy. And there's a link with Glam because at a certain point he tells his guitarist Jacques Racine, 'Why don't you make a song that sounds like 'Buick MacKane' by T. Rex, Marc Bolan? And 'Nancy Beaudoin' comes from the 'Buick MacKane' influence, and there's the link with Glam."

You certainly can hear that link in "Nancy Beaudoin," but it is more raw, more late night, synth washes, nasty licks, Francoeur yelling the lyrics about a go-go dancer he knew from a strip club. In the pub, he describes her to me: "She was good-looking. She was nice. She

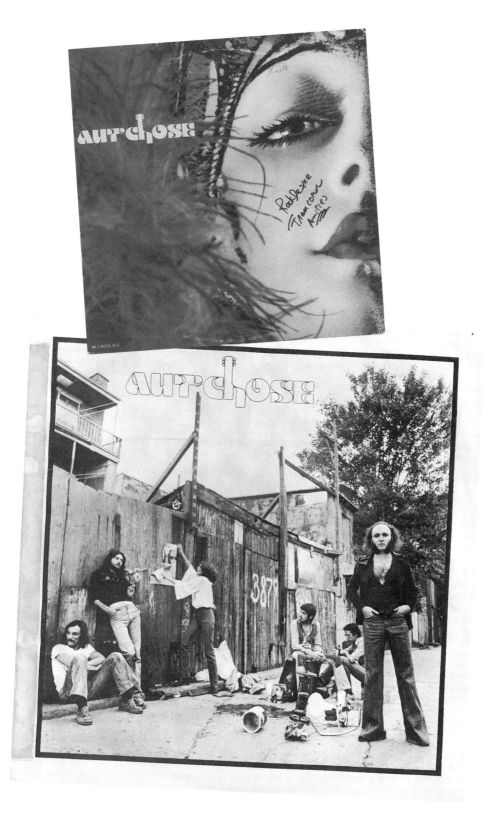

Front cover and lyric booklet of *Une nuit comme une autre* by Aut'Chose (CBS, 1975). Author's collection.

Front cover of *Le Cauchemar Américain* by Aut'Chose (CBS, 1976). Author's collection.

liked me, she loved me." It is "Nancy Beaudoin" which opens the second album *Une nuit comme une autre* followed by the delicate piano and synths of "Vancouver, une nuit comme une autre." More flange and synth mood rockers. A couple brooding epics. Aut'Chose does a radical cover of Brigitte Fontaine's 1969 song "Comme à la radio," taking the jazz and turning it into a massive synth wall played by the keyboardist Jean-François St-George, Francoeur half-rapping, adding in new lyrics: "AM, FM, underground, overground . . . "

Francoeur describes how their producer came back from London in 1975 with the master tapes of the Troggs' cover of the Beach Boys' "Good Vibrations." He had just stolen them and wanted Aut'Chose to rush into the studio and replicate the song, then quickly get it out in Quebec before the Troggs released theirs. Afterwards Francoeur's friend told him, "How amazing, the band Aut'Chose doing a Beach Boys song, their own version in

English and French. And then we received a week after: the Troggs." The producer loved it. Francoeur notes, "Just that power of major labels, they could do anything they want to." The similarities to the Troggs version is mostly in the pounding drums played by the special guest, Richard Tate. I do prefer the Aut'Chose version: they can't resist adding odd flourishes and synths and flange and Francoeur singing "Sexe fiction." Vibing to a variation on "Good Vibrations" but make it *sexe,* make it *fiction,* Francoeur adding the simulated moans of coitus, the only English phrase being "I've got to keep those good vibrations happening with her."

The album cover is a photo from an art deco book that they found in the garbage—cropping it and adding a feather boa to cover their asses (no asses on the cover this time) and not get sued. Gauthier was thrown out of the band some time during this album. Many of the songs from this album were performed in the live video that he was in. Racine, a great musician himself, became the band leader. Francoeur had a terrible falling out with Gauthier. It's clear that it was over money. Hell, maybe throw drugs and alcohol into the mix—ego, too. Vitriolic quotes have been removed for clarity. The lyric-booklet photo replicates the first album cover, except now a woman is ripping Gauthier out of the Aut'Chose poster. The revised band sits in front, Francoeur standing in the foreground. It has been said that the proggier elements of the first two albums were due to Gauthier, who is certainly open to such things, along with all other sorts of music. However, these albums are not, by any means, prog albums. And the third album from 1976—done without Gauthier—is not radically different, keeping to the template.

For the third Aut'Chose album cover, it is just Francoeur and Francoeur alone on the cover, front and center, shirtless, painted completely in silver from head to toe, even the sunglasses are silver, like Goldfinger but he's got silver fingers. Racine co-wrote many of the songs with Francoeur, as did St-George. The first two albums are classics. The third album, not so much, but still quite good.

After Aut'Chose folded, Francoeur did a solo album in 1978 using just his last name Francoeur with the album itself called *Aut'Chose,* retaining only the keyboard player, St-George, from the band Aut'Chose. Calling the album *Aut'Chose* is certainly a savvy—even ballsy—move on either his or the label's part. Name recognition! That said, this album is a personal fan favorite. It's certainly him at his most pop, loaded with little nuggets, though very Francoeur: one song is downright bubbly, contrasting with his voice. Opening with the Brigitte Bardot number "Contact," he takes the op-art silver space-age kinetics of the Serge Gainsbourg–written original and gives it a vocoder vocal. How fitting to cover a sex symbol—Francoeur is a sex symbol in his own way. The album art, again faux hand-tinted, has a soft-focus Polaroid of Francoeur's face tucked into a woman's stocking, with the entire focus being again rather ass-centric. "Pin-Up," "Bubble Gum," "Paris Rock 'n' Roll," a modernized version of that old rock 'n' roll chestnut "Be-Bop-A-Lula." This whole album is Glammy!

Performing live at that time, Francoeur was given a brief make-over to be more up to date. He says, "I tried my best." A designer made him a suit jacket out of a shower curtain, paired with faux leather pants. "It was all black. And then I walked and all they see is that fucking jacket with black, white square. I was kind of an asshole at the time." The spot followed him as he approached the mic to say, "You want to rock and roll?" Bang!

Alan Lord met Lucien when he interviewed him for the early punk zine *Surfin' Bird*. Alan is a Montreal punk alumnus from the bands the Marauders and then the Pagan Gurus, who continue to release new music. In 1980, Lord produced and did all the music for Francoeur's second solo album and named it *Le Retour de Johnny Frisson*. It is total rock 'n' roll, punky with synths, occasionally feeling '50s, like Gainsbourg's *Rock Around the Bunker*. Francoeur is described here as "Poète rock," black spandex pants Lucien, very bouncy synthy new wavin' but still very, very Francoeur. Throwing in an impeccably chosen cover of the French garage pop singer Antoine and doing an ode to Françoise Hardy.

The impresario concert promoter Donald K. Donald called to say, "There's only one band that can do the first opening act for the Ramones." Francoeur replied, "Yeah, but what's the problem?"

"It's gonna be hard because there's no opening act that lasts more than five minutes."

"Well, I'm going to tell you something, they'll be lucky if they last ten minutes after me. I was a motherfucker."

Lord was excited to open for these legends. The audience was full of kids from the suburbs. Francoeur elaborated: "Mother drove them in station wagons. They put the diaper pin in their nose." Things went sideways. Francoeur explains, "So I didn't know at the time when they spit on you it was because they liked you." Francoeur then goes on to describe himself attacking the crowd with his pointy boots.(He is known for his hyperbole. Others who were there have no recollections of such incidents of violence.)

In the middle of these Francoeur albums, a mysterious single co-written with Lord was released in 1982 under the name Aut'Chose. It sounds rec-room dinge with a basic rock groove, Francoeur singing about the hit parade. Deep, ugly voices come in chanting, "Rock rock, rock 'n' roll . . ."

The first Quebec rap song, "Rap-à-Billy," followed. Francoeur rapping is not a stretch by any means—he had been pretty much rapping all along—the rhythm is just amped and hardened here, using the musical rap style with French Canadian rock flourishes. More Francoeur rap followed. All along, he continued his focus on poetry and was teaching at the Rosemont and John Abbott CEGEPs. He even has a Quebec music award named after him, the Lucien, for the best acts that don't fit the industry norms.

After Aut'Chose, Gauthier was still with the record label CBS, reforming his original band, Genèse, now renamed Eclipse. As with Aut'Chose, John J. Williams was the executive producer. The resulting 1976 album sounds like they really, really, really loved Pink Floyd, particularly *The Dark Side of the Moon*—total prog overload when you listen to

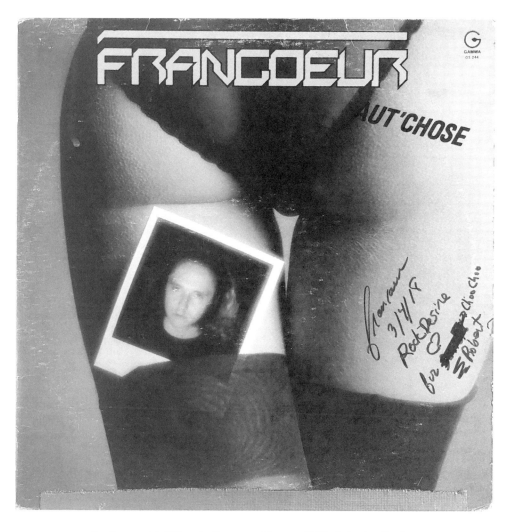

Front cover of *Aut'Chose* by Francoeur (Gamma, 1978). Author's collection.

it—the split makes sense, as this is everything Francoeur hates. The back cover features a photo of Gauthier's massive Moog synthesizer, the first Moog synthesizer in Quebec, which he purchased after hearing Wendy Carlos' *Switched-On Bach*—"That blew me away. So I said, 'I have to get that synthesizer.'" In 1973, he and a friend drove to New York to Manny's Music Store where they were told that it wasn't in the store, that they were all hand-built by Mr. Robert Moog himself. They then drove to Trumansburg where he lived, stopped at a Denny's phone booth, looked him up in the phone book, and gave him a call: "Bob Moog? We're a band from Montreal and we're really, really interested in using your synthesizer but not the way that people might use it. We want to use it as a percussion instrument." Moog said, "Wow, come on down. Here's my address." They went to his home where he was building a synth drum. Gauthier explains, "I was there at the right

Front cover of *Night and Day* by Eclipse (Casablanca, 1977). Author's collection.

time. So, he was very happy that we wanted to use the Moog as a percussion because he was just building this synth—doo doo doo—that you hear all over the place in the disco." Alas, Moog had just sold his company to Norland. To get the three-cabinet modular system Gauthier needed, he drove to Chicago. "It's huge. So, at that time, you could have bought a house with that money, but I said, I want that because I'm sure it's gonna make some nice sounds that nobody's heard."

This system and other gear, including a vocoder, got Gauthier a lot of work throughout the '70s and '80s, including deep disco work with Kebekelektrik, Bombers, and Lime, programming the Montreal disco king Gino Soccio's synths, recording numerous commercial jingles that needed robot voices, and also lending the Glam band Danger equipment to make their recordings.

Gauthier created all kinds of music. Recording at Le Studio in Morin Heights, Eclipse were asked to do a song for the big-budget disco movie *Thank God It's Friday*. Though the song wasn't used, Gauthier had now formed a whole new lineup of Eclipse bandmembers, creating an album so utterly audacious that many prog-heads despise it—especially after the first Eclipse album. After hearing Donna Summer's "I Feel Love," Gauthier became inspired by Giorgio Moroder's production. Already owning a Moog, he now added sequencers. This second Eclipse album, *Night and Day,* was released on Casablanca Records, the big American disco label, in 1977.

Now with entirely English lyrics, they were total Glam disco, mixing up original spacey anthems like "Space Love" and turning Gauthier's love of the '60s rock classics "Born to Be Wild," "Sunshine Superman," and "You Really Got Me" into dance-floor thumpers—the latter goes on for eight minutes with a total percussive breakdown—whistles too! Yes, it's cheese, but it's the kind of cheese you bring to impress at a fun party to get everyone dancing. And the synth work is phenomenal.

Eclipse wore custom-made chest-baring silver outfits surrounded by cosmic lights, Gauthier drew pupils on his eyelids so that when he closed his eyes for the cover photo they still looked open—a real alien effect. For the shows they placed big boxes filled with car lights behind the band, beaming and blinding the audience. Some of these venues that Eclipse played, such as discotheques, were not set up for live bands, so they had to lip-sync. Before long, the singer Jesse Otten was forced to return home to the United States. For the final single, a demo single, Eclipse did the ridiculous by taking a song that represented what was gauche about the late '60s, the lengthy—yet dunderheaded—"In-A-Gadda-Da-Vida" and made it disco. They also got a new singer, Peter Beau. The band broke up soon after.

Gauthier then went on to form Le Show in 1978 with the other players from the second Eclipse lineup, and they have continued for many years. Trivia: the singer, Michel St-Clair, whose real name is Michel Dion, is Céline Dion's brother. The first two album covers show Gauthier in drag in blond wig, bobby-socks, and poodle skirt. For the promotional video "Viens ce soir" (a cover of Rocky Burnette's "Tired of Toein the Line"), each band member is in their persona: the letterman-sweater nerd, the leather man (greaser?—no, more leather man), with a focus on the suave-suited Italian singer singing to Gauthier in drag. The video opens with Gauthier in a spacescape-patterned long-sleeved shirt getting made up. Le Show was definitely in the showband mold, covering "Little Darling" and "Let's Twist Again," but also doing Hollies, Bee Gees, Beatles, and Beach Boys medleys on their live album. Flash forward to the '80s: Le Show have a twelve-inch called "Super D.J."—heads up, it's a banger—and albums where they are now doing po-faced AOR synth pop, all jumpsuits and lasers. Le Show formed a label, Tokyo Records, releasing various Hi-NRG singles by other acts.

In 2000, the unthinkable happened: Francoeur and Gauthier reunited to make a new Aut'Chose album with them both front and center smiling together, their names highlighted. This reunion was not to last. The rift deepened and remains to this day. The resulting Aut'Chose CD, *Dans la Jungle des villes* was released as the label Les Disques Star Records was going bankrupt.

Francoeur came back with Aut'Chose again, with one of the original members, Jacques Racine, rejoining, along with members of Voivod, a revered band who acknowledge the influence of Aut'Chose. In 2005, this lineup recorded an album of the old Aut'Chose hits done in a more straight-up heavy rock style, Francoeur's voice further up in the mix. Jacques Racine died in 2024.

LEWIS FUREY

BEHOLD, LISTEN TO THE MANY CHARMS, the dazzling, unique expression defying convention: the music of Lewis Furey. Now, imagine that your first name is Lewis and as your first single, your announcement to the world of music, is the song "Lewis Is Crazy." Imagine that. How audacious. Picture sleeve done up to look like a mental-hospital file. Doctor's notes state, "Lewis is Crazy!" Yeah, sure he's crazy—crazy good! And the song? Same! Lewis wasn't really crazy, but more "crazy" in the context of this romantically obsessive song. Furey says, "I used that line because I was running after this girl that was working at a bar in Montreal that I used to go to and she was very hard to get. It's just everybody saying that I'm crazy to be running after somebody that you're not going to have a relationship with." He adds, "I really didn't know what the hell I was doing. I was just enjoying myself."

The song is so good that Furey re-recorded it three years later for his first album (self-titled, 1975), and his partner Carole Laure recorded an "answer song" version in French in 1979, "Tout le Monde dit," from the perspective of the woman in the original, singing what happened after she left everything for a guy named Billy who dressed like a cowboy.

Lewis Furey may have always been Lewis but he wasn't always Furey. Born Lewis Greenblatt, Furey was the stage name required for his recording career, putting necessary distance between the two for this candid persona to dwell in a heightened sense of reality. The name was born in the new Métro of Montreal, Furey theorizes: "I guess it was the feeling of the other trains rushing by and the excitement of the beginning of a new career and, and there was something sort of furious about it. I imagine now that's how it was." A classically trained violinist, Furey was drawn to theatrical music, stating, "I liked to be able to get away from the restraint of classical music and into the possibility of talking about my life through music, but in a theatrical way, so that it's not really autobiographical, but it's something about the feeling of what I was going through in my teens and early twenties." These songs are not necessarily straightforward confessionals so much as dwelling sideways and into metaphorical regions of feeling: "It was autobiographical, but taking a

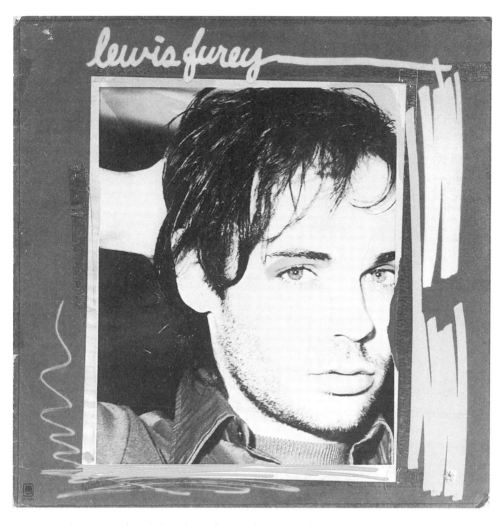

Front cover of *Lewis Furey* by Lewis Furey (A&M Records, 1975). Author's collection.

lot of freedom in how it expressed itself, so that each song was a kind of character in my mind that I was creating. I just enjoyed it. I enjoy tremendously writing songs. I still do."

He chose Gamma Records to release the first single because it was the great Robert Charlebois's label. Gamma had put out that wildly unique Robert Charlebois and Louise Forestier album from 1968 which was a new take on psychedelic music, distinctively French Canadian and very influential. Charlebois was one of the first pop shows Lewis had seen as a late teen, a very theatrical show that left an impact on him. Gamma seemed like a good fit. However, Furey says, "Later, I regretted it and when I got to meet Robert he said he had so much trouble getting out of the contract and it was too bad that we hadn't known each other; he would have told me and, in fact, I had trouble getting out of it too. But finally I did and was able to get a contract with A&M Records, who basically bought me out of the contract before."

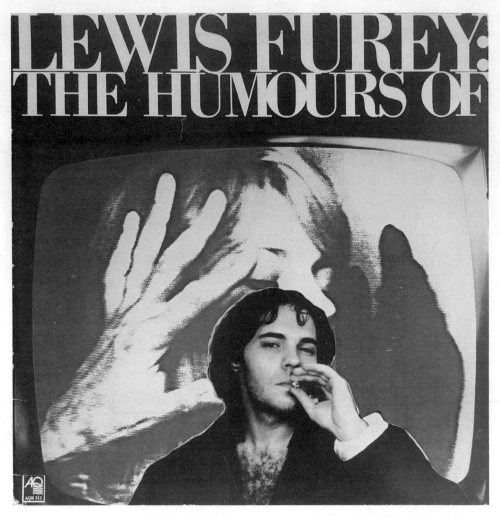

Front cover of *The Humours of Lewis Furey* by Lewis Furey (A&M Records, 1976). Author's collection.

Both the single and the later first album were produced by John Lissauer. Furey speaks glowingly of him: "John absolutely understood. He doesn't come from a rock-and-roll background. He's a really good arranger and he tries to be sensitive to all sorts of music. I've seen that in his career as a producer, what he's come up with, and he understood that kind of arrangement that would be right for me. He understood it better than I did in the specifics. And I told him things like, 'I don't really feel like guitars and the things that a rock record would have, you know, drums and guitars and then electric bass.' So he said, 'You don't really like guitars?' I said, 'Not particularly.' And so, there's no guitars on that album. There's absolutely none. I don't think there was a rock album that came out that year that didn't have guitars. There's banjos, like Kurt Weill used. So, I really enjoyed working with John."

Lissauer also produced a few Leonard Cohen albums, including *New Skin for the Old Ceremony,* which features many of the same musicians, including Furey himself, who says, "Leonard and I knew each other quite well. He had been very helpful to me when I was younger and starting to write poems. And so he was following what I was doing in music, and he came to see it. He asked to meet John, and he asked him to do some work with him. And they got along really well. And I think John was a very good producer for Leonard."

Furey's vocal tone is seductively high nasal. If you are a Peter Ivers fan (and you very well should be), chances are you will grow enamored of this; you will detect unique singing similarities, both unintentional and unknowing, contemporary, highly intelligent but certainly not distant—it's engaging. With his violin, Furey leads us into a midnight world of sexually hazy cabaret, tattered tux 'n' tails. "This is my magic circle . . . enter." Magick references seeping in through the arcane interests of Crowley-obsessed friends. This album has delicate dynamics—again, read the sign on the lightly cracked door: NO GUITARS. Theatricality without posturing. Definite Romantic Glam. The production offers up a sense of space and casual mystery, streaks of candlelight atmosphere, light debauchery in the evening. The haunting ballad "Louise" brings in strings and screams. Lines like "Take two, man, they're small" are sung fliply. Maybe I'll casually misuse the descriptor "Brechtian" right about now. No, not Brecht. Well, maybe? Genet? Absolutely. Definitely Weill. The song "Huster's Tango" was absolutely influenced by Weill's *Threepenny Opera,* which Furey explains was "probably my favorite group of songs at that point when I was starting out as a songwriter. It was a big, big influence for me at that point, you know, it took me a while to get free of it. I mean, I never get free of it, because it was so important." Tangos and waltzes and other dances that he enjoys pervade Furey's work.

Tim Curry popped by for a gang vocal, along with Cat Stevens. Furey had a gas seeing *The Rocky Horror Show* in Los Angeles in 1974, where he had been spending a lot of time. He and Curry had mutual friends and became friends. Furey was a guest star himself on the eccentric French pop star Michel Polnareff's self-titled 1975 English-language album debut for Atlantic, an album of appropriately scrumptious excess. With his wry voice interluding descriptions of the entertainment world, Furey is curiously credited as the "Show" personified in "Fame à la mode." À la mode? This song is an entire ice-cream shop.

The artist Stephen Lack, a close friend of Furey's, designed the cover for Furey's debut album and subsequent Furey albums and materials. Bordered by bright swaths of paint, his face is adorned with hand-tinted mascara on the album sleeve. I first heard of the music of Furey through the book *Lost in the Grooves,* where Richard Henderson described the album art as "faux-Warhol." This isn't too far off. In high school, Lewis went to New York to study violin with the great teacher Ivan Galamian at the Juilliard extension school. A little later he went back to New York. When I asked Furey about "pornography star" mysteriously popping up in a bio of his, he recalled, "I got interested in what the people were doing around New York . . . It was Warhol's period and the Factory. And they were making these sort of porn

Lewis Furey and Carole Laure in *Fantastica* t-shirts.
Image courtesy of the *Ottawa Citizen*,
February 23, 1980.

films. It wasn't so much Warhol, but the filmmaker that worked with Warhol." Paul Morrissey? "Yes. Exactly. So, I said, 'Jesus, I could do this too. This is a great way of making money.' It's easy. It's a formal style. The more I learned about it, the more I saw: this has to happen after five minutes, that has to happen after ten minutes, and then you're out by fifteen minutes, right? It felt like a sonnet. It had very formal rules, you know. And I had the whole thing in my mind about it being like sonnets to make these. At the time, they were doing shorts. And so, I went to auditions for a couple and I did a couple of them. And I was so proud of myself that I was able to do that, they were really pretty softcore at that time. But I thought it was very romantic. So I put it in my biography. That's all it was really, as exciting as it sounds. I always liked Warhol. I like those movies that they were making. It was very refreshing, his philosophy of art. It was sexy, it was playful and profound. I worked at Max's Kansas City as a busboy for, you know, two minutes, maybe like two months or something like that. And they would all come in there, you know? It was around the corner. The back room at Max's Kansas City. And the Factory was across the park."

Many of the songs on his debut were appropriately used for Allan Moyle's feature film *Rubber Gun,* released in 1977, a gritty and funny Montreal street drama centered on a sharp-witted drug dealer and user charismatically played by Stephen Lack, who co-wrote it. (Lack would later star in David Cronenberg's *Scanners.*) *Rubber Gun* candidly depicts sexually fluid mores and casually communal drug use with unflinching near-verité realism—lots of hanging out—art making, too.

Though not used for the film, the song "Rubber Gun Show," from Furey's 1976 follow-up album, *The Humours of Lewis Furey,* is him at his most rock opera. Lissauer was not involved with the second album. Furey explains, "Unfortunately, A&M didn't want me to do my next record with him because we didn't sell enough copies. And they wanted me to work with a producer that made records that sold a lot of copies." They went with Roy Thomas Baker, famed for producing Queen, of whom Furey says, "They were selling lots and lots of records. And my record was a kind of Queen-like album because Roy took me in that direction. I really didn't like it for the longest time. It didn't feel like me, but I guess it was like, you know, working for a director or a photographer that does his interpretation of you. And Roy was certainly a very capable person in the recording studio.

And the six weeks I spent with him flew by. It was really interesting. But that's what sounds Glam. Of course it sounds Glam. Queen was probably one of the defining groups of Glam Rock. Now I can live with it. I mean, I'm not embarrassed by it or anything and I know some people really like it and it's done well." *The Humours of Lewis Furey*—and it is not without humors, if you want to get all Shakespeare—runs the gamut, there's even a proto-disco number, "Top Ten Sexes" ("do you like it on the top or on the bottom?"), a "Cops Ballet," and a "Lullaby," all somehow cohesively flowing along, bombastically so. Yes, there are guitars. But it doesn't sound like a watered-down compromise, there is no second-album fatigue, it's a potent beast with bite.

Lewis Furey and Carole Laure in *Fantastica*. Image courtesy of the *Gazette*, November 1, 1980.

Of this period Furey says, "It was a time in my life when I would sort of do a round between Los Angeles, New York, and Montreal. I couldn't stay still. I was about a month in each city for about three or four years. And I had my hotels where I would stay that had pianos in the hotel and who would let me play on the pianos during the daytime when they weren't in use. And so it was that kind of life for me. You know, I wasn't married. I could travel all the time. I would go around from city to city, maybe for about four or five years, until I ran away from Los Angeles and the music scene in America and moved to Paris to get away from being told that my songs weren't selling enough copies. Which I really didn't want to hear. I mean, I really didn't care if they sold a lot of copies or not, as long as I was able to make them and there were people who enjoyed them and that I could make a living out of it. I really didn't care. And they did. The people that were, you know, like my agent, he was Cat Stevens' agent. They were expecting me to make millions of dollars."

The actor Carole Laure met Furey while she was shooting a film in Montreal. One evening she went to one of his shows at the Hotel Nelson. She wanted him to do the music for her next film, *La Tête de Normande St-Onge* (1975), so she brought the director, Gilles Carle, to see him perform. "And that's actually how we met and became friends," Furey recalls, "Friends at first and she's my wife still. It's fifty-two years later or something like that." Carle directed Laure and Furey for the 1977 movie *L'Ange et la femme* (brief synopsis: after a young woman is shot to death by mysterious snowmobilers, an angel revives her in a cabin in the woods). The film was controversial for showing what was then regarded as explicit sex. These scenes were respectfully filmed on a very closed set; the cam-

The Hooded Fang from *Jacob Two-Two Meets the Hooded Fang*. Image courtesy of *The Montreal Star*, February 23, 1979.

era lens was on a snake far from the crew, who stayed outside the room. I asked him if the two of them were still just friends by then. "I think that we were a little more than friends. Yeah. Definitely more than friends. Yes. Very, very friendly."

Furey and Laure would again act together—as well as sing—in the 1980 musical *Fantastica*, also directed by Carle. Furey's *Fantastica* movie soundtrack is more the lush stuff of musicals in a Van-Dyke-Parks-ian manner, with Lissauer doing the orchestral arrangements. *Fantastica* is a great movie showcase for Furey's music—softer-edged than before, so soft that the title number is a visual explosion of pastels amidst a light-hearted, sexy drama about capitalist destruction. After those two movies, Furey made the conscious decision to never act on film again. In fact, when he later directed and did the music for the difficult-to-find 1985 movie musical *Night Magic*, the actor Nick Mancuso lip-synched all of Furey's vocals to this noble experiment, a Faustus story with all of the extensive lyrics by Leonard Cohen.

A number of years later, in 2015, the acclaimed director Guy Maddin asked Furey to be in the unrestrained and heavily worked (yet not mannered) hypnagogic fantasy *Forbidden Room*, a must-see film drawing inspiration from old lost films and then running with it or, more appropriately, floating away with it, plus: an un-credited musical cameo by Sparks. Really, the best movies have "forbidden" in the title, just daring you to watch (*Forbidden Zone, Forbidden Planet,* uhhh . . . *Forbidden Dance*). What brought about this return? "Absolutely everybody said yes. He has such a good reputation. And any actor I had spoken to said you can't say no to him. It's just not done!" Not only that, but appearing in the movie with him was his daughter Clara Furey.

Furey has certainly done more than a few film scores, including a couple of children's movies. *Jacob Two-Two Meets the Hooded Fang* (the original 1978 version) was based on the Canadian author Mordecai Richler's first venture into the children's-lit game. This bad dream of discipline and authority features a wrestler as villain, playing the heel to the hilt: Glam Rock and wrestling do have overlaps. Such an odd and unique film, a low budget fantasy: that's Glam right there! Why, the costumes alone—the Hooded Fang's

Front cover of *The Sky Is Falling* by Lewis Furey (Aquarius Records, 1979). Author's collection.

elaborately decorated gold and crimson glittery robe is so bright it practically vibrates, hood coming up like a half shell. A mask covers half of his face. His lackeys are a silver fish man and a frizzy red-haired chicken lady. Much ridiculous, evil laughter. Like all the best children's movies (and books), this gets a bit dark. When not hidden by smog, the sets are intentionally askew. Lots of slime, too. The Slime Squad gets into abstract nightmare recesses, creatures that were inventively designed on a dime.

Furey's soundtrack, however. is softly saccharine sweet, with hints of edge and more tangos. Three Penny Cabaret sounds, ya da ya da da—fishnet stockings and tails would not be out of place. The opening of *Two-Two* has Furey's off-screen vocals introduce the plot of the movie: "Little boy, make your own way in the world . . . what if, what if, so many what ifs . . . " A fantasy where everything is heightened with grit and wildly made-up char-

Sleeve of "Sauverais-tu Ma Vie?" single by Les Petites Filles (RCA Victor, 1979). Author's collection.

acters—bumbling, old authority figures out to put kids in jail; adults change into weird villain personas; two superhero kids with capes and blue satin pants who represent Child Power, their t-shirts and musical theme proclaiming it, here to help Jacob Two-Two. It was all a dream!

The 1985 Canadian children's movie *The Peanut Butter Solution* is similarly dream-logical, not following conventional movie plot norms. A boy goes into an abandoned house and catches "the Fright," losing all his hair. In his sleep, ghosts visit him and give him a hair-growth formula containing peanut butter that works a little too well; the excess hair is then harvested by kidnapped children to make magic paintbrushes. Furey's soundtrack for *The Peanut Butter Solution* marks the English-language debut of a young Céline Dion.

Furey's third album, *The Sky Is Falling*, from 1979, was recorded partly in France, where Furey and Laure now lived. Lissauer returned to produce and arrange. The differences between the first two albums are split with an orchestral Glam strut. Yes, there is guitar: it's flanged. The epic rock opener "Jacky Paradise" was written as the theme for the Jean-Michel Ribes play *Jacky Parady*. Boundaries still get nudged with such songs as "Desire Machine" contending with itchy stuff of an array of addiction. "Thieves" is sung from the thieves' perspective, with rootin' tootin' gusto. The hit Robert Charlebois ballad "Ordinaire" is the perfect closer, with its massive orchestral wall and tinkled ivories, translated by Furey into "Ordinary Guy" with the lyric "My life is poetry. My life is song." This translation itself dates to his early Gamma days but he has been doing translation, French to English and English to French, all his life. "Translation is a great way to learn a language deeply," he says. Both Lissauer and Furey worked on Laure's debut album *Alibis* (1978), with some of Furey's earlier songs getting translated into French.

Together, Laure and Furey did a series of theatrical shows performing songs and monologues that Furey wrote. "Carole was a very popular movie star in France that also brought in a public of her own," Furey explained, "and we did very well doing shows in France and Quebec and Belgium and all the French territories." Also performing were three or four young girl singers from a ballet school. The main song that they sang in the show, "Sauverais-tu ma vie?", became a single for RCA in 1979 under the name Les Petites Filles. Furey and Laure also sing—they're practically rapping—to a disco beat. He notes, "Now they come to my shows and they're these adults. And it's really funny. They were lovely, these kids."

After much discussion of his albums, Furey admits, "I've never been that interested in records. I'm really interested in writing songs. And performing songs or having them performed. What I don't really enjoy is locking in an arrangement. I don't consider myself a classical songwriter like a Schubert or Brahms or somebody and their arrangements are never touched. These are popular songs and every time I've done a show, I've always done them a little differently. I've never done them in the same way exactly. I always feel I haven't had my last say on the arrangement of the song. About ten years ago, I did a series of concerts for a couple of years called 'Selected Songs Recital.' I had songs from my beginning to the latest ones I've written, including Brahms songs because I just did an album a couple of years ago on Brahms's *Lieder* that I translated into English and I play at the piano and sing [*Haunted by Brahms*, 2018]. I renewed again the arrangements that felt right to me at the time; some were very different. And I found the influences to some of the songs—like 'Hustler's Tango' I know was Jacob who was wrestling with the angel, from the Bible, and so I changed the way of singing the song so that there was an introduction with those passages from the King James Version about Jacob wrestling with the angel and his thigh was hurt. And, of course, he lives forevermore after that experience. And, even though I came from a Jewish family, I grew up in Protestant Montreal, in English Montreal, which was really a pretty conservative Protestant city. And when I studied poetry with

Louis Dudek[7] at McGill University, the Bible was a really important part of the studies that I had. And not to mention being taught songs, not at nursery school maybe, but in grade school. So that was a big influence in my feeling for poetry and song-writing in a way."

As much as Furey prefers the mutability of songs in live performance, his albums still feel very much alive; the performative quality comes out. And as much as I would love to see Furey in his live element, I am grateful for these albums. They are accessible and very considered recordings. The songs take hold in any setting.

THE WACKERS AND ALL THE YOUNG DUDES

THE WACKERS WERE AN AMERICAN BAND. California boys who toured everywhere in their van, they toured so much that they became everywhere's favorite local band—be it Portland or Seattle, they were voted as such and won. Early on they'd put their finger on a map and go! And once they got there they'd hit a phonebooth and find the teen dancehalls in the Yellow Pages and play.

Flash forward to recording their second album in Montreal. They liked the city so much that they all decided to move there—all but the guitarist, Mike Stull, who stayed in California. These kinds of rock band stories are usually told in reverse, with Canadian bands moving to the USA. But the Wackers loved Montreal, and the feeling was mutual. They were already all over the radio and the gigs were always packed, and the real incentive: girls chased them once—maybe twice—through the big shopping center, Alexis Nihon—the Wackers were running for their lives, and they liked it. They loved the food and the people, too.

Look, the band name is not what you think: it's British slang for "friends." The Wackers' chief songwriters were Bob Segarini and Randy Bishop. Of his and Bishop's dynamic, Segarini says, "And usually, if I'm singing it, I wrote the majority of the song; if Randy was singing, he wrote the majority, but everything he did musically was invaluable." Signed to Elektra Records, the label head, Jac Holzman, once came to visit them at their home in Eureka, California. As they took him back to the airport, he tossed them a cassette and said, "Listen to this guy. Thinking about signing him." It was *Hunky Dory* by David Bowie. Segarini says, "So Randy Bishop and I listened to the cassette over and over and over and over and over; it totally changed Randy's life; he became David Bowie and I pretty much was in awe of the writing and everything about it was incredible. And this was on a Friday night; we called Jac on Monday and went, 'Sign him! Sign him!' RCA just beat him to it; they just got him for the U.S." Released in 1971, *Hunky Dory* is pre-Ziggy, the softer side

---

7   The instructor Louis Dudek was a massive influence on the poetry world. He published Cohen's first chapbook, as part of the McGill Poetry Series.

Front cover of *Wackering Heights* by the Wackers (Elektra, 1971). Author's collection.

of Bowie, three-ply and gloriously pretty. There's no denying the influence that it had on the Wackers, along with the even stronger Beatles influence. Hey, they can get away with it: Segarini had already been in a few bands (including the Family Tree and Roxy—which the Wackers sprang out of). He says, "I know a lot of people and I don't know why, but everybody I know wasn't famous when I knew them. Harry Nilsson—you're looking at the only guy ever co-wrote a song with Harry Nilsson except for John Lennon. Only our song that we wrote together was great. He wrote one on my piano."

Being the frontmen, Segarini and Bishop dressed up to the hilt. Segarini notes, "We were up there in feather boas and glitter in our hair. One of us [Spencer T. "Ernie" Earnshaw] looked like a hippie because he was a hippie—one of the greatest drummers in North America. The rhythm section was a serious fucking thing." Segarini elaborates on

Bishop: "He really got into it. We did Carnegie Hall. I have a picture. He's wearing a full-length purple bodysuit, a pair of hot pants, and these wooden high heeled sandals—he had this guy making them. Long hair and a rhinestone scarf. Melanie Bishop, his first wife, encouraged that a lot. They were off to the Lime Light[8] every fifteen minutes in Montreal. It's the lifestyle, man, David Bowie. I mean, I was impacted more by Lennon at that time and he was impacted more by David Bowie. And it worked out."

Melanie Bishop loved Glam and really pushed the aesthetic limits for the Wackers. Randy wanted to mess with gender conventions and shock people.[9] Segarini was no slouch either: just pick up the August 1973 issue of *Creem* magazine with its headline "MEET ROCK'S DECA-SEXUAL ELITE!", flip to the article "The Androgyny Hall of Fame"—amongst the many photos of the luminaries the Sweet, the GTOs, Bowie, etc. is a photo of Segarini in makeup. The article describes the Wackers: "As the first mainstream American rock & roll band into makeup, a fairly accurate barometer of the acceptability of deca-rock's accoutrements." Oh, so much makeup, gobs and gobs. Randy got a shag haircut, framing his high—and well blushed—cheekbones perfectly.

And clothing. Living in Montreal, they would hit the St. Vincent de Paul thrift store and the then more au courant Le Château. Segarini noted, "I spent more money in that place buying girly fucking clothes. But at the time it wasn't girly. It was cool." About such aesthetics of Glam etc., Segarini says, "It's just inherent: little girls love boys that are little girls. Go figure. It's not a sexual thing, it's taking down a barrier." When I call his attire "costumes," I am swiftly corrected: these weren't costumes.

As for Montreal's nightlife, Segarini says, "There was a big gay community there, the Lime Light—remember this, there were dance clubs there that five thousand people would be at and it was very chic. Compared to anywhere else that we had been—New York, Boston, blah blah—even New York paled to the cosmopolitan feel of Montreal—very sophisticated city. And everybody was well dressed. I mean the women in Montreal—if I got dragged into a bathroom for some girl to blow me, she'd be in a fucking twelve-hundred-dollar pale green suede skirt and coat—I mean, they dressed beautifully, everybody was coiffed and turned out, you know?" He says of the recording studios, "There wasn't a bad studio. None of them were bad." When not hanging out in bars with the Montreal musicians, Segarini was regularly seeing shows by this community of incredible talent: Nanette Workman, Pagliaro, all of Walter Rossi's bands, Moonquake . . .

They used their stage moves to let the music talk. And personable banter. And glitter. Pounds of glitter. Opening for the Ventures in Montreal, their set began in darkness with a loud recording of their own spacey music on the PA about an alien rock 'n' roll being, with the band quietly and oh so secretly hitting their marks, individual spotlights coming

---

8 The massive and diverse Montreal discotheque that opened in 1973.

9 YouTube interview with Randy Bishop, "Wack in the Saddle Again," Bob Segarini blog, 1/26/2019.

up and hitting them like they had literally teleported on stage, materializing from parts unknown à la *Star Trek* amidst a shower of glitter let loose from a snow-bag made of cheesecloth. Adds Segarini, "I was pulling glitter out of my fucking pubes for two years after this shit." And then they rocked. Yes, they believed in putting on a show, but they also put the music first. As Segarini says, "You better have something behind the dressing-up thing that works."

The Wackers were getting tons of great press—but it wasn't for the albums. Their first album, *Wackering Heights,* released in 1971, was named for their not-for-much-longer gorgeous Eureka, California, home, an album that is oh so 'Luded out mellowwwww that it would be Laurel Canyon landfill, apart from a couple of moments. Their first two albums were produced by the legendary producer Gary Usher. Segarini explains, "The people that wrote about us saw us live. So they'd rave about us and the records would never match what they're talking about. A rock and roll band? These guys sound like Crosby, Stills, and Nash—you know, slick, and that was Usher—which is weird because he co-wrote 'In My Room' with Brian Wilson; he mixed a lot of Beatles stuff for America—the singles, the Byrds' *Sweetheart of the Rodeo, Younger Than Yesterday*: the best Byrds album. He did all that stuff. We figured he would do that with us." Segarini does mention two shining moments with Usher on their 1972 album *Hot Wacks*: the well-produced and -arranged rocker "Wait and See" and their John Lennon cover "Oh My Love," done in such a faithful *Abbey Road* style that it wound up on Beatles bootlegs.

Though this album had much more oomph, with the Beatles and *Hunky Dory* Bowie influences coming more to the fore, the album cover that they wanted for *Hot Wacks* was rejected. The reason? They said, "You look like girls, you're gonna turn off your core audience." Segarini said, "No, know we're not gonna turn off anybody, we get more pussy than you can possibly imagine!" It was no use, "because Randy and I looked too much like girls and then five minutes later: David Bowie, Alice Cooper. We were ahead of the curve and they stopped us from being ahead of the curve!" The actual cover shows the band hanging out on the corner. The more effective back cover goes for the faux hand-tinting, adding blush artifice to their cheeks amidst the very tight clothing, plush velvet pants made for Segarini by Pamela Courson,[10] the bassist Kootch casting spells in a star-spangled wizard robe, Mike Stull in a satin jacket borrowed from Randy.

While recording their 1973 album *Shredder*, Segarini says, "Jac Holzman comes up with his replacement for *Shredder*—Mark Abramson. Mark Abramson is Judy Collins' producer. This is a twee folk guy with glasses; tall, lanky. The guy's wife was a soap star actress. And he lived in a fucking chalet in Vermont, just completely the antithesis of what I wanted to have. And then he made *Shredder* and the only problem I ever had with that record was we had three great songs and he insisted on putting that jam on there—which

---

10 Pamela Courson had a boutique called Themis across the street from Elektra Records. Jim Morrison was her long-term companion.

some people like, so go figure. But so, we went in to do the fourth album, which was going to be called *Wacker High* because we played so many high schools."

More representative of what they really were, *Wacker High* became *Wack 'n' Roll*, with most of the bed tracks recorded live. The opening track, a live track, has a proto–Juicy Fruits intro with a "Fuck off" into an adrenalinized '50s rock 'n' roll nod all about, you guessed it, rock 'n' roll, with a Chuck Berry–style solo. "In the Aisles," with its very T.-Rexy groove, is saying, "Rise and stomp, we'll put the bomp" with "Glammy slammy," "rock is grand," and "stardust is the style," a half-belched "Yeahhh," a half-anthem touching the sky, getting all the queenies and "fledgling freakies" up to dance in the aisles. Then there's a smoky, sultry ballad, "Juvenile Delinquent," trying to go all "Hey Jude" on us at the end.

Some of these songs were recorded after *Shredder* and some were recorded during *Hot Wacks*: when the producer's away the mice will play; they had the keys to the studio and the impetus, after dinner and drinks down the street, recording an all-nighter of eight songs, four of which were to be on *Wack 'n' Roll*.

With *Wack 'n' Roll,* the band knew that they had something special and true that would break them big. Everyone was poised—the bands, the fans, the press. Holzman sold Elektra Records but loved the Wackers so much that before he left he gave them a seven-album deal. Then the band's manager, Norman Schwartz, messed it all up with just one phone call to the new label head, David Geffen, that was so offensive (details I shan't be printing here—allusions to the manager's ignorant foot-in-mouth homophobia and epithets) they were dropped, with the band only finding out why years later. They were now persona non grata and that was that, though they packed a lot into a short three and a half years. *Wack 'n' Roll* languished. One song came out as a single on Bomp! The album remains unreleased, other than two hundred copies made for the Wackers reunion show at Cherry Cola in Toronto in 2011—very much an event, as it had been thirty-eight years since they had played together.

After the Wackers broke up, Randy went on to a solo career and had a couple of top-ten singles. Ernie Earnshaw went back to California. Segarini was down; he was hurting. He loved the Wackers, a band that never fought and had fun. He was in a funk. His wife asked, "When are you going to leave the house?" Booking time at Studio 6, what was then the cheapest and diviest—though quite open-minded—studio, he used their innovative drum machine—built from a plywood box using pushpins to make the drum sounds—and recorded the warmest power-pop ballad with strummed guitar and synth, half French and half English vocals and multi-track harmony. This song has that warm early-drum-machine sound that I love Robin Gibb's *Robin's Reign*, Timmy Thomas, and Sly and the Family Stone's *There's a Riot Goin' On* for. His wife asked, "Well?" Playing her the tape, he replied, "Oh yeah, I'm back on." Segarini then set about putting together a refurbished Wackers 2.0, with Kootch. They auditioned a kid named Wayne Cullen who knew all of Earnshaw's drum parts and recorded a single for Polydor, a mid-tempo rocker with

Back and front cover of *Hot Wacks* by the Wackers (Elektra, 1972). Front cover, author's collection. Back cover courtesy collection of Ian Marshall.

Inner gatefold of *Shredder* by the Wackers (Elektra, 1972). Album courtesy collection of Ian Marshall.

cowbell and handclaps. Out of that sprang forth their band All the Young Dudes, adding the future April Wine member Brian Greenway and two former April Wine members, the Henman brothers, David and Ritchie, whose band Silver was just breaking up. This meant not just two brothers but also two guitarists and two drummers who were so in sync that they could have been brothers.

David and Ritchie Henman were founding members of April Wine, the classic Canadian coke-'n'-cock-rock band that had a reputation for creating arena rock hits, songs that sounded like a back-of-the-newsprint-magazine ad for a dual coke-spoon mustache comb, they were a soundtrack for your custom van waterbed springing a leak and smelling up the shag. April Wine cruised out from their birthplace of Nova Scotia to Montreal in 1970 and cut an album. There they stayed and cut more albums. The April Wine B-side "I Get Bad" really bangs a gong; other than the direct and typical come-on-baby lyrics, there's no mistaking the T. Rex sound, written by David Henman: this is the band at their most Glam. Henman clearly loved Glam, even forming a later band called the Debutantes. Segarini says, "I have a picture of David Henman wearing what looks to appear to be a pixies top with little tassels on it." Those Nova Scotian Henman brothers were the Glam-loving weapons, and in between April Wine and All the Young Dudes they did just one single as Silver in 1973. This song, "Serpent in the Street," has got Glam in it along with some other stuff as well—caramel, nuts, wafers, sweet riffin' . . . I'd have loved to have heard more from them. That song was actually supposed to be on the 1973 April Wine album *Electric Jewels*,[11] but the Henmans left the band during the album sessions. After they left, April

---

11 *Electric Jewels* is a very good album of stoner rock with a Glammed out cover: a sparkly guitar zooms out from the stars of hyper-space and right out atcha—poke an eye out. The song "Just Like That" is a Glammy stomper.

Wine released *The Whole World's Goin' Crazy*,[12] with two songs falling into the Velvet Tinmine niche of Glam.

When they came up with the band name, All the Young Dudes got excited. They were named after the pivotal Glam anthem "All the Young Dudes," which David Bowie wrote for Mott the Hoople when they were on the verge of breaking up and, well, giving up. Bowie blessed Mott with the song and it saved the band. It was a hit! And Mott the Hoople's Ian Hunter gave his blessing to All the Young Dudes the band! And became a friend—a friendship helped along by Hunter and All the Young Dudes sharing a manager—the pleasure of business.

All the Young Dudes recorded a bunch of powerful demos that Segarini expertly produced. Cowbell clops in on one with big rock riffs and a twangy vocal, a city driving song. A cover of Chuck Berry's "Little Queenie" done as '70s rock and still loads of lively fun with lots of posing in the vocals. Some prerequisite ersatz reggae (everyone seemed to be doing that then), with both drummers ricocheting like steel drums. Another one where you hear the riffs, the vocal character, and the big big beats. Followed by some pure AM gold. A country rocker called "Sugar" going fully on the double drums—the big dynamics of the two drummers were used so well. Then there was a song that Henman wrote, causing Segarini to go, "We got to do this man, this is the greatest Alice Cooper song never written." Called "Meet You After School," it is heavy dank shock and doom rock riff and thunder drums and a purely villainous mustache-twirling voice: "Can I meet you after school? Can we take the long way home?" as the two lead guitars build and wail, driving it home—then, just when you think it is over—no, it comes back! A right nasty bit of camp, heightened horror musical that caused silence from everyone after playback.

April Wine and Thundermug live concert ad. Image courtesy of *The Ottawa Citizen*, June 12, 1976.

These were solid, well-produced demos, and, on the strength of them, All the Young Dudes got signed to CBS for a quarter of a million dollars cash U.S. It was a massive signing, yet Segarini says, "And it didn't even make news here. The Dudes couldn't get a deal in Canada. We signed with New York, man." And the label made them shorten their name to Dudes—just Dudes.

Dudes recorded a cover of the girl-group classic "Please Mr. Postman" by the Marvelettes with big drums and hand claps and jangly guitar and sent it to CBS, telling them, "Put

---

12 With a cheap-looking drawing of the Mad Hatter on the cover, the record label marketing department got some poor soul to dress up as the character and hit the record stores.

The Dudes: From left, Wayne Cullen, Kootch Trochim, Bob Segarini, Brian Greenway, Ritchie Henman and David Henman.

All the Young Dudes. Image courtesy of the *Gazette*, September 6, 1975.

it out, man. It should be our first single." The label refused. Six weeks later the Carpenters had a number-one hit with it.

Kim Fowley was sending Segarini songs all the time. Segarini explains, "Him and Mars Bonfire would send me a reel-to-reel tape describing the next big thing and it was going to be a rock–disco hybrid. And he was convinced that the Dudes were going to be this thing, constantly sending me lyrics. The one thing I remember in the fucking reel-to-reel where they're just talking to me about what's going to happen in music. None of it accurate. At the end of it, Kim's still talking, and I hear the fucking toilet flush. And they start laughing. And that is because while he was talking, Mars went into the bathroom, had a leak, I guess. The door was right there. So, I think we all went, you know, this is bullshit, we all know it. It was fun. It was funny."

With their album about to be released, Dudes were selected to open for the Bee Gees on the eastern-Canada leg of their 1975 Main Course tour. Barely anyone knew it when Dudes were booked, but this was the Bee Gees' massive comeback, with the number-one disco hit "Jive Talkin'." Segarini says, "They were a dream to work with. I've never been treated that well before. I can tell you a million stories of how nice these guys were. We got an encore at the Montreal Forum: 15,000 people stood up and all three brothers were standing on the stage. And I looked over and Barry went, 'Take it.' They told us to take the encore. That doesn't happen." After the Montreal Forum show, there was a big party in a suite at the Ritz Forum with the likes of Ian Hunter and Kim Fowley flying in for it. Buckets of Kentucky Fried Chicken were everywhere at the hotels on tour, a current fixation of Barry's. Segarini asked Barry if he had any advice about songwriting. Barry replied, "If it takes longer than three minutes, don't bother."

Dressing casual, being funky and funny, and kicking ass on stage, the label gave Dudes money for some threads: the suits gave them cash for some suits for the album and suits they got. Three-piece suits, dressed for success, or, in the case of this 1975 album, a funeral. It looked like all the elements for greatness were there. They were album-cover poised and ready for their session with Art Kane, head photographer for *Penthouse* magazine as well

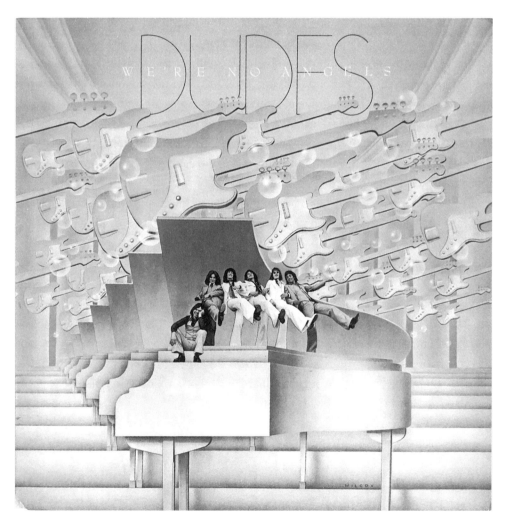

Front cover of *We're No Angels* by Dudes (Columbia, 1975). Album courtesy collection of Ian Marshall.

as *Viva,* an erotic magazine for women (including a pictorial that the probably all-male bullpen came up with of women's pubic hair coiffed and trimmed into hearts and arrows).

The album jacket has numerous touches that scream Glam: an art-deco-style cover in dusty rose and cream of repeated guitars and pianos, liner notes by Greg Shaw of *Bomp!* talking them up to the high heavens, and a song co-written by Kim Fowley that gave the album its name: *We're No Angels.*

A Montreal super-duper group in the best sense of the word, with all those frontmen, guitars, and drums, nothing getting in the way of each other, they were working together, and what could stand in their way? Segarini says flat out, "CBS destroyed that band with the worst record I've ever been part of. And so bad that André Perry and Nick Blagona (of the very reputable Le Studio) said, we will give you $75,000 worth of studio time in the studio, so you can recut this. CBS said no. The only good thing about it was the engineer from New York and Mark [Spector], the guy that produced it, never worked again. Oh my God, they sucked the life out of the band, they wouldn't let us use both drummers." No double drums?!? "There aren't any because they said, 'We can't. It'll sound weird.' Yeah, that's the point, asshole!"

That's right, the album sounded so bad that another studio offered to step in and recut it for free! What a dud of an album, a wet fart. The album did not play to their strengths. The songs "Teenage Love," "Sugar," and "Meet Me After School" were all left off. Honestly, they should have just released the demos. Dudes even had material for their second album, *Gotta Have Pop*, recorded, including a title track done later to lesser effect on a solo Segarini album. And so Dudes dissolved. Segarini broke the band up because, what's the point?

In 1997 these songs finally got released on CD as *All the Young Dudes . . . All the Old Demos*. Bob Segarini died in Toronto in July 2023 at the age of seventy-seven.

STANLEY FRANK

AT JUST TWO AND A HALF MINUTES, "S'cool Days" by Stanley Frank packs a punch. Feelin' good, this is Creamsicle rock. Yum! Tight tees, tight jeans, and empty bottles of peroxide strewn about a lacquered bathroom. It pops! It's pop. "School Days" is a song title and trope oft-used throughout Glam because hey, Chuck Berry did it, but throw in an apostrophe so it is now like two words in one? Why, that kind of double meaning playfulness and creative spelling just makes it more Glam. And it is a capper here. It wins the Glam achievement award; the metric-system equivalent is a Solid Gold Participaction badge for eating the most Creamsicles at recess. We're all winners! The British single sleeve even looks like a Creamsicle—popping all orange and white, bubble lettering, and showing us their etching of Stanley Frank looking right at us, collar popping. It's a hit! In the USA, Greg Shaw put "S'cool Days" in his All-Time Power Pop Records list in *Bomp!* magazine.

Sleeve of "S'Cool Days" single by Stanley Frank (Power Exchange Records, 1976). Author's collection.

Despite the title, it isn't telling us that school is cool—no, like the others of the form, it is saying to us kids that school can be a real drag, man. Rapid fire lyrics—"Teacher says what teacher knows and in his face you know it shows the feeling that he's growing old"—only slowing down enough at points to sarcastically ask, "Ain't that nice?" "S'cool Days" roolz with sweet oolas and dit dit dit dit multi-tongued intonations, screams, a crackling riff, Morse-code piano, hand claps and toms and chant-along chorus. We can't keep up! This is his most Glam song and wow, what a song. How did it get made?

Good question! Well, back in 1975, in Montreal—where he was born and raised—Stanley Frank hit Studio 6 in the East End, a studio that did production deals—a cut of the profits in exchange for studio time. To back him up the studio got a band called Cockroach, uncredited probably because of the name—Frank sarcastically notes, "Chicks really go for

Front cover of *Rejected* by Stanley Frank (Polydor, 1977). Author's collection.

that." Frank told them what he wanted and they laid it down. When he finished laying down the impressive vocals in one take, the studio guys in the booth applauded.

When "S'cool Days" was written it was to be one section of a four-part suite inspired by the 1971 movie *Carnal Knowledge*: 1. the wonderment of childhood, 2. "S'cool Days," 3. turning thirty, and finally, 4. much older. The first time he recorded it as a demo, there was no guitar so he just went, "Dit dit dit dit dit dit," with his mouth and it worked. Those dit dit dits stuck.

He then took a train to Toronto and hit the record companies who acted all Goldilocks and the Three Bears on him: some said, "It's too hard," and others said, "It's not hard enough." Frank says, "Anyway, here's the story. I think it's pretty good. I was just walking around and my train left at six o'clock to go back to Montreal and I have an hour and a half to kill, it was snowing and it was lousy. So, I went to this record company called Attic Records. And I called them up and the lady says, 'Well, sorry, Mr. Williams can't see you today.' I said, 'Listen, I got something really good for him.' You know, basically, I just wanted a warm place to sit for a while. 'Well, he's not going to see you.' And I said, 'Well, you know what, I'm coming down anyway.' So, I came down and she says, 'He's not going to see you.' And I said, 'Well, I'm here, maybe he'll come out.' Anyway, he finally did come out. He didn't look very happy about it. And I gave him the song and he went in, he came out, and he looked at me and says, 'I can't believe it,' he says. 'It's incredible!' And that was the start."

It was now 1976. Attic Records put their weight on it and released it in Canada, they pushed it, they believed in it. And it flopped. It did nothing. Canada didn't know and didn't care what it had. The end.

No! Not the end. Never the ever-loving end. Enter the taste-maker Robert Charles-Dunne, who knew a good thing when he heard it. He loved it and he loved Attic Records. Charles-Dunne explains, "When a pal in the U.K. sent me a new single called 'I'm Stranded' by the Saints, from Australia, I noticed that the label releasing it in the U.K. was run by someone with whom I was distantly acquainted. I thought if they had good enough ears to hear the brilliance of Australia's Saints, maybe they'd have good enough ears to hear the brilliance of Canada's Stanley too. So I sent them a copy, unsolicited, cold calling. They phoned to say that the female label staff would not stop playing it and dancing to it. Could I put them in touch with the guys at the Attic label?"

Before shipping it off to England, Attic Records got Willi Morrison and Ian Guenther of the THP Orchestra and other disco productions to remix it. They sprinkled a bit of pixie dust on it and, to make him sound younger, they sped it up. It was already a whole lotta words packed in to almost three minutes, but now with the sped-up recording, doing it live was almost too much to handle. Others have tried to cover it, but you ever scale Mount Everest? Look at all those bodies on the way up—you could be next.

Influenced by the versatility of the Beatles and seeing that as a plus, the B side "On a Line" was his take-off of a country song, but really it jangles. The label, Power Exchange Records, also released a split EP version with Frank's songs on one side, the Saints on the other side.

And, sure enough, it was climbing up the charts, earning great reviews in the British press with the *New Musical Express* calling it "Superfine!" and *Sounds* saying that it had more energy than the Sex Pistols and Ultravox combined. Frank got cred, the kind of Canadian cred that only happens when you are first validated in another country. Attic called him up and said, "Get over to England, it's happening over there!" Stanley couldn't go over just yet. Why? "The reason was I was with a girl I just met and we went through this whole drama where she was kicked out of her family's home because she was with me." I asked him, "You were a bad influence?" "I don't blame them. I didn't want to leave her alone."

In the meantime, Attic got him in the studio. He did an all-nighter, recording eight songs in twelve hours, recorded live off the floor with his new big muff distorting the hell out of everything, guitars overdriven, it rumbles. It is raw and reckless right from the first song, with him screaming, "You're doing alright!" Another song, "Hey Stupid," was stark, full of anger that no one gave him the time of day until "S'cool Days." His cover of choice was John Lennon's "Cold Turkey." One writer thought that this version more accurately conveyed the harrowing pains of addiction than the original did. How did he capture this gut-wrenching intensity? Through actual gut-wrenching. Frank explains, "Well, the truth is, is that at about three in the morning, we wanted to get something to eat so we went over to this smoked meat place called Dunn's and I had this smoked meat and I came back to this studio and I puked my guts out, totally, my stomach wasn't ready for that kind of meat or whatever. And then I went out and sang 'Cold Turkey.'" Post smoked meat puke mixed with adrenaline—the session was dripping with attitude. Looking on in the studio as well were David Henman and Bob Segarini from Dudes, with Henman joining in on vocals for what may be the best song from the session, "I Want to Really Care." You know that feeling you get when you are desperate to feel something—anything—and will just go for it? This song captures that tension. It slices, it dices, it doesn't blink—the song was ahead of its time.

Frank was going to have a management team, including an odd man who elbowed his way into the picture and pushed the others out: Ihor Fu Fangio was his name, an obvious pseudonym. Tellingly, his company was called Piranha Productions. Once it ended with Attic, Fangio bought the demo tapes from them, then took just four of those songs, seemingly at random, to Polydor. Polydor loved the rawness of the demos and released them as is, no sweetening. They could have fit more songs on this twelve-inch EP—shockingly, "I Want to Really Care" went unreleased until years later when Frank's daughter Christine posted it to YouTube. The sleeve art, by Fangio himself at his graphic arts studio, went high contrast: Frank porcelain-skinned, ciggie hanging out of his mouth, slicking his hair back, with bright ruby red lipstick and yellow mascara added in post, a faux hand-tinted touch—though he was no stranger to makeup and chains around his neck, the title *REJECTED* stamped along the side: ouch.

A full-page ad for *Rejected* in *Billboard* (January 14, 1978), with uncredited copy but seemingly written by Fangio, mentions the handshake deal with Polydor and then how, when Fangio presented Frank with the record, he smashed it over his knee.

Frank had no say; Polydor released *Rejected* without his permission. Frank explains the situation with Fangio: "So, Polydor and he had a worldwide release and he never had a contract and so about two months into our contract I sued him, I got out of it. I was throwing up, I was so stressed out. He read a book about Colonel Tom Parker, the guy that managed Elvis Presley, and Parker really exploited Elvis. But, also his Bible, and I should have known this, you just don't think sometimes, but his Bible was a book called *Winning*

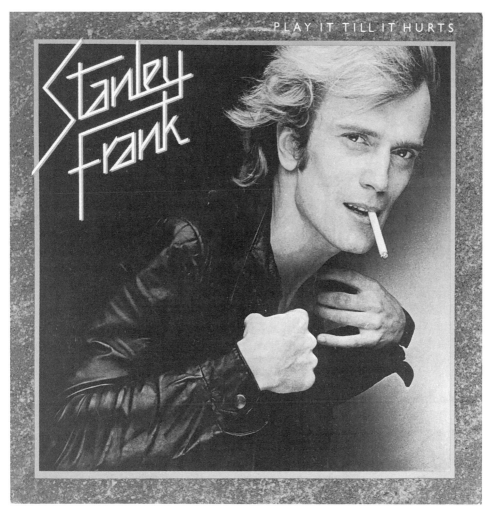

Front cover of *Play It Till It Hurts* by Stanley Frank (A&M Records, 1980). Author's collection.

Through Intimidation. It was kind of a bestseller there for a bit, that basically you screw everybody, get them to sign, don't pay them until . . . , give them some bones, don't give them all the money they're supposed to get. And he thought this was the way to do it. He was like the Donald Trump of pop music or something."

Mess in the courts means no better time to finally get away to England for a few months. Frank had a reputation from "S'cool Days" over there—though, admittedly, the British label that released it went bankrupt and no one saw a penny. But he did go over to Polydor and got a few bucks out of them. In England, he soaked up the culture and saw some teddy boys listening to "Summertime Blues" by Eddie Cochran. This inspired his first full-length album. As he put it, "My idea was to write an album that had the rock-and-roll way of expressing modern ideas, you know, like, not the old rock-and-roll lyrics." After

Stanley Frank. Image courtesy of the *Vancouver Sun*, January 27, 1981.

he got signed by Mike Godin at A&M, this became the crux of his 1980 album *Play It Till It Hurts,* produced by Robin Cable, who had worked with Roy Thomas Baker on *Queen II*. A few years prior, Godin had wanted to release "S'cool Days" but was too new at A&M to make it happen. *Play It Till It Hurts* is a hodge-podge of styles, with songs like "Rock Crazy,", a cover of "Good Lovin'," a pogo-ing curiosity called "Nylon Meat Dreams," and some ersatz reggae that later landed on a *Rock'n'Reggae Party* comp. Frank toured the album across Canada and over to Europe, where he played forty-one shows.

    A&M later called him up to renew their contract with him and set up a demo recording session with the Glam god guitarist Mick Ronson over at Bearsville Studios in Woodstock, New York. Frank had nothing but glowing things to say about him: "Ronson with his arrangements—and he was able to do string arrangements—added a dimension to Bowie's stuff." Frank stayed with Ronson and his wife Suzi in New York. When Ronson picked him up he asked him, "Are you hungry?" and cooked Frank up a steak—"A little peppah! A little of this!" Ronson loved to cook. Frank did two separate sessions with him, about nine songs total, all officially unreleased, including a song named "Canadian Boy." "Run for the Sun" is the perfect summer song that Ronson also sings and plays on, a power-pop gem. And then there's "Scum Heaven," a nasty take-off on the well-worn "all the rock stars are jamming together up in heaven" trope, sharply jabbing at the idol in idolatry.

    Frank kept recording demos into the '90s. He gets called power pop, he gets called new wave, rock too, a real slip through the pavement cracks, but the Glam is there and you can contact him to cover his songs through his website, where a good number of these demos are posted. Hold on a sec. The website is down. Sorry.

The guy who wrote "S'cool Days" became a teacher, an ESL teacher teaching refugees from Rwanda, the Balkans, and Nicaragua. Frank wrote a book, *This World of Ours*, filled with activities to help advanced level ESL students gain fluency on more of a cultural level.

For fifteen years, Frank has been an in-demand working musician playing for seniors in retirement homes, hospitals, palliative care, and long-term care facilities doing standards like "As Time Goes By." One year he played three hundred shows. He'd still throw in the odd kick and, in a similar move to the old days when he'd leap off the stage scaffolding, get up on the furniture.

BONUS TRACKS!

THE ANGRY YOUNG DUCKS

Montreal's Angry Young Ducks were popular for Tubes-like performances. The music is saxophone-driven art rock moving into a realm of dreamy Romantic Glam. A Halifax poster on the Steve Hoffman site says: "The Angry Young Ducks. They were from Montreal. I saw them in '79 or '80 and they played a crazy mix of originals, Zappa, the theme to Hockey Night in Canada, you name it. I remember the guitar player wore an Expos batting helmet with a whirling propeller on top."

STUART SATURN, THE SINGING ASTROLOGER

Hailing from Miami, Stuart Saturn the Singing Astrologer landed in Montreal and hooked up with some young Montreal prog musicians who probably played on his rather groovy and cosmic rock album released in 1979, though he credits himself for pretty much everything—so many synths—even though the cover hyperbole says that there are guest appearances by "George Harrison, Eric Clapton, Donna Summer, . . . "—the casual and suspicious name-drops go on. God is also thanked: "Enclosed the secrets of my power to success." With waxed and creative facial hair, he holds a crystal ball up close and personal. In the insert he says that he has done readings for many famous people, including David Bowie. Believe the hype—believe everything you read. If you are looking for verification, do understand that it was self-released. One song is "What's Your Sign in the Zodiac?" And, yeah, it's Glammy! What happened to the Singing Astrologer? He disappeared! The music historian Pascal Pilote and friends have undertaken trying to find him . . . have they? The mystery deepens.

LPS AND 45s

LA BANDE À BENNY LP
(MULTI-POP, 1975)

Led by Pierre "Benny" Gervais, the vocals are soft and sweet like a younger brother politely asking for more of that delicious butterscotch pudding. Quebec's Bay City Rollers but as a much gentler laxative. Yet the cover to their eponymous 1975 album has them in action poses—one could misconstrue it as belonging to the "wrestler as singer" genre—monogrammed satin robes getting loose, baring a shoulder, a nipple, some calf. Is the song "Vivre à l'Américaine" sarcastic? Surely "Sexy Baby" isn't. Produced by Les Sinners' drummer, Louis Parizeau. Their song "Super Lady" was later covered by Stereo Total on their *Carte postale de Montréal* album.

CONNEXION—*UN EMPLOYÉ* LP
(1975, RCA)

The Montreal band Connexion's 1975 RCA album does the heavy guitar rock *en français*, with lot of soloing, but one song, "Un Employé," has got Glam thud, probably by accident.

WITCH QUEEN—"BANG A GONG
(GET IT ON)" 12"
(UNISON, 1979)

After proving himself with the pulsing disco minimalism of Kebekelektrik and working on Guy Lafleur's odd hockey instructional disco hybrid,[13] the noted Montreal dance music producer Gino Soccio recorded with the Muscle Shoals rhythm section in 1979 as the studio band Witch Queen to release a ten-minute, by-the-numbers disco version of the T. Rex classic. A TV appearance featured lip-synchers and weightlifters flexing their muscles.

---

13 Released in both French and English versions.

NEW YORK DOLLS IN CANADA: JOHNNY (THUNDERS) APPLESEEDS

New York Dolls inspired so many bands to form. Danger formed after seeing them play to fewer than a hundred people in Montreal on June 16, 1974. The guitarist Walter Rossi's heavy rock band Charlee opened. Angelo Finaldi, who was Charlee's bassist that night, says, "The sound was awful in that fucking place. And Walter, he played loud. He played very, very loud." New York Dolls were loud too, in a venue that sounded like a tin can, very unpleasant. Finaldi bonded with Sylvain Sylvain of New York Dolls: "He was cultured. He read, this guy—he's no fucking dummy, this guy Sylvain Sylvain. Smart fucking guy, man. Very smart. We got along."

In Vancouver on March 13, 1974, New York Dolls played a sold-out show at the fabulous Commodore and fittingly Sweeney Todd opened. In true Pied Piper fashion, New York Dolls again left their mark on another city, this time influencing the formation of the key Vancouver punk band the Modernettes and the Young Canadians. The *Province* music columnist Jeani Read wasn't having it, though; her scathing review of the Commodore concert ended, "If glitter rock isn't dead yet, groups like the Dolls are definitely going to kill it."

In Sylvain's memoir *There's No Bones in Ice Cream,* he mentions their first Canadian show in Toronto, on October 27, 1973, stating that the opening act, Rush, "was scarcely a blend we'd have chosen for ourselves."¹ Future members of the Toronto punk bands the Diodes and the "B" Girls excitedly showed up. Lucasta Ross of the "B" Girls states, "Yes, I was at every single Glam show and yes . . . I am forever scarred by Rush opening for the Dolls!!!!!" John Catto of the Diodes notes, "Basically, the people who put together the first Toronto punk bands and formed most of the core audience and the front row of any glam show from 72-74 are exactly the same people! It's a comparatively small group really, 50 to 100 people."

Much has been written about the influential Hamilton punk band Teenage Head. They were deeply rooted in Glam, having formed early on in 1974. In an interview with the CBC Radio show Q from

Ad for New York Dolls in Montreal. Image courtesy of the *Montreal Star*, September 14, 1974.

June 16, 2019, the bassist, Steve Mahon, mentions how he clipped everything he could find of New York Dolls from magazines into scrapbooks and even attempted to make his own platform boots in shop class. Teenage Head's self-titled first album is a pivotal Canadian punk classic and one can ever so clearly hear a more straight-ahead take on the Dolls template. Released in 1978, *Teenage Head* had the Glam hallmarks of big frizzy hair and pink shirts.

Their next Toronto date, June 15, 1974, had KISS, who were influenced greatly by New York Dolls, as the openers.

MORSE CODE TRANSMISSION— "SATAN'S SONG" 7" (RCA, 1972)

This French Canadian prog rock band stretches wayyyy out on their second album, a double album from 1972, but this single B side keeps it down to three minutes. Still, the evil cannot be contained—this is scary stoner Glam thud. Are they playing the chords to conjure up the Devil himself? That is an ominous riff, to be sure!!!! Or is just spy music gone "woooooo"? No matter what, my chalice runneth over with sticky sweet stage blood! Back it up—I hear voices. It's actually the double album closer, what a way to end a trip . . . screaming! How's the A side? Oh, it's rather pleasant: "Satan's Song" is the closest they got to Glam—maybe they should have offered up more music to the Dark Lord instead of tapping away all those dots and dashes.

RICK E. BLUE AND SONIC STEW— "SUMMERLOVE SENSATION" 7"(PLANET RECORDS)

When people say that they hate musical comedy, "Canada's favorite musical comedy duo" (their term), Bowser and Blue, are the epitome of that unfortunate feeling, with their forced Canada-specific political material. Prior to that ill-fated team-up, the Blue in Bowser and Blue released a single as Rick E. Blue and Sonic Stew. Side B features an ersatz Caribbeana steel-drum instrumental which sure sounds nice, thanks to the skilled production of Montreal Sound, who previously did *Canadian Christmas,* an over-the-top lavish disco album that took tons of musicians and studio time— Santa riding a rocket with a glittery silver disco diva on the cover. For the A side, Rick E. Blue covered the Bay City Rollers hit "Summerlove Sensation," which had a bubblegum sweetness. Rick E. Blue and Sonic Stew take it and just add water, simmer for far too long, and serve when tepid.

Front cover to *La Bande à Benny* album by La Bande à Benny (Multi-Pop, 1976). Author's collection.

TINKER'S MOON—"SHANG-A-LANG" 7" AND "TING A LING DING"/"NOW THAT SUMMER IS OVER" 7" (POLYDOR, 1974)

1974's "Shang A Lang" is a Bay City Rollers cover from a Montreal studio band. It's nice. The B Side, "I'm Sad," written by Rosina Bucci, feels like a Rollers ballad but it's not. They had a couple other singles, written by Bucci, as well: the very AM-radio-sounding "Ooh Baby Baby" and "Ting A Ling Ding," an obvious sound-alike follow-up to "Shang-A-Lang," with guitar blasts and piano tinkle, about a song that was just too catchy. The B side is even better, with bigger Glam drums, smashes, and big bells ringing. Alas, it still has that showband vocal—it's almost like the musicians are trying their best to wipe him out, but he is just too high in the mix.

SLASH—"JACK THE RIPPER" 7" (1974, UNITED ARTISTS)

A mystery 45 from 1974 on United Artists Canada... super fuzzed-out with the "Rock and Roll Part 2" rhythm and handclaps and vocal ahhhhhs that could totally take over the dancefloor. The lead vocal is so fazed. "Jack the Ripper gonna rip ya up . . . "—much maniacal laughter. This thing is nasty! Definitely from the unsavory, shock-value side of Glam, provocative for the sake of being provocative. Performed by the rock group Slash but written and produced by Paul Gross, who did a lot of work for United Artists.

CHAPTER 7
THE MARITIMES

IN THE MARITIME PROVINCES OF NOVA SCOTIA, New Brunswick, and Prince Edward Island, nary a Glam Rock sound could be heard. That being said, Glam elements flower up in unlikely ways. From New Brunswick, Alexander Varty left for Vancouver, British Columbia, in 1977. Before that, the closest band that he could think of to Glam in that area was April Wine, who formed in 1969 in Nova Scotia, the next province over, then took off the next year to Montreal. As for attire, Varty says, "I remember at the time I had long reddish-brown hair and I would stomp around Fredericton [New Brunswick] in the snow in four-inch caramel platforms and a little green plaid bum-freezer jacket. And that was Glam fashion in Fredericton. It was probably sourced at Le Chateau if I remember correctly. My explanation of it is that we were too young to be proper hippies and too old to be proper punks and so we were left with Glam as a kind of generational marker to hold on to and, unfortunately, we're all too ugly for Glam, but we tried to seize on it anyway. We really felt like outsiders—hippies still felt like outsiders—so when we started wearing colorful, sexualized clothes people were furious. It reinforced the feeling of being aliens and outliers. New Brunswick is basically the Alabama of Canada; it still is . . ."

An early incarnation of Halifax born and bred, April Wine playing live in Halifax on August 31, 1973. Photographer unknown.

In Fredericton there was the influential Wayne Little, who eventually co-started Little Records in the University of New Brunswick's Student Union Building where Varty had his first record-store job. Prior to the record store, Little was more portable: he would go from house to house with a rucksack full of import LPs. Varty explains, "Wayne would come by with things like King Crimson, and I first heard Nick Drake when he brought, I think, *Pink Moon* to the house and I put it on and absolutely fell in love. I'll backtrack a bit: Wayne was half-indigenous and lived with his mother in a literal hovel outside of Maliseet reserve near Jemseg, New Brunswick. So, he was an interesting character. How he got involved in adventurous music I don't know, but he was definitely a kind of literal Pied Piper for creative music in New Brunswick. Anyway, he showed up at our house with the Roxy Music record. And all of us just absolutely fell in love with different aspects of it. We were Bowie fans, we were Velvet Underground fans, but there was this thing, it had new energy, it had abstract sound and playfulness and strangeness and an outer-space rockabilly edge to it. We were all attracted to it immediately and that was kind of the model for the little fake band that we put together. All those people, myself, my roommates, Tony Bergmann-Porter and Bruce Oliver, and two brothers whose last name was Anand who were the rhythm section. I don't know whatever happened to the one of the Anand brothers. The one, Alan Anand, went on to become a professional astrologer. I don't know how you can extrapolate from being exposed to Roxy Music to that. Tony Bergmann-Porter has become a rabid libertarian gun crank in the United States. And Bruce Oliver ended up working for the New Brunswick government and building synthesizers as a hobby and he died last year, I believe, or two years ago, a lovely man. I'm, you know, whatever. I think that age did have an influence on our ongoing trajectories in different ways. Interesting that Tony was the singer and became a libertarian crank. I think we can see Bryan Ferry following the same sort of pattern—maybe this is the singer's trajectory."

Their band never played any gigs outside of their house and went through countless names. After moving across the country to Vancouver, Varty played in the great jazzy art rock band A.K.A. and in so many other musical projects, including a stint with Tim Ray and A/V. A passionate music lover, he has written about music for many years and put on pivotal shows in Vancouver at the Savoy, the Pitt Gallery, and the Western Front—including Wales's Young Marble Giants, Snakefinger, and Pink Section from San Francisco. He has done far more but he is also far too modest.

I asked others about Glam in these provinces. I scoured, I yelled, I posted on boards and came up so empty . . . some folks mentioned acts that were much more generic rock, often later, like Titan from Nova Scotia that briefly caught Kim Fowley's interest to be the next Loverboy, or 1980's Bon Jovi cover bands, or cover bands that were into the skinny-tie new-wave cover-act sound, like Taquila from Prince Edward Island. And that was a lot of reaching—even on tippy-toes it wasn't working. Now if there were platform boots handy, well then . . .

CHAPTER 8
NEWFOUNDLAND AND LABRADOR

Front cover to *Newfoundland Mummers* (Snocan, 1975). Author's collection.

OVER ON THE EASTERNMOST SIDE OF THE CONTINENT, the large island of Newfoundland and the adjacent mainland, Labrador, became the last province to join Canada, in 1949, reluctantly so. Both Newfoundland and the mummering tradition predate the nation-state of Canada. For a time, the Newfoundland residents were an unfortunate butt of many "Newfie" jokes that were made by Canadians much less funny than them. Mummering's murky Newfoundland origins date at least to the nineteenth century, perhaps further, brought from Britain and Ireland where it may have started hundreds of years earlier—pagan folk-horror meeting gleeful Glam with a strong anarchic sentiment.

It can be cold around Solstice, a time of change, yet out people come throughout Newfoundland and Labrador, freed from their old identities for the Mummers Parade, disguising themselves by grabbing whatever's handy around the house, keeping it cheap and accessible,[1] making do with creativity as the limit—be it underwear on the outside, all manner of brightly colored cross-dressing, new faces made up and painted on old linens, knocking on neighbors' doors with their voices disguised to a peculiar pitch asking, "Any mummers 'lowed in?" causing identity guessing games, singing folk songs in their molasses "stick a fork in it" thick accents (voted thickest in the country), dancing, gumboot stomping, and drinking up the homebrew. There were also ribbon fools extensively ribboned from head to toe prodding people with their ribbon sticks. In the northern part of Labrador, the Inuit tradition of Nalujuk Night brings out the *nalujuit* wrapped in furs and masks banging sticks, bearing similarities to the Krampus tradition. Children would have to sing in Inuktitut to the *nalujuit*s, who'd reward the good children with candy and presents and chase after the naughty.

Mid-nineteenth-century authorities unsuccessfully tried to kibosh mummering due to incidents of violence, including rubbing blubber on people's faces, and intimations of social unrest often pointedly attacking the wealthy and powerful. Who is that knocking on our door? A stranger, a neighbor, or what? Mummering mellowed. In 1972, Chris Brookes returned from the United States with a theater degree to his home of St. John's, Newfound-

---

[1] Unlike the much more lavish and expensively costumed mummers down in Philadelphia.

Mummers. Image courtesy of the *Ottawa Citizen*, December 12, 1966.

land, inspired by the Living Theatre, the San Francisco Mime Troupe, and the Chicago Seven. Brookes resurrected *The Mummers Play* after its fifty-year absence, performing it across the region in homes, pubs, and even on a city bus until the troupe dissolved in 1982. Both Mary Walsh and Tommy Sexton, later of the Newfoundland comedy group CODCO, performed in the Mummers' Troupe in its first couple of years. Brookes saw mummering as transformative, an inversion of the social order.[2]

Today, mummering is going strong with festivals and parades.[3] For the two years I joined in the parade, I noticed just how egalitarian and non-exclusive it was. There were far more participants than spectators, with both young and old (and young dressed as old) joining in.

There was one album, called *The Newfoundland Mummers,* released in 1975. The artwork for this record by Bruce Rawlins is really something else: brightly colored stylized characters hoisting mugs looking like they stepped off of a Halloween album with bright red lips and fangs. But there's no spooky sounds—it's a party, a real corker, full of accordion and twang and hooting and a-hollering. One of the musicians, Reg Watkins, also did a country album as Cam Canuck.

The song "Shock Absorber" by Peter Francis Quinlan is pure Newfoundland Glam. This confused sexual metaphor comes on strong with its rock riff, synth squeal, steady drum thump, and group shout of "rock." The word "shock" prominently echoes all Glam as "absorber" soon follows side-mouth-enunciated Newfoundland-style: "I'm gonna be your shock absorber tonight!" Described as Newfoundland's first rock star in the December 4, 2005 issue of the *Newfoundland Herald*, Quinlan says, "Artists in Newfoundland were not doing rock. They were doing country or Newfoundland music. So me trying to be different I made it rock 'n' roll. I think I was the first person to drive from Burgeo to St. John's up the highway, and I beat two or three shock absorbers out of my truck and went back and wrote that song. It had nothing to do with romance at all. Can you throw in a set of tires with that shock absorber?" The *Shock Absorber* album from 1979, its name labeled in an electrifying shock font, showcases Quinlan clad in a most-probably-rented tux with big bowtie and hair half-feathered and flattened, holding out a rose and a snifter of burgundy liquid. Behind him is the profile of a woman in a backless dress signaling all manner of classy. The title song comes on strong but the rest of the album steers off in various directions away from Glam into a steel-guitarified cover of Robin Gibb's "Saved by the Bell," an unusually modulated trucking song, an obsessively unbalanced song "Nancy," singing to her that he'll put a gun to his head if she doesn't come back to him, and a very tripped-out ode to Newfoundland. The rest of the album is a bunch of Legion pleasers ("The Night the Ladies' Dart League Had the Fight"). He performed "Shock Absorber" on NTV and on

---

2   Chris Brookes's book, *A Public Nuisance* (Memorial University Press, 1988.)

3   I highly recommend the 2014 book *Any Mummers 'Lowed In?* by Dale Jarvis (Flanker Press, 2014) as an exceptional mummers resource.

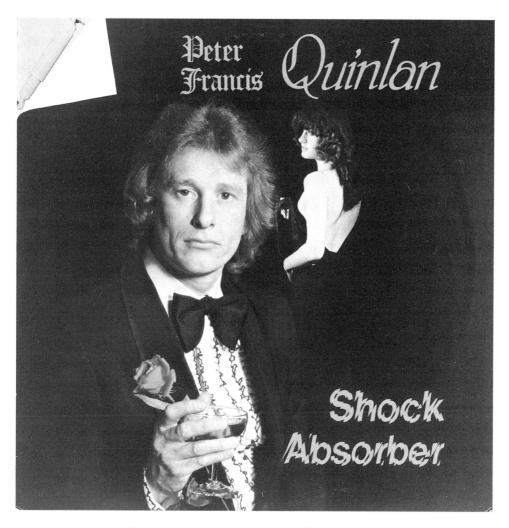

Front cover to *Shock Absorber* by Neil Francis Quinlan (Cod, 1979). Author's collection.

the Newfoundland club circuit, then moved away early on to perform at Newfoundland themed pubs in other regions. In 1987 Quinlan was the St. John's East candidate for the Rhinoceros Party, a long-running satirical political party. I have been told that Quinlan is alive and well and back in St. John's.

After a mind-expanding trip to learn from gurus in India, the wealthy media mogul Geoff Stirling, the co-founder of Newfoundland's TV station NTV, started free-form after-midnight broadcasts in the mid-'70s as a way to propagate his ideas of higher consciousness with lectures, music, and early computer animation. Viewers were introduced to dubious vitamin supplements and interviews with gurus, including Ram Dass, and conspiracy theorists such as David Icke going on about powerful lizard people. NTV's profoundly mystical content introduced a psychedelic superhero named Captain New-

Atlantis, page 26, art by Danny Bulanadi (Herald Publishing Company, 1983). Author's collection.

foundland, a cowled "spirit of Newfoundland" with the map of Newfoundland for a face: his "ancestors came from beyond the stars" and he "travels through different dimensions and different times" as a means to promote meditation to the young (quotes lifted from a Captain Newfoundland NTV spot). A rare 1980 TV movie *Captain Newfoundland and the Tip of Atlantis,* has been rumored to exist, though the longtime NTV news director and historian Jim Furlong told me that if there were such a movie he'd know of it. Three scarce graphic novels of Captain Newfoundland and his protégé Captain Canada were released. These were very professionally drawn by the Filipino-American superhero artist Danny Bulanadi, who had worked for Marvel Comics, yet written pseudonymously by Stirling himself, propagating a mix of Eastern spirituality and libertarianism.[4] These graphic novels collected the comic strips that ran in the *Newfoundland Herald*. One volume is divided into chakras, with Captain Newfoundland introducing Captain Canada to a ten-foot-high stone book titled *Holy Gospel of Consciousness* to prepare him against the Super-Mafia's giant robot that was sent to disrupt a royal visit from Queen Elizabeth and Prince Charles. The hockey player Wayne Gretzky tries to defeat the robot, and Captain Canada ultimately wins using the power of love. Captain Canada was known to make public appearances in the real world as well.

The comedy group CODCO began as a theater company in 1973, encompassing multi-media, improv, music, and more with a distinctly Newfoundland feel. *CODCO* landed on the CBC in 1986, airing alongside *The Kids in the Hall* for much of its run. The head of costumes was Juul Haalmeyer, a '70s variety-show veteran and, importantly, of the Juul Haalmeyer Dancers fame from SCTV. CODCO had much cross-dressing but were also very co-ed with Cathy Jones and Mary Walsh, as well as two openly gay cast members, Tommy Sexton and Greg Malone. The CODCO member Andy Jones, with his brother Michael

---

4   In the National Film Board documentary *Waiting for Fidel,* Newfoundland's premier, Joey Smallwood, and Geoff Stirling fly to Cuba with the filmmaker Michael Rubbo (*The Peanut Butter Solution*) (see Lewis Furey section) to argue about Communism and capitalism and to try and get a meeting with Fidel Castro (they don't).

Atlantis, inside back cover, art by Boris Vallejo (Herald Publishing Company, 1983). Author's collection.

The Wonderful Grand Band, Tommy Sexton in satin jacket on the far right.
Image courtesy of the *Vancouver Sun*, November 17, 1983.

Jones, made *The Adventure of Faustus Bidgood*, the first fully made-in-Newfoundland movie, which also featured members of CODCO. Begun in the mid-1970s and released in 1986, *Faustus Bidgood* is an absurdist masterpiece about a desk clerk who has hallucinations of becoming ruler of Newfoundland. Highly recommended for fans of Flann O'Brien, the Firesign Theatre, and the films of Guy Maddin.

The *CODCO* television series ended in 1992, and a year later Tommy Sexton died of complications from AIDS; he had performed even while in dire health. A housing center for people living with HIV and AIDS was named after him in 2006.

Sexton sang with the Wonderful Grand Band for their comedy rock hit "Babylon Mall" on their 1980 television variety show. "Babylon Mall" is pure Newfoundland Glam, with Sexton frenetically wiggling his hips in a half-buttoned satin jacket and tight blue jeans, no shirt, hair greased back except for a curl in front—backed up by twin Chipmunks rip-off puppets, flashpots a-popping, with one version featuring CODCO and the Grand Band cast member Greg Malone dancing along. This paean to the artificial environment of capitalism was about the Avalon Mall in St. John's, and they even performed the song there live. In

2017, the Wonderful Grand Band brought the song back for a video to raise funds for AIDS research through the Tommy Sexton Centre. Cutting from the mall to the studio settings, Sexton's satin jacket hangs proudly.

Wet Cheeze Delirium formed in 1977 as an art-rock band named after a Gong song. Although they did not consider themselves Glam, for their one and only show as a rock band they did cover "Editions of You" by Roxy Music complete with a saxophone player, along with songs by John Cale and King Crimson. Two of the members, Wallace Hammond and Craig Squires, have been playing together since 1974 and used the name Wet Cheeze Delirium for various different incarnations over the next two decades, working with loops and tape machines, with Doug Ivey replacing Squires, who was away in Toronto throughout the '90s. Their last show was in July 2001, with Squires, Hammond, and Ivey. Ivey passed in 2015. Squires and Hammond continue to play together in an experimental band called the Black Auks formed in 1992.

Hammond and Squires also formed Da Slyme, Newfoundland's first punk band, in 1977, with Peter Morris. Their 1980 (recorded 1978-1979) album could only loosely be called punk; other aspirations, like having too much fun, took precedence. Da Slyme made it a double album at that, thriftily reusing old record sleeves and spray-painting their name overtop with a stencil. The live show incorporated a toilet as smoke machine. Later shows were theme-oriented: when a touring production of Beatlemania came to town, they did their own production of Bagelmania, retooling Beatles songs to be about bagels with a bag of bagels thrown at the audience. For their twentieth-anniversary show, God appeared in a white robe. In God's honor, they released a second album called *The 20 Year Scam*. A Da Slyme compilation was released by Celluloid Lunch records in 2023.

CHAPTER 9
NUNAVUT AND THE REST OF CANADA

Jimmy Ekho in seal skin jumpsuit. Image courtesy of *The Gazette*, March 28, 1990.

JIMMY EKHO

UP NORTH IN IQALUIT, THE CAPITAL CITY of the Inuit-governed territory Nunavut, there is a beautiful mural of the musician Jimmy Ekho, who died of lung failure in 2008 at the young age of forty-eight. Known as Arctic Elvis, Ekho had a unique take on rock 'n' roll. He started performing in the early '80s in a full sealskin jumpsuit sewn by his adoptive mother, shaking his hips and singing Gene Vincent's "Be-Bop-A-Lula" in the Inuktitut language. All of his songs were in Inuktitut. The 1993 CD *Guti* featured Ekho singing his own dreamy, emotional ballads on acoustic guitar accompanied by dramatic and unearthly washes of synths by Dave Boileau. It was dedicated to his young friend Tikivik King, who had died of AIDS. Ekho performed at numerous concerts and festivals and appeared on Polish, German, and American TV. He was a guide at Iqaluit's Nunatta Sunakkutaangit Museum for over twenty years. Jimmy Ekho's obituary in the June 26, 2008, edition of *Nunatsiaq News* states that he was buried in his sealskin jumpsuit.

Canada's three territories include Nunavut, the Northwest Territories, and the Yukon located in the Northern part of the country. I searched and I searched for Glam in the Northwest Territories and the Yukon and found nothing, but it doesn't mean it's not there -- I'd love to be proven wrong on this matter.

OUTRO
CANADIAN GLAM NOW AND FOREVER

GOING TO BED, LAZILY FOREGOING the cold-cream rituals, my makeup still slathered, I had wicked dreams of everything up to now and into the future and then some. Upon awakening I saw my own reflection caused by my own "face" slathered across the pillow. My puffy white shroud opened its lipstick mouth to speak. This is what it said: "Canadian Glam NOW!" Why NOW? It's needed, man, it's needed. Why so uptight? Loosen up. The vestiges of Glam keep on pushing forward. So here we go, from 1980 to as far as we can take it—what year is it?

King Rockit was a 1980 synth-pop alien with silver skin wanting to take you on a "Rocket Trip," releasing a rare seven-inch EP on King Rockit Music. A film composer named Larry Steinberg patented the name King Rockit in 1978, stating that the name is "fanciful and does not identify a particular individual."

The musician and performance artist Glen Meadmore was part of the Winnipeg cable-access television world and played in the punk band the Psychiatrists. He moved to L.A. in the early '80s and formed a band with Vaginal Davis, where they both performed in drag. Meadmore's solo albums are a perfect mix of synths and bluegrass and avant-garde humor. The album *Chicken and Biscuits,* with the songs "Girlene" and "Do Me Baby" being a pure delight.

Both Ensign Broderick and Glamatron come from Toronto from around the same time and are self-described as Glam but really have far more subdued trappings making moody music, low-key, nice suits. Reissued in 2017, Glamatron's 1981 album is very New Romantic.

Tonetta is the persona of Toronto-based Tony Jeffries, who started making his own original music in 1983 after the break-up of his marriage, eventually finding his audience on YouTube despite getting repeatedly shut down for numerous violations. His countless videos show incredible creativity with costumes, masks, wigs, and makeup, recording all of the music and videos in his apartment using curtains and video effects, distorted beats and meats, dollar synth, guitar, and homemade percussion, be it ballads about his dead brother, "Drugs Drugs Drugs," or "G n B Showers," about water sports and coprophilia.

James Harcourt's hyper-obscure mid-'80s independent *Emotional Blackmail* LP has a fake hand-tinted photo of him with ultra-blond hair and ruby red lips. The giddy "You Make My Thing Ping" is my favorite track, with Harcourt's high-pitched sensual voice. Harcourt may have had a financial backer to get him into the studio to make an album and a video, produced by the Atlantic Records hitmaker Bob Gallo during his mysterious Canadian stint. The rock 'n' roll pioneer Bo Diddley did indeed sit in on the album, but his name is misspelled in the credits as "Bo Diddely." Charlie Calvo, the guitarist, told me that Harcourt is successfully working in blockbuster movies today under a different name.

Outrageous is an incredible character-driven Canadian movie from 1977 starring the late Craig Russell, who not only played a female impersonator but also was one, performing quite often. Russell was a massive influence on drag culture in general, and this movie was ground-breaking all over the world. Ten years later, Russell released a twelve-inch single called "Glamour Monster," which opens with "Ladies and gentlemen, Mr. Craig Russell!" The beats come on and Russell speaks about how great it is getting older: People no longer yell homophobic slurs on the street anymore, "They just think I'm a middle-age girl with her Walkman and two dogs." Then on to the chorus and call-outs to cities all over the world.

Melleny Melody has done voice-over work for numerous cartoons, including *Rock & Rule,* which has her song with Patricia Cullen, "Hot Dogs and Sushi." She makes cartoony music on her labels Play and Gay Records and did a remix of Carole Pope from Rough Trade's 2005 album *Transcend.* In the '90s she put on *The Bubbalicious Lounge,* a regular variety show hosting in her own countless brightly colored outfits and wigs with her sidekick Kyree Vibrant. Her pink art car with its zebra interiors covered in jewels of Baghdad, toys and dolls, and bowling trophies made the newspapers in 2005 when she was pulled over by the cops for "driving a dangerous vehicle."

The Shangs, from Hamilton, were named after the Shangri-las, with a girl-group and soft-psych sound made by men, containing a former member of the legendary Simply Saucer. The 1990 video for "Never Know" is a tribute to the Shangri-Las, recorded in that style appearing in girl-group drag. The Shangs came back in 2022 with a new album. The lead-off track refers to the murdered androgynous boy from *Day of the Locust*, that acidly critical book and film about old Hollywood.

Forming in 1991, the Leather Uppers were—and still are—purveyors of "scarf rock." This duo in matching outfits consisted of Classy Craig and Groovy Greg, who would switch instruments mid-set with their own stompers, such as "Sugar Sandwich."

Platinum Blonde's self-released 1980 single showed them looking more Glam than punk and sounding more punk than Glam. They'd cover Gary Glitter and T. Rex in their live set. The band broke up right after; then Mark Holmes put together a whole new lineup. The addition of synths would soften their sound; their look softened too, making them very visually appealing for the music-video medium. The original bassist, Joey Ciotti, quickly formed Trixie Goes Hollywood. His current band, Still 18teen, is a mother–father–daughter trio that has a Glam and alternative sound. Toronto's Cosmic Saints started in the late '80s, with their plan to take Glam further using elements of shock, and were closer to Glam punk. Vancouver's Flash Bastard were on the Glam punk spectrum. Loaded up on eyeliner, duct-tape on nipples, they formed in the very early '90s, were hand-selected by Mötley Crüe to open a massive tour for them, then subsequently thrown off the tour for bad behavior (they were too bad for Crüe). Their video for "Rock n' Roll Must Be Destroyed" pays tribute to *Rocky Horror* with nothing but red lips singing and floating on a black backdrop. The Vancouver Glam punkers the Black Halos have performed as the New West Dolls, a New York Dolls tribute slow-nodding to a Vancouver suburb. Spinning out of the "punkaoke" and "new-wave-aoke" live karaoke band phenomenon in Vancouver was Glamaoke—all Glam covers. The band, consisting of members of Art Bergman's Poisoned and Tankhog, wore elaborate Glam costumes: the bassist Hamm spray-painted his gumboots gold—a very Canadian Glam move.

Allow me to take a moment in this chronology to add some late-in-the-book context and an honest admission: I am a multi-disciplinary artist and performer born in Canada. Strong elements of Glam pervade my work. My band July Fourth Toilet—formed in Vancouver in 1994—had the mandate of "No two shows the same," and we stuck to that un-stickability, shape-shifting lucidly, wearing elaborate costumes and makeup, depending on the evening's theme in our long history while our albums would shift sounds sometimes, going full Glam, and as unreal as we seemed, contrary to one recent book we were real and did exist for many years. As well, I was/am Lil' Hamm, half of the comedic song-and-dance duo Canned Hamm (Big Hamm was/is the other half; his current solo project as Theremin Man takes it to mystical space, often adorned in a robe), of full persona in matching outfits, changing looks with each successive synthy album. There's also my character the Canadian Romantic, with glitter on his belly and everywhere else, face all made up. In 2006 I formed a Romantic Glam band called Hallmark that lasted for a handful of years.

Wiggle, an annual wearable-art wig and performance extravaganza, is all about bringing the glamor, starting in Windsor, Ontario, in 1994, then on to Vancouver and now Montreal. The club/drag scene in New York was a huge inspiration, with Wiggle's Venus Girls performing at Wigstock in 1999, "a Canadian first." Lady Bunny hosted two Wiggle festivals in Vancouver. It's a wondrous event with all kinds of performers. Its organizer, the performer Michael Venus, does and has done so much, including the important documentary *Snow Queen: A Herstory and Exposé of Drag Culture in Canada*.

Peaches is the persona of Merrill Nisker, making pure personality music, pushing boundaries as she sings sexually progressive and funny lyrics overtop of her electronic music, while easily incorporating performance art and an array of costumes. The cover art to her 2003 album *Father Figure* features Peaches in lustrous fake beard. On the late Hal Willner's T. Rex tribute album she sings "Solid Gold, Easy Action." Peaches has united the freaks from all over (case in point: she connected my act Canned Hamm with the art/Glam/garage/synth rocker the World Provider, causing us to become long-time pals and play shows together).

The late artist and activist Will Munroe's monthly nights called Vazaleen were wild queer music events with Nina Hagen, Lesbians on Ecstasy, and Peaches performing. These were inclusive community events with a diverse crowd, showing possibilities. With Lynn MacNeil, he co-founded the Beaver before he died way too young of brain cancer in 2010. In the midst of looming condos, the Beaver felt inclusive for anyone who felt different. This special Toronto bar would have a lot of fun events, including the Bands and Drag events hosted by Tago Mago. The pandemic hit it hard and, like many important spaces, it closed.

In the MySpace era, Robin Black and the Intergalactic Rock Stars were Toronto hairdresser metal, with two members in that profession—lots of purple and piercings, with the guitarist Christopher "Starboy" Cunnane wearing platforms. The song "More Effeminate Than You" was released as a star-shaped single. Cunnane has an encyclopedic knowledge of Glam. His new album *Electric Tiger* has a Glam influence. Self-described as "Glam Rock Revival," Sugar Coated Killers from Kelowna, British Columbia, formed in 2001. They have an ode to the local lore of the Okanagan lake monster Ogopogo and, like Ogopogo, there are still sightings of this band!

Montreal's Les George Leningrad, from the early 2000s, were so delightfully freaky and funny! This was the only time I ever saw a wig put on with an elastic, and it would be pulled up and down while the band members tattooed themselves with magic marker. Their music is definitely uniquely unpredictable—there was nothing quite like them. Their names were Poney P, Mingo L'Indien, and Bobo Boutin. There were visual artists in the band, giving it all a mystical, cartoony design.

Max Turnbull's persona of Slim Twig delivered his take on Glam with 2015's *Thank You for Stickin' with Twig*, right down to the fake hand-tinted look of the album cover.

The production is very *now* in its digitally compressed and distorted splendor and keeps me coming back. This will only get more highly regarded with time. Cindy Lee, who has been described as a "gender-bending experimental rock artist" (*Toronto Star*), is the persona of Patrick Flegel. Cindy Lee's seventh album, *Diamond Jubilee,* is a dream-like opus containing thirty-two incredible poppy songs (with excellent guitar work). It features an Alberta grain elevator and shuttle train on the cover. Cherry Hooker formed in Toronto in 2015, with the singer Madge Colleran, who has the biggest collection of Glam singles I have seen in Canada, and her brother T-Bone on heavy wah-wah guitar, all unified in glitter and faux fur, with Colleran's fearless emotional stage performances. They currently have two singles out and an album in the can. The Vancouver band Clone is all in wigs and makeup, using the Glam stomper sound as template with lots of digital pink, describing themselves as a "lush Neo-Glam collage." Based in British Columbia, Art d'Ecco's fashion, makeup, and soft voice are impeccably styled, no question—everything is just so with a thick veneer and a sensual voice like Nick Gilder on 'ludes and synthy New Romantic trappings. Frosty Valentine is real deep persona, almost unreal, an anthropomorphic dancefloor diva dalmatian with long lashes, nails, digital sparkles, and amazing red outfits. Slash Need features Dusty Lee, often costumed in bouffant wig, makeup, knee-high boots, and exaggerated latex non-implants, commandingly singing about art-gallery spaces—"I came for the free food" and "What's your practice?" then replying, "Uhhhhhhhhh whaaaahhhh!!!!" while Alex Low operates grinding electronics and deeply incognito panty-hose-headed dancers cavort. Trans-Canada Highwaymen are a band made up of members of Sloan, the Pursuit of Happiness, Odds, and Barenaked Ladies who released a very K-Tel-looking album of Canadian cover songs originally by such acts as Stampeders and Pagliario. They also threw in a self-referential original Glam stomper "Theme from Trans-Canada Highwaymen."

There's surely more and more to come. Much of the aforementioned acknowledge their Glam history while exploring possibilities, an openness. Go Glam yourself and add your name in lights—go on!

No matter where you are, flower forth and forward and flourish. This cruel world needs more fun and fabulousness. It's not the easiest road, but it's not dull and perhaps less lonely. Give it some PIZZAZZAMATAZZ!

Xoxoxoxoxoxo,
Robert

Oh, and if you are curious about me and my shenanigans, go here:
http://www.robertdayton.com

THANK

MY OLDEST BROTHER FRANK for buying Sweeney Todd's records and bringing them home all those years ago, making for my introduction to this world; Steve Krakow, a.k.a. Plastic Crimewave, for coining the term "Canadian Glam" and sending me off on this journey; Christina Ward and Jessica Parfrey at Feral House for believing in me at a time when I'd lost hope and for having *Cold Glitter* be a part of their incredible roster of books and guiding me along to make this a much better book; Kevin Howes for his wisdom and countless single suggestions—likewise Ian Marshall for Flivva and Toby Swann and more; Madge Colleran for suggesting Lynx and more; Sandy Gordon for suggesting Stanley Frank; Allison Thompson for suggesting Baby Strange and helping me with research; Glenn Salter for introducing me to the music of Justin Paige; John Armstrong for suggesting Toys; Mark Oliver for so many Vancouver places and fashion; 1000 Songs people: Adam Sobolak for suggesting Chikkin and Kurt Swinghammer for suggesting Brutus; Terry Dawes for introducing me to "Glamour Boy"; Jan Haust for suggesting Johnnie Lovesin and more; Heather Cameron for suggesting Buick McKane; Mark Kleiner and Terry Hoknes for the Nerve; Alexander McDonald for the Wackers. Many thanks to Kier-La Janisse and *ByNWR* for running the La Troupe Grotesque piece. Even more thanks to Kier-La Janisse for greatly improving the *Rock & Rule* and *Phantom of the Paradise* sections through setting up the original interviews and more and for believing in me and pushing my writing, greatly improving it; Guy Maddin for making the Lewis Furey section really happen, greatly improving it; Mike McGonigal for running Doug Henning and Breathless in *Maggot Brain* and just *knowing* that this book would come out; *Vulcher* for running a couple pieces in their earlier forms; Jesse Locke for running an earlier version of Chikkin in *Zine Obscura*; Kira Sheppard for believing in me and patiently reading it all; John Bertram and Jeffrey Nagel for giving me a shift to get me out of rock bottom; Dan Bejar and Gregg Turkington for reading and giving great feedback and support; Lester Smolenski for his title push towards *Cold Glitter* and logo pixie dust; Sue Frumin for the use of her archive of photos and letters and clippings and Mike Gabel for getting them in England; Christina Rice for doing some difficult transcribing work on La Troupe Grotesque; John Mackie, Alan Zweig, David Dedrick, Leora Kornfeld, Elizabeth Semmelhack (Bata), Paul Corupe, Dan Rocca, Charlie Huisken, Michael Venus, Lex Vaughn, Dane Goulet, Mimi Bonhomme, Sebastien Desrosiers, Otis Fodder, Alan Lord, Shaunna Moore (archivist at Belkin), Kristy Farka (archivist at Western Front), the Toronto Reference Library, Andrew Paterson, Gary Topp, Erella Ganon, Scott McGovern, John Catto, Marty Topps, David Bertrand, Ben Frith and Rob Frith at Neptoon, Courtenay Webber, Jaimie Vernon, Dan Brisebois, Bruce Mowat, Jake Austen, Barbara Bernath, Erin McMichael, Jim Betts, David Ferry, James Dyck, Ivan Sayers, John Davis, Thor, Wallace Hammond and Peter Morris, Celluloid Lunch Records, David Bertrand, Clint Enns, Jeff Khonsary, Richard Chapman at Northern Electric, Linda Walley, Pat Braden, Bob Mersereau, Jason Flower at Supreme Echo, Marc Bell, Trish Lavoie, Reg Harkema, David Marriott, Chris Seguin, Jessie Nagel, Peter Wolchak, Ann Kennard, Ron Obvious, Phil Smith, Neil Wedman, Jeff Silverman, Leatrice O'Neill. Thank you to the Canadian Glam Patreon subscribers Alexander Varty, Stephen Hamm, Julie Pomerleau, Marjorie Robbins, Lisa Macleod, Jody Franklin, Allison Thompson, Susan Ferguson, Grayson Walker, Ron McFarlan, Barb and Mike, Devlan Nicholson, Joyce McBeth, Emily Gove, Jeremy Singer, Soren Brothers, Carlos Yu, Caroline Selkirk, Jennifer DeCresce, Jennifer, Jessica Yateman, Julian Lawrence, Eli Speigel, FLA, Cathy Illman, Squidra Em, Adam Boysen, Neal Armstrong, Claudia Greaves, and Jennifer Akkermans. Big thanks to everyone who so kindly loaned photos for use and giving that visual sparkle. And to all the amazing people who I interviewed for this book who were so giving of your time and incredible memories, thank you for sharing your PIZZAZZAMATAZZ!

This project has been years in the making and I am sure I've missed some very deserving people and I apologize; it's a horrible oversight and I feel terrible about it.

AUTHOR'S NOTE

SO MUCH GREAT Canadian Glam has been uncovered for inclusion in *Cold Glitter* that it is simply too jam-packed! We created a supplemental PDF for the complementary Glam elements that made innovation across the spectrum beyond music itself. This PDF covers Fashion (Beau Brummell, Evelyn Roth, Long John's, Master John's platform boots, Amelia Earhart, and so much more), Magic (Doug Henning accompanied by John Mills-Cockell and Breathless), Comedy (La Troupe Grotesque), Movies (*Metal Messiah*, *Rock & Rule*, and *Phantom of the Paradise* in Winnipeg), and Art (The Hollywood Decca Dance —including Anna Banana, Eric Metcalfe a.k.a. Dr. Brute, and more). You can find this PDF on the Feral House website or via contacting info@feralhouse.com.